Human Rights: Integrated Approaches

Human Rights: Integrated Approaches

Alfie Thomas

MURPHY & MOORE
www.murphy-moorepublishing.com

Murphy & Moore Publishing,
1 Rockefeller Plaza,
New York City, NY 10020, USA

ISBN: 978-1-63987-316-6

Cataloging-in-Publication Data

Human Rights : integrated approaches / Alfie Thomas.
p. cm.
Includes bibliographical references and index.
ISBN 978-1-63987-316-6
1. Human rights. 2. Right to development. I. Thomas, Alfie.
JC571 .H86 2022
323--dc23

For information on all Murphy & Moore Publications
visit our website at www.murphy-moorepublishing.com

MURPHY & MOORE

Contents

Preface

This book aims to highlight the current researches and provides a platform to further the scope of innovations in this area. This book is a product of the combined efforts of many researchers and scientists, after going through thorough studies and analysis from different parts of the world. The objective of this book is to provide the readers with the latest information of the field.

The moral principles that describe the standards of human behavior and are protected in international and municipal law are referred to as human rights. These are the same for everyone and are applicable everywhere at any point of time. The right to development is central to the concept of human rights and development. It entitles all the people to participate in and enjoy the social, economic, political and cultural development of their country. It is exercised collectively but enjoyed individually. The topics included in this book on human rights and developments are of utmost significance and bound to provide incredible insights to readers. Some of the diverse topics covered herein address the varied branches that fall under this category. This book will serve as a valuable source of information for those interested in this field.

I would like to express my sincere thanks to the authors for their dedicated efforts in the completion of this book. I acknowledge the efforts of the publisher for providing constant support. Lastly, I would like to thank my family for their support in all academic endeavors.

Alfie Thomas

1

Introduction

By their very nature, economic and social [including cultural] rights imply that conditions of poverty and deprivation will be satisfied. By recognising these rights, the eradication of poverty becomes not merely a policy choice for the state, but a legally binding responsibility for which it is accountable.[1]

1 Introduction and overview

1.1 Some background discussions

While the aggregation of national growth rates in the overall conditions of world populations in the years that followed the Cold War led to the hasty suggestion that Africa had recorded 'rapid improvement' in human development indices,[2] a more thorough analysis reveals sharp contradictions. Before, and particularly since the end of the Cold War, a gloomy picture of human development indices in Africa consistently radiated through all the scientific standards of measuring human growth and progress around the world. A quick look at any of the *Human Development Reports* (Reports) produced by the United Nations Development Programme (UNDP) since 1990 shows that the plight of most Africans has remained parlous in terms of the overall trends of poverty and human deprivations.[3]

1 S Liebenberg & K Pillay *Poverty and human rights report of the national 'speak out on poverty' hearings* (1998) 2.

2 See generally RA Easterlin 'The globalisation of human development' 570 *Annals* (2000) 35-38.

3 All UNDP's *Human development reports* are available at http://www.undp.org. See particularly UNDP *Human development report 2007-2008: Fighting climate change: Human solidarity in a divided world* (2008). Other instruments of global human development measurement include the 'World development reports' and 'World development indicators' (both produced annually by the World Bank), http://www.worldbank.org; United Nations Educational, Scientific and Cultural Organisation (UNESCO) *Statistical yearbook*; United Nations Children's Fund (UNICEF) *State of the world's children*; and the World Health Organisation (WHO)

Despite tremendous gains made by other regions of the world in the post-Cold War era, African countries, constituting the larger quota of the world's most impoverished peoples, especially sub-Saharan Africa, remain in free fall as against other regions in *per capita* incomes.[4] The human development challenges confronting Africa are indeed formidable. With the vast millions of people living on less than US $1 per day in several African countries, the massive human misery in Africa cannot be more graphic.[5] The 2007-2008 edition of the UNDP reports depicts Africa as not only failing to eliminate poverty, but also as experiencing an increase in the number of people living in extreme poverty.[6] Based on empirical data, the current UNDP report registers Africa as having the bottom 22 countries among the 177 countries listed on the human development index;[7] while the 2003 edition had shown that the 25 lowest countries on the human development index were African states among the 175 listed worldwide.[8] When compared to other regions of the world, Africa lags far behind in all measurements of human growth.[9] This bleak description of Africa's performance on global human development charts is reinforced by a quick review of some major indicators of human deprivation in most recent times.

According to the 2007-2008 UNDP report, the average life expectancy in sub-Saharan Africa is 49,6 years, a marginal increase from the 2002 mark of 48,7 years, and the lowest for all world regions.[10] The situation with respect to health, food and education is a grim tale. Percentages of the population having access to safe water and sanitation are 48% and 55%, respectively.[11] In the sphere of

'World Health Report', among others. See also UNDP 'Human development report 2002: Deepening democracy in a fragmented world' 48-49 (Table A1.3 Progress towards millennium development goals).

4 See *Human development report 2007-2008* (n 3 above) 24-25.

5 For studies showing the consistent poverty trends in Africa, see K Roe 'Sub-Saharan Africa and extreme poverty' presented at North American Association of Christians in Social Work (NACSW) conference, Philadelphia, October 2006; UN Economic Commission for Africa Millennium Development Goals in Africa: Progress and challenges (2005). See also NJ Udombana 'The summer has ended and we are not saved! Towards a transformative agenda for Africa's development' (2005) 7 *San Diego International Law Journal* 5 7-12.

6 See *Human development report 2007-2008* (n 3 above) 240 (Table 3 Human and Income Poverty). See also UNDP 'Human development balance sheet 2002' http://www.undp.org/hdr2002/presskit/HDR%20PR_balance.pdf (accessed 12 June 2009).

7 See *Human development report 2007-2008* (n 3 above) 231-232 240 (Table 1 human development index). The report shows only two African nations (Seychelles and Mauritius) on the list of nations with high human development indices.

8 UNDP *Human development report 2003* (2003) 239-240 (Table 1 Human development index). The report retains Seychelles as the only African nation on the list of nations with high human development indices.

9 *Human development report 2007-2008* (n 3 above).

10 As above.

11 *Human development report 2003* (n 8 above) 254 (Table 7 Water, sanitation and nutritional status).

education, while 60,3% of adults are literate, the combined primary, secondary and tertiary gross enrolment ratio is stated as 50,6%, indicating a low level of human capital formation in Africa as compared to other world regions. At the quoted US $1 998, Africa's real gross domestic product (GDP) *per capita* is the lowest among all regions compared to an average of US $5 282 for all developing countries, and US $9 543 for the whole world.[12] Not surprisingly, over 50% of human beings in sub-Saharan Africa live below the global poverty line.[13]

As critical as the general situation is, it is more pathetic for children and women.[14] Out of the estimated 54 million people living with HIV/AIDS in sub-Saharan Africa, the vast majority of these are women and children.[15] The mortality rates for infants (those under one year) and children (between ages one to five years) are 102 and 172 per thousand live births, respectively, the highest among all regions of the world.[16] Besides this, only 76% and 65% of infants in sub-Saharan Africa are fully immunised against tuberculosis and measles, respectively, a dismal comparison to other world regions.[17] The situation of women is much worse than that of men in Africa. While the life expectancy of women is slightly higher than that of men, all other indicators of human development weigh in favour of men.[18]

Significant for a broader view of these critical human conditions are unmistakable imbalances in the allocation of fiscal resources. The 2007-2008 Report shows that between 1990 and 2007, many African countries occupying the bottom ladder of the global human development index committed a considerable amount of public funds to military expenditure.[19] Conversely, for the nations listed as having

12 *Human development report 2007-2008* (n 3 above) 232.

13 *Human development report 2007-2008* (n 3 above) 240 245-247 (Table 3 Human and income poverty). The UNDP defines population below poverty line as those living on income of US $1 per day according to the 'purchasing power parity' rate.

14 The UNDP *Human development balance sheet 2002* noted that child immunisation rates in sub-Saharan Africa had fallen below 50%, and that 90% of the more than 40 million people living with HIV/AIDS in the world were in developing countries with 75% of them in Africa as at 2000. The current report shows no marked improvement. See *Human development report 2007-2008* (n 3 above) 25.

15 UNAIDS '*2006 Report on the global AIDS epidemic* http://www.unaids.org/en/KnowledgeCentre/HIVData/GlobalReport/Default.asp (accessed 12 June 2009); UNICEF 'More HIV-positive children and pregnant women getting AIDS treatment' press release 3 April 2008 http://www.unicef.org/media/media_43458.html (accessed 12 June 2009); *Human development report 2003* (n 8 above) 258-261 (Table 7 Leading global health crises and challenges), 253 (Table 5 Demographic Trends).

16 See *Human development report 2007-2008* (n 3 above) 264 (Table 10 Survival: progress and setbacks).

17 *Human development report 2007-2008* (n 3 above) 250 (Table 6 Commitment to health: Access, services and resources).

18 *Human development report 2007-2008* (n 3 above) 326-329 (Table 28 Gender-related development index). These are in respect of the indices of literacy and earned income.

the highest human development index, there was a drastic decline in military expenditure in favour of social services over the same period.[20]

Notwithstanding these indicators of gloom, there have been some 'bright rays' in the human development situation in Africa. Life expectancy has slightly increased from 46 years to 49,1 years and infant mortality declined from 144 to 102 per thousand births between 1970 to 1975 and 2000 to 2005, respectively.[21] In similar vein, there was a projected increase in adult literacy from 54,2% in 1985 to 59,3% in 2005.[22] However, even against the relative progress recorded for Africa in the twilight of the last century, there remain sharp and deep contradictions.[23]

In the midst of the deplorable human conditions described above, can the *ordinary* African be said to be free in any way? What sort of freedom can be expressed amidst the suffocating living conditions described above? This book sets out to establish a theoretical and practical concept on *how* economic, social and cultural rights could become affirmative channels of human development in Africa. Being a holistic effort, this book considers all economic, social and cultural rights as an interactive, interrelated, and indivisible whole. My premise is that social rights are just as valid and vital as economic rights, and cultural rights in many instances might entail social and economic values that often intersect the realm of human rights. [24]

19 While it is to be noted that some African nations slightly reduced their military expenditure between the 1990 and 2000-2001 statistics, a considerable number of the most 'impoverished African states' increased or sustained the level of their military spending over the same period. Angola, Burundi, Eritrea, Ethiopia, Mali, Mozambique, Nigeria, Rwanda and Sudan, at various times within the same time scale, spent more resources on the military than on education or health; n 18 above 295-298 (Table 17 Priorities in public spending).

20 *Human development report 2007-2008* (n 3 above) 294-297 (Table 19 Priorities in public spending). For a finding that Africa recorded comparatively lower growth in GDP in years when military expenditure increased, see NK Kusi 'Economic growth and defence spending in developing countries: A causal analysis' (1994) 38 *Journal of Conflict Resolution* 152-159.

21 *Human development report 2007-2008* (n 3 above) 264 (Table 10 Survival: Progress and setbacks).

22 *Human development report 2007-2008* (n 3 above) 272 (Table 12 Literacy and enrolment). This improvement, however, still fell far short of the 77,1% for all developing countries.

23 See M Ramphele 'Human rights and human development: Fulfilling the basic needs of people' (2000) http://www.hawkecentre.unisa.edu.au/speeches/lecture3.htm (accessed 12 June 2009).

24 For illuminating jurisprudence on this line of argument, see *Ominayak v Canada* Communication 167/1984, Report of the Human Rights Committee, UN Doc A/45/40, Vol II, GAOR 45th sess, Suppl No 40 1-30; Communication 511/1992, *Länsman v Finland*, Report of the Human Rights Committee (26 October 1994) UN Doc A/50/40, Vol. II, GAOR 50th Sess, Supplement No 40 66 76. See also J Symonides 'Cultural rights' in J Symonides (ed) *Human rights: Concepts and standards* (2000) 175-227, for critical arguments on the significance of cultural rights in the global integrative human rights discourse.

Since both human rights and human development are concepts essentially concerned with the empowerment of human beings and the enhancement of their capabilities,[25] a linkage between the two concepts is necessary and desirable, if not inevitable. Human rights generally, and economic, social and cultural rights in particular, can become veritable vehicles for human development in Africa if concrete intellectual foundations are laid, nurtured and sustained for such an experience to positively materialise. Hence, the overarching thrust of my rights-based approach.

One of the most elaborate international agenda for human development and the eradication of poverty in Africa was the Second Tokyo International Conference on International Development (TICAD II) in 1998, which established human development and poverty reduction as goals that must be attained for Africa between 2005 and 2015.[26] Although those goals represent the plan of action adopted by the international community for Africa, each African government is obliged to evolve strategies for their realisation at the domestic level, within TICAD II time-frames.[27] On the home front, African leaders and eminent development experts have evolved diverse platforms of action to confront the massive human development challenges facing the continent.[28] All these objectives demanded, and still demand, a synergy of efforts, approaches and strategies for success.

Considering these broad developmental designs, and yet, worsening living conditions, this book raises some critical questions: How well is Africa prepared to meet its global and regional human development responsibilities? In quantitative and qualitative terms, how many positive effects have those efforts had on Africa and Africans? To what extent have governments in African states evinced concrete commitment to the goals of human development? How well have states and non-state actors in Africa articulated their responses to the challenges of human development? What are the impediments that militate against the efficacy of development efforts, and how have these been addressed and/or should be addressed? What

25 See AK Sen 'Capability and well-being' in M Nussbaum & AK Sen (eds) *The quality of life* (1993) 30; AK Sen 'Development thinking at the beginning of the XXIst century' in L Emmerij (ed) *Economics and social development into the XXIst century* (1997) 531 540-542; AK Sen *Development as freedom* (1999) 75 297. See also UNDP *Human development report 2000: Human rights and human development* (2000) 1. See also J Paul Martin 'Development and rights revisited: Lessons from Africa' (2006) 4 *SUR - International Journal of Human Rights* 91 97.

26 See TICAD II 'Special feature on Africa' http://www.unu.edu/hq/ginfo/media/ticad-articles.html (accessed 12 June 2009).

27 For a historical perspective on the concerted collaborative efforts among experts that led to TICAD II, see G Carceles *et al* 'Can sub-Saharan Africa reach the international targets for human development?' (2001) *African Region Human Development Working Paper Series* 5-6. See also n 26 above.

28 See ch 2 and text accompanying footnotes 273-288 and 1218, for a further discussion of the various African regional initiatives.

implications could a human rights praxis portend for the current state of human development in Africa, and *vice versa*? How well have intellectual efforts responded to these onerous challenges? What should define the thematic province of a human rights focus in Africa's development goals?

Critical to the questions outlined above and the problems considered in this work is the underlying existence of a broad range of human rights instruments within the United Nations (UN) human rights system, within the African regional human rights system, and within various domestic systems in Africa, all of which hold implications for human development in Africa. However, despite the overwhelming convergence of all these instruments on the obligation of African states to take all appropriate measures to secure the implementation of their valued contents, the evolution of a coherent rights-based approach to development has generally been stunted across Africa, if existent at all.

Apart from the incidence of institutional apathy, the negative impact of non-state actors and the impediment of non-justiciability, this book posits that the very low-level awareness, promotion and implementation of economic, social and cultural rights in Africa – critical to the development process - have largely been the result of the under-theorised and under-explored profile of economic, social and cultural rights within the African human rights discourse.

A particularly problematic factor in evolving a rights-based approach in African development discourse is the unmistakable devaluation of economic, social and cultural rights as *legal* entitlements. While the legal systems of many African states are replete with constitutional provisions and multiples of treaty provisions that give positive recognition to the implementation of economic, social and cultural rights, these rights are generally less protected, less implemented, and even generally less discussed. The outcome has been an unmistakable incoherence in the interpretation of economic, social and cultural rights at diverse fora in Africa. I seriously contend that the continued devaluation of economic, social and cultural rights will render human rights practically irrelevant to whatever development agenda Africa embarks upon. It is therefore critical that for economic, social and cultural rights to attain relevance in Africa's human development efforts, the discipline must be properly grounded on firm theoretical and conceptual parameters. So far, intellectual intercourse towards this direction is lacking. To that end, this book advances the pursuit of human development in Africa beyond the traditional confines of macro-economic and political propositions. It thus assesses the concept of *human* development within the broader discourse on the role of human rights in global *development*, with emphasis on the African context of the subject.

1.2 Linking human rights to development discourses

Events over the last decade, particularly following the demise of the Cold War, have remarkably opened new vistas to activity in the field of economic, social and cultural rights by scholars, jurists and non-governmental organisations (NGOs) across the globe. Beyond the theoretical debate as to whether economic, social and cultural rights are justiciable, human rights scholars and activists are beginning to examine the potentials of securing the implementation of these rights at the domestic level, and their implications for human development.[29] Such rights-based discourses encompass civil and political rights, economic, social and cultural rights, and other rights found in diverse human rights instruments. The approach works in tandem with international development targets, focusing on the twin issues of poverty alleviation and human development. In that regard, *all* human rights are to be perceived as components of human development as well as platforms for achieving it.[30]

However, while scholars in many other nations of the world have done extensive work in defining economic, social and cultural rights implementation as an effective platform for development, the contribution of African scholars on the African context of the subject has been relatively paltry and incomprehensive.[31] This phenomenon

29 See eg International Commission of Jurists *Development, human rights and the rule of law* (1981); J Donnelly 'The "right to development": How not to link human rights and development' in CE Welch Jr *et al* (eds) *Human rights and development in Africa* (1984) 261-283; A Rosas 'The right to development' in A Eide *et al* (eds) *Economic, social and cultural rights: A textbook* (2001) 119-130.

30 See Martin (n 25 above) 97-99; J Donnelly 'Human rights and Asian values: A defence of "Western universalism"' in JR Bauer & DA Bell (eds) *The East Asian challenge for human rights* (1999) 74-75; SSC Tay *et al* 'Economic, social and cultural rights ASEAN: A survey' 12 Background Paper at the Friedrich Ebert Stifung Conference on Human Rights, held in Manila, The Philippines, 24-25 January 2000). See also UNDP 'Human rights and development - An emerging nexus' http://www.undp.org/rbap/rights/Nexus.htm (accessed 12 June 2009).

31 See, eg, E Ankumah *The African Commission on Human and Peoples' Rights: Practice and procedures* (1996) 143; S Liebenberg 'The protection of economic and social rights in domestic legal systems' in Eide *et al* (n 29 above) 55 71-75; CA Odinkalu 'Implementing economic, social and cultural rights under the African Charter on Human and Peoples' Rights in M Evans & R Murray (eds) *The African Charter on human and peoples' rights: The system in practice 1986-2000* (2002) 178; C Obiagwu & CA Odinkalu 'Combating legacies of colonialism and militarism' in AA An-Na'im (ed) *Human rights under African constitutions: Realising the promise for ourselves* (2003) 211; GW Mugwanya *Human rights in Africa: Enhancing human rights through the African regional human rights system* (2003) 209; J Oloka-Onyango 'Beyond the rhetoric: Reinvigorating the struggle for economic and social rights in Africa' (1995) 26 *California Western International Law Journal* 1; CA Odinkalu 'Analysis of paralysis or paralysis by analysis? Implementing economic, social and cultural rights under the African Charter on Human and Peoples' Rights' (2001) 23 *Human Rights Quarterly* 327.

of scholarly inertia is traceable to the preoccupation of African leaders, governments, jurists, human rights researchers and other strata of society with post-colonial governance conflicts and other related problems (for example, democratisation, transitional justice and reconciliation processes, foreign Commission on Human and Peoples' Rights (African Commission) in elaborating the economic, social and cultural rights content of the African Charter on Human and Peoples' Rights (African Charter);[32] the general reluctance among national judicial organs to engage these rights; and the erroneous perception debt crises, and intra-national conflict resolution); the ambivalent attitude of the African, among many African and non-African human rights scholars working on Africa, that human development is strictly determined by the dynamics of global trade and entails the fine details of macroeconomics.[33]

While I acknowledge the efforts of economists and political scientists in theorising the impact of economic policies on human conditions in Africa, there yet remains their obvious inability to integrate their ideas with intersecting human rights ethos. Similarly, while human rights activists and scholars convey genuine concern about the implications of economic policies on human rights in Africa, they fail to comprehensively articulate integrative rights-based responses to arguments based on considerations of economic or political expediency. Proper intellectual responses to Africa's myriad human development problems cannot work in isolation, but must consider interdisciplinary and multidimensional approaches to translate theory into practice, establishing an empirical nexus between rhetoric and stark realities.

As its objectives, therefore, this book seeks to develop a theoretical basis for understanding and analysing all human rights as they relate to the challenges of poverty, human deprivation and underdevelopment in African states; to define a human rights praxis for human development discourse in Africa; to evaluate the capacity of existing as well as evolving human rights law standards and mechanisms in meeting the challenges of human development in Africa; to determine how these standards and mechanisms can be translated into platforms for effectively addressing the problems of underdevelopment and mass deprivation in Africa, defining remedial strategies that will ensure that end; and to fill the gap in the existing

32 OAU Doc CAB/LEG/67/3 Rev 5 (1981) 21 ILM 58 (1982), entered into force on 21 October 1986.

33 See, eg, Economic Commission for Africa (ECA) and Africa Action *International policies and African realities* (2000) 1 25. See also J Tan *et al* 'Enhancing human development in the HIPC/PRSP context' African Region Human Development (2001) World Bank Working Paper Series 9-14.

human rights literature in relation to the implementation of economic, social and cultural rights in Africa.

Notwithstanding age-long circumstances, perceptions and practices that have kept economic, social and cultural rights as the undignified partners of civil and political rights, the present discourse seeks to squarely place economic, social and cultural rights on the African human rights agenda, and make them central subjects in defining integrative rights-based strategies for human development. In that light, despite the protracted allegation that economic, social and cultural rights are imprecise and vague, I portray them as rights not only capable of substantive interpretation, but also as human rights of ubiquitous relevance in the evolution of any realistic human development programme.

Without equivocation, I argue that economic, social and cultural rights are human rights equipped with ample normative substance and institutional frameworks that can guarantee their application at the domestic level just like any other human right, irrespective of any African state's legal tradition. Within the UN, regional and national human rights systems, I highlight how diverse institutions (including traditionally less identifiable fora) can strengthen the implementation of economic, social and cultural rights and contribute to a rights-based approach to human development in Africa.

An underlying argument in this work is that economic, social and cultural rights are human rights that have a special role to play in the protection of democratic principles.[34] It is pivotal in this book that civil and political rights are themselves better protected when economic, social and cultural rights are accorded adequate recognition within domestic legal systems. This book asserts that the effective protection and implementation of economic, social and cultural rights constitute a veritable pedestal for addressing the plight of the most vulnerable people of Africa; vital instrumentality in ensuring the accountability of African governments to their peoples; and a platform for strengthening every other human right. I seek to demonstrate that the effective implementation of economic, social and cultural rights has the potential of promoting socio-economic justice that could form the bedrock for the establishment of truly participatory democratic societies in Africa. In essence, it shows how the substance of economic, social and cultural rights could widen the ambits of emerging and existing liberal democratic regimes in Africa and allow the interests of traditionally marginalised groups (for example peasants, workers, women, children, youths, the landless,

34 See IE Koch 'Good governance and implementation of economic, social and cultural rights' in H Sano *et al* (eds) *Human rights and good governance* (2002) 73-93.

people with disabilities and people living with HIV/AIDS) to become mainstream issues in African political and socio-economic discourses and programmes.

I also seek to disprove the justiciability and resource constraint arguments against the implementation of economic, social and cultural rights and to demonstrate that the alleged lack of funds cannot always justify African governments' neglect or failure in fulfilling their basic legal obligations. Beyond the traditional conceptualisation of human rights as entitlements that must absolutely be judicially enforceable to qualify as 'legal' rights, this book identifies a range of other mechanisms for the remedial implementation of economic, social and cultural rights, for example, budgetary processes, social action, administrative justice and basic needs prioritisation, which are not necessarily connected to juridical mechanisms.

Equally critical to my argument is the question of calibrating the possible effect of legislation and bureaucracies on the integrative human rights approach. This is particularly crucial for any well-grounded inquiry into the intersection of constitutionalism, human rights and human development in Africa where, before and after independence, governance and development had largely been fixated on the ideals of centralised state system and monolithic planning.[35]

This book generally considers the conceptual and practical problems experienced in giving efficacy to economic, social and cultural rights in Africa, particularly the critical questions of justiciability and resources as they relate to issues of appropriateness, availability of and accessibility to remedies. In that regard, I examine juridical responses to human rights in African countries toward the protection and realisation of economic, social and cultural rights in order to identify how juridical attitudes contribute or have contributed to the marginalisation and devaluation, or the implementation and promotion of economic, social and cultural rights. That effort is helpful in understanding the new remedial approach to the implementation of economic, social and cultural rights canvassed in this book.

For analytical purposes, and to a lesser extent for comparative understanding, I consider the significance of positive trends in the UN, European and Inter-American human rights systems as well as in various national contexts around the world. By so doing, I present an

35 See JS Wunsch 'Centralisation and development in post-independence Africa' in JS Wunsch *et al* (eds) *The failure of the centralised state: Institutions and self-governance in Africa* (1995) 43; R Murray *Human rights in Africa: From the OAU to the African Union* 2004) 73-115.

analysis of the operational experiences of key institutions with respect to their relevant normative frameworks, the efficacy of their interpretive mandates for the implementation of economic, social and cultural rights, and highlights the lessons that can be learnt in stimulating a rights-based approach to human development in Africa.

Although African rights-based discourses generally resonate with the obligations of states, I accentuate the significant impact of non-state actors on the implementation of economic, social and cultural rights in Africa. Relating their activities to the theme of this book, I highlight the legal basis of the economic, social and cultural rights responsibilities of a wide range of significant non-state actors in Africa.

This book focuses on the broad spectrum of the normative and institutional frameworks for the implementation of economic, social and cultural rights within the UN human rights system, the African regional human rights system, and at the domestic level. While some African states are central case studies (for example Libya, Mauritania, Nigeria and South Africa), I highlight trends in many other African and non-African states where applicable.

Following the background introduction of the conceptual concerns, approach, form and contents of this book, in chapter II I define the normative and institutional frameworks of economic, social and cultural rights at the UN and the African regional levels, and their implications for the effective implementation of economic, social and cultural rights at the domestic level in Africa. The chapter underscores the reality of ample economic, social and cultural rights protection mechanisms and yet, the asymmetry of weak implementation. It points out a range of the legal problems that have arisen in the course of the textual elucidation of economic, social and cultural rights norms. This chapter indicates that, despite observable constraints, economic, social and cultural rights consist of protective and promotional elements that can strengthen their value as legal rights. Against the backdrop of increasing global efforts aimed at establishing human development as a human rights theme, this chapter evaluates the capacity of existing and emerging human rights frameworks relevant to Africa, and accentuates their weaknesses and prospects in the conceptualisation of an integrative rights-based approach to the appalling socio-economic conditions in Africa.

Chapter III entails an extensive analysis of the consequences of national legal systems, constitutional models and institutional mechanisms for the implementation of economic, social and cultural rights in African states. It considers the operational effects of human rights treaties, bills of rights, directive principles and national legislation on economic, social and cultural rights in Africa. This chapter strongly argues that, in view of the interplay of treaties, constitutional and other statutory provisions, economic, social and cultural rights can indeed assume significant value as legal entitlements within and outside juridical fora. The chapter critically evaluates the roles of hitherto recondite national institutions (for example, human rights commissions and ombudsmen) in the implementation of economic, social and cultural rights in Africa, and strongly emphasises their capacities to serve as purveyors of integrative rights-based approach to human development in Africa.

Without doubt, economic, social and cultural rights constitute an object of considerable debate. Despite their recognition in many human rights instruments in affirmative language, the controversy rages on. The debate among writers has persistently revolved around the volatile questions of justiciability and resource implications. While one school of thought argues that these rights are 'programmatic' and merely aspirational,[36] the other contends that these rights can be subjects of judicial review and implementation.[37] Chapter IV therefore critically addresses the justiciability question that has dogged economic, social and cultural rights implementation for long and accentuates the trends toward giving content and vigour to economic, social and cultural rights through indirect and direct interpretive application before UN, regional and national human rights bodies. It argues that, apart from the Second World Conference on Human Rights held in Vienna, Austria, in June 1993, that explicitly reaffirmed the *indivisibility, interdependence* and *interrelatedness* of human rights,[38] some national courts, UN human rights treaty monitoring bodies and human rights monitoring institutions within the European and Inter-American regional arrangements have, to a large extent, effectively disproved the overworked contention that economic, social and cultural rights are not justiciable. This chapter further demonstrates that economic, social and cultural rights are not esoteric entitlements in Africa, and that these rights are indeed critical subjects to African human development goals and human

36 EW Vierdag 'The legal nature of the rights granted by the International Covenant on Economic, Social and Cultural Rights' (1978) *9 Netherlands Yearbook on International Law* 69; M Cranston *What are human rights?* (1973) 65-71; GJH van Hoof 'The legal nature of economic, social and cultural rights' in P Alston *et al* (eds) *The right to food* (1984) 100-101; S Holmes & CR Sunstein *The cost of rights: Why liberty depends on taxes* (1999) 45 118-121.

37 H Shue 'Rights in the light of duties' in PG Brown *et al* (eds) *Human rights and US foreign policy* (1979) 65 66-78; H Shue *Basic rights: Subsistence, affluence and US foreign policy* (1980) 24-25; A Rosas *et al* 'Categories and beneficiaries of human rights' in R Hanski *et al* (eds) *An introduction to the international protection of human rights: A textbook* (1999) 49-62; A Eide & A Rosas 'Economic, social and cultural rights: A universal challenge' in Eide *et al* (n 29 above) 3-7; I Merali & V Oosterveld *Giving meaning to economic, social and cultural rights* (2001)

38 See World Conference on Human Rights, Vienna 14-25 June 1993 Vienna Declaration and Programmeme of Action, UN GAOR, 48th Sess, 22nd Plenary Mtg, UN Doc A/CONF 157/23 (12 July 1993) para 5 (Vienna Declaration).

rights implementation at both the regional and domestic levels in Africa. The chapter thus juxtaposes emerging jurisprudence from every geo-political zone of the world and highlights their implications for Africa and African states. The chapter emphasises the need to develop a vibrant body of economic, social and cultural rights jurisprudence in Africa to enhance their value as *legal* entitlements.

Chapter V presents a broad view of the difficulties in the effective remedial implementation of human rights generally and economic, social and cultural rights in particular. Critical to the discourse on the justiciability of economic, social and cultural rights has been the question of remedies. However, within global, regional and many national contexts, these rights are increasingly being accorded positive recognition as legal rights. Here, I emphasise how, despite observable constraints, Indian, South African and other national juridical entities across diverse world regions have, through the expansive interpretation of civil and political rights and commitment to the tangible delivery of the promises of human rights, considerably charted a path for the theoretical and practical appreciation as well as the jurisprudential development of economic, social and cultural rights in Africa. The chapter posits that the Indian experience is particularly instructive for many African states where the neo-Nigerian constitutional model of Directive Principles holds sway.

In respect of resource limitations, the state can simply not evade its obligations with respect to the realisation of most economic, social and cultural rights, irrespective of its level of resources or financial ability. This is because in many domestic contexts in Africa, the critical questions on these rights relate to equality and non-discrimination (on grounds of sex, race or other social status), priority setting (concerning budgetary allotments and imperatives) or accessibility (relating to normative, structural and institutional frameworks). I contend that these dynamics do not necessarily entail fiscal commitments. In terms of fiscal prioritisation, for instance, empirical survey shows in this work that many African states commit more funds to military expenditure or other bogus development projects than to social services like housing, education, water resources and health. The implication of this discovery is for closer public scrutiny of budgetary processes. This chapter also evaluates the import of current approaches to the implementation of economic, social and cultural rights and identifies gaps in those approaches as well as their weaknesses in meeting the peculiar normative and practical challenges in the African context. Drawing on plausible experiences from diverse backgrounds, I propose *a new remedial approach* to economic, social and cultural rights, founded upon state performance evaluation; basic needs prioritisation; and administrative process. This approach essentially defines a rights-based platform for realising the *legitimate expectations* of human beings in Africa.

While most literature on human rights in Africa generally evades direct engagement with the impact of diverse non-state actors on economic, social and cultural rights, chapter VI advances the human rights discourse in Africa by extensively examining a broad spectrum of such direct and remote actors that should become subjects of monitoring in the evolution of an integrative human rights response to development in Africa. It recognises that, even though states are primarily responsible for human rights protection, the effective implementation of economic, social and cultural rights in Africa will largely depend on the level of accountability deductible from numerous non-state actors, including transnational corporations (TNCs), multinational enterprises (MNEs), international financial and trade institutions, development agencies, aid donors, small-scale entrepreneurs, and even private persons and, of particular significance, the level of responsibility that civil society in Africa assumes in that task.

Chapter VI therefore argues that, in securing the implementation of economic, social and cultural rights in Africa, and in evolving a rights-based approach to human development, the impact of non-state actors must be subjected to evaluation, and thus proceeds to an analysis of the *legal* responsibilities of well-known and less identifiable role actors – derivable from a broad spectrum of instruments – and linking these to their programmes, policies and initiatives. The chapter also appraises the significance of African civil society in the theme of the present discourse and *why* the civil society's embrace of the challenges posed is historic, inevitable and non-negotiable at this stage of Africa's development experience.

Chapter VII sums up the entire discourse, drawing conclusions from the arguments and inferences in preceding chapters. A new insight emerges that within the corpus of international human rights law and other relevant instruments, economic, social and cultural rights are not abstractions but are legal entitlements consisting of enforceable elements in African states. The chapter reiterates the need for the advancement of Africa-specific standards of interpreting economic, social and cultural rights obligations in such a way that avoids the legalistic impediments of the International Covenant on Economic, Social and Cultural Rights (ICESCR). It concludes that traditional conceptualisations of economic, social and cultural rights as marginal rights are untenable in the African context, having regard to the convergence of the African Charter and a range of other human rights instruments.

Although it recognises the point of departure of this work as one located in the realm of *law*, the chapter nonetheless accentuates the interplay of diverse non-legalistic parameters that would directly and indirectly affect the value of economic, social and cultural rights in Africa. In its strategic outlook, chapter VII indicates a horizon of prospects for a vibrant economic, social and cultural rights culture and sustainable rights-based human development agenda in Africa as it presents recommendations to diverse sectors of the human family in securing the aims of this work. In defining trajectories for the actualisation of the approaches it canvasses, the chapter identifies civil society in Africa as the primary purveyor of the activism required to secure my goals in this book. Recognising some of the perceived limitations and problems of civil society groups in Africa, I explore new ways of repositioning the African civil society to effectively champion this evolutionary process within existing legal frameworks.

This book represents an effort to address some of the salient challenges to the African human rights and development agenda, both from legal and multidisciplinary perspectives. An invaluable outcome of my rights-based approach is its articulation of practical ideas for galvanising economic, social and cultural rights advocacy in other developed, developing countries, and states in transition.

1.3 Concepts and definitions

All through this book, the reader will encounter some concepts and terminologies that may or may not have assumed a technical meaning in scholarly works. To clarify whatever ambiguities may arise, I set out the connotations of these twin expressions, 'rights-based approach' and 'integrative rights-based approach'.

Beginning in the 1990s, it has increasingly become commonplace for development theorists, policy experts, global institutions and, lately, human rights advocates to address development in the language of rights. Today, with the formal commitment of a range of intergovernmental agencies and international non-governmental organisations (INGOs) towards integrating a human rights ethos into their development work, the prevalent thinking in development discourses is the *rights-based approach*. Although there is divergence in the outlook of what each agency or institution perceives as representing the 'rights-based approach', certain elements have crystallised over the years as representative of the central attributes of the concept.[39]

There is thus an unmistakable consensus among the various theories on the rights-based approach that the full realisation of human rights should be a vital goal of development efforts. The approach canvassed in this book therefore perceives human rights as vital components of development programmes and policies that must necessarily be integrated in all processes designed to deliver the promises of development. Taken together, the integrative rights-based approach to human development contemplates people-centred modalities for development in ways that emphasise equality and non-discrimination; accountability and transparency; and popular participation.

[39] For an in-depth scholarly insight into the emergence of human rights themes in development theory and the various definitions proffered by writers, see P Gready & J Ensor 'Introduction' in P Gready & J Enson (eds) *Reinventing development? Translating rights-based approaches from theory into practice* (2005) 1 12-14; AL Sarel in 'Human rights-based approaches to development co-operation, HIV/AIDS, and food security' (2007) 29 *Human Rights Quarterly* 460 475-478.

2

Normative and Institutional Frameworks of Human Rights in the UN and African Regional System

We affirm that economic, social and cultural rights are not hierarchically below civil and political human rights. They are at an equal level. We are tired of having to put up with situations where successive governments justify dictatorship by stating that in widely asymmetrical societies, curtailing the fundamental freedoms is justified in order to guarantee social and economic progress ... it is better for us to live in an era that guarantees the basic freedoms ... this means that dealing with human rights is dealing with civil, political, economic, social and cultural human rights.[40]

1 Human development in a rights-based context

It is important to note from the onset that rights-based frameworks for human development exist in Africa at multiple normative levels. The channels for determining these rights are to be found in a matrix of international, regional and national legal mechanisms. Platforms for human rights contestation in Africa are not, however, limited to the interplay of 'legal' regimes. Because I consider the theme of this discourse in holistic fashion, its scope extends beyond the putative ideal of locating human rights validation within the narrow confines of legalism.

Therefore, I examine a complex of non-legal political and social processes that hold the capacity effectively to confer legitimacy on the enjoyment of human rights in African states. Specifically, I argue that the definition, interpretation and effective implementation of economic, social and cultural rights, as rights critical to human development, require the inputs of political, administrative, social, and private sector systems because the promotion, protection and

40 PC Carbonari 'Human dignity as a basic concept of ethics and human rights' in BK Goldewijk *et al* (eds) *Dignity and human rights: The implementation of economic, social and cultural rights* (2002) 35 40.

implementation of economic, social and cultural rights depend more on policy mechanisms than on narrower reliance on legalism.[41]

Based on the foregoing premise, I proceed to analyse my concerns as they relate to a human development praxis located within the frameworks of international and African regional human rights systems.[42] While not oblivious of the works of various authors in diverse civilisations addressing some of the theoretical aspects of this theme, in its own uniqueness, my effort here reflects on the broad spectrum of the human rights standards and instruments relating to the theme of our present discourse at international and regional levels. I make a conscious attempt to draw attention to the problematic theoretical and practical issues that have been

41 See C Moser *et al To claim our rights: Livelihood security, human rights and sustainable development* (2001) 22.

42 I acknowledge the philosophical questions surrounding the conceptualisation of economic, social and cultural rights as 'rights' within the mainstream discourse on human rights. Such questions include the founding of economic, social and cultural rights on the notion of human dignity; the place of economic, social and cultural rights in the 'trichotomisation' or tri-generational approach to human rights; the converging debate on the interconnectedness of all human rights; and the volatile issue of whether economic, social and cultural rights, or indeed, all human rights, are universal. The dialectic of this book, however, goes beyond the quest for philosophical foundations or the abstract origins of these rights. For background reading, see JJ Shestack 'The philosophical foundations of human rights' in Symonides (n 24 above) 31 53-54; T Fernyhough 'Human rights and pre-colonial Africa' in R Cohen *et al* (eds) *Human rights and governance in Africa* (1993) 39 42; PG Lauren *The evolution of international human rights: Visions seen* (1998) 14-20; OC Eze 'Human rights and social justice: An African perspective' EMPAC Annual Lecture IV, 21-22 (Empowerment and Action Research Centre, Lagos, Annual Lecture Series 4 1998); C Wellman *The proliferation of rights* (1999) 13-4; P Meyer-Bisch 'D'Une Succession de Générations A UN Système des Droits Humains' [Of a series of generations in the UN system of human rights] in A Fernando *et al* (eds) *Human rights at the dawn of the twenty-first century* (1999) 333-359; K Kumado 'Africa and human rights since Karel Vasak's three generations' in Fernando *et al* (eds) 273; M Cranston (n 36 above) 65-71; V Kartashkin 'The socialist countries and human rights' in K Vasak *et al* (eds) *The international dimensions of human rights vol ii* (1982) 633-635; A Eide 'Economic and social rights' in Symonides (n 24 above) 111; D Matas *Economic, social and cultural rights and the role of lawyers: North American perspectives* (1995) 55 *The Review of the International Commission of Jurists* 123 126; KJ Guest *Exploitation under erasure: Economic, social and cultural rights engage economic globalisation* (1997) 19 *Adelaide Law Review* 77 82; JB Lima Jr 'The expanding nature of human rights and the affirmation of their indivisibility and enforceability' in Carbonari (n 40 above) 4 47; Shue (n 37 above); H Shue 'Rights in the light of duties' in PG Brown *et al* (eds) *Human rights and US foreign policy* (1979) 65 66-78; K Tomaševski 'Justiciability of economic, social and cultural rights' (1995) 55 *The Review of the International Commission of Jurists* 203 218; M Mutua *Human rights: a political and cultural critique* (2002) 64-67 137-139; F Ouguergouz *The African Charter on Human and Peoples' Rights: A comprehensive agenda for human rights and sustainable democracy in Africa* (2003) 9-10; W Benedek 'Peoples' rights and individual duties as special features of the African Charter on Human and Peoples' Rights' in P Kunig *et al* (eds) *Regional protection of human rights by international law: The emerging African system* (1985) 59 94; R Cohen 'Endless teardrops: Prolegomena to the study of human rights in Africa' in R Cohen *et al* (eds) *Human rights and governance in Africa* (1993) 13-16; R Howard 'Evaluating human rights in Africa: Some problems of implicit comparisons' (1984) 6 *Human Rights Quarterly* 160 175.

confronted in giving life to these norms, particularly in Africa. With the hindsight of contemporary developments in the field of human rights, I examine implementation mechanisms for economic, social and cultural rights and endeavour to evaluate the prospects for translating human rights norms into concrete benefits for all Africans.

1.1 The United Nations system

The UN has since 1948 churned out an array of treaties and other instruments that set global standards for human rights protection.[43] Moreover, since the 1990s, the body has also promoted series of global conferences that have advanced an integrative human rights discourse.[44] It should be noted, however, that its recently increased attention to economic, social and cultural rights arose out of the appalling conditions of poverty and deprivation that have continued to plague a vast portion of the human family, long after World War II.[45] Interest has been rekindled among researchers and civil society activists that the realisation of economic, social and cultural rights could be a viable platform for addressing diverse socio-economic and human development challenges.[46]

43 The original core of UN human rights treaty-making efforts is contained in what is known as the 'International Bill of Rights'. These are the Universal Declaration of Human Rights (Universal Declaration), UNGA Res 217 A (III), UN Doc A/810 (1948); the International Covenant on Civil and Political Rights (ICCPR), UNGA Res 2200A (XXI), UN Doc A/6316 (1966), 999 UNTS 171, entered into force on 23 March 1976, and the International Covenant on Economic, Social and Cultural Rights (ICESCR), UNGA Res 2200A (XXI), UN Doc A/6316 (1966), 993 UNTS 3, entered into force on 3 January 1976. See K Drzewicki 'Internationalisation of human rights and their juridisation' in Hanski *et al* (n 37 above) 25 32-35; M Robinson 'Making human rights matter: Eleanor Roosevelt's time has come' (2003) 16 *Harvard Human Rights Journal* 4.

44 Some of these were the UN Seminar on Appropriate Indicators to Measure Achievements in the Progressive Realisation of Economic, Social and Cultural Rights' (Geneva 1993), UN Doc A/CONF.157/PC/73 (1993); the Second World Conference on Human Rights' (Vienna 1993) (n 38 above); the World Conference on Population Development (Cairo 1994); the World Summit on Social Development' (Copenhagen 1995); the Fourth Women's Conference (Beijing 1996); and the World Summit on Sustainable Development (Johnnesburg 2002).

45 See BK Goldewijk *et al Where needs meet rights: Economic, social and cultural rights in a new perspective* (1999) viii-ix; AR Chapman 'A "violations approach" for monitoring the International Covenant on Economic, Social and Cultural Rights' (1996) 18 *Human Rights Quarterly* 23. See also I Cotler 'Human rights as the modern tool of revolution' in K Mahoney *et al* (eds) *Human rights in the twenty-first century: A global challenge* (1993) 7-11.

46 See eg K Raes 'The philosophical basis of social, economic and cultural rights' in P van der Auweraert *et al* (eds) *Social, economic and cultural rights: An appraisal of current European and international developments* (2002) 43 52-53. See also P De Vos 'Transformative justice: Social and economic rights in the South African Constitution' in Van der Auweraert *et al* 243-260. See also SC Agbakwa 'Reclaiming humanity: Economic, social and cultural rights as the cornerstone of African human rights' (2002) 5 *Yale Human Rights and Development Law Journal* 177 178; Guest (n 42 above) 93; SC Agbakwa 'A path least taken: Economic and social rights and the prospects of conflict prevention and peace building in Africa' (2003) 47 *Journal of African Law* 38 57-63.

Alongside UN forum, there has been an impressive civil society activism in the field of economic, social and cultural rights.[47] In June 1986, a group of activists and professionals met in Limburg, the Netherlands, and produced what is now known as the Limburg Principles on the Implementation of the International Covenant on Economic, Social and Cultural Rights.[48] There have also been a series of other equally significant and relevant instruments.[49]

The basis of the UN's involvement in human rights is its Charter.[50] The UN Charter affirms the faith of all member states of the body 'in fundamental human rights, in the dignity and worth of the human person, in equal rights of men and women and of nations large and small'.[51] The UN's commitment to human rights, broadly speaking, can also be distilled from other provisions in its Charter. Under article 13, the UN General Assembly is obliged to 'initiate studies and make recommendations for the purpose of ... assisting in the realisation of human rights and fundamental freedoms for all without distinction as to race, sex, language, or religion'.

Of greater significance to our discourse, however, are the provisions of articles 55 and 56 of the UN Charter. Article 56 creates an obligation for all UN member states to co-operate and collaborate, jointly and severally, with the UN 'for the achievement of the purposes set forth in article 55.' Article 55, in turn, commits the UN to the promotion of '(a) *higher standards of living, full employment,*

47 The 1990s witnessed a redirection of the efforts of many otherwise conservative human rights non-governmental organisations (NGOs) towards addressing human rights violations in holistic fashion at their various levels of activism. See eg 'Indivisible human rights: The relationship of political and civil rights to subsistence and poverty' *Human Rights Watch* September 1992 1-80. See also 'Evil days; 30 years of war and famine in Ethiopia' *Africa Watch* September 1991; 'Mozambique: Conspicuous destruction - War, famine and the reform process in Mozambique' *Africa Watch* July 1992; A McChesney *Promoting economic, social and cultural rights* (2000) 21.

48 UN Doc E/CN.4/1987/17, Annex, reprinted in (1987) 9 *Human Rights Quarterly* 122-135. For a scholarly analysis of the evolution of the Limburg principles and how these principles have impacted the economic, social and cultural rights discourse since 1986, see 'Economic, social and cultural rights: Limburg principles' in E Lawson (ed) *Encyclopaedia of human rights* (1991) 416; DL Martin 'The Limburg principles turn ten: An impact assessment' in T van Boven (ed) *The Maastricht guidelines on violations of economic, social and cultural rights: Proceedings of the workshop of experts,* organised by the International Commission of Jurists (Geneva, Switzerland), the Urban Morgan Institute on Human Rights (Cincinnati, USA) and the Maastricht Centre for Human Rights of Maastricht University 22-26 January 1997 (1988) *Netherlands Institute for Human Rights SIM Series* No 20 191-205.

49 See eg 'The Bangalore declaration and plan of action' (1995) 55 *The Review of the International Commission of Jurists* 5-227; 'The Maastricht guidelines on violations of economic, social and cultural rights' reprinted in (1997) 15 *Netherlands Quarterly of Human Rights* 244-252, UN Doc E/CN.4/Sub.2/1991/55.

50 UN Charter 1945. For a concise history of the evolution of the UN Charter, see A Yoder *The evolution of the United Nations system* (1997) 25-37.

51 n 59 above, Preamble para 2.

and conditions of economic and social progress and development; (b) solutions of international economic, social, health, and related problems; and international cultural and educational co-operation; and (c) universal respect for, and observance of, human rights and fundamental freedoms for all without distinction as to race, sex, language, or religion'.[52]

It is interesting to note that in identifying the crux of human rights in the UN Charter, scholarly attention has dwelt almost exclusively on article 55(c). That focus is not surprising as only that sub-section explicitly mentions 'human rights.' Nevertheless, article 55(a) pointedly stresses the central responsibility of the UN and its member states for the pursuit of 'higher standards of living, full employment, and conditions of economic and social progress and development'.[53] The UN Charter thus 'globalises' certain fundamental concerns for human well-being.[54]

The first comprehensive instrument to elucidate the depth and content of the human rights provisions in the UN Charter was the

52 My emphasis. For the controversy about the legal status of the human rights provisions in the UN Charter, see L Henkin *The age of rights* (1990) 51; P Alston 'Critical appraisal of the UN human rights regime' in P Alston (ed) *The United Nations and human rights: A critical appraisal* (1992) 25; K Drzewicki 'The United Nations Charter and the Universal Declaration of Human Rights' in Hanski *et al* (n 37 above) 65 70. Another group of scholars, however, argues that because of the imprecise nature of the language of the provisions, the fact that these provisions do not list any of the rights contemplated, and the absence of enforcement machinery, those provisions do not confer any rights on the individual. According to the writers in this group, the Charter provisions merely allude to human rights aspirations which member states hope to achieve within the scope of national resources and development. See J Dugard *International law: A South African perspective* (2001) 236-237. See also J Dugard 'The legal effect of United Nations resolutions on apartheid' (1966) 83 *South African Law Journal* 44.

53 Delving into the *travaux préparatoires* of the provisions in art 55, Goodrich, Hambro and Simons contend that '[t]his phraseology had reflected a twofold preoccupation of ... leaders in particular: first, a belief resulting from the circumstances leading to World War II that it was necessary to take effective measures by international co-operation to restore and maintain conditions of economic stability and general well-being if war was to be avoided in future; second, a conviction that respect for basic human rights and fundamental freedoms should be achieved not only as an end in itself but also as a condition favourable to the maintenance of international peace and respect for law.' See LM Goodrich *et al Charter of the United Nations: Commentary and documents* (1969) 371.

54 To demonstrate that the UN Charter did not envisage a cosmetic human rights profile, its art 62 empowers one of the principal organs of the UN, the Economic and Social Council (ECOSOC) to 'make recommendations [to the UN General Assembly] for the purpose of promoting respect for, and observance of, human rights and fundamental freedoms', while art 68 goes further to empower ECOSOC to 'set up commissions ... for the promotion of human rights ...'. It was pursuant to this mandate that ECOSOC established the Commission on Human Rights in 1946. See RE Asher *et al The United Nations and the promotion of the general welfare* (1957) 664; LB Sohn 'Human rights: Their implementation and supervision by the United Nations' in T Meron (ed) *Human rights in international law: Legal and policy issues* (1984) 368 384-389.

Universal Declaration of Human Rights (Universal Declaration), 1948.[55] A treaty containing 30 articles, the Universal Declaration opens with the unequivocal provisions on *equality* and *non-discrimination*, two vital principles that have become hallowed concepts in defining every other human right.[56] Articles 3 to 21 cover the traditional civil and political rights,[57] while articles 22 to 27 deal with economic, social and cultural rights.[58] What is particularly outstanding about the Universal Declaration, at least from the perspective of our discourse, is that it is devoid of any language of hierarchy among human rights. On the same footing and with equal potency, the Universal Declaration guarantees the protection of civil and political rights and economic, social and cultural rights.

Notwithstanding divergent arguments on the legal status of the Universal Declaration, an undeniable fact is that it is an instrument that has become the most influential and most authoritative global reference for human rights, considering the multitude of UN and regional human rights treaties, national constitutions, municipal cases and statutes, and private sector initiatives that have unabashedly drawn inspiration from it.[59]

To translate the ideals of the Universal Declaration into concrete legal obligations, two distinct instruments were later drafted,

55 For a vivid insider description of the drafting processes and political intrigues that culminated in the adoption of the Universal Declaration on 10 December 1948, see MA Glendon *A world made new* (2001). See also J Morsink *The Universal Declaration of Human Rights: Origins, drafting, and intent* (1999) 1-88.

56 See Universal Declaration, arts 2 & 3, respectively. Virtually all human rights treaties since World War II emphasise the cardinal principles of equality and non-discrimination. See EW Vierdag *The concept of discrimination in international law with special reference to human rights* (1973) 1 83-139. See also A Eide *et al* *Equality and non-discrimination* (1990) 17-25.

57 The right to life, liberty and personal security (art 3); prohibition of slavery and servitude (art 4); prohibition of torture, cruel, inhuman or degrading treatment or punishment (art 5); recognition as a person (art 6); equal protection before the law (art 7); the right to effective judicial remedy for violations (art 8); freedom from arbitrary arrest, detention or exile (art 9); the right to a free and fair trial (art 10); presumption of innocence in criminal proceedings (art 11); the right to privacy and family life (art 12); freedom of movement (art 13); the right to seek and enjoy asylum (art 14); the right to a nationality (art 15); the right to marry and found a family (art 16); the right to property (art 17); freedom of thought, conscience and religion (art 18); freedom of opinion and expression (art 19); freedom of peaceful assembly and association (art 20); and the right to political participation (art 21).

58 These are the rights to social security (art 22); to work and to free choice of employment and employment standards and conditions (art 23); to rest and leisure, including holidays with pay (art 24); to adequate living standards (art 25); to education (art 26); and to cultural life (art 27).

59 For discussions on the legal significance and influence of the Universal Declaration at global, regional and national levels, see Asher *et al* (n 54 above) 674-677; LB Sohn *et al International protection of human rights* (1973) 514-522; HJ Steiner *et al International human rights in context* (2007) 152.

namely, the International Covenant on Civil and Political Rights (ICCPR) and ICESCR, both of 1966.[60]

Although ICCPR obviously addresses traditional civil and political rights, the treaty is not without implications for economic, social and cultural rights. Like the Universal Declaration, ICCPR emphasises the cardinal principles of equality and non-discrimination.[61] Article 22 of ICCPR guarantees the right to freedom of association, including the right to form and join trade unions.' ICCPR goes further in article 23 to guarantee the protection of the right to marry and to equality in marriage, a subject that would naturally be considered as belonging to the social and private realm. Furthermore, ICCPR recognises and protects cultural and linguistic rights.[62]

It is, however, not only from ICCPR that one can glean economic, social and cultural rights within the UN human rights treaty framework. They are also found in a series of other UN human rights treaties. Some of these are the Convention on the Elimination of All Forms of Racial Discrimination (CERD), 1965;[63] the Convention on the Elimination of All Forms of Discrimination Against Women (CEDAW), 1979;[64] the Convention on the Rights of the Child (CRC), 1989;[65] and the Convention on the Rights of All Migrant Workers and Members of their Families (MWC), 1990.[66]

60 See Drzewicki (n 43 above) 32-35.

61 See ICCPR, arts 2-3. Similarly, art 26 of ICCPR reinforces the principle of equality. See Human Rights Committee, General Comment No 28 para 31 UN Doc HRI/GEN. 1/Rev 6 (2000).

62 Art 27. For a wealth of jurisprudence emanating from this provision, see R Hanski & M Scheinin *Institute for human rights, leading cases of the Human Rights Committee* (2003) 325-374.

63 CERD, UNGA Res 2106, UN Doc A/6014 (1965), 60 UNTS 195, entered into force on 4 January 1969. These include the right to marry and choice of a spouse (art 5(d)(iv)); the right to property (art 5(d)(v)); the right to freely-chosen employment conditions and standards (art 5(e)(i)); the right to form and join trade unions (art 5(e)(ii)); the right to housing (art 5(e)(iii)); the right to social security (art 5(e)(iv)); the right to education (art 5(e)(v)); and the right to equal participation in cultural activities (art 5(e)(vi)).

64 CEDAW, UNGA Res 34/80 (1979), 1249 UNTS 13, entered into force on 3 September 1981. These include the rights to own land and property (art 16 (1)(h)); to education (art 10); to health (art 12); to freely-chosen employment conditions and standards (art 11(a)); to marry and equality in marriage (arts 16(1)(a)-(c)); to reproductive health services (art 12(2)); to social security (art 11); and to cultural life (art 13(c)).

65 CRC, UNGA Res 44/25 (1989), 28 ILM 1456, entered into force 2 September 1990. These include the right to own land and property (art 16 (1)(h)); the right to education (art 10); the right to health (art 24); the right to a healthy environment (art 24); the right to food (art 24)(2)(c)); the right to reproductive health services (arts 24(1)(d) & (f)); the right to social security (art 26); and the right to cultural life (arts 30-31).

66 MWC, UN Doc A/Res/45/158 (1990), entered into force on 10 December 2002. These include the right to privacy and family life (art 14); the right to property (art 15); the right to freely-chosen employment conditions and standards (art 26(e)(i)); the right to form and join trade unions(art 26); the right to social security (art 27); the right to education (art 30); and the right to equal participation in cultural activities (art 31).

Outside these UN treaty-based instruments, the International Labour Organisation (ILO) equally has a cornucopia of instruments that guarantee aspects of economic, social and cultural rights.[67]

While there are now numerous international treaties, plans and programmes that seek to secure, directly and indirectly, the protection and implementation of economic, social and cultural rights, it is no overstatement that the UN human rights system is the most significant for Africa. This cannot but be so. In the light of the underdevelopment of economic, social and cultural rights jurisprudence within the African regional human rights system, the infancy or rather imprecision of economic, social and cultural rights jurisprudence within the European and Inter-American regional human rights systems as against the fast-paced definitive elaboration on the scope and content of human rights by the various human rights treaty monitoring bodies within the UN, it is only logical and instructive for the African regional human rights system to seek guidance, albeit cautiously, in the UN human rights model.[68] As would be seen in subsequent chapters, this same *raison d'être* explains why some domestic legal regimes in Africa have begun to have recourse to the UN human rights interpretative model.

67 Some of these are the ILO Convention Concerning Freedom of Association and Protection of the Right to Organise, ILO Convention 87, 9 July 1948, 68 UNTS 17, entered into force on 4 July 1950; the ILO Convention Concerning the Prohibition and Immediate Action for the Elimination of the Worst Forms of Child Labour, ILO Convention 182, 17 June 1999 ILO/Gen Con, 87th Sess, entered into force on 19 November 2000; the ILO Convention Concerning Equal Remuneration for Men and Women Workers for Work of Equal Value, ILO Convention 100, 29 June 1951, 165 UNTS 303, entered into force on 23 May 1953; the ILO Convention Concerning Minimum Standards of Social Security, ILO Convention 102, 28 June 1952, 210 UNTS 131, entered into force on 27 April 1953; the ILO Convention Concerning Discrimination in respect of Employment and Occupation, ILO Convention 111, 25 June 1958, 362 UNTS 31, entered into force on 15 June 1960; the ILO Convention Concerning the Abolition of Forced Labour, ILO Convention 105, 25 June 1957, 320 UNTS 291, entered into force on 17 January 1959; and the ILO Convention Concerning the Principles of the Right to Organise and Bargain Collectively', ILO Convention 98, 1 July 1949, 96 UNTS 257, entered into force on 18 July 1951. All these instruments are available at http://www.ilo.org (accessed 12 June 2009). For an extensive scholarly analysis of the direct implications of the ILO's activities for the protection of economic, social and cultural rights, see K Samson 'The protection of economic and social rights within the framework of the International Labour Organisation' in F Matscher (ed) *The implementation of economic and social rights: National, international and comparative aspects* (1991) 123-140.

68 See D Harris *et al The European Social Charter* (2001); L Samuel *Fundamental social rights: Case law of the European Social Charter* (2002). See also K Lenaerts *et al* 'Social rights in the case law of the European Court of Justice: The impact of the Charter of Fundamental Rights of the European Union on standing case law' in Van der Auweraert *et al* (eds) (n 46 above) 159-185; AC Baspineiro 'Inter-American tools for the enforceability of economic, social and cultural rights' in Carbonari (n 40 above) 99-110.

1.1.1 The International Covenant on Economic, Social and Cultural Rights

Normative content

ICESCR[69] consists of a Preamble and five other parts. The Preamble sets out the broad concerns and principles underlying the rights guaranteed in its provisions. Apart from stressing its recognition of the inherent dignity and of the equal and inalienable rights of all members of the human family',[70] the Preamble emphasises the enjoyment of civil and political rights and economic, social and cultural rights as a precondition for the 'freedom from fear and want.'[71]

Part I of ICESCR contains only one article of three subsections that proclaim the right of self-determination for all peoples and the right to freely dispose of their natural wealth and resources.[72] Part II (articles 2-5) defines the obligations of state parties to ICESCR and the scope of the lawful restrictions permissible under the treaty. The most significant, yet most controversial provision of ICESCR is in article 2. I shall examine this provision in detail in a short while.

Part III (articles 6-15) contains the cluster of rights that ICESCR guarantees to 'everyone.'[73] Part IV (Articles 16-25) deals with the

69 For an insight into the drafting history of ICESCR, see M Craven 'The International Covenant on Economic, Social and Cultural Rights' in Hanski *et al* (n 37 above) 101. ICESCR serves its purpose in that, rather than just listing rights in their nominal form as seen in the Universal Declaration, ICESCR gives descriptive and definitive details about most of the rights it guarantees. See generally T Buergenthal *International human rights in a nutshell* (1995) 52-53. Since 1966 when ICESCR was adopted, 159 states have become parties to it, including 47 African states. See United Nations 'Status of ratifications of the ICESCR' at http://www2.ohchr.org/english/bodies/ratification/3.htm (accessed 12 June 2009).

70 Preamble para 1-2.

71 Preamble para 3. This is an obvious allusion to the famous 'four freedoms' expression of former US President Franklin Roosevelt prior to the establishment of the UN. See Franklin D Roosevelt's Address to Congress 6 January 1941 (1941) 87(1) *Congressional Records*.

72 Art 1(1)-(3). For an interpretation of this article as conferring an economic rather than a political right, see Craven (n 69 above) 103-104.

73 These rights are the right to work (art 6); the right to the enjoyment of just and favourable conditions of work (art 7); the right to form and freely join trade unions (art 8); the right to social security (art 9); the right to the protection of family and family life (art 10); the right to an adequate standard of living (art 11); the right to the enjoyment of the highest attainable standard of physical and mental health (art 12); the right to education (art 13), including steps towards its implementation (art 14); and the right to take part in cultural life and to enjoy the benefits of scientific progress (art 15). For an array of literature where each of these rights have been subjected to rigorous analysis, see MCR Craven *The International Covenant on Economic, Social and Cultural Rights* (1995) 153-351; Eide 'Economic and social rights' (n 42 above) 128-155; A Eide 'The right to an adequate standard of living including the right to food' in Eide *et al* (n 29 above) 133-289.

treaty's monitoring and implementation mechanisms, while Part V (Articles 26-31) contains the customary treaty provisions on signature, ratification, entry into force, accession, transitional period, amendment procedure and treaty authenticating clauses.

I would have considered the rights guaranteed in ICESCR to have meaningfully met the socio-economic quintessence of the Universal Declaration but for the gaping *lacuna* in respect of the right to property. Whereas Article 17 of the Universal Declaration positively guarantees the right to individual or joint ownership of property, ICESCR does not replicate that provision in any way.[74]

Apart from the contentious issue of the scope and content of obligations under ICESCR, the treaty has been subjected to other subtle criticisms. While Craven decries the 'excessive generality' of the terms of the rights provided,[75] Trubek remarks that the treaty only 'recognises' rights, without more.[76]

Nature and scope of obligations created

The kernel of the obligations created for the protection of the rights in ICESCR is the provision of article 2(1), which states:

> Each state party to the present covenant undertakes to take steps, individually and through international assistance and co-operation, especially economic and technical, to the maximum of its available resources, with a view to achieving progressively the full realisation of the rights recognised in the present Covenant by all appropriate means, including particularly the adoption of legislative measures.

The above provision encapsulates the nature of state parties' obligations under ICESCR and determines how they must approach the implementation of the substantive rights contained in articles 6 to 15.[77] The wording of article 2(1) of ICESCR has remained a subject of great controversy among government officials, scholars and human rights activists. There have been robust arguments suggesting that, rather than constituting binding obligations for state parties, the

74 See generally Craven (n 73 above) 25.

75 As above.

76 DM Trubek 'Economic, social and cultural rights in the third world: Human rights law and human needs programmes' in Meron (n 54 above) 206 213.

77 By virtue of arts 26 and 31 of the Vienna Convention on the Law of Treaties, UN Doc A/CONF.39/28 (1969) 8 ILM 679 (1969), entered into force 27 January 1980, the provisions of ICESCR are binding on all parties to it and must be performed in good faith. See MW Janis *An introduction to international law* (1999) 27-30.

rights in ICESCR are but mere 'aspirations' or idealistic goals to be achieved over the course of time.[78]

Under article 2, state parties have expressly undertaken to be legally bound to take steps, to the *maximum* of their *available resources*, to *achieve* progressively the full realisation of the rights in ICESCR. One critical misconstruction that has resulted from the language of that provision is that the actualisation of economic, social and cultural rights strictly necessitates state provisions. This was why many writers, such as Vierdag and Cranston, berated economic, social and cultural rights on the assumption that the rights are costly, would undermine creativity, would remove incentives, and would lead to bloated state apparatus.[79]

While there remains a lot of work to be done in the elaboration of the exact scope and content of article 2, a clearer understanding of the obligations of a state party to ICESCR has increasingly crystallised over the years. Human rights experts and scholars have, by growing consensus, identified the tripartite levels at which the obligations of a state operate in regard to any human right. These are that the state must *respect*, *protect* and *fulfil*. The obligation to fulfil further contemplates the duty to *facilitate*, to *provide* and to *promote*.[80]

The UN Committee on Economic, Social and Cultural Rights (ESCR

78 See generally Vierdag (n 36 above) 80. See also I Brownlie *Principles of public international law* (2003) 539. For others like Sunstein, civil and political rights are negative in that they only require abstention by states whereas the ESCR Committee are positive because they demand expenses by states. See CR Sunstein 'Against positive rights: Why social and economic rights don't belong in the new constitutions of post-communist Europe' (1993) 2 *East European Constitutional Review* 35-38.

79 See Vierdag (n 36 above) 80. See also Cranston (n 36 above).

80 Although Shue originally conceived the idea of a 'tripartite typology' in 1980, many human rights scholars and experts in subsequent years have advanced the idea. While there are variants of the levels of obligations, such as those proposed by Van Hoof (1984), the *Maastricht Guidelines* (n 49 above) and Steiner & Alston (2000), the most elaborate and most influential are those found in the pronouncement of the treaty monitoring body of ICESCR, the ESCR Committee in its General Comment No 14 'The right to the highest attainable standard of health (art 12)', UN Doc E/C.12/2000/4 (GC No 14). For a scholarly analysis of these typologies, their variants, significance and connotations, see M Sepulveda *The nature of the obligations under the International Covenant on Economic, Social and Cultural Rights* (2003) 157-248. The ESCR Committee's typology has itself found further development in the works of the UN Special Rapporteur on the Right to Food (A Eide). See A Eide 'The right to adequate food as a human right' UN Sales S89.XIV2, New York, 1989; A Eide *et al* 'Food security and the right to food in international law and development' (1991) 1 *Iowa Journal of Transnational Law and Contemporary Problems* 415-467; Report updating the study on he right to food prepared by A Eide UN Doc E/CN.4/Sub.2/1998/9; 'The right to adequate food and to be free from hunger', updated report by Special Rapporteur A Eide UN Doc E/CN.4/Sub.2/1999/12 paras 51-52; and A Eide 'The right to food in theory and practice' http://www.fao.org/docrep/ (accessed 12 June 2009). See Shue (n 37 above) 65 66-78.

Committee) has consistently addressed many of the rights in ICESCR from the perspective of these typologies as evident in the jurisprudence emanating from its work.[81] Thus, with regard to the obligation to *respect*, state parties are required to *refrain* from taking actions that result in the denial of economic, social and cultural rights. This means, for example, that a state must not interfere with the livelihood of its subjects or their capabilities as well as their means of subsistence, including land. A number of the ESCR Committee's Concluding Observations on the reports of some African states illustrates the ESCR Committee's concern in this regard.[82]

It is thus arguable, for instance, that where national legislation or policy adversely affects human livelihood, the state must rectify it.[83] Literally, therefore, the obligation to respect means a state should not promulgate a law or adopt a policy that would deprive individuals of their rights or carry out any act that would jeopardise the choices and freedoms of individuals. While complex experiences in modern governance might provide contestable justification for state restraint on individual liberties, the essence of the *respect* quotient is to negate arbitrary actions. This element certainly demands no such fiscal commitment as economic, social and cultural rights critics are wont to assume. To secure the right to housing, for instance, a state

81 Although it was in respect of the right to food that the ESCR Committee first applied the test of this typology in 1999, it has equally applied it in defining the right to education (1999), the right to the highest attainable standard of health (2000), and the right to water (2002). See ESCR Committee General Comment No 15 'The right to water (arts 11 & 12)' (2002*)*, UN Doc E/C.12/2002/11 (GC No 15) reprinted in Compilation of General Comments and General Recommendations adopted by Human Rights Treaty Bbodies UN Doc HRI/GEN/1/Rev6, 12 May 2004 106-123.

82 See eg ESCR Committee Consideration of reports submitted by state parties under arts 16 & 17, Senegal (2001) para 31 http://www.umn.edu/humanrts/esc/senegal2001.html (accessed 12 June 2009), where the ESCR Committee lamented the incidence of forced evictions in Dakar and other districts; ESCR Committee, Consideration of Reports Submitted by States Parties under Articles 16 and 17, Sudan (2000) para 25 http://www.umn.edu/humanrts/esc/sudan2000.html (accessed 12 June 2009) (ESCR Committee – Sudan) where the ESCR Committee decried the 'bombardment of villages and camps of the civilian population, in the war zones in Southern Sudan, including the bombing of schools and hospitals. The ESCR Committee also expressed concern about the resort to 'deprivation of food and the creation of a man-made famine as an instrument of war, coupled with the diversion of humanitarian food aid supplies from groups of the population in need'. See also ESCR Committee, Consideration of reports submitted by states parties under Arts 16 & 17, Morocco (2000) para 21 http://www.umn.edu/humanrts/esc/morocco2000.html (accessed 12 June 2009), where the Committee expressed concern about the 'absence of legislation for 'domestic workers ... who are ill-treated and exploited by their employers'. The Committee had also criticised the clampdown on the right to strike, para 2.

83 See Sepulveda (n 80 above) 212-222; Moser *et al* (n 41 above) 48; Eide (n 42 above) 127.

should not enact a land use legislation that would arbitrarily dispossess landowners of what they have, as was the case in Robert Mugabe's Zimbabwe between 2000 and 2005.[84] Similarly, therefore, to escape reprimand for violating the right to food, the Sudanese government should have refrained from the diversion of food items meant for its most vulnerable civilians to dubious locations.[85] Concerning the right to education, the Congolese government had violated its obligation to *respect* the right to education in light of the deplorable condition of the educational system arising principally from 'economic mismanagement'.[86] It is equally reprehensible for any state to enact a law that would deprive peasant families of their land rights in favour of influential persons and TNCs as Angolans recently experienced.[87]

Concerning the obligation to *protect*, states are beholden to prevent non-state actors (third parties) from interfering with the enjoyment of economic, social and cultural rights. This might entail a number of measures by the state, depending on which right is involved.[88] In respect of the right to water, for instance, a state should, on the one hand, avoid macro-economic policies and trade conditionalities that would deprive the people of access to clean water as the government of Ghana recently embarked upon,[89] and, on the other hand, secure its dams and water resources against industrial pollutants.[90]

84 See generally S Romero 'Mass forced evictions and the human right to adequate housing in Zimbabwe' (2007) 5 *Northwestern Journal of International Human Rights* 275; PD Ocheje 'In the public interest: Forced evictions, land rights and human development in Africa' (2007) 51 *Journal of African Law* 176 181-182. See also K Pillay 'The rights to accommodation, housing and shelter in South Africa' in G Bekker (ed) *Economic and social rights series* (2000) 9. The defunct military regime in Nigeria had carried out a series of arbitrary evictions of large portions of the Nigerian populace in the 1990s under the controversial Land Use Decree No 6 of 1978. Both Nigeria and Zimbabwe are state parties to ICESCR.

85 See ESCR Committee – Sudan (n 82 above) para 25.

86 See ESCR Committee, consideration of reports submitted by state parties under arts 16 & 17 Congo (2000) para 23 http://www.umn.edu/humanrts/esc/morocco200.html (accessed 12 June 2009).

87 See C Foley *Land rights in Angola: Poverty and plenty* Overseas Development Working Papers (2007) 14-17.

88 See Sepulveda (n 80 above) 222-239; Moser *et al* (n 41 above) 48.

89 D Olowu 'Privatisation and water governance in Africa: Implications of a rights-based approach' (2008) 4 *TD: Journal for Transdisciplinary Research* 59 68-70.

90 See ESCR Committee, General Comment No 15 (n 81 above) paras 23-24. This component of the three levels of the obligation of state parties under art 2 has become helpful a pedestal for the human rights movement to address the adverse effect of the activities of international financial institutions (IFIs) as well as TNCs and MNEs from a critical human rights perspective. See eg SS Åkermark 'International development finance institutions: The World Bank and the International Monetary Fund' in Eide *et al* (n 29 above) 515-530; 'Economic, social and cultural rights, the right to food: Report by the Special Rapporteur on the Right to Food', J Ziegler, submitted in accordance with Commission on Human Rights Resolution 2000/10, Addendum, UN Doc E/CN.4/2003/54/Add.1 (3 January 2003) paras 41-43; I Houghton 'Report of the workshop on human rights

The obligation to *fulfil* requires that states adopt the proper legislative, administrative, fiscal, juridical, educational and other practical measures to secure the protection and promotion of these rights.[91] The inverse obligation to *facilitate* (fulfilment) involves proactive measures by a state to strengthen the existing structures and institutions that guarantee individuals' access to the resources necessary for their well-being.[92] In the same vein, the obligation to *provide* (fulfilment) entails that where all circumstances show the distress of individuals in meeting the necessities for human survival, the state should exert measures to offer assistance *as much as it is practically able to afford.*[93]

The obligation to *promote* (fulfilment) connotes the general duty of states to create awareness among the citizenry about their rights, their remedies and how best to secure their freedoms.[94] The *fulfilment* component of the tripartite levels of obligations perhaps explains why economic, social and cultural rights have sometimes been assumed to necessitate the creation of 'social welfare' states.[95] I reject such a supposition. The idea behind state responsibility for the obligation to fulfil by provision finds robust foundation in three

and the intergovernmental agencies' (24 September 2002, Washington, DC, USA); SI Skogly 'Structural adjustment and development: human rights – An agenda for change' (1993) 15 *Human Rights Quarterly* 751-778. See also J Symonides 'Globalisation and human rights' (2000) 4 *Mediterranean Journal of Human Rights* 145 154-161. For an appraisal of the efforts of the ESCR Committee in bringing the dealings of state parties with IFIs, TNCs and MNEs under the scrutiny of the ICESCR monitoring mechanism, see J Tooze 'Aligning states' economic policies with human rights obligations: The ESCR Committee's quest for consistency' (2002) 2 *Nottingham Human Rights Law Review* 229. In ch VI, I critically examine the role of these and other non-states actors.

91 See Sepulveda (n 80 above) 239-246; Moser *et al* (n 41 above) 48; Eide (n 42 above) 128. In contextualising the purport of the obligation to fulfil, while some of its elements are indeed programmematic, time must not defeat the overall objective of ICESCR. The ESCR Committee had interpreted the phrase 'progressive realisation' as follows: '[T]he phrase must be read in the light of the overall objective, indeed the *raison d'être*, of the Covenant which is to establish clear obligations for state parties in respect of the full realisation of the rights in question. It thus *imposes an obligation to move as expeditiously and effectively as possible towards that goal ...*'. See ESCR Committee 'General Comment No 3 The nature of state parties' obligations' (art 2 para 1 of the Covenant) UN Doc E/C.12/1990/8 (E/1991/23) (GC No 3) para 9, reprinted in *Compilation of general comments* (n 81 above) 16.

92 In respect of the right to food, eg, the state is expected to work towards improving the processes and infrastructure underlying the production, distribution and consumption of food. See Eide (n 80 above).

93 See D Olowu 'Conceptualising a rights-based approach to poverty alleviation in Africa: The platform of social security' (2003) 43 *Indian Journal of International Law* 67 73. See also ESCR Committee 'General Comment No 19 The right to social security' (art 19 of the Covenant) UN Doc E/C.12/GC/19 (4 February 2008) (General Comment No 19) para 50.

94 Eg, in the case of the right to an adequate standard of living, a state should provide vocational training programmemes that would help individuals to earn their own living. Similar programmemes should be designed for persons with disabilities.

95 See Trubek (n 76 above) 214-215.

indispensable assumptions that I deduce from the consequences of modern governance: (i) that poverty, inequality and discrimination are threats to human well-being and the dignity of the human person; (ii) that human misery, inequality and deprivation are not beyond alleviation, and since these conditions often result from political decisions, they can be controlled by political processes; and (iii) that governmental power has often been used to construct and sustain economic institutions and systems that favour certain groups or classes in the human society.[96]

Apart from the tripartite obligation typology, some human rights scholars have proposed the 'minimum core content' approach as another way of understanding the nature of state obligations under ICESCR.[97] Thus, against the background of the overworked plea of resource constraints by many states for the evasion of their economic, social and cultural rights obligations, the ESCR Committee adopted an 'objective' standard for measuring the minimum level of compliance of state parties.[98] Applying that approach, the ESCR Committee identifies the very minimum essentials of the rights in ICESCR.[99] This is what the ESCR Committee has termed the 'minimum core obligation' of each state party.[100] The minimum core approach has continued to attract rigorous scholarly analyses and propositions on many provisions of ICESCR, the details of which should not detain us here.[101]

96 See HI Clarke *Social legislation* (1957). See also J Nickel *Making sense of human rights* (1987) 8-9; PCC Bocayuva 'Social subjects, human rights and their political relevance' in Carbonari (n 40 above) 49 154-158; EA Kolodziej *A force profonde [profound force]: The power, politics, and promise of human rights* (2003) 1 20-27.

97 For my analytical discussion of the evolution and development of the 'minimum threshold approach' and its critique, see ch V.

98 As above.

99 ESCR Committee, General Comment No 3 (n 91 above) para 10.

100 As above.

101 See eg RL Siegel 'The right to work: Core minimum obligations' in A Chapman *et al* (eds) *Core obligations: Building a framework for economic, social and cultural rights* (2002) 21 32-36; C Fenwick 'Minimum obligations with respect to article 8 of the International Covenant on Economic, Social and Cultural Rights' in *Core obligations* 53 69-75; L Lamarche 'The right to social security in the International Covenant on Economic, Social and Cultural Rights' in Chapman *et al* (eds) 7 103-104; RP Claude 'Scientists' rights and the human right to the benefits of science' in Chapman *et al* (eds) 247 264-268; AR Chapman 'Core obligations related to ICESCR Article 15(1)(c)' in Chapman *et al* (eds) 305 317-320. This approach is a subject of critical analysis in ch V.

While there still remains quite a long way to go in arriving at an objective 'universal' standard of minimum essentials for each right in ICESCR,[102] it is obvious that the central concern of the ESCR Committee is to ensure that state parties demonstrate their unwavering commitment to the protection of vulnerable members of society.[103]

If the above exposition proffers a plausible answer to the question of *what* constitutes the obligation of a state party under ICESCR, the more volatile question would then be *how* the state should implement its obligations, with exactitude. It is thus inevitable to explore further the formulative content of the provision in article 2, because doing so will accentuate a convergent praxis from various approaches to the obligations of states.

Central to any interpretation of the obligatory content of ICESCR is the arduous task of analysing the key phrases 'to take steps', 'achieving progressively the full realisation', and 'to the maximum of available resources'.[104] The ESCR Committee has pointed out that, while the concept of 'progressive realisation' constitutes a recognition of the fact that the full realisation of *all* economic, social and cultural rights will generally not be achievable in a short period of time, the phrase must be seen in the light of the overall objective, namely, that state parties must move 'as expeditiously and effectively as possible' towards the realisation of these rights.[105] All state parties thus have an obligation to immediately begin to take steps towards the full realisation of the rights in ICESCR through all appropriate means, including legislative, administrative, judicial, economic, social and educational measures, consistent with the nature of the rights, in order to fulfil their obligations under the Covenant.[106] This is the basis of what the Maastricht Guidelines identify as indicating a

102 The ESCR Committee has not issued any General Comment in respect of the right to take part in cultural life (art 15(1)(a)) and, thus, the 'minimum core content' of the right remains fuzzy. See SA Hansen 'The right to take part in cultural life: Toward defining minimum core obligations related to article 15(1)(a) of the International Covenant on Economic, Social and Cultural Rights' in Chapman *et al* (eds) (n 101 above) 279 299-301.

103 See General Comment No 3 (n 91 above) paras 9 & 11. See also Limburg Principles (n 48 above) paras 25-28, declaring that the scarcity of resources will not relieve a state of its certain minimum obligations under ICESCR. For a further extensive discussion of the 'minimum core obligation' concept, see Sepulveda (n 80 above) 311-378.

104 Art 2(1).

105 See General Comment No 3 (n 91 above).

106 n 91 above, paras 2, 3 & 7. See also the Limburg Principles (n 48 above) para 38.

twin obligation of *conduct* and obligation of *result*.[107]

I contend that the obligation of progressive achievement within the maximum limits of available resources does not essentially entail an accumulation of fiscal resources, but relates more to an increasingly *effective and transparent use of the available resources* which must be optimally prioritised to fulfil the enumerated rights, taking into account the need to ensure for everyone the satisfaction of basic subsistence requirements as well as the provision of essential services.[108]

In similar vein, it is obvious that ICESCR acknowledges the uneven fiscal capacities of states with its provision in article 2(1) that they are to 'take steps, individually and *through international assistance and co-operation, especially economic and technical*'.[109] It therefore behoves a state party to demonstrate a 'no-fault' position by showing that it has fairly exhausted all possible international economic and technical assistance and co-operation in meeting its economic, social and cultural rights obligations.

Another notable scholar has also contended that 'the latitude to achieve the realisation of the rights "progressively" should not be interpreted as an invitation for the state to drag its feet interminably'.[110] Today, there is positive appreciation of the concept of 'progressive realisation' as implying the avoidance of retrogressive measures that reduce either the number of beneficiaries who have access to the rights or the substance of the benefits.[111] Rather than being considered a structural weakness or a leeway from responsibility, the wording of article 2(1) should be viewed as a conscious effort to create an objective international standard for

107 Maastricht Guidelines (n 49 above) para 7. It defines the obligation of conduct as requiring '*action reasonably calculated* to realise the enjoyment of a particular right [while] ... the obligation of result requires states to achieve *specific targets* to satisfy a detailed substantive standard' (my emphasis). See A Eide 'Making human rights universal: Achievements and prospects' in H Stokke *et al* (eds) *Human rights in development yearbook. The millennium edition* (2001) 23-26.

108 See A Eide 'Economic, social and cultural rights as human rights' in Eide *et al* (n 29 above) 26-28; Chapman *et al* 'Introduction' in Chapman *et al* (eds) (n 101 above) 11-12, for other interpretations of the 'available resources' phraseology.

109 My emphasis.

110 S Liebenberg 'Socio-economic rights' in M Chaskalson et *al* (eds) *Constitutional law of South Africa* (1999) 40. See also Limburg Principles (n 48 above) para 21.

111 See International Human Rights Internship Programmeme (IHRIP) *Circle of rights economic, social and cultural rights activism: A training resource* (2000) 163-166. See also General Comment No 3 (n 91 above) para 9; Limburg Principles (n 48 above) para 72; the Maastricht Guidelines (n 49 above) paras 14(e)-(f).

measuring a state's performance of its obligations, while acknowledging disparities among states.[112]

Implementation mechanisms

Under ICESCR, the responsibility for monitoring the implementation of the treaty provisions is vested in the UN Economic and Social Council (ECOSOC).[113] At an early stage, ECOSOC had delegated this task to a Working Group of Government Experts. However, in 1985, ECOSOC decided to convert the Working Group into the ESCR Committee.[114] The prime function of the ESCR Committee is to assist and guide state parties in complying with their obligations under ICESCR. Over time, the ESCR Committee has performed this function through a combination of activities, including the consideration of the periodic reports submitted by state parties; the issuance of Concluding Observations and Recommendations; the adoption of General Comments; and by conducting *in-situ* visits.[115]

States' periodic reports

Under articles 16 and 17 of ICESCR, state parties undertake to submit periodic reports to the ESCR Committee within two years of entry into force of ICESCR for each state party, and thereafter once every five years, setting out the legislative, judicial, policy and other measures that they have taken to ensure the enjoyment of the rights guaranteed therein.[116] The ESCR Committee has provided assistance in this process by issuing a set of guidelines specifying the types of information it requires in order to monitor the implementation of ICESCR.[117] The objectives of the reporting system in the ESCR Committee are to ascertain, through 'constructive dialogue', that states are monitoring their own progress, promoting the adoption of detailed implementation plans, and facilitating public participation in

112 It is also worthy to note that, unlike other UN human rights treaties, ICESCR contains no derogation clause. For an argument on the non-derogability from ICESCR provisions, see Craven (n 69 above) 111.

113 See ICESCR arts 16-17.

114 ECOSOC Res 1985/17, 28 May 1985 para B. For a comprehensive discussion of the history and operational structures of the ESCR Committee, see Craven (n 73 above) 35-56; and for a pragmatic critique of the ESCR Committee, see S Leckie 'The Committee on Economic, Social and Cultural Rights: Catalyst for change in a system needing reform' in P Alston *et al* (eds) *The future of UN human rights treaty monitoring* (2000) 129-144.

115 See ICESCR, art 17(2). It is apt to note that these activities follow the practices of the other key UN human rights treaty monitoring bodies.

116 ECOSOC Res 1988/4, 24 May 1988.

117 See Revised Guidelines Regarding the Form and Contents of Reports to be Submitted by State Parties under Articles 16 and 17 of the ICESCR' UN Doc E/C.12/1989/SR.8. See ESCR Committee, Report on the fifth session, ECOSOC, Official Records, 1991, Suppl No 3 (E/1991/23), Annex IV (Reporting guidelines).

policy development and evaluation.[118] The reporting mechanism of ICESCR has been described by Leckie as 'the most important means of monitoring compliance with this instrument at the international level'.[119]

However, the reporting mechanism has been criticised for becoming ineffective in view of the backlog of overdue state reports.[120] As at 31 December 2008, there were 194 overdue reports.[121] In an effort to curb this trend of delay, the ESCR Committee now invites *all concerned bodies and individuals* to submit relevant and appropriate documentation to it,[122] an approach that has given a boost to participation by civil society groups in the work of the ESCR Committee.[123] For instance, in 2001, the ESCR Committee proceeded to examine the alternative reports submitted by civil society groups in Togo after numerous invitations to the Eyadema government had been rebuffed.[124] Although the ESCR Committee was not an establishment of the treaty it monitors, unlike other UN human rights treaty bodies, the body has been able to develop flexible and qualitative monitoring methods in carrying out its supervisory mandate.[125]

In the absence of a mechanism for individual complaints as found under ICCPR, CERD, CAT and CEDAW, the reporting procedure has

118 ESCR Committee, General Comment No 1, Reporting by state parties, UN ECOSOC Doc E/1989/22 (General Comment No 1) paras 1-4, reprinted in *Compilation of general comments* (n 81 above) 8-9.

119 S Leckie 'The appearance of the Netherlands before the UN Committee on Economic, Social and Cultural Rights' (1989) 7 *Netherlands Quarterly of Human Rights* 308.

120 See Craven (n 69 above) 114.

121 See Reports Overdue by Treaty http://www.unhchr.ch/tbs/doc.nsf/RepStatfrset?OpenFrameSet (accessed 12 June 2009). Among these overdue states reports, the 47 African state parties share 85 among themselves, approximately representing 50%.

122 ESCR Committee Report of the sixth session, UN Doc E/1992/23, Suppl No 3 para 386 (my emphasis).

123 For a detailed discussion and critique of the impact of the new role fashioned for civil society groups by the ESCR Committee, see K Arambulo *Strengthening the supervision of the International Covenant on Economic, Social and Cultural Rights: Theoretical and procedural aspects* (1999) 41-44.

124 See ESCR Committee 'Review of the implementation of the ESCR Committee: Concluding observations - Togo' UN Doc E/C.12/Add.61, 21 May 2001, paras 2-5, http://www.unhchr.ch (accessed 12 June 2009). The ESCR Committee noted that, although Togo became a state party to ICESCR in 1984, it had not filed its initial report as of 2001.

125 The ESCR Committee has demonstrated its willingness to consider alternative reports in the absence of a state's report, after giving due notice to the state involved. This it has done consistently and successfully after 1991. See ESCR Committee, Report of the fifth session, UN Doc E/1991/23. See also ESCR Committee, Report of the seventh session, UN Doc E/1993/22, paras 39-41, where the ESCR Committee adopted a formal procedure to establish this practice. The ESCR Committee has ever since applied the procedure against a number of African states — Gambia, Kenya, Mali, and Mauritius. See Arambulo (n 123 above) paras 2-5.

steadily emerged as the most viable instrumentality for monitoring the implementation of economic, social and cultural rights at the international level, similar to a judicial setting to identify critical issues in dispute.[126]

How far then has the reporting procedure assisted in the evolution of a regime of economic, social and cultural rights protection in African states? As at 31 December 2008, 47 African states had ratified ICESCR, with three others being mere signatories and another two being neither signatories nor state parties.[127] Compared to other countries of the world, the few reservations and declarations entered by African state parties are largely interpretative and do not constitute a significant deviation from ICESCR obligations.[128] This might be a pointer to the formal commitment of the preponderance of African states to the core values of ICESCR, more so when its basic provisions and purpose do not radically depart from relevant African regional human rights instruments. It must be noted, rather regrettably, however, that African state parties to ICESCR have generally shown a lackadaisical attitude towards *compliance* with ICESCR reporting obligations in many instances.

Out of a total of 405 state reports filed before the ESCR Committee as at 31 December 2008, only 132 originated from Africa, and out of the total of 194 overdue state reports worldwide, 96 accrued from Africa.[129] Thirteen African state parties had three

126 Instructively, civil society groups are now permitted to make brief oral submissions and may submit written briefs to the Pre-Sessional Working Group of the ESCR Committee. See B Porter 'Judging poverty: Using international human rights law to refine the scope of charter rights' (2000) 15 *Journal of Law and Social Policy* 117-162.

127 Comoros, São Tomé and Principe and South Africa are signatories while Botswana and Mozambique are neither signatories nor state parties. See Status of Ratification (n 69 above).

128 To date, there are eight reservations and two interpretative declarations entered by Algeria, Egypt, Guinea, Kenya, Libya, Madagascar, Rwanda and Zambia; and Algeria and Egypt respectively. Eg, that of Libya says: 'The acceptance and accession to this Covenant by the Libyan Arab Republic shall in no way signify a recognition of Israel or be conducive to entry by the Libyan Arab Republic into such a dealing with Israel as are regulated by the Covenant.' The Declaration by Madagascar says: 'The government of Madagascar ... reserves the right to postpone the application of article 13, paragraph 2, of the Covenant ... particularly as it relates to primary education, since ... the financial implications are such that full application of these principles in question cannot be guaranteed at this stage.' See Reservations and declarations to ICESCR http://www2.ohchr.org/english/bodies/ ratification/3.htm (accessed 12 June 2009). For other reservations, interpretive declarations and objections filed by African states to UN human rights treaties, see C Heyns *Human rights law in Africa* (1998) 4-22.

129 See Reporting Status – Overdue by Treaty http://www.unhchr.ch/tbs/doc.nsf/ newhvoverduebytreaty?OpenView&Start=1&Count=250&Expand=7#7 (accessed 12 June 2009).

overdue reports each, while there were 21 African states that had never submitted any report.[130] In the same vein, very few African state parties do fully comply (if at all) with the Concluding Observations and Recommendations that the ESCR Committee issues at the end of the reporting process.[131] Apart from the lackadaisical attitude of states, the contribution of African civil society groups has been relatively insignificant in the activity of the ESCR Committee. I contend that without effective civil society input, the ESCR Committee will have little grasp of the issues of critical concern in Africa.

Concluding Observations

At the end of the thorough consideration of a state's report, the ESCR Committee usually issues a set of Concluding Observations, which are essentially an official evaluation of the progress made by a state party, the difficulties faced, other subjects of concern to the ESCR Committee as well as suggestions and recommendations for improvement.[132] The practice of the ESCR Committee in adopting Concluding Observations after each report has not only given a quasi-judicial value to ICESCR, but also reinforces the efficacy of the ESCR Committee.[133]

While the ESCR Committee's Concluding Observations and Recommendations are not legally binding in the strict sense, they are nonetheless potent pronouncements that might define the assessment of a state's disposition toward responsible governance within the international arena.[134] In the repressive military years in Nigeria, for instance, the ESCR Committee was able to express what might be considered as the opinion of the international community about the

130 These were Angola; Burkina Faso; Cape Verde; Central African Republic; Chad; Côte d'Ivoire; Djibouti; Equatorial Guinea; Eritrea; Ethiopia; Gabon; Ghana; Guinea Bissau; Lesotho; Malawi; Namibia; Niger; Sierra Leone; Somalia; and Uganda. See above.

131 See CE Welch Jr *Protecting human rights in Africa: Strategies and roles of non-governmental organisations* (1995) 56-60. See eg ESCR Committee Review of the implementation of the ESCR Committee: Concluding observations - Nigeria, UN Doc E/C.12/1/Add.23, 13 May 1998, where the ESCR Committee berated the general failure of states to implement its recommendations in previous reports.

132 For a historical background to the adoption of this procedure and the continuing process of elaboration and clarification, see Craven (n 73 above) 88.

133 See S Leckie 'An overview and appraisal of the fifth session of the UN Committee on Economic, Social and Cultural Rights' (1991) 13 *Human Rights Quarterly* 539 547.

134 For a particularly dramatic effect of the ESCR Committee's approach, see M Craven 'The Committee on Economic, Social and Cultural Rights' in Eide *et al* (n 29 above) 455 466-467, showing how the ESCR Committee succeeded in dissuading the government of the Philippines from carrying out an imminent eviction of 200 000 families in 1995.

persecution of opposition leaders, labour and democracy activists and students on the pretext that they were security threats.[135] The ESCR Committee particularly criticised the incessant massive evictions of underprivileged Nigerians from their homes.[136]

The ESCR Committee has also used its Concluding Observations to expose some of the most egregious but usually latent human deprivations in Africa.[137] These Concluding Observations and Recommendations can have a significant impact if they are followed up by civil society and the media at the domestic level.[138]

General Comments

In view of the paltry amount of jurisprudence on economic, social and cultural rights at international, regional and national levels, the absence of an individual complaint machinery, and the contested language of ICESCR, the ESCR Committee prepares and issues pronouncements that are known as General Comments to assist state parties in the implementation of their treaty obligations under ICESCR.[139]

These General Comments are based on the experience that the ESCR Committee has garnered over a long period of examining states'

135 See Concluding observations - Nigeria (n 131 above) paras 10, 15 & 33.

136 n 135 above, para 42.

137 See eg ESCR Committee Review of the Implementation of the ESCR Committee: Concluding Observations - Zimbabwe UN Doc E/C.12/1/Add.12, 20 May 1997 para 11, where the ESCR Committee observed that, pursuant to the amended Constitution of Zimbabwe, public servants, teachers and nurses could not join professional unions, and that doctors and nurses who had organised strikes had been subjected to arrest and dismissal. The ESCR Committee has also had occasion to highlight the devastating impact of foreign debts and Structural Adjustment Programmemes (SAPs) in the enjoyment of economic, social and cultural rights in Africa. See ESCR Committee Review of the Implementation of the ESCR Committee: Concluding Observations - Sudan' UN Doc E/C.12/1/Add.48 para 15; ESCR Committee 'Review of the Implementation of the ESCR Committee: Concluding Observations - Morocco' UN Doc E/C.12/1/Add.55 para 10; ESCR Committee 'Review of the Implementation of the ESCR Committee: Concluding Observations - Egypt' UN Doc E/12/1/Add.44 paras 10 & 28; ESCR Committee 'Review of the Implementation of the ESCR Committee: Concluding Observations - Cameroon' UN Doc E/C.12/1/Add.40 para 10; ESCR Committee 'Review of the Implementation of the ESCR Committee: Concluding Observations - Senegal' UN Doc E/12/1/Add.62 para 10; and ESCR Committee 'Review of the Implementation of the ESCR Committee: Concluding Observations - Congo' UN Doc E/12/1/Add.45 para 11. All the concluding observations of the ESCR Committee referred to in this book are also available at http://www.unhchr.ch (accessed 12 June 2009).

138 See generally Porter (n 126 above) 130-145.

139 See ESCR Committee 'General comments adopted by the ESCR Committee' (UN Doc E/1989/22) para 3, reprinted in *Compilation of general comments* (n 81 above) 8.

periodic reports, as elaborated through the contributions of experts, specialised bodies and civil society groups.[140]

While these General Comments are not binding, they carry substantial weight in the interpretation of the rights they address. In respect of a human rights treaty that was drafted in such a way as to accommodate disparities among state parties, the interpretations given to its contents by the ESCR Committee are indeed invaluable.[141] In the words of Meron, albeit relating to another UN human rights treaty, while 'such interpretation *per se* is not binding on states parties ... it affects their reporting obligations and their internal and external behaviour ... the practice of states in applying [human rights treaties] and may establish and reflect the agreement of the parties regarding its interpretation'.[142]

A striking feature of the General Comments is the consistent effort of the ESCR Committee at identifying aspects of each right that are capable of immediate implementation. The juridical importance of the General Comments issued by the ESCR Committee can certainly not be lost on African human rights advocates and researchers. Over the course of time, the General Comments of the ESCR Committee have become highly instructive and materially instrumental in the interpretation of conventional human rights law at regional and national levels.

In *Social and Economic Rights Action Centre (SERAC) and Another v Nigeria (Ogoni)*,[143] for instance, the African Commission on Human and Peoples' Rights (African Commission) extensively relied on General Comments Nos 3, 4, 7, and 14 to hold that the Federal Government of Nigeria had violated the rights to housing, food and health. Prior to the *Ogoni* decision, in interpreting the 'reasonableness' of the housing policy of the South African government, the Constitutional Court of South Africa applied General Comments Nos 3 and 4 in *Government of the Republic of South Africa and Others v Grootboom and Others*[144] to define the nature and scope of the constitutional provisions on the subject. Similarly, outside Africa, in determining the obligations of the Latvian government in

140 As of 31 December 2008, the ESCR Committee has issued some 19 General Comments on various provisions of ICESCR. Most of these General Comments are contained in the *Compilation of general comments* (n 81 above) as well as on the web pages of the ESCR Committee.

141 See generally Sepulveda (n 80 above) 73-112.

142 T Meron *Human rights law making in the United Nations* (1986) 10. Although Meron's assertion was in respect of the powers of the treaty-monitoring body of CERD, the thrust of his reasoning is nonetheless relevant to the subject here.

143 (2001) AHRLR 60 (ACHPR 2001). I analyse this case in detail in the course of this discourse.

144 *Grootboom* 2000 11 BCLR 1169 (CC). These and other relevant cases will be analysed in detail in a subsequent chapter on ESCR jurisprudence.

implementing effective programmes and policies to realise economic, social and cultural rights, in this case the right to social security, the Constitutional Court of Latvia relied on General Comments Nos 3 and 9.[145]

Furthermore, in *Ex parte Azanca Alhelí Meza García*, the Supreme Court of Peru interpreted the right to health under the Peruvian Constitution of 1993 in light of General Comment No 14 to grant *amparo* remedy to several applicants who were HIV/AIDS victims by ordering the Ministry of Health to supply them with anti-retroviral drugs prescribed by their doctors.[146]

In-situ *visits*

The ESCR Committee has adopted the practice of conducting *in-situ* (investigative) visits to the territories of state parties, although this is contingent on invitation by the state concerned. The first of such visits was to Panama in 1995.[147] Another such visit was to the Dominican Republic in 1997.[148] One common denominator in these two visits was that the ESCR Committee had considered the information produced by the two states involved to be inadequate responses to the grave allegations of economic, social and cultural rights violations in their respective territories: specifically, massive forced evictions.[149] While this mechanism might appear at first to be negligible because it is dependent on state co-operation, its potency for gathering first-hand information and raising international awareness must not be underestimated. Regrettably, however, no such visit has been conducted to any African state, because of the intransigence of some of those states.[150]

145 Case 2000-08-0109, 'On compliance of item 1 of the Transitional Provisions of the Law on social insurance with articles 1 and 109 of the Satversme (Constitution) of the Republic of Latvia and articles 9 and 11 (the first Part) of the 16 December 1966 International pact on economic, social and cultural rights' (*Latvian* decision) http://www.satvtiesa.govlv/Eng/ Spriedumi/08-0109(00).htm (accessed 12 June 2009).

146 Case 2945-2003-AA/TC, *Tribunal Constitucional*, Peru, 20 April 2004.

147 See ESCR Committee *Report on the technical assistance mission to Panama by the ESCR Committee, Report of the Twelfth and Thirteenth Sessions*, UN Doc E/ 1996/22, Annex V.

148 See ESCR Committee *Report on the technical assistance mission to Dominican Republic by the ESCR Committee Report of the Sixteenth and Seventeenth Sessions*, UN Doc E/1998/22, Annex VI.

149 See Craven (n 69 above) 116-117.

150 As an illustration, at the peak of the Niger-Delta crisis in Nigeria in the 1990s, the military junta rebuffed every idea of publicised country visits by regional or UN human rights treaty-monitoring bodies. When the African Commission and UN monitors were eventually allowed access in 1997, only some groups enjoying the Abacha-led government's patronage participated. The entire visit was farcical. It will be recalled that the infamous Mobutu Sese Seko of Zaire (now Democratic Republic of Congo) had also declined to accede to requests for visitation by the HRC to Zaire in the twilight of his repressive rule.

Individual complaints procedure

Unlike several other UN human rights treaties that have complaint procedures for aggrieved individuals, ICESCR did not contain an individual complaints mechanism. To rectify this shortfall, there were vigorous efforts to evolve such a procedure. While the idea of an Optional Protocol to ICESCR had earlier surfaced within the ESCR Committee itself in 1990, it was at the World Human Rights Conference in 1993 that it became an item on the global human rights agenda.[151]

This task was later spearheaded by human rights experts and civil society groups who continue to lobby for the adoption of such an instrument. Those efforts culminated in the adoption of a Draft Optional Protocol to ICESCR at the fifteenth session of the defunct UN Commission on Human Rights.[152] For a long time thereafter, however, the Draft Protocol remained enmeshed in controversy and institutional ambivalence. While there was broad consensus in principle among diplomats and jurists on the desirability of an Optional Protocol to ICESCR, the content and scope of the Optional Protocol had been problematic.[153] Consequently, many versions of the draft Optional Protocol were proffered at various fora while

151 See ESCR Committee *Report of the Fifth Session of the Committee on Economic, Social and Cultural Rights* UN Doc E/1991/23, para 285. The Vienna Declaration and Programmeme of Action (Vienna Declaration) had urged the UN Commission on Human Rights to collaborate with the ESCR Committee in the examination of optional protocols to ICESCR. See Vienna Declaration (n 38 above) para 75.

152 Draft Optional Protocol to the International Covenant on Economic, Social and Cultural Rights, UN Doc E/CN.4/1997/105, Annex, 18 December 1996. For a historical description of the Optional Protocol, see UN Human Rights Fact Sheet No 16 (Rev 1) 'Committee on Economic, Social and Cultural Rights'; E de Wet 'Recent developments concerning the Draft Optional Protocol to the International Covenant on Economic, Social and Cultural Rights' (1998) 13 *South African Journal on Human Rights* 514-548. The UN Commission on Human Rights has since 2006 been replaced by the UN Human Rights Council. See P Alston 'Reconceiving the UN human rights regime: Challenges confronting the new UN Human Rights Council' (2006) 7 *Melbourne Journal of International Law* 185.

153 See P Alston 'No right to complain about being poor: The need for an Optional Protocol to the Economic Rights Covenant' in A Eide *et al* (eds) *The future of human rights protection in a changing world* (1991) 86; W Vandenhole 'Completing the UN complaint mechanisms for human rights violations step by step: Towards a complaints procedure complementing the International Covenant on Economic, Social and Cultural Rights' (2003) 21 *Netherlands Quarterly of Human Rights* 423.

proposals for changes have been vast.[154] Fortunately, all the prerequisites for the presentation of the final draft of the Optional Protocol to the UN General Assembly for adoption were eventually completed with the resolution of the Assembly's Third Committee (Social, Humanitarian and Cultural) to that effect. It is gratifying to note that the UN General Assembly formally adopted this instrument on International Human Rights Day 2008.[155]

While the political questions around the Optional Protocol are beyond the scope of this book, I must state that it is critical to stronger human rights efficacy that an international economic, social and cultural rights complaint mechanism be put in place. Its eventual adoption will not only bring the UN human rights system up to date with emerging economic, social and cultural rights trends at regional and domestic levels, but will also allow the UN to address some of the pronounced problems of inequality, deprivation and discrimination in the territories of many state parties than the existing mechanisms presently avail.

Whatever the cacophony of arguments around the Optional Protocol might be, I contend that more than any other UN human rights treaty, the complaints mechanism in the recent Optional Protocol will be a veritable channel for exposing latent egregious acts, policies and omissions by states and non-state actors that threaten human survival and livelihood, that repress human capabilities, and more importantly, that deprive human beings of the unfettered ability to enjoy all other human rights. Without doubt, the adoption of an Optional Protocol holds significant promise for effective economic, social and cultural rights protection in Africa, just as much as in other world regions.

154 See Arambulo (n 123 above) 235-236 348-350; Craven (n 73 above) 98-102; International Network on ESCR (INESCR) *Report to the Working Group on Adjudication and Enforcement on Work at the 2001 session of the Commission on Human Rights: Work on the Optional Protocol to the ICESCR* October 2001; R Brett 'Shadow play: Report on the 59th session of the United Nations Commission on Human Rights' Geneva, 17 March-25 April 2003 7 (Quaker United Nations Office, Geneva June 2003). See also MJ Dennis 'Human rights in 2002: The annual sessions of the UN Commission on Human Rights and the Economic and Social Council' (2003) 97 *American Journal of International Law* 364 374-379; M Scheinin 'The proposed Optional Protocol to the Covenant on Economic, Social and Cultural Rights: A blueprint for UN human rights treaty body reform - Without amending the existing treaties' (2006) 6 *Human Rights Law Review* 131-142. For a more recent analysis, see International Service for Human Rights Human Rights Monitor No 65/2007 (2008) 87-88.

155 See 'UN General Assembly adopts Optional Protocol to International Convention on Economic, Social and Cultural Rights' UN Press Release, 10 December 2008.

1.2 Other United Nations human rights mechanisms

Beyond ICESCR, I observe that a spectrum of other instruments and mechanisms exist through which the implementation of economic, social and cultural rights and a rights-based approach to human development can be promoted and secured.

1.2.1 Treaty bodies

I have pointed out earlier in this chapter that economic, social and cultural rights guarantees are to be found in a plethora of other UN human rights instruments, beyond ICESCR itself. The implication of this observation is that there exists an array of mechanisms through which to vindicate economic, social and cultural rights. A case in point is the CRC.[156]

Although the treaty-monitoring body of CRC has not issued a General Comment in respect of the general nature of the obligations of state parties under CRC, it has stated in unequivocal terms that state parties have a positive and immediate duty to develop comprehensive national plans of action with regard to children's education[157] and treatment for HIV/AIDS.[158]

In yet another vein, the economic, social and cultural rights provisions in CERD[159] are without qualifications whatsoever and the individual complaints mechanism created under its article 14 does not delimit the human rights in respect of which a complaint may be brought.[160] These are cogent provisions that implicitly admit of economic, social and cultural rights complaints.

Even though it might appear to be a groping in the dark for thematic synergies within the UN human rights system, there are reasons to suggest that a veritable platform exists within the broad corpus of UN human rights instruments to strategise a holistic monitoring response that could give more efficacy to economic, social

156 The economic, social and cultural rights content of CRC is not expressed in the language of 'progressive realisation' as it is in ICESCR. Under CRC, the obligations are *immediate* although their implementation is still qualified by the phrase 'to the maximum extent of their available resources'. See CRC art 4.

157 CRC, General Comment No 1, UN Doc HRI/GEN/1/Rev6 (2001), reprinted in *Compilation of general comments* (n 81 above) 287 para 23.

158 CRC, General Comment No 3, UN Doc HRI/GEN/1/Rev6 (2003), reprinted in *Compilation of general comments* (n 81 above) 287, paras 15 & 25.

159 CERD, art 5(e)(i)-(vi) & 5(f) (n 63 above).

160 Art 14 only provides for the optional declaration by a state party to recognise the competence of the CERD Committee to receive individual petitions. Art 14(1) speaks of 'victims of a violation by that state party of any of the rights set forth in this Convention', while art 6(a) refers to 'any communication' and 'violating any provision of this Convention'.

and cultural rights. Illustrative of this argument is the Convention Against Torture and Other Cruel, Inhuman or Degrading Treatment or Punishment (CAT).[161] I strongly contend that there are compelling moral and legal grounds, by the extension of our traditional understanding of 'inhuman' and 'degrading' treatment or punishment, to begin to view some of the deliberate and unjustifiable acts of states and non-state-actors that starve people and devastate their livelihood (as with land mines in Angola, or massive evictions in Kenya, oil spillage in Nigeria, and environmental pillaging in the Democratic Republic of Congo) as inhuman and or degrading treatment. The phrases 'inhuman' and 'degrading' cannot be confined to the narrow meaning of what physically and directly hurts a person, because it is just as humiliating and degrading to be locked up *incommunicado* without food, light and water as it is to be disallowed from farming on one's ancestral land or to be disallowed from participating in a trade union to voice out one's professional or trade concerns. It is difficult to draw any meaningful line of distinction between the 'degradation' of overcrowded and unkempt prisons and the 'humiliation' generated by a nationwide six-month delay in the payment of workers' salaries for no justifiable reason.[162] While I recognise that not every arbitrary act or omission of states that violates human rights would automatically constitute 'inhuman' or 'degrading' treatment, it is helpful to the cause of protecting the human rights of the most vulnerable that the peculiar circumstances of such acts and omissions be investigated, analysed and documented with a view to internationalising their reprehensible consequences.

It is gratifying to note that some awareness is already developing in understanding the implications of CAT for economic, social and cultural rights violations. In 2002, a coalition of civil society groups and INGOs submitted a complaint to the treaty-monitoring body of CAT in respect of the incessant, deliberate and large-scale forced evictions and house demolitions carried out against the poor and vulnerable by the Mubarak government in Egypt.[163] The CAT Committee has also been playing a dynamic role in conceptualising the economic, social and cultural rights implications of its mandate.

[161] CAT, UN Doc UNGA Res 39/46 (1984), 23 ILM 1027, entered into force 26 June 1987.

[162] See generally J McBride 'The violation of economic, social and cultural rights as torture or cruel, inhuman or degrading treatment' in G van Bueren (ed) *Childhood abused* (1998) 107 110.

[163] See World Organisation Against Torture (OMCT) and The Egyptian Centre for Housing Rights 'The policy of forced eviction and house demolitions in Egypt: A form of cruel, inhuman or degrading treatment or punishment' http://www.echr.org/en/ asd/02/rep1.htm (accessed 12 June 2009). It is equally pertinent to note that the OMCT also convened a conference on 'Economic, social and cultural rights and the emergence of violence, including torture and other forms of cruel, inhuman or degrading treatment' in April 2003 in Geneva that focused extensively on the problem in Zimbabwe.

In its Concluding Observations on Israel in 2001, the Committee declared that 'Israeli policies on house demolitions ... amount to cruel, inhuman or degrading treatment or punishment'.[164]

Another significant UN human rights treaty is ICCPR. Whatever the scepticism might be about the nature and language of economic, social and cultural rights, there can be no denying their crosscutting linkages with civil and political rights norms. This is what some writers have labelled the 'organic interdependence' of human rights.[165] The denial of access to treatment for a terminable disease could just be as much a violation of the right to life (civil right) as it is a violation of the right to health (social right). The proscription of a professional body in a country could very well amount to a violation of the right to freedom of association (political right) as it would be a denial of the right to freely form and join trade union (economic right). These are indeed what constitute the core of the indivisibility and interdependence principle of the Vienna Declaration.[166]

What then should be the appropriate implementation approach to these concerns? The emerging jurisprudence from the work of the treaty-monitoring body of ICCPR, the Human Rights Committee (HRC), would seem to indicate the willingness of this UN human rights body to embrace the integrative human rights approach. Although it is essentially charged with the supervision of ICCPR, its mandate portends considerable implications for economic, social and cultural rights on many fronts. As early in its existence as 1982, the HRC had expanded its interpretation of the right to life as follows:

> [T]he right to life has been too often narrowly interpreted. The expression 'inherent right to life' cannot properly be understood in a restrictive manner, and the protection of this right requires that states adopt positive measures. In this connection, *the Committee considers that it would be desirable for states parties to take all possible measures to reduce infant mortality and to increase life expectancy, especially in adopting measures to eliminate malnutrition and epidemics.*[167]

Beyond this radical interpretation, the HRC has also advanced the justiciable implementation of economic, social and cultural rights

164 See Conclusions and recommendations of the Committee against Torture: Israel (23 November 2001), UN Doc CAT/C/XXVII/Concl.5, para 6(j). See also CAT, art 16.

165 See eg C Scott 'The interdependence and permeability of human rights norms: Towards a partial fusion of the International Covenants on Human Rights' (1989) 27 *Osgoode Hall Law Journal* 771. See also IE Koch 'Social rights as components in the civil right to personal liberty: Another step forward in the integrated human rights approach' (2002) 20 *Netherlands Quarterly of Human Rights* 29 35.

166 See Vienna Declaration (n 38 above) para 5.

167 HRC, General Comment No 6 UN Doc HRI/GEN/I/Rev6, reprinted in *Compilation of general comments* (n 81 above) 129 para 5 (my emphasis).

through some of its quasi-judicial pronouncements. In *Zwaan-de Vries v The Netherlands*,[168] the HRC established the right to freedom from discrimination (article 26), a right found in all UN human rights treaties, as a self-standing human right. That pronouncement settled, in resounding fashion, the debate about whether one could complain about this right without linking it to another right in ICCPR.[169] The complaint in that case had been in respect of state legislation in the Netherlands under which married women were denied unemployment benefits that were granted to unmarried women as well as married and unmarried men. This was a clear case of the right to social security being given content.

The HRC was to advance its progressive integrative approach in yet another case, *Broeks v The Netherlands*,[170] when it said:

> Although article 26 requires that legislation should prohibit discrimination, it does not of itself contain any obligation with respect to the matters that may be provided for by legislation. Thus, it does not, for example, require any state to enact legislation to provide for social security. However, when such legislation is adopted in the exercise of a state's sovereign power, then such legislation must comply with article 26 of the Covenant.[171]

The attitude and pronouncements of the HRC are of immense help in understanding and theorising economic, social and cultural rights in Africa and in defining strategy for the promotion of a rights-based approach to human development. This is particularly so because discrimination constitutes one of the foremost impediments to this agenda for Africa.[172]

1.2.2 Charter-based mechanisms

Although the UN system has no formal complaint system specifically designed for the protection of economic, social and cultural rights, nevertheless, I find that there are diverse mechanisms within the framework of the UN that could be of tremendous value in advancing a rights-based human development discourse. Of note in this regard are the two UN Charter-based mechanisms: (a) the Public 1235 Procedure and the Confidential 1503 Procedure created in 1967 and 1970, respectively, to respond to 'violations of human rights and

168 Communication 182/1984 UN Doc CCPR/C/OP/2, 209 (9 April 1987).
169 For an analysis of this communication, see Hanski & Scheinin (n 62 above) 325.
170 Communication 172/1984 UN Doc CCPR/C/OP/2 196 para 12.5 (9 April 1987).
171 As above.
172 See generally Oloka-Onyango (n 31 above) 57.

fundamental freedoms',[173] and (b) the 'thematic' procedures.[174] Since all UN human rights treaties couch their provisions in the language of preventing violations, it is logical and unassailable to posit that economic, social and cultural rights complaints can be brought within the purviews of these special mechanisms. I acknowledge, however, that the 1235 and 1503 mechanisms have not been used for economic, social and cultural rights protection because of normative or structural deficiencies, or a combination of both.[175] Nevertheless, in light of the largely settled province of civil and political rights, focus should shift towards invigorating the integrative human rights approach *via* these mechanisms.

With regard to the thematic procedures, although most of the thematic mandates are obliged to implement their mandates with discretion, their mandates are usually couched in general terms, giving them considerable latitude to develop their own working modalities.[176] The strength of these mechanisms lies in their ability to expose human rights violations in any part of the world, notwithstanding the fact that the government involved is not a state party to a particular human rights treaty.[177]

Because of the exceptional fact-finding functions of these mechanisms, I consider them as strategic vehicles for cross-pollination of information and ideas between the UN human rights system and civil society groups such that could ensure the report of economic, social and cultural rights complaints before the UN, even

173 See generally C Flinterman 'Extra-conventional standard-setting and implementation in the field of human rights' in Hanski *et al* (n 37 above) 143-150.

174 These are some of the 'special procedures' adopted by the UN Commission on Human Rights and its Sub-Commission on the Promotion and Protection of Human Rights under the auspices of ECOSOC, to look into specific types of human rights violations wherever they might be occurring in the world. Some of these procedures are called 'Country Mandates', meaning they are to monitor human rights situation in specific countries, while 'Thematic Mandates' are for specific *themes*, regardless of territories. These could be called Special Rapporteur(s); Representative(s); Independent Expert(s); or Working Group(s).This system of appointing thematic mechanisms started in 1980. See Office of the High Commissioner for Human Rights *United Nations special procedures: Facts and figures 2007* (Geneva 2007).

175 See generally M Scheinin 'Economic and social rights as legal rights' in Eide *et al* (n 29 above) 29 31-32.

176 There has been an effort at streamlining the conduct of each mandate. See 'Further promotion and development of human rights and fundamental freedoms, including the question of programme and methods of work of the Commission follow-up to the world conference on human rights: note by the United Nations High Commissioner for Human Rights' UN Doc E/CN.4/1998/45 20 November 1997.

177 See 'Special procedure of the commission on human rights: Thematic mandates' http://www.unhchr.ch/html/menu2/7/b/tm.htm (accessed 12 June 2009). I examine the work some of these mandates in the course of my analysis in subsequent chapters as they pertain to my sub-themes.

when a country is not a state party to the applicable treaty.[178] The thematic mandates also hold the promise of deepening the cross-cutting capabilities of the various treaty-based human rights regimes. As a pointer, Sir Nigel Rodley, former Special Rapporteur on Torture, took a broader view of human rights when he said:

> [A]s long as national societies and the international community fail to address the problems of the poor, the marginalised and the vulnerable, they are indirectly, and as far as exposure to the risk of torture is concerned, directly contributing to the vicious circle of brutalisation that is a blot on and a threat to our aspirations for a life in dignity and respect for all.[179]

Regrettably, UN thematic mandates remain largely unknown to most Africans and African civil society groups. Little or nothing has ever been done to draw the attention of these elaborate mechanisms to the unspoken violations of human rights that denigrate the dignity of many Africans. The moral for the African human rights movement is to engage the UN thematic mechanisms as complementary strategies in internationalising many of the economic, social and cultural rights abuses in the region.

1.3 Relevant specialised agencies

Within the global system, particularly since the end of the Cold War, there has been increased collaboration among the UNDP, the defunct UN Commission on Human Rights (now the UN Human Rights Council), multilateral development institutions, governments, and civil society groups such as research institutions and trade unions, towards the ends of economic growth, development and creating a better world for all human beings.[180] At the UN level, these concerns are gradually being translated into structured multi-dimensional approaches linking socio-economic development to human rights and freedoms.[181] In this category are the various specialised agencies of the UN, such as the UNDP, the Economic Commission for Africa (ECA), the Food and Agricultural Organisation (FAO), the International Labour

178 See generally BW Ndiaye 'Thematic mechanisms and the protection of human rights' in Y Danieli *et al* (eds) *The Universal Declaration of Human Rights: Fifty years and beyond* (1999) 67 69-70 73-74.

179 'Question of torture and other cruel, inhuman or degrading treatment or punishment: Note by the Secretary-General Interim Report to the General Assembly' UN Doc A/55/290, 11 August 2000 para 37 http://www.unhchr.ch (accessed 12 June 2009).

180 See A Rosas 'The right to development' in Eide *et al* (n 29 above) 119-130.

181 T van Boven 'Human rights and development: the UN experience' in DP Forsythe (ed) *Human rights and development: International views* (1989) 121-135. See also K Tomaševski *Development aid and human rights revisited* (1993) 45-56; S Shetty 'Millennium Declaration and Development Goals: Opportunities for human rights' (2005) 2 *SUR International Journal of Human Rights* 7.

Organisation (ILO), the United Nations Conference on Trade and Development (UNCTAD), the United Nations Environment Programme (UNEP), the United Nations Educational, Scientific and Cultural Organisation (UNESCO), the United Nations Population Fund (UNFPA), and the United Nations Children's Fund (UNICEF), the United Nations Development Fund for Women (UNIFEM), the World Health Organisation (WHO), and many others.[182]

As early as 1979, Alston, who later became the first Chairperson of the ESCR Committee, had stressed that, apart from the 'fundamental responsibility to promote the realisation of human rights in all the facets of their work ... the primary thrust of the implementation procedure [of ICESCR] is directed at the agencies'.[183] In addition, in fairness to many of these agencies, their efforts through data collection, policy recommendations and involvement in form of direct assistance projects at national levels have had positive impact on economic, social and cultural rights across the world.[184] The work of WHO has been significant in relation to the right to health, the work of UNICEF in relation to children's rights, the work of ILO in relation to labour rights, the work of FAO in relation to the right to food, the work of UNESCO in relation to the right to education and cultural rights, the work of UNIFEM in relation to the rights of women, the work of UNEP in relation to environmental rights, and of particular importance in the context of our discourse, the all-embracing work of the UNDP in spearheading the interactive discourse on a global development agenda that revolves around the UN.

In varying degrees, these entities play significant but often ignored roles in human development in Africa.[185] From all that I have discussed, it becomes evident that the normative framework for a rights-based approach to human development is thus to be found in a mass of international *legal* obligations embedded in customary international law and treaties. It could also result from diverse policy

182 The roles of these agencies as purveyors of human rights have received notable scholarly attention. See eg P Alston 'The United Nations' specialised agencies and implementation of the International Covenant on Economic, Social and Cultural Rights' (1979) 18 *Columbia Journal of Transnational Law* 79; D Türk 'The United Nations and the realisation of economic, social and cultural rights' in F Matscher (ed) *The implementation of economic and social rights: National, international and comparative aspects* (1991) 95-121; JCN Paul 'The United Nations and the creation of an international law of development' (1995) 36 *Harvard International Law Journal* 307-328; A Gallagher 'Human rights in the wider United Nations system' in Hanski *et al* (n 37 above) 153-167.

183 See Alston (n 182 above) 117.

184 See LA Rehof 'Development assistance from the point of view of human rights' in LA Rehof *et al* (eds) *Human rights in domestic law and development assistance policies* (1989) 7.

185 In ch VI, I extensively explore the impact of the operational activities of non-state actors and how they positively or negatively affect economic, social and cultural rights and human development in Africa.

statements, recommendations, plans of action, declarations and principles as emanate from time to time within the international arena.[186]

While the latter species of instruments may not be binding, they do have strong implications for states.[187] After all, a preponderance of today's binding international human rights treaties were preceded by hortatory declarations.[188] Beyond their long-term objectives, non-binding human rights instruments can serve as a powerful instrumentality of political compulsion, through 'the mobilisation of shame'.[189] Moreover, scholars and state institutions recognise that these moral obligations are capable of metamorphosing into state practice, and invariably, into customary international law.[190]

2 The African regional human rights system

When, in 2000, Steiner and Alston described the African regional human rights system as 'the newest, the least developed or effective ... the most distinctive and the most controversial,[191] they must have had in their minds the picture of an ambivalent regional system, of the helplessness of human rights standards to tame the vicious spirit of *génocidaires*, age-long rebels and brutal dictators, as well as the unmistakable pangs of human misery, in a continent replete with manifest contradictions between human rights norms and effective human rights protection. There have indeed been many volumes of

186 Pertinent to our discourse is the UN Declaration on the Right to Development, adopted on 4 December 1986, UNGA Res 41/128, UN GAOR, 41st Sess, Suppl No 53, Agenda Item 101 186, UN Doc A/41/53 (1987). See generally Moser *et al* (n 41 above) 11; International Commission of Jurists (ICJ) 'Development, human rights and the rule of law', report of a conference held in the Hague 27 April-1 May 1981 (ICJ, Geneva, Switzerland, 1981).

187 By the principles enunciated in the *North Sea Continental Shelf case (The Netherlands v Germany and Denmark v Germany)* 1952 ICJ 3 44, and the *Nicaragua v United States* (Merits) 1986 ICJ 98-104, paras 187-195, such standards can attain the status of customary international law if they are repeated in state practice. See MN Shaw *International law* (1997) 66-69; Brownlie (n 78 above) 12-14; ID Seiderman *Hierarchy in international law: A human rights dimension* (2001) 27.

188 Eg, the UN Convention on the Elimination of All forms of Discrimination Against Women (CEDAW), adopted in 1979, had its precursor in the UN Declaration on the Elimination of All forms of Discrimination Against Women (1967), and the UN Convention on the Elimination of All forms of Racial Discrimination (CERD) adopted in 1965 was preceded by the UN Declaration on the Elimination of All forms of Racial Discrimination (1963).

189 See generally Janis (n 77 above) 50-52.

190 Under art 38(1) of the Statute of the International Court of Justice, the three main sources from which international law is derived are: international conventions and treaties; international custom; and the 'general principles of law as recognised by civilised nations'. See S Rosenne *The law and practice of the International Court of Justice* (1965) 603 611; S Yee 'Notes on the International Court of Justice (Part 1): Arguments for the publication of the rule-making materials' (2008) 7 *Chinese Journal of International Law* 691.

191 Steiner *et al* (n 59 above) 920.

scholarly works on the subject of human rights in Africa ranging from the philosophical, the moral and the historical, to the legal, structural, and the normative.[192]

It has been an engaging endeavour for scholars to contend about universalism and the alien origins of human rights in Africa;[193] the weaknesses, ambivalence or Utopian goals of the African regional human rights system;[194] the impracticability of certain categories of human rights in and for Africa;[195] and the mass of impediments to human rights protection in African states.[196] Yet others have concentrated on documenting the history and spate of state-sponsored violations of civil and political rights, particularly as they relate to democratisation, electioneering and the political process.[197]

The conceptualisation of human rights within the narrow confines of civil and political rights by African scholars is even manifested in the perceived role of civil society. Consequently, prescriptions for governance and nation building are usually defined in limited terms of increased involvement in constitutionalism and the electoral process in ways that would engender more political democratisation.[198]

192 See generally IG Shivji *The concept of human rights in Africa* (1989) 10-30, describing how human rights scholarship on Africa has continued to revolve around such questions as universalisation, theorisation and prioritisation of human rights.

193 See eg J Cobbah 'African values and the human rights debate: an African perspective' (1987) 9 *Human Rights Quarterly* 309-331; R Howard *Human rights in Commonwealth Africa* (1986) 23; NKA Busia Jr 'The status of human rights in pre-colonial Africa: implications for contemporary practices' in E McCarthy *et al* (eds) *Africa, human rights and the global system* (1994) 225-250.

194 See eg RA Baah *Human rights in Africa: The conflict of implementation* (2000) 39-41; E Bondzie-Simpson 'A critique of the African Charter on Human and Peoples' Rights' (1988) 31 *Howard Law Journal* 643-665; R Murray 'The African Charter on Human and Peoples' Rights 1987-2000: An overview of its progress and problems' (2001) 1 *African Human Rights Law Journal* 1-17; SBO *Gutto* 'The reform and renewal of the African regional human rights and peoples' rights system' (2001) 1 *African Human Rights Law Journal* 175 181-185.

195 See eg Busia (n 193 above) 225-250; O Eze *Human rights in Africa: Some selected problems* (1984) 5-6; J Donnelly 'The right to development' in CE Welch Jr *et al* (eds) *Human rights and development in Africa* (1984) 261-273; EA El-Obaid *et al* 'Human rights in Africa — A new perspective on linking the past to the present' (1996) 41 *McGill Law Journal* 819 846-847.

196 See eg O Eze 'Human rights issues and violations: The African experience' in GW Shepherd Jr *et al Emerging human rights: The African political economy context* (1990) 95-103.

197 See generally SBO Gutto *Human and peoples' rights for the oppressed: Critical essays on theory and practice from sociology of law perspectives* (1993) 47-49, ascribing the 'backwardness' in the African human rights discourse to 'historical' and 'sociological' factors.

198 See eg A Aidoo 'Democracy without human rights' (1993) 15 *Human Rights Quarterly* 703 - 715; PM Walubiri 'Liberating African civil society: Towards a new context of citizen participation and progressive constitutionalism' in J Oloka-Onyango (ed) *Constitutionalism in Africa: Creating opportunities, facing challenges* (2001) 83 86-88.

The historical dimensions of human rights violations and the ubiquitous scepticism about the efficacy of human rights in Africa are, however, at variance with the essence of our discourse: a forward-looking effort in all ramifications and the central dialectic of *how* to evolve a stronger economic, social and cultural rights profile across the African continent in a way that would make a positive impact on the lives of vulnerable and ordinary Africans. This segment therefore examines the normative, institutional and structural aspects of the African regional human rights system and particularly accentuates the novel stance of the system on *implementation* and its capacity to sustain a vibrant integrative rights-based approach to human development in Africa. Here, I adopt a descriptive approach to the African regional human rights system, highlighting its critical capabilities along the line.

2.1 The African Charter on Human and Peoples' Rights[199]

Regional human rights mechanisms are commonly thought to be potentially more effective than UN mechanisms, because they are able to take better account of regional conditions.[200] In another significant way, the UN itself has always encouraged the creation of regional mechanisms to deal with security and human rights, which should complement UN mechanisms.[201] African human rights instruments are, therefore, Africa-specific, and should naturally be expected to take into consideration certain values and customs peculiar to the continent.

In terms of its conceptualisation, the African Charter bears greater semblance to the contents of the Universal Declaration than to the outlook of the European and Inter-American regional human

199 For an extensive description of the drafting history of the African Charter up to its adoption in 1981, see CR Mahalu 'Africa and human rights' in Kunig *et al* (n 42 above) 1-30; BG Ramcharan 'The *travaux preparatoires* of the African Commission on Human and Peoples' Rights' (1992) 13 *Human Rights Quarterly* 307-314. The following documents are also very vital to a proper understanding of the philosophical and historical basis of the African Charter: [Mbaye] Draft African Charter on Human and Peoples' Rights' OAU Doc CAB/LEG/67/1 (1979) reprinted in C Heyns *Human rights law in Africa* (1999) 65-77; '[Dakar] Draft African Charter on Human and Peoples' Rights' OAU Doc CAB/LEG/67/3/Rev1 (1979) reprinted in Heyns 1999 81-91; *Report on the Draft African Charter presented by the Secretary-General at the 37th ordinary session of the OAU Council of Ministers*, held in Nairobi, Kenya, 15-21 June 1981 OAU Doc CM/1149 (XXXVII) (1981) reprinted in Heyns 1999 92-105.

200 See D Shelton 'The promise of regional human rights systems' in BH Weston *et al* (eds) *The future of international human rights* (1999) 351. See also A Rosas *Economic, social and cultural rights in the external relations of the European Union* in Eide *et al* (n 29 above) 479 484-487.

201 See BH Weston *et al* 'Regional human rights regimes: A comparison and appraisal' (1987) 20 *Vanderbilt Journal of Transnational Law* 585.

rights systems.[202] The philosophical foundation for the equal emphasis of *all* human rights in the African Charter is expressed in its seventh Preambular paragraph as follows:

> Convinced that ... civil and political rights cannot be dissociated from economic, social and cultural rights in their conception as well as universality and that the satisfaction of economic, social and cultural rights is a guarantee for the enjoyment of civil and political rights.

Apart from its eloquent Preamble, which underscores the importance traditionally ascribed to human rights notions in Africa, the instrument is divided into three focal parts of 68 articles. Part I contains a set of 'Rights and Duties' (articles 1-29); Part II covers 'Measures and Safeguards' (articles 30-63) sub-divided into 'Establishment and Organisation of the African Commission on Human and Peoples' Rights' (articles 30-44), 'Mandate of the Commission' (article 45), 'Procedure of the Commission' (articles 46-59) and 'Applicable Principles' (articles 60-63); and Part III deals with 'General Provisions' (articles 64-68). I limit the analysis of the African Charter to its normative and implementation aspects as are relevant to the purposes of this book.[203]

While various distinctive characteristics of the African Charter have been identified by many writers, what is particularly striking and significant for our discourse is the overarching endorsement of the *interdependence* and *indivisibility* principles in the African Charter, long before the Vienna Declaration. The African Charter, which is the foremost African human rights instrument, makes provision for all human rights within the same context, and with equal force.

202 For comparative distinctions between the Universal Declaration, the African Charter, the European Convention and the Inter-American Convention, see BO Okere 'The protection of human rights in Africa and the African Charter on Human and Peoples' Rights: Comparative analysis with the European and American systems' (1984) 6 *Human Rights Quarterly* 141-159; P Kunig 'Regional protection of human rights: A comparative introduction' in Cohen *et al* (n 42 above) 31-58; T Buergenthal 'International human rights law and institutions: accomplishments and prospects' (1988) 63 *Washington Law Review* 1-19; GM Wilner 'The status and future of the customary international law of human rights: Reflections on regional human rights law' (1995-1996) 25 GA *Journal of International and Comparative Law* 407-426; JD Boukongou 'The appeal of the African system for protecting human rights' (2006) 6 *African Human Rights Law Journal* 268 273.

203 For detailed analyses and a critique of the provisions of the African Charter, see C Flinterman *et al* 'The African Charter on Human and Peoples' Rights' in H Hannum (ed) *Guide to international human rights practice* (1992) 159-169; OU Umozurike 'The African Charter on Human and Peoples' Rights' (1983) 77 *American Journal of International Law* 902-912; Ankumah (n 31 above) 111-177.

2.1.1 Normative content

The African Charter enumerates a long list of human rights couched as the entitlements of 'every individual' (articles 2-18) and of 'all peoples' (articles 19-24). The individual rights emphasise the prohibition of discrimination;[204] the principle of equality before the law and equal protection of the law;[205] the inviolability and integrity of the human person;[206] the protection of 'human dignity' through the prohibition of all forms of exploitation and 'degradation';[207] the prohibition of arbitrary arrest and detention;[208] the right of fair trial and enabling rights;[209] freedom of conscience and religion;[210] freedom of information and expression of opinion;[211] the right of association;[212] the right of assembly;[213] the right to freedom of movement and asylum;[214] the right to participate in the political process, including access to public affairs and facilities;[215] the right to property;[216] the right to fair conditions of work;[217] the right to health;[218] the right to education and cultural life;[219] and the protection of the family, especially women, children, the elderly and the disabled.[220]

The African Charter thereafter proceeds to list a number of what are regarded as 'peoples' rights',[221] the inalienable right to self-

204 Art 2.
205 Art 3.
206 Art 4.
207 Art 5.
208 Art 6.
209 Art 7.
210 Art 8.
211 Art 9.
212 Art 10.
213 Art 11.
214 Art 12.
215 Art 13.
216 Art 14.
217 Art 15.
218 Art 16.
219 Art 17.
220 Art 18. The economic, social and cultural rights provisions in the African Charter have been subjected to analysis in a series of scholarly writings. See Ankumah (n 31 above) 143-155; VOO Nmehielle *The African human rights system* (2001) 121-138; Ouguergouz (n 42 above) 183-198; and CA Odinkalu 'Implementing economic, social and cultural rights under the African Charter on Human and Peoples' Rights' in Evans & Murray (n 31 above) 178 187-194. Since the interpretations given to the content of each of the rights are not problematic for our present discourse, the endeavour here focuses on the *nature of obligations* created. It is in respect of the conceptions about the nature of state obligation that the present discourse seeks to differ.
221 For discussions of the idea of 'peoples' rights' in the African Charter, see RN Kiwanuka 'The meaning of "people" in the African Charter on Human and Peoples' Rights' (1980) 82 *American Journal of International Law* 80-101; M Mutua 'The Banjul Charter and the African cultural fingerprints: An evaluation of the language of duties' (1995) 35 *Virginia Journal of International Law* 339-380; Benedek (n 42 above) 85-94.

determination and socio-economic development,[222] the right to exercise autonomy over their wealth and natural resources,[223] right to economic, social and cultural development as well as the right to development,[224] right to national and international peace and security,[225] and the right to a satisfactory environment.[226]

It is significant to note that throughout the African Charter, there is a marked absence of any explicit derogation clause as is customary in human rights treaties generally. The plain meaning of this is that no African government is permitted to abridge these rights, even during emergencies.[227]

While so much has been written about the 'claw-back' clauses found in the body of the African Charter,[228] it seems to have escaped the scrutiny of scholars that there are no such claw-back clauses in respect of the economic, social and cultural rights provisions in articles 15 through 24. They are in plain, unrestricted and unqualified language.

2.1.2 Nature and scope of obligations created

The rudimentary obligation of state parties under the African Charter is identical to what obtains under the International Bill of Rights - to protect human rights and freedoms. Article 1 of the African Charter establishes the fundamental obligation of states to 'recognise the rights, duties and freedoms enshrined in this Charter and ... undertake to adopt legislative or other measures to give effect to them'. A corollary of this obligation is found in article 62, which makes it mandatory for state parties to submit biennial reports 'on the legislative or other measures' they have put in place to give effect to the African Charter.

The African Charter goes further to spell out the promotional obligations of state parties. Under article 25, it is the duty of state parties 'to promote and ensure through teaching, education and

222 Arts 19-20.
223 Art 21.
224 Art 22.
225 Art 23.
226 Art 24.
227 See Umozurike (n 203 above) 910. See also *Media Rights Agenda & Others v Nigeria* (2000) AHRLR 200 (ACHPR 1998) para 67, where the African Commission held that '[i]n contrast to other international human rights instruments, the African Charter does not contain a derogation clause. Therefore, limitations on the rights and freedoms enshrined in the Charter cannot be justified by emergencies or special circumstances.' Compare Buergenthal (n 69 above) 233-234.
228 See eg Ankumah (n 31 above) 8 176-177; Buergenthal (n 69 above); C Flinterman et al 'The African Charter on Human and Peoples' Rights' in Hanski *et al* (n 37 above) 390-391.

publication, the respect of the rights and freedoms' in the Charter. Complementing this is another provision in article 26 obliging state parties 'to guarantee the independence of courts and ... allow the establishment and improvement of appropriate national institutions entrusted with the promotion and protection of the rights and freedoms' in the Charter.

Some critical points emerge from a synchronised reading of these provisions. The language employed in articles 1 and 62 reveals the overall intention of creating an *active* human rights posture in African states rather than a mere set of idealistic goals. A state will thus be in violation of its obligation under the African Charter if it fails to '*adopt* legislative or other measures' to give effect to the provisions.[229]

It is evident, *a priori*, that the human rights profile created by the African Charter equates *all* its provisions: Civil and political rights are just to be given as much priority as economic, social and cultural rights as well as 'peoples' rights'. It is, however, regrettable to note that the interpretation and analysis by scholars tend to disparage the value of the economic, social and cultural rights content of the African Charter. While commentators who suppose that the African Charter gives no room for programmatic realisation are few, far between and recent,[230] there is an overwhelming number of activist scholars who either strongly or subtly canvass the idea of economic, social and cultural rights being inferior to the civil and political rights in the African Charter, or of being incapable of implementation.[231] As an illustration, while acknowledging 'the indissoluble link in the conception and universality of civil and political rights ... and economic, social and cultural rights', Rembe concluded his analysis of the African Charter by saying that '[i]t is difficult to make the latter group of rights [that is, economic, social and cultural rights]

229 Art 1 African Charter (my emphasis).

230 See eg NKA Busia Jr & BG Mbaye 'Filing communications on economic and social rights under the African Charter on Human and Peoples' Rights' in Institute for Human Rights and Development in Africa (IHRDA) 'Procedures of the African regional human rights system workshop materials' (2001) 107-108 (Centre for Human Rights, University of Pretoria, South Africa); Ouguergouz (n 42 above) 200; Odinkalu (n 31 above) 327.

231 See Gutto (n 197 above) chs 2, 3 & 6; Ankumah (n 31 above) 144; F Jhatuala 'Human rights and the socio-economic context' in FE Snyder *et al* (eds) *Third world attitudes towards international law* (1987) 293-319; Mugwanya (n 31 above) 209; M Mutua 'The African human rights system in comparative perspective' (1993) 3 *Review of the African Commission on Human and Peoples' Rights* 5 10; R Gittleman 'The African Charter on Human and Peoples' Rights: A legal analysis' (1982) 22 *Virginia Journal of International Law* 667 687.

justiciable in the same way as [civil and political rights]'[232] – without providing any empirical, legal or moral validation for that assertion.

Thus, despite the clear language of the African Charter, the abundant *travaux préparatoires*,[233] and the views of the most distinguished African jurists, the *implementation* question has remained an albatross in vitalising the economic, social and cultural rights provisions in the Charter. The reasons for this are not far-fetched. With the protracted historical and ideological debates in which international human rights were enmeshed in the Cold War years; the eventual emergence of a segregated human rights treaty system within the UN; together with the interminable consequences of colonialism, brutal dictatorship and culture of maladministration to which African intellectuals have for long been exposed and accustomed, African human rights scholarship could not have escaped pessimism in its appreciation of the promise and uniqueness of a home-grown human rights system. After all, many consider the African Charter to be a product of oppressors and neo-colonialists.[234] That cynical attitude to human rights concerns is just one of the myriad symptoms of the skewed intellectualism that pervades the African human rights terrain.[235]

The misconception about the nature of economic, social and cultural rights obligations under the African Charter has also rubbed off on states. My scrutiny of some of the reports filed by states under article 62 of the African Charter reveals the wrong perception among many African states in equating their obligations under the African Charter with the 'progressive realisation' requirements under

232 NS Rembe 'The system of protection of human rights under the African Charter on Human and Peoples' Rights: Problems and prospects' (1991) 12 *Human and Peoples' Rights Monograph Series* No 6.

233 See n 199 above and accompanying text.

234 See generally Mahalu (n 159 above) 1 14-23; Rembe (n 232 above) 3; J Harrington 'Human rights in Africa' http://www.africana.com/Articles/tt_798.htm (accessed 22 November 2008).

235 An erudite African history scholar, Professor Iwe, eloquently described the tragedy of the African human rights movement as follows: '[T]he march of human rights movement on the African continent [is] a story of hypocrisy, a farce, and an endlessly tortuous pilgrimage of contradictions and negations.' See NSS Iwe *The history and contents of human rights: A study of the history and interpretations of human rights* (1986) 134. See also CG Caffentzis 'Professional academic ethics and the structurally adjusted African university' in McCarthy-Arnolds *et al* (n 193 above) 173 181.

ICESCR.[236] This perception is erroneous considering the Guidelines issued by the African Commission on the reporting process.[237]

Under the General Guidelines Regarding the Form and Contents of Reports on Economic and Social Rights, the African Commission prescribes that:

> As under civil and political rights it is suggested that the reports under economic and social rights should be of two types: Initial Reports and Subsequent Periodic Reports. The rights, duties and *fundamental freedoms* to be reported on should include the following: the right to work, just and favourable conditions of work; right to form and belong to free and independent trade unions, right to social security and social insurance; right to protection of family; right to highest attainable standard of physical and mental health; right to education; right to compulsory primary education; right to economic development; right to equal pay for equal work; etc.[238]

It was not fortuitous that the African regional human rights treaty monitoring body described economic, social and cultural rights as 'fundamental freedoms' that must be reported as comprehensively as civil and political rights. I contend that while economic, social and cultural rights are subject to progressive realisation under ICESCR, in the absence of any textual inference to the contrary, the spirit and letters of economic, social and cultural rights provisions connote immediate implementation under the African Charter. For Africa, the 'programmatic' argument of the Vierdag school of thought as well as the 'generations' paradigm of the Vasak school of thought are more remote and far-fetched. My view finds articulation in the all-inclusive and classification-neutral framework of human rights in the African Charter. Since the African Charter was conceived and designed as a unified whole,[239] it would amount to a disservice to its drafters for the instrument to be subjected to normative severance through sheer cynicism and stereotyped pessimism.

While it will require tremendous efforts to disentangle nuanced thoughts on the *nature* of obligation of states under the African

236 Illustrations of this trend abound in many states' reports where state obligations on economic, social and cultural rights are perceived as being of 'progressive' and not 'immediate' implementation. See eg the Mauritius and Zimbabwe reports to the 20th session of the African Commission, ACHPR/PR/MAU/XX and ACHPR/PR/ZIM/XX, respectively, 1996; and Namibia's report to the 29th session of the African Commission, ACHPR/PR/NAM/XXIX, 2001; the Democratic Republic of Congo's eighth, ninth and tenth periodic reports to the African Commission, June 2007; the Federal Republic of Nigeria's third periodic report to the African Commission, September 2008, all available at http://www.achpr.org/english (accessed 12 June 2009).

237 See African Commission on Human and Peoples' Rights State Reporting Procedure Information Sheet 4.

238 n 237 above, 178 para II(1) (my emphasis).

239 See Kumado (n 42 above) 277; Shivji (n 192 above) 25-29.

Charter, the *scope* of states' obligation to 'undertake measures' has been interpreted as implying that a state must take pre-emptive steps to prevent rights violations even when such a state is not the direct cause of the violations.[240] This obviously holds implications for evolving an appropriate human rights response to the activities of third parties, in particular, non-state actors engaged in Africa.

2.1.3 Implementation mechanisms

The principal mechanism that exists in the African Charter to ensure and monitor the compliance of state parties with their treaty obligations is the African Commission. Article 30 of the African Charter establishes the African Commission with the tripartite mandate *to promote, to ensure* and *to interpret* the human and peoples' rights in the African Charter.[241] The African Commission fulfils its mandate in a number of ways: through the state reporting procedure, the complaints procedure, and its promotional activities.[242]

The state reporting procedure enables the African Commission to examine what measures a state party has put in place to secure the provisions of the African Charter. The complaints procedure is bifurcated as it allows the Commission to consider inter-state complaints[243] as well as individual complaints.[244] The Commission's promotional mandate enables it to 'undertake studies and researches on Africa's problems in the field of human and peoples' rights' and to pursue educative programmes; to formulate normative human rights standards and to embark on co-operative programmes that would enhance human rights protection in Africa.[245]

240 See Communication 74/92, *Commission Nationale des Droits de l'Homme et des Libertés v Chad* (2000) AHRLR 66 (ACHPR 1995); *Zimbabwe Human Rights NGO Forum v Zimbabwe* (2006) AHRLR 128 (ACHPR 2006).

241 Arts 45(1), (2) & (3). For a comprehensive background discussion and procedural structures of the Commission, see Ankumah (n 31 above) 13-110; Rembe (n 232 above) 21-43; and for a pragmatic critique of the work of the Commission, see F Viljoen 'Overview of the African regional human rights system' in Heyns 1998 (n 128 above) 128- 205; F Viljoen *International human rights law in Africa* (2007) 310-317.

242 See generally IAB El-Sheikh 'Human rights development in Africa' (1992) 2 *Review of the African Commission on Human and Peoples' Rights* 46 52-54.

243 Arts 47-54.

244 Arts 55-56.

245 Art 45.

States' periodic reports[246]

Although the reporting procedure has become the mainstay of the African Commission,[247] it remains a system fraught with many impediments to efficacy. Just as it affects other regional human rights systems, a major problem that hampers the effectiveness of this procedure is the sheer failure of states to submit their reports as and when due.[248]

Another problem lies in that, even when states do submit reports, they frequently fail to send competent representatives to present such reports.[249] This explains why, for instance, the reports of Ghana and Namibia could not be examined at the 28th ordinary session of the African Commission held in Cotonou, Benin, in 2000.[250] This phenomenon leads to long delays, and some reports would have run out of date by the time they were examined.[251]

246 For a discussion of the reporting mechanism within the African regional system, see F Viljoen 'State reporting under the African Charter on Human and Peoples' Rights: A boost from the south' (2000) 44 *Journal of African Law* 110 112-113.

247 See IB El-Sheikh 'The African Commission on Human and Peoples' Rights: Prospects and problems' (1989) 7 *Netherlands Quarterly of Human Rights* 272-283.

248 See 'Status of submission of state initial/periodic reports to the African Commission on Human and Peoples' Rights' (updated March 2008) http://www.achpr.org/english/_info/statereport_considered_en.html (accessed 28 June 2008), showing that 12 African states had never submitted any report as of March 2008). The states were Botswana, Equatorial Guinea, Ethiopia, Eritrea, Gabon, Guinea-Bissau, Liberia, Madagascar, Malawi, São Tomé and Principe, Sierra Leone and Somalia.

249 See Viljoen (2007) (n 241 above) 378 383.

250 See 'Final communiqué of the 28th ordinary session of the African Commission on Human and Peoples' Rights' 23 October-6November 2000, Cotonou, Benin, http://www.africaninstitute.org/html/28th_session.html (accessed 12 June 2009). The evasive conduct of states towards the reporting system had become so rampant that at the 25th ordinary session of the African Commission, held in Bujumbura, Burundi, 26 April-5 May 1999, the African Commission had become so exasperated that it called on the defunct OAU Assembly of Heads of State and Government to express their disapproval at the persistent refusal of the Republic of Seychelles to submit its report and to consider the conduct a deliberate violation of the African Charter. Seychelles had refused to submit its initial report despite all invitations to do so since the 17th session of the African Commission, held in Lome, Togo, in March 1995. See K Quashigah 'The African Charter on Human and Peoples' Rights: Towards a more effective "reporting mechanism"' (2002) 2 *African Human Rights Law Journal* 261 277; Viljoen (2007) (n 241 above) 383-384.

251 See Social and Economic Rights Action Centre's interview with EVO Dankwa, a member of the African Commission on Human and Peoples' Rights, 1 *Access Quarterly* (Lagos, Nigeria 1999), Magazine 16-17. The African Commission later adopted a radical approach to this question of default in filing reports. At its 23rd session in 1998, the Commission decided that it would thenceforth consider states' reports without the presence of representatives once the affected state had been given adequate opportunity to attend and had failed to respond. See R Murray 'The African Commission on Human and Peoples' Rights (Report of the 23rd session)' (1998) 16 *Netherlands Quarterly of Human Rights* 394 395.

Other problems have been identified relating to the administration of the reporting procedure. For example, it has been shown that states frequently submit their reports in only one language, English or French, while the Arab states submit in two languages, including Arabic. The consequence is that, since not all commissioners are able to read those reports, this hampers their ability to ask meaningful questions.[252]

Beyond these procedural impediments, the African Commission lacks any effective follow-up mechanism. Once the African Commission closes its consideration of a state party's report and makes its recommendations, no clear device exists to ensure or monitor what the affected state does with the recommendations. In fact, the African Commission's manner of handling states' reports has been satirised as lacking 'seriousness [and] incisiveness' and as constituting 'a reduction of the whole exercise into a rigmarole'.[253]

Invariably, what should have been time for active constructive dialogue that would enhance the African Commission's capacity to develop a well-informed basis for holistic human rights monitoring ends up being routine processes around sedentary human rights perceptions. With this type of scenario, coupled with the low level of understanding of economic, social and cultural rights among state parties and civil society groups, the integrative human rights approach has been a retarded experience within the African regional system.

Individual complaints procedure

The individual complaints procedure of the African Commission has been kept remarkably active in responding to a wide range of human rights abuses in African states. However, there is an inextricable pointer to the imbalance in the causes of action in the communications brought before the Commission. A survey of the communications handled by the African Commission between 1994 and 2001 reveals a huge gap between the number of communications dealing with civil and political rights and economic, social and cultural rights in the African Charter.[254] Even where there were communications that involve cross-cutting rights within the African Charter, the African Commission had traditionally been pliable to

252 See Ankumah (n 31 above) 97 - 108; Odinkalu 'Analysis of paralysis' (n 31 above) 355-358.

253 Quashigah (n 250 above) 278.

254 Among all the 146 communications documented before the African Commission between 1994 and 2001, only five of them related to the economic, social and cultural rights provisions in the African Charter, and they were tangential to the main violations alleged.

excise the economic, social and cultural rights quotient from its remedial consideration.[255]

The ambivalence of the African Commission becomes evident when one weighs the manner in which it handles communications on the various rights in the African Charter. Two particular decisions would illustrate the point. In *Malawi African Association and Others v Mauritania,*[256] the African Commission showed its ability to elaborate on the civil and political rights content of the African Charter and to pronounce concrete and specific remedies in unequivocal language. The African Commission had, in that case, held that the government of Mauritania must establish an independent enquiry into the fate of disappeared persons, take diligent measures to replace the national identity documents seized from the expelled Mauritanian citizens, ensure appropriate compensation for the violations, reinstate persons dismissed from their jobs without due process, carry out assessment of the deep-rooted causes of the degrading practices in the Mauritanian society, and enforce its legislative measures on the abolition of slavery.[257]

Conversely, in *Free Legal Assistance Group and Others v Zaire,*[258] although the African Commission held the government of Zaire (now Democratic Republic of the Congo) to have violated the right to health and the right to education as guaranteed in the African Charter by failing to provide basic services such as 'safe drinking water and electricity and ... medicine' to the complainants during their detention as well as 'the closures of universities and secondary schools',[259] the Commission only ended an otherwise lucid decision with '[f]or these reasons, the Commission holds that the facts constitute serious and massive violations of the African Charter, namely of articles ... 16 and 17'.[260] That was one of the numerous opportunities the African Commission had missed to elaborate on the content of economic, social and cultural rights as well as to chart the path of remedial implementation.

Moreover, even though some notable scholars have hailed the decision of the African Commission in *Ogoni* as groundbreaking,[261] the

255 See n 706 and accompanying text for the basis of this assertion.
256 (2000) AHRLR 149 (ACHPR 2000).
257 n 256 above 190-191.
258 (2000) AHRLR 74 (ACHPR 1995).
259 n 258 above, paras 47-48.
260 As above.
261 See eg D Shelton 'Decision regarding Communication 155/96 *SERAC v Nigeria*. Case No ACHPR/COMM/A044/1' (2002) 96 *American Journal of International Law* 937 942; F Coomans 'The *Ogoni* case before the African Commission on Human and Peoples' Rights' (2003) 52 *International and Comparative Law Quarterly* 749; G Bekker *The Social and Economic Rights Action Centre and the Centre for Economic and Social Rights v Nigeria* (2003) 47 *Journal of African Law* 107 132.

pronouncement loses flavour as the African Commission uncritically adopted and endorsed the 'progressive realisation' paradigm of the ESCR Committee. Apart from a bare finding on economic, social and cultural rights violations and the usual tenuous language of 'appeals to' and 'urges' to the government of Nigeria, the decision is bereft of any remedial substance. Little wonder that there has been no tangible outcome from the decision within the troubled Niger Delta region, long after its delivery.[262]

The African Commission's pronouncements on economic, social and cultural rights have thus generally remained terse and incoherent, perpetuating misconceived notions about the justiciability of economic, social and cultural rights within the African human rights discourse.[263]

The other complaints procedure recognised in the African Charter is the inter-state mechanism. For all practical purposes, the inter-state complaints mechanism has remained dormant, just as in other regional human rights systems. African states have generally shied away from accusing one another of violating the rights in the African Charter, quite understandably.[264] In his assessment of the first decade of the African Commission in 1997, the Chairperson, Isaac Nguema, chided African states for not bringing any complaint against themselves despite widespread human rights violations across the continent.[265]

Confidence has also been dismal in the efficacy of the individual complaints system because of its inherent bottlenecks. After considering a communication, rather than making public its findings and making swift contact with the state party where violations of human and peoples' rights have been established, the African Charter

262 Apart from the Niger-Delta Development Commission (NDDC) Act 2000, that had been enacted prior to the African Commission's decision in *Ogoni*, the incumbent civilian regime has not met any of the actual demands of the peoples of the Niger-Delta. So embittered have the people of that sub-region of Nigeria been that no elections were held there during the general elections in April 2003. *Ogoni* might at best remain a testimony to the emasculated practicum of the African regional human rights system as is presently constituted. I critically examine the jurisprudential value of the *Ogoni* decision in ch IV. For my extensive critique of *Ogoni*, see D Olowu 'Emerging jurisprudence on economic, social and cultural rights in Africa: A critique of the decision in *SERAC and Another v Nigeria*' (2004) 2 *Turf Law Review* 29.

263 See generally Odinkalu (n 31 above) 362.

264 States would naturally be reluctant to point accusing fingers at other states to avoid reprisal. The only ever recorded inter-state communication was that between the Democratic Republic of the Congo against Burundi, Rwanda and Uganda, in 1999, alleging the violations of African Charter provisions by the bellicose activities of those states within its territory. See U Essien 'The African Commission on Human and Peoples' Rights: Eleven years after' (2000) 6 *Buffalo Human Rights Law Review* 93 103 n 28; Viljoen 2007 (n 241) 361-362.

265 G Oberleitner '22nd ordinary session of the African Commission on Human and Peoples' Rights' (1998) 16 *Netherlands Quarterly of Human Rights* 97 98.

prohibits the African Commission from publishing its findings and decisions until it has been considered by the Assembly of Heads of State and Government.[266] This invariably translates into the delay of public scrutiny of information available to the Commission.[267]

Promotional mandate

In terms of its promotional mandate, the African Commission is to be commended for the numerous interactive programmes it has conducted with national human rights institutions in various states as well as with African and non-African civil society groups. The activities of the African Commission in this regard have been well documented over the years.[268] It is regrettable, however, that the African Commission has not yet designed or implemented any concrete promotional programme for economic, social and cultural rights in Africa.[269]

The African Commission has extended its promotional mandate to cover the appointment of special rapporteurs to investigate, monitor and report on specific human rights issues under the African Charter. The first of such appointment was that of the Special Rapporteur on Arbitrary, Summary and Extra-Judicial Killings, in 1994.[270] Thereafter, there have been others, on Prisons and Conditions of Detention in Africa, in 1996; and another on Women's Rights in Africa, in 1999.[271] While the innovative activity of the African Commission in

266 Art 59.

267 However, see Viljoen (n 241 above) 154, noting that, since its Seventh Annual Activity Report in 1994, the African Commission has steadily departed from that culture of 'rigid secrecy' as it now attaches its review of individual communications as Annexure to its reports.

268 See Essien (n 264 above) 95-98. For a comprehensive list of the seminars and conferences organised by the African Commission, see Seminars of the African Court on Human and Peoples' Rights http://www.achpr.org/html/seminarsconferences.html (accessed 12 June 2009).

269 A quick view at the various programmemes of action designed by the African Commission reveals the absence of any positive commitment to the promotion of economic, social and cultural rights. See, eg, Programmeme of Action of the African Commission on Human and Peoples' Rights, OAU Doc 1987-1988 ACHPR/RPT/1st (8-13 February 1988) reprinted in Heyns 1999 (n 199 above) 169; African Commission on Human and Peoples' Rights Programmeme of Activities 1992-1996', OAU Doc 1992-1993 ACHPR/RPT/6th (1-9 March 1992), reprinted in Heyns (n 128 above) 170-173; and Mauritius Plan of Action 1996- 2001, reprinted in (1996-1997) 6 *Review of the African Commission on Human and Peoples' Rights* 215. A proposed seminar on the rights to education and development has been in limbo since 1988.

270 The practice of appointing Special Rapporteurs by the African Commission is based on the components of its promotional functions under art 45(1), namely, 'to collect documents, undertake studies and research'. See Essien (n 264 above) 99-102; Viljoen (2007) (n 241 above) 392-401.

271 The mandates of the three existing Special Rapporteurs are reproduced in Heyns (1999) (n 199 above) 223-226. For a discussion of these mandates and a critique of their efficacy, see J Harrington 'Special Rapporteurs of the African Commission on Human and Peoples' Rights' (2001) 1 *African Human Rights Law Journal* 247.

these regards is indeed commendable, it is perturbing that the Commission has not deemed it fit to appoint a special rapporteur for the elaboration and effective implementation of economic, social and cultural rights in Africa.

Furthermore, since article 45(1)(b) of the African Charter obliges the African Commission 'to *formulate* and *lay down*, principles and rules ... *upon which African governments may base their legislations* [*sic*]',[272] it is rational for the African Commission to embark on the formulation of indicators and benchmarks that would govern the interpretation of all rights in the African Charter. If certain rights have been problematic for the African Commission to interpret and enliven, it is not helpful for the Commission to ignore them or subject them to unhealthy disparity. The retardation of a class of rights within the African Charter might indeed imperil the whole.

2.2 Other African regional human rights mechanisms

Although the African Charter is the *grundnorm* of human rights within the African regional milieu, there are a number of other regional instruments that could influence rights-based human development in Africa. Some of these are: the African Charter on the Rights and Welfare of the Child (African Children's Charter),[273] the Additional Protocol to the African Charter on Human and Peoples' Rights on the Establishment of the African Court on Human and Peoples' Rights (African Court Protocol),[274] and the Protocol to the African Charter on Human and Peoples' Rights concerning the Rights of Women (African Women's Protocol).[275]

2.2.1 Applicable regional instruments

The African Children's Charter guarantees in unqualified language that '[e]very child shall have the right to an education'[276] and that '[e]very child shall have the right to enjoy the best attainable state of physical, mental and spiritual health'.[277] The obligation of state

272 My emphasis.

273 OAU Doc CAB/LEG/153/Rev2 reprinted in (1993) 1 *African Yearbook on International Law* 295-309, entered into force on 29 November 1999.

274 OAU/LEGAL/MIN/AFCHPR/PROT (I) Rev2. AHG/Res 230 (XXX) (1998) reprinted in (1997) 9 *Africa Journal of International and Comparative Law* 953-961, entered into force on 25 January 2004.

275 OAU Doc CAB/LEG/66.6, adopted 11 July 2003, entered into force 25 November 2005.

276 African Children's Charter art 11(1).

277 n 276 above, art 1(1). See generally A Lloyd 'A theoretical analysis of the reality of children's rights in Africa: An introduction to the African Charter on the Rights and Welfare of the Child' (2002) 2 *African Human Rights Law Journal* 11 14, conceding that the African Children's Charter offers a higher level of protection than that offered by CRC.'

parties is to take all 'the necessary steps, in accordance with their constitutional processes and with the provisions of the present Charter, to adopt such legislative or other measures as may be necessary to give effect to the provisions of this Charter'.[278]

To monitor the implementation of this treaty, a Committee of Experts is established to consider periodic states' reports as well as individual complaints. The Committee's disposition to the integrative human rights approach is yet to be tested because of its newness in the African regional human rights system.[279] The African Women's Protocol equally recognises and obliges state parties to take legislative and other measures to protect, among others, certain economic, social and cultural rights for women in Africa.[280] The contents of this Protocol fall under the supervisory jurisdiction of the African Commission. It is pertinent to note that, besides treaty obligations, there is a broad assemblage of 'soft law' instruments in which African leaders have reaffirmed their faith in human rights, in the need to protect the dignity of Africans, and in an integrative human rights approach to human development. Some of the most recent and far-reaching are the Grand Baie Declaration and Plan of Action, 1999;[281] and the Kigali Declaration, 2003.[282]

At Grand Baie in 1999, the First Organisation of African Unity (OAU) Ministerial Conference on Human Rights in Africa had unanimously affirmed 'the principle that human rights are universal, indivisible, interdependent and inter-related' and demanded of all African 'governments, in their policies, to give parity to economic, social and cultural rights as well as civil and political rights'.[283] Furthermore, as if to denounce and repudiate the protracted conceptual quagmire in which the integrative human rights approach

278 n 276 abobe, art 14(1).

279 See D Olowu 'Protecting children's rights in Africa: A critique of the African Charter on the Rights and Welfare of the Child' (2002) 10 *International Journal of Children's Rights* 127-136; A Lloyd 'The African regional system for the protection of children's rights' in J Sloth-Nielsen *Children's rights in Africa: A legal perspective* (2008) 33 41.

280 These are: the right to education and training (art 12); the right to economic and social welfare (art 13); health and productive rights (art 14); the right to food security (art 15); the right to adequate housing (art 16); the right to a healthy and sustainable environment (art 18); and the right to sustainable development (art 19). For a critical assessment of the capacity of the Africa Women's Protocol to advance a rights-based approach to human development in Africa, see D Olowu 'A critique of the rhetoric, ambivalence and promise in the Draft Protocol to the African Charter on Human and Peoples' Rights on the Rights of Women in Africa' (2006) 8 *Human Rights Review* 78-101.

281 OAU First Ministerial Conference on Human Rights in Africa 12-16 April 1999 OAU Doc CONF/HRA/DECL. (I) (16 April 1999) reprinted in (1999) 8 *Review of the African Commission on Human and Peoples' Rights* 255-260.

282 AU First Ministerial Conference on Human Rights in Africa AU Doc MIN/CONF/HRA/Decl.1 (I) (8 May 2003).

283 The Grand Baie (Mauritius) Declaration and Plan of Action (n 281 above) para 1.

has for long been entangled in Africa, the African Union (AU)'s[284] First Ministerial Conference on Human Rights in Africa, in 2003, reinforced the universality, indivisibility, interdependence and interrelatedness of *all* human rights,[285] and proceeded to direct 'member states and *regional institutions* to accord the same importance to economic, social and cultural rights, and apply, at all levels, *a rights-based approach to policy, programme, planning, implementation and evaluation*'.[286]

The inevitable consequence from the above description of binding and non-binding human rights instruments in Africa is the manifestation of an adequate legal and moral framework for strategic activism for a rights-based approach to human development in Africa. The challenge remains how to galvanise same.

2.2.2 The emerging African Human Rights Court

Many African and Africanist scholars are enthusiastic about an increased relevance for economic, social and cultural rights with the emergence of the African Court Protocol that recently ushered in the African Court on Human and Peoples' Rights (African Court).[287] The details of the composition, structure and jurisdiction of the Court need not detain us here, other than to stress that the Court might be able to perform judicial functions *stricto sensu* beyond the traditional

284 The AU is the successor body to the Organisation of African Unity (OAU). For an elaborate discussion of the background processes that led to the emergence of the AU, see NJ Udombana 'A harmony or a cacophony? The music of integration in the African Union Treaty and the New Partnership for Africa's Development' (2002) 13 *India International and Comparative Law Review* 185 206-214.

285 Kigali Declaration (n 282 above) para 1.

286 n 285 above, para 4 (my emphasis).

287 The African Court Protocol entered into force on 25 January 2004, having obtained the 15 ratifications required from Algeria, Burkina Faso, Burundi, Comoros, Côte d'Ivoire, The Gambia, Libya, Lesotho, Mali, Mauritania, Rwanda, South Africa, Senegal, Togo and Uganda. See List of countries which have signed, ratified/acceded to the Protocol to the African Charter on Human and Peoples' Rights on the Establishment of an African Court on Human and Peoples' Rights' http://www.african-union.org (accessed 12 June 2009). For an elaborate review and critique of the emerging African Court, see GJ Naldi *et al* 'Reinforcing the African system of human rights: The Protocol on the Establishment of a Regional Court of Human Rights' (1998) 16 *Netherlands Quarterly of Human Rights* 431-456; NJ Udombana 'Towards the African Court on Human and Peoples' Rights: Better late than never' (1999) 8 *Review of the African Commission on Human and Peoples' Rights* 338-358; VOO Nmehielle 'Towards an African Court on Human Rights: Structuring of the Court' (2000) 6 *Annual Survey of International and Comparative Law* 27 49-52; Viljoen 2007 (n 241 above) 419.

purview of the African Commission's promotional functions, more so as the Protocol makes no distinction in the nature of the rights protected.[288]

A particularly innovative element that is expected to invigorate rights-based development process in Africa, as I envisage, is the explicit competence of the proposed African Court to entertain cases from individuals and civil society groups in respect of the breach of the African Charter 'and any other relevant human rights instrument ratified by the states concerned'.[289] The proposed African Court will therefore, expectedly, be able to interpret and apply *all* relevant human rights treaties in Africa in a way that would give them judicial meaning and define their enforceability quotient. The recent entry into force of the African Court Protocol certainly promises a viable platform for Africans, and in practical terms, African civil society groups, to spearhead the dynamic advocacy that would bring about the anticipated juridical response to the challenges of rights-based development.

How this emerging African Court will handle its historic responsibility once it comes into operation can only, at least for now, remain a matter of conjecture.[290]

3 Contextualising the rights-based discourse in Africa

In view of the elaborate treaty provisions and inter-governmental policy statements at the African regional level, particularly such as

288 Art 3(1) of the African Court Protocol confers jurisdiction on the African Court in respect of 'all cases and disputes submitted to it concerning the interpretation and application of the Charter, this Protocol and any other relevant human rights instrument ratified by the states concerned'. According to art 5(3), '[t]he Court may entitle relevant non-governmental organisations (NGOs) with observer status before the Commission, and individuals to institute cases directly before it, in accordance with article 34 (6) of this Protocol'. Art 34(6), in turn, provides that '[a]t the time of the ratification of this Protocol or any time thereafter, the state shall make a declaration accepting the competence of the Court to receive cases under article 5(3) of this Protocol. The Court shall not receive any petition under article 5(3) involving a state party which has not made such a declaration.' See generally Ankumah (n 31 above) 198, noting that the establishment of the Court would generally enhance human rights protection in Africa.

289 For a critique of the jurisdictional competence of the proposed African Court, see RW Eno 'The jurisdiction of the African Court on Human and Peoples' Rights' (2002) 2 *African Human Rights Law Journal* 223-233. See also GJ Naldi *et al* 'The proposed African Court of Human Rights: Evaluation and comparison' (1996) 8 *African Journal of International and Comparative Law* 944 947.

290 See generally K Hopkins 'The effect of an African Court on the domestic legal orders of African states' (2002) 2 *African Human Rights Law Journal* 234 235, pointing out that the 'success of [the] African Court is mostly dependent on the willingness of states to embrace, with a real sense of obligation, the core values of the African human rights system that it is intended to serve'.

those found in the very recent African Women's Protocol and the Kigali Declaration, it is no longer plausible to suggest that economic, social and cultural rights still lack the status of *legal* rights within the African regional arrangement, nor that economic, social and cultural rights are of such negligible nature as to be irretrievably consigned to the status of mere marginalia within the African human rights and development discourse. Yet, in real life, it is evident that the extensive array of instruments and mechanisms in this area has produced more rhetoric than results.

Analysts of African political economy, especially bureaucrats, readily cite the incapacity of African states to fulfil the full promises of global development goals, stressing that economic development must come before human rights can be secured in Africa.[291] In 1995, the UN Secretary-General had summed up the arguments of many governments on the question of human rights and human development as follows:

> Most governments, in their replies, drew attention to the intimate link between economic development and the enjoyment of human rights and the danger posed by the problem of foreign debt to the conceptual values of democracy, to the proper enjoyment of all human rights and to national sovereignty ... The devastating effects of the debt crisis have, for almost a decade, prevented the economic and social development of many developing countries, threatening the basic human rights and fundamental freedoms, including the right to development.[292]

Thus, ranging from the cataclysmic consequences of indebtedness to the IMF and the World Bank, the albatross of neo-colonial corruption and patrimonial political leadership, the infinite frequency of human and capital flight from Africa and, lately, the ill-wind of globalisation, the natural reaction of intelligentsia has generally been one of uncanny pessimism about the role of rights in addressing peculiar African socio-economic challenges.[293] This is the context in which I locate my rights-based approach to human development in Africa.

291 See eg FX Njenga 'The African debt problem: Legal and institutional dimensions' (1994) 2 *African Yearbook on International Law* 95-107; M McMorrow 'Global poverty, subsistence rights, and consequent obligations for rich and poor states' in McCarthy-Arnolds *et al* (n 193 above) 37-60; AH Robertson *Human rights in the world: An introduction to the study of the international protection of human rights* (1982) 8-9.

292 Report of the Secretary-General to the Commission on Human Rights, 30 January-10 March 1995, UN Doc E/CN.4/1995/25, para 15.

293 See B Okunade 'Democracy and human rights in the context of twenty-first century Africa in O Oladipo (ed) *Remaking Africa: Challenges of the twenty-first century* (1998) 127-144; Robertson (n 291 above) 8-9. See also EG Bello 'Human rights: Rule of law in Africa' (1981) 30 *International and Comparative Law Quarterly* 628 634 636; A Essy, 'Don't drive Africa to despair' *Le Monde* [The World] (Paris),10 November 1994, translated and published in *Africa Analysis* 25 November 1994 5.

As already mentioned, the cacophony of arguments about the core rights that are most critical to human development has always revolved around the questions of justiciability and resources. The first relates to the essence, content and scope of those rights while the second relates to the fiscal capacity of states to meet the obligations created under them. It has even been argued by some African and non-African scholars alike that African states are generally too weak and poor to fulfil economic, social and cultural rights obligations.[294]

These seemingly formidable issues are often over-emphasised. In this regard, I am making two points clear: For one, what the rights-based approach to human development essentially entails is a holistic consideration of all human rights. Scholarly discussions often fail to note that all six UN human rights treaties emphatically oblige state parties to ensure the protection of the provisions of those treaties without any form of distinction or discrimination.[295] Quite often, it is in complying with the equality and non-discrimination principles that many African states default in their treaty obligations. The second point is that, more than the question of resources, what the implementation of economic, social and cultural rights would require of African governments is the exertion of political will.[296] The so-called cost-free civil and political rights have not fared well in Africa, and it would be difficult to ascribe the spate of gross and subtle state-sponsored violations of civil and political rights to the poverty of African states.[297]

In the case of the integrative human rights paradigm that would enhance human development in Africa, this does not have to be interpreted strictly in terms of direct claims on specific items in state fiscal budgets. The obligations contemplated and created are much more about appropriate *policies* than about monetary entitlements. All that will be required to meet the duties imposed in this respect, in the first instance, is for a state to put credible, equitable and effective regulatory frameworks in place. These have generally been lacking or tenuous in much of Africa. An analogous question illustrates the point: To what extent has the Nigerian government taken 'appropriate steps' to fulfil its obligations under article 11 of ICESCR

294 See eg R Howard 'The full-belly thesis: Should economic rights take priority over civil and political rights? Evidence from sub-Saharan Africa' (1983) 5 *Human Rights Quarterly* 467 470-482; Baah (n 194 above) 92-95; M Haile 'Human rights in Africa: Observations on the implication of economic priority' (1986) 19 *Vanderbilt Journal of Transnational Law* 299 300-301.

295 See eg art 2(1) ICCPR; art 2(1) ICESCR; arts 1 & 4 CERD; CEDAW; arts 2(1) & (2) CAT; art 2 CRC.

296 See generally SS Mahmud 'The state and human rights in Africa in the 1990s: Perspectives and prospects' (1993) 15 *Human Rights Quarterly* 485 492-93.

297 See generally Human Rights Watch 'Africa: Human rights review, ambiguity and duplicity on human rights: Human Rights Watch World Report 2003' http://www.hrw.org/wr2k3/africa.html (accessed 12 June 2009).

(the right to housing), taking cognisance of the fact that the entire land constituting the territory of each state of the Federal Republic of Nigeria is vested in the governor of such a state on the pretext that he or she holds it 'in trust' for the citizens of the state?[298] Alternatively, to put it more broadly, how well do the urban population policies in Cameroon, Côte d'Ivoire, Egypt, Ethiopia, Kenya, Nigeria, Tanzania and Zambia (to mention but a few) evince the commitment of the governments involved to guarantee *equal access* to the means of decent housing facilities as contemplated by CRC, ICESCR and the African Charter to which they are all parties?[299]

The bottom line of my contention here is that the rights that will make life worth living for Africans do not necessarily entail fiscal commitment. Where they do, it is often in the manifestation of the friction between misdirected prioritisation and profligacy, on the one hand, and prudent, accountable public spending, on the other.

It is of critical importance to the foregoing proposition, therefore, that there must be some structure of power that would confer legitimacy on the right-duty relations engendered by the rights-based approach to human development as envisaged in this discourse. This is where the rights-based approach attains its point of entry amidst the broad range of international and regional frameworks.

4 Concluding remarks

I have attempted to analyse some of the legalistic impediments to the proper conceptualisation of economic, social and cultural rights obligations with regard to African states in the broader human rights

298 See sec 1 Land Use Decree 6 of 1978 (now Land Use Act Cap 202), Laws of the Federation of Nigeria (LFN) 1990, which provides: '[A]ll land comprised in the territory of each state in the federation are hereby vested in the Military Governor of that state and such land shall be held in trust and administered for the use and common benefit of all Nigerians.' This statute essentially divested customary landowners of tenure and created technical mechanisms that make land acquisition more arduous for less privileged Nigerians. The Act runs contrary to ICESCR provisions. The UN Committee that monitors the implementation of ICESCR has elaborated on the 'minimum core obligation' in the right to adequate housing, stressing that state policies should increase access to land and not diminish it. See ESCR Committee General Comment No 4 'The right to adequate housing (art 11(1) of the Covenant)'. See also S Leckie 'The human rights to adequate housing' in Eide *et al* (n 29 above) 149 153-158. It is worthy to note that Tanzania adopted the Nigerian legislative approach to land ownership in 1999. See sec (4)1 Land Act, 1999 (Tanzania). For a discussion of the human rights implications of this Act, see R Palmer 'The Tanzanian Land Acts 1999: An analysis of the analyses' (1999).

299 See generally AA Gordon 'Population, urbanisation and AIDS' in AA Gordon *et al* (eds) *Understanding contemporary Africa* (2001) 204-206, describing how, in the attempt to discourage rural-urban migration, some African governments resorted to destroying squatter camps in the major cities, without providing alternatives, thereby compounding urban congestion and public health hazards.

discourse, and attempted disproving the critical theoretical legal questions, namely, justiciability and resource constraints. In the course of the above, I highlighted the broad assemblage of international and regional human rights frameworks that could promote an integrative rights-based approach to human development in Africa, indicating the legal and political considerations that should guide the performance of human development-oriented human rights obligations.

My effort here has been about elaborating the basic normative and institutional frameworks of economic, social and cultural rights at the UN and the African regional levels, and their implications for the effective implementation of economic, social and cultural rights at the domestic level in Africa, in a way that enhances human development. Here, I underscored the reality of ample economic, social and cultural rights protection mechanisms and yet, the asymmetry of weak implementation. It points out a range of the legal problems that have arisen in the course of the textual elucidation of economic, social and cultural rights norms. In the final analysis, therefore, I have indicated that, despite observable constraints, economic, social and cultural rights consist of protective and promotional elements that can strengthen their value as legal rights. Against the backdrop of increasing global efforts aimed at establishing human development as a human rights theme, this chapter evaluates the capacity of existing and emerging human rights frameworks relevant to Africa, and accentuates their weaknesses and prospects in the conceptualisation of an integrative rights-based approach to the appalling socio-economic conditions in Africa.

3

Domestic Implementation of Human Rights

The struggle for human rights will be won or lost at the national level. Unless we begin to study such struggles, we will neither understand the most important issues nor be able to make the most effective possible contribution to the realisation of internationally recognised human rights.[300]

1 Overview of the domestic effect of treaties

The efficacy or otherwise of a human rights treaty, or any treaty for that matter, can only be assessed on the basis of its domestic effect, that is, its status within a particular legal system. Ordinary reasoning would dictate that it is always more desirable and preferable for individuals who complain about the violation of their rights to have the opportunity to seek relief or remedy in their own national courts and related institutions. However, in many legal systems, African states inclusive, the formalities prescribed by constitutional law determine the effect of treaties.[301] Further, in most states of the world, a written constitution's provisions are supreme. As Gonidec discovered concerning African states:

> [T]he Constitution is, as a rule, sacrosanct, that is, it is very often considered as the supreme and fundamental law of the state ... the supremacy of the constitution is guaranteed by a system of control of the constitutionality of the laws.[302]

The effect of treaties within the hierarchy of laws in different legal systems has been a subject of great debate among international

300 J Donnelly 'Post-Cold War reflections on the study of international human rights' in JH Rosenthal (ed) *Ethics and international affairs: A reader* (1995) 236 252.

301 See D Olowu 'Human rights and the avoidance of domestic implementation: The phenomenon of non-justiciable constitutional guarantees' (2006) 69 *Saskatchewan Law Review* 39.

302 See PF Gonidec 'The relationship of international law and national law in Africa' (1998) 10 *African Journal of International and Comparative Law* 244 247.

lawyers and scholars and will continue to be so.[303] Contentious issues in debate include the implications of the rights contained in a treaty *vis-à-vis* the prevailing constitutional order in a state party; whether the provisions in a treaty automatically become an integral part of the state's internal laws; whether a state party is obliged to enact new laws or to amend its existing statutes to *transform* a treaty into domestic law; and the stage at which a treaty becomes cognisable for human rights adjudication in the regular courts of the state.

Answers to those questions vary in Africa as in other parts of the world. Traditionally, the legal methods for resolving the issues have been classified by using the roughly dichotomised theories of 'dualism' and 'monism'.[304] In states of the dualist tradition, the understanding of municipal law and international law place them as distinct legal systems, requiring the performance of a formal legislative process to give effect to a treaty. Conversely, in the monist tradition, international law and municipal law together form a unified legal system, often characterised by the primacy of international norms.[305]

Scheinin has argued that the divergence of scholarly opinions about the theoretical construction of human rights treaties – monism, dualism, adoption, incorporation, transformation, and reference – is the outcome of approaches predicated on differing legal traditions.[306] Scheinin's observation could not have found a better ground for credence than in Africa where, by consequence of history,

303 See M Sorensen 'Obligations of a state party to a treaty as regards its municipal law' in Robertson (n 291 above) 11.

304 A Angwenyi *et al* 'How to ensure the judiciary enforces treaty obligations' (1999) 6 *Innovation: Journal of the African Centre for Technology Studies* 20. See also ME Adjami 'African courts, international law, and comparative case law: Chimera or emerging human rights jurisprudence?' (2002) 24 *Michigan Journal of International Law* 108.

305 M Scheinin 'International human rights in national law' in Hanski *et al* (n 37 above) 417-419. See Gonidec (n 302 above) 245-246 for a concise analytical description of the treaty-formulation procedures in francophone and anglophone African states.

306 See Scheinin (n 305 above). For other views on the analytical discussions of the monism-dualism polarities among some legal scholars, see JG Starke 'Monism and dualism in the theory of international law' (1936) 17 *British Yearbook on International Law* 66; H Kelsen *Principles of international law* (1966) 553-588; GM Silverman 'Dualistic legal phenomena and the limitations of positivism' (1986) 86 *Columbia Law Review* 823-851; Janis (n 77 above) 85-86; D Kennedy 'International law and the nineteenth century: history of an illusion' (1997) 17 *Quinnipiac Law Review* 99; DJ Bederman *International law frameworks* (2000) 151-152; J Morgan-Foster 'The relationship of IMF structural adjustment programmemes to economic, social and cultural rights: The Argentine case revisited' (2003) 24 *Michigan Journal of International Law* 577.

all the conflicting legal traditions in the world converge.[307] This might indeed be another unexplored factor for the manifest weaknesses in the implementation of many human rights treaties in Africa.[308]

I do not intend to unearth all the intricate issues involved in the debate on the legal effect of every treaty at the domestic level in Africa. My design here is to identify *how* relevant human rights treaties can become instruments of human development at the national level in Africa even when the constitutional order is weak or structurally encumbered for such outcome. As I have indicated earlier, since no African Constitution is problematic about the normative framework of civil and political rights, it is to ICESCR and the African Charter that I turn for my present thematic enquiry. The ESCR Committee has had cause to expound the effect of ICESCR within domestic legal systems. In its General Comment No 9 (1998), the ESCR Committee declared:

> In general, legally binding international human rights standards should operate *directly and immediately* within the domestic legal system of each state party, thereby enabling individuals to seek enforcement of their rights before national courts and tribunals. The rule requiring the exhaustion of domestic remedies reinforces the primacy of national remedies in this respect. The existence and further development of international procedures for the pursuit of individual claims is important, but such procedures are ultimately only supplementary to effective national remedies.[309]

However, what is the status of ICESCR *vis-à-vis* its domestic application in the jurisdiction of state parties to it? It would appear that the ESCR Committee itself had been hesitant in pronouncing on

307 See M Hansungule 'Domestic implementation of human rights in African constitutions' (2001) 9-11 (unpublished manuscript); Gonidec (n 302 above) 245-246. Although the wealth of literature on the scholarly debates in Africa is concentrated on the Southern African experience, there have generally been considerable contributions from African scholars on this subject. See eg O Umozurike *Introduction to international law* (1993) 29-36; T Maluwa 'The incorporation of international law and its interpretational role in municipal legal systems in Africa: An explanatory survey' (1998) 23 *South African Year Book on International Law* 45; O Tshosa *National law and international human rights law: Cases of Botswana, Namibia and Zimbabwe* (2001); Adjami (n 304 above) 106-112; D Olowu 'The effect of human rights treaties in domestic courts: The Nigerian Supreme Court decision in *Sani Abacha v Gani Fawehinmi* revisited' (2002) 3 *Nigerian Supreme Court Monthly* 172-178. For a legal analysis of the effect of ICESCR in South Africa that has only signed the treaty, see S Liebenberg 'The International Covenant on Economic, Social and Cultural Rights and its implications for South Africa' (1995) 11 *South african journal on Human Rights* 359 371-374.

308 See generally Gonidec (n 302 above) 248.

309 ESCR Committee 'The domestic application of the Covenant' General Comment No 9 UN Doc E/C 12/1998/24 3 December 1998 para 4 in *Compilation of general comments* (n 81 above) 54 55 (my emphasis).

the self-executing or non-self executing status of ICESCR when it went further to say:

> The Covenant does not negate the possibility that the rights it contains may be considered self-executing in systems where that option is provided for. Indeed, *when it was being drafted, attempts to include a specific provision in the Covenant to the effect that it be considered 'non-self-executing' were strongly rejected.* In most states, the determination of *whether or not a treaty provision is self-executing will be a matter for the courts*, not the executive or the legislature ... Thus ... when governments are involved in court proceedings, they should promote interpretations of domestic laws which give effect to their Covenant obligations ... *It is especially important to avoid any* a priori *assumption that the norms should be considered to be non-self-executing*. In fact, many of them are stated in terms which are at least as clear and specific as those in other human rights treaties, the provisions of which are regularly deemed by courts to be self-executing.[310]

In one stroke, the ESCR Committee seems to suggest 'Yes, the treaty is self-executing', and yet, in another stroke, it says the self-executing status of ICESCR should be a decision for the courts. The ambivalence of the ESCR Committee has not been helpful.[311]

While some scholars have suggested that, as a result of the cross-fertilisation of ideas about liberal treaty implementation methods (for example, incorporation), the trend towards unified legal effect of international norms, the increasing openness of judiciaries to a wide use of international norms even without their formal status as norms of domestic law, and the growing heterogeneity of international norms, the traditional distinction between 'dualism' and 'monism' has diminished in relevance,[312] the reality within domestic legal systems in Africa portrays a distant reality from such a conclusion.

Even with some 47 odd African state parties to ICESCR, the treaty is yet to make any tangible impact within those domestic jurisdictions, including francophone countries that belong to the 'monist' tradition. Moreover, even the African Charter, that I have

310 n 309 above, para 11 (my emphasis).

311 For an analysis of the debates regarding whether or not ICESCR is a self-executing treaty or not, see M Scheinin 'Direct applicability of economic, social and cultural rights: A critique of the doctrine of self-executing treaties' in K Drzewicki *et al* (eds) *Social rights as human rights: A European challenge* (1994) 73-90.

312 See eg Scheinin (n 305 above) 418; R Bahdi 'Globalisation of judgment: transjudicialism and the five faces of international law in domestic courts' (2002) 34 *George Washington International Law Review* 555; JV Lanotte *et al* 'Economic, social and cultural rights in the Belgian Constitution' in Auweraert *et al* (eds) (n 46 above) 253 274-275.

shown to be autochthonous and of 'universal' acceptance and recognition in every African state, is yet to receive the level of engagement that one would have expected. The failure of human rights treaties in Africa has been a perennial phenomenon.[313]

While African states are generally disposed to ratifying or acceding to human rights treaties, putting the required machinery in place that would secure their implementation has always been problematic.[314] Empirical research has shown that the non-domestication of human rights treaties has stultified the growth of human rights jurisprudence in dualist and monist states of Africa alike.[315]

Without doubt, the burden of implementing economic, social and cultural rights provisions in both ICESCR and the African Charter primarily lies on states that are expected to provide a legislative framework for their implementation. This is consistent with the provisions of the treaties themselves as well as international law and practice.[316] However, where governments are reluctant about initiating positive legislative changes, what then are the options in implementing the economic, social and cultural rights provisions in these two treaties – and by extension, the economic, social and cultural rights provisions in African constitutions?

Rossi has vividly described how international legal norms have been applied as interpretive tools before courts and governmental agencies in Bangladesh, India, Nepal and Pakistan even when there were weak or non-existent economic, social and cultural rights

313 See generally GJ Naldi *et al The African Economic Community: emancipation for African states or yet another glorious failure?* (1999) 24 *North Carolina Journal of International Law and Commercial Regulation* 601. See also Maluwa (n 307 above) 46-47.

314 See Baah (n 194 above). See also W Onzivu 'Public health and the tobacco problem: International legal implications for Africa' (2001) 29 *Georgia Journal of International and Comparative Law* 223 235, addressing the non-chalance of African governments to confront the menace of tobacco abuse, says that while 'African countries usually complain of an inability to implement [health] rights due to lack of funds ... the prohibition of advertisement, increased taxes on tobacco sales and mass education about the dangers of tobacco will be less costly to implement'.

315 Adjami (n 304 above) 124-125; CA Odinkalu 'The judiciary and the legal protection of human rights in common law Africa: Allocating responsibility for the failure of post-independence bills of rights' (1996) 8 *African Society of International and Comparative Law Proceedings* 124; II Dore 'Constitutionalism and the post-colonial state in Africa: A Rawlsian approach' (1997) 41 *St Louis University Law Journal* 1301 1302.

316 See art 2(1) ICESCR; art 1 African Charter; and art 27 Vienna Convention on the Law of Treaties, 1969, UN Doc A/CONF.39/27 (1969), 8 ILM 679 (1969), entered into force 27 January 1980 (VCLT), providing that 'a party may not invoke the provisions of its internal law as justification for its failure to perform a treaty'. Art 26 of the VCLT also demands that state parties to a treaty must perform their obligations under it in good faith.

frameworks.[317] I must quickly add, however, that committed, well-trained and motivated human rights groups spearheaded those experiences described by Rossi.[318]

Through public interest litigation, and greater educational and research-based activism, African human rights groups can also begin to urge economic, social and cultural rights on judiciaries, policy makers and even private sector actors within their various domestic systems. Generally, so far, this type of effort has remained at low ebb.

2 The promise of constitutionalism

Although recent empirical studies readily trace the roots of modern political systems from the philosophical ideas of the Greek republics all the way through eighteenth and nineteenth century intellectual enquiries, it has never been an easy task delimiting the fine details of law-ordered societies.[319]

With the enduring debates on the latitude of governmental power and the determination of the relationship between the government and the governed, the narrow passage of compromise among liberal-welfarists, contractarian constitutionalists, strict constructivists, realists, conventionalists and minimalists alike, had largely been the need for a *formalised set of restrictions* on those officials who wield political power — restrictions that must be founded on the rule of law.[320]

Notwithstanding the fact that *constitutionalism* continues to mean different things to different writers in different political

317 J Rossi 'Strategies for enforcing ESC rights through domestic legal systems' in IHRIP (n 111 above) 418 430-431.

318 n 317 above 422 430.

319 See generally R Hardin *Liberalism, constitutionalism and democracy* (2003) 41-81; AP Blaustein *Constitutions of the world* (1993) 2-4; S Gordon *Controlling the state: Constitutionalism from ancient Athens to today* (1999); GM Hodgson 'The evolution of institutions: An agenda for future theoretical research' (2002) 13 *Constitutional Political Economy* 111-127; A Gifford 'The evolution of social contract' (2002) 13 *Constitutional Political Economy* 361-379; AL Bendor 'On Aristotelian equality, the fundamental right to equality, and governmental discretion' (2003) 8 *Review of Constitutional Studies* 1-19.

320 See Hardin (n 319 above) 80-81 84; NB Reynolds 'The ethical foundations of constitutional order: A conventionalist perspective' (1993) 4 *Constitutional Political Economy* 79-95; SL Elkin 'Constitutionalism: Old and new' in SL Elkin *et al* (eds) *A new constitutionalism: Designing political institutions for a good society* (1993) 20-37; KE Soltan 'Generic constitutionalism' in Elkin *et al* 70-93; JR Rudolph 'Constitutional governments' in FN Magill (ed) *International encyclopaedia of government and politics* (1996) 299; Gordon (n 319 above) 58-59.

contexts, certain notions have become invariable.[321] In today's legal parlance, constitutionalism implies governance according to the rule of law, an important universal norm that negates arbitrary rule.[322] Closely linked to this neo-liberal conception is the existence of a *written constitution* that stipulates separation of governmental powers, checks and balances, judicial review, accountable governance, rule of law and, of course, a bill of human rights.[323]

With the collapse of communism following the dramatic socio-economic and political events of 1989, the ground had been laid for radical global policy reforms that would assert the earlier day values of liberalism, free market economy and human rights as opposed to the collectivist ideology of the defunct Eastern bloc.[324] What became obvious, however, in the process of supplanting the old ideological divide was the realisation of the inadequacy of merely ousting the old communist order as a guarantee for sustainable reforms. The consensual path was the gradual ascendancy of a global culture of human rights and the rule of law, enhanced through the instrumentality of constitutionalism.[325]

In the post-Cold War era, the ideals of democracy, rule of law and a culture of human rights, rooted in constitutionalism, have become entrenched in the consciousness of states.[326] In the light of those tremendous changes that marked the end of the Cold War, Fukuyama had exclaimed:

> As mankind approaches the end of the millennium, the twin crises of authoritarianism and socialist central planning have left only one competitor standing in the ring as an ideology of potentially universal validity: liberal democracy, the doctrine of individual freedom and

321 There has been a remarkable level of discussions among scholars about the elements of constitutionalism. While some contend that it requires a set of codified norms in *written* form, others have argued that the unwritten constitutional model of the United Kingdom dispenses with the necessity of a written constitution. Constitutionalists on these arguments usually canvass various reasons. See eg J Rubenfeld 'Legitimacy and interpretation' in L Alexander (ed) *Constitutionalism: Philosophical foundations* (1998) 214 216; J Kis *Constitutional democracy* (2003) 112 119 131; S Woolman & M Bishop *Constitutional conversations* (2008).

322 L Henkin 'Elements of constitutionalism' (1998) 60 *Review of International Commission of Jurists* 11 12; Woolman *et al* (n 321 above).

323 Henkin (n 322 above) 12-15. See also E Petersmann 'Human rights and international economic law in the 21st century: The need to clarify their inter-relationships' (2001) 4 *Journal of International Economic Law* 3 11-16.

324 See K Pistor 'The demand for constitutional law' (2002) 13 *Constitutional Political Economy* 73 81-84.

325 Pistor (n 324 above) 77-80.

326 See generally D Larry 'Is the third wave over?' (1996) 7 *Journal of Democracy* 20-37; SBO Gutto 'Current concepts, core principles, dimensions, processes and institutions of democracy and the inter-relationship between democracy and modern human rights seminar' on the 'Interdependence between democracy and human rights', Geneva, 25-26 November (2002) 7.

> popular sovereignty. Two hundred years after they first animated the French and American revolutions, the principles of liberty and equality have proven not just durable but resurgent.[327]

An enduring normative idea since the age of the earlier liberal thinkers has been the overarching imperative of human rights protection and promotion through constitutional provisions. Some scholars have argued that, since individuals are themselves prone to abusing the liberties of others just as those who govern can abuse their powers, human rights constitute the best safeguards for the defence of individual liberties against tyranny.[328]

The desirability of including human rights provisions within the body of a national constitution or as an appendage to it is an idea that has found robust validation in ample scholarship. There is a contention that the inclusion of a bill of rights in a constitution translates such rights into a device for 'legitimacy ... and political stability in pluralistic societies'.[329] Gavison also argues that '[t]he high visibility and solemn nature of most constitutions help in making the commitment to human rights a part of *civil religion* and civil-shared culture'.[330]

While critics of the constitutionalisation of human rights contend that the inclusion of a bill of rights is neither necessary nor adequate to secure human rights protection,[331] there is no denying the fact that the mere existence of such explicit provisions are potent in building, institutionalising and sustaining the processes that would ensure their promotion and protection as they gain more popular and informed cognition.[332]

As De Waal, Currie and Erasmus have argued, beyond strengthening the rule of law, democratic accountability, separation of powers as well as checks and balances – all fundamental principles of a constitutional order:

327 F Fukuyama 'The end of history?' (1989) 16 *The National Interest* 3; F Fukuyama 'Second thoughts: The last man in a bottle' (1999) 56 *The National Interest* 16.

328 See Petersmann (n 323 above) 10. See also PC Ordeshook 'Are "Western" constitutions relevant to anything other than the countries they serve?' (2002) 13 *Constitutional Political Economy* 3 8-11.

329 Ordeshook (n 328 above) 17.

330 R Gavison 'What belongs in a constitution?' (2002) 13 *Constitutional Political Economy* 89 96 (emphasis in the original).

331 See eg H Pitkin 'Obligation and consent - I and II' (1965) 59 *American Political Science Review* 990-991; TM Scanlon 'Human rights as a neutral concern' in PG brown *et al* (eds) *Human rights and US foreign policy* (1979) 83-92.

332 See Gavison (n 330 above) 86 96. See also E Scarry 'On philosophy and human rights' in Koh *et al* (eds) (n 327 above) 71 75-76.

> [a] bill of rights overrides ordinary law and conduct inconsistent with it. In addition, subject to considerations of justiciability and constitutional jurisdiction, the bill of rights generates its own set of remedies ... At the same time [it] contains a set of values that must be respected whenever ordinary law is interpreted, developed or applied. This form of application, which aims at creating harmony between the bill of rights and ordinary law, is termed the indirect application of the bill of rights.[333]

The 1787 Constitution of the United States (together with the subsequent Bill of Rights, 1791)[334] has been credited with the pride of being the first written constitution to have an entrenched bill of rights.[335] Although the Constitution was enacted as an amplification of the promises of 'life, liberty and the pursuit of happiness' proclaimed in the US Declaration of Independence on 4 July 1776, it fell short of defining which rights would ensure those ends.[336] Pollock provides an insight into this shortfall:

> The founders believed in individual rights, and they held that the primary concern of government should be the protection of these rights ... Jefferson and Madison did not envision a federal government that would be heavily involved in promoting health, education, and welfare ... Their ideal was a small, limited government, not the bloated monster we have today.[337]

The missing link in Pollock's argument is *what* makes the contemporary US government a 'bloated' institution. Pollock must have realised over time, however, that it is not the promotion of

333 J de Waal *et al The bill of rights handbook* (2001) 27. See also I Currie & J de Waal *The bill of rights handbook* (2005).

334 Constitution of the United States of America and Bill of Rights, reprinted in L Wolf-Phillips (ed) *Constitutions of modern states: Selected texts and commentary* (1968) 207-217.

335 See Blaustein (n 319 above) 4; N Strossen 'United States ratification of the international Bill of Rights: A fitting celebration of the bi-centennial of the US Bill of Rights' (1992) 24 *University of Toledo Law Review* 203. See also AT Arnason 'Constitutionalism: Popular legitimacy of the state?' in M Scheinin (ed) *The welfare state and constitutionalism in the Nordic countries* (2000) 29 44-45. In his letter to President James Madison, urging the incorporation of a bill of rights in the US Constitution, Thomas Jefferson had written, *inter alia*: 'Let me add that a bill of rights is what the people are entitled to against every government on earth, general or particular, and what no just government should refuse or rest on inference.' See T Jefferson's letter to J Madison 20 December 1787 quoted in TA Aguda *The judiciary in the government of Nigeria* (1983) 41.

336 A leading American constitutional scholar, Hardin, has suggested that the US Constitution was meant to create a 'neutral economic policy', as an indication of why that Constitution and its Bill of Rights were devoid of any reference to 'proprietary' rights. See Hardin (n 319 above) 228. Earlier, in his dissenting judgment in *Lockner v New York* 198 US 45 (1905), Justice Holmes had defined the 'non-ideological' posture of US constitutionalism as follows: 'A constitution is not intended to embody a particular economic theory, whether of paternalism and the organic relation of the citizen to the state or of *laissez faire*', quoted in Hardin above.

337 L Pollock *The free society* (1996) 73.

'health, education and welfare' that has made it so.[338] Whereas the US Constitution and Bill of Rights only guarantee civil and political rights, a wide range of subsequent national constitutions were to give positive recognition to 'the other category' of rights – economic, social and cultural rights. The Mexican Constitution of 1917[339] recorded the first comprehensive attempt at con-stitutionalising economic, social and cultural rights.[340] The Constitution not only guaranteed the traditional civil and political rights as were enumerated in the US Bill of Rights, but also made *justiciable* the rights to literacy,[341] to employment and fair conditions of employment,[342] and to social security.[343]

Many other European nations, particularly from the end of World War II, incorporated economic, social and cultural rights in their constitutions. Remarkable in this regard are the Nordic states of Denmark, Finland, Norway and Sweden, which have not only constitutionalised economic, social and cultural rights, but have also sought to promote them through the establishment of elaborate social welfare systems.[344]

Other nations have also adopted similar constitutions, containing economic, social and cultural rights in extensive or limited terms.[345]

338 See generally K Farris 'Human rights and US military interventions' in T Wagner *et al* (eds) *Fifty years after the declaration: The United Nations' record on human rights* (2001) 145 147, showing how the cost of US military expeditions have impacted domestic social policies adversely; CL Mann 'Perspectives on the US current account deficit and sustainability' (2002) 16 *Journal of Economic Perspectives* 131-152, describing how government's policy options and priorities have led to a sustained budget deficit in the US despite a drawdown on social services.

339 The Constitution of the Mexican United States 1917, reprinted in Wolf-Phillips (ed) (n 334 above) 138-165.

340 Blaustein (n 319 above) 56. The Constitution made justiciable the right to literacy, the right to employment and fair conditions of employment, the right to an adequate standard of living and the right to health care. For a scholarly exposition on the history of constitutional transformation in the Latin American region and its impact on the economic, social and cultural rights provisions in the Mexican Constitution, see PG Carozza 'From conquest to constitutions: Retrieving a Latin American tradition of the idea of human rights' (2003) 25 *Human Rights Quarterly* 281 303-311.

341 Art 3.

342 Arts 4-5.

343 Art 123(xi).

344 For an extensive discussion of the interplay of constitutionalism, legislative intervention and judicial review in the Nordic countries, see JE Rytter 'Judicial review of legislation - A sustainable strategy on the enforcement of basic rights' in M Scheinin *The welfare state and constitutionalism* (2001) 137-174.

345 Such states include Belgium, Germany, Argentina and a host of others. I discuss the jurisprudence emanating from various national courts around the world in the next chapter. For an assemblage of literature that examine national constitutional provisions on economic, social and cultural rights, see V Hart *et al* *Writing a national identity: Political, economic and cultural perspectives on the written constitution* (1993). The African dimension of economic, social and cultural rights constitutionalisation is discussed in the next segment of this chapter.

Despite the tendency to presumptuously regard the collapse of communism as a tacit abrogation of economic, social and cultural rights values, the constitutional reform processes in Central and Eastern Europe (among other places) demonstrate that, rather than signalling the end of economic, social and cultural rights, what is prevalent is the convergence of liberal free-market economy and the human and social dimensions of governance.[346] Communism and the preservation of human dignity through the language of rights are certainly two divergent subjects.[347]

Even though the United States is often criticised for giving exclusive constitutional recognition to civil and political rights and for not ratifying ICESCR,[348] it has been conceded at various fora that it is a state that has metamorphosed into a 'quasi-welfare state by popular will rather than constitutional compulsion ...'.[349]

I contend that today, the dividing line among states and within states is no longer about economic or political ideology: It is much more about humanity, human survival and the preservation of human dignity, through *the rule of law* – a process that is adding new vistas to the juridical status of economic, social and cultural rights.[350] It is in this light that I address the dimension of constitutionalism and its attendant implications for Africa in this book.

346 See K Drzewicki *et al* 'Social rights in a United Europe' in *Social rights as human rights* (n 311) 11 12-13; V Dimitrijevic 'The human dimension of post-totalitarianism' in A Eide *et al* (eds) *The future of human rights protection in a changing world: Fifty years since the four freedoms speech* (1991) 32; Z Kędzia 'Social rights in the (Draft) Constitutions of Central and Eastern Europe' in *Social rights as human rights* (n 311 above) 203-209. See also Henkin (n 322 above) 18; KYL Tan 'The making and remaking of constitutions in South East Asia' (2002) 6 *Singapore Journal of International and Comparative Law* 1 33; Carozza (n 340 above) 305.

347 It had been a strong point of argument, during the Cold War, for antagonists of US ratification of ICESCR to label the treaty as a communist programmeme in disguise. That chequered argument can no longer withstand the demands and social pressures of the world of the twenty-first century. See B Stark 'Economic rights in the United States and international human rights law: Towards an "entirely new strategy"' (1992) 44 *Hastings Law Journal* 79 82.

348 See T Buergenthal 'Modern constitutions and human rights treaties' (1997) 36 *Columbia Journal of Transnational Law* 211; LC Backer 'Human rights and legal education in the Western hemisphere: Legal parochialism and hollow universalism' (2002) 21 *Pennsylvania State International Law Review* 115.

349 RB Lillich 'The United States Constitution in its third century: foreign affairs: Rights – here and there: The Constitution and international human rights' (1989) 83 *American Journal of International Law* 851 852. See also the brilliant exposition of SA Barber *Welfare and the constitution* 55 (2003).

350 See generally N Haysom 'Constitutionalism, majoritarianism democracy and socio-economic rights' (1992) 8 *South African Journal on Human Rights* 451 459. See also M Baderin & R McCorquodale *Economic, social and cultural rights in action* (2007) 15.

3 Rights-based frameworks in African domestic legal systems

Many volumes of scholarly works have assessed the impact of colonisation on constitutionalism, democratisation, governance and the process of evolving a human rights culture in Africa,[351] and I do not intend to add to that wealth of literature.

Since the demise of the Cold War, the quest for a constitutional order has gained tremendous momentum in Africa. Many African countries are democratising, at least in the formal sense, while giant strides have also been recorded in the establishment of governments based on the rule of law.[352] What is, however, more significant is that across the African continent, there is a gale of constitutional reform processes sweeping through some 20 African countries.[353]

Complementing these processes has been a series of national conferences, high-level colloquia and various other political and intellectual fora.[354] The new era of a 'globalised' culture of constitutionalism, democratisation and human rights would seem to

351 A select bibliography on this point will include the following: C Welch *et al Human rights and development in Africa* (1984); KA Maope *Human rights in Botswana, Lesotho and Swaziland survey* (1986); RE Howard *Human rights in Commonwealth Africa* (1986); Shepherd Jr *et al* (n 196 above); Gutto (n 197 above); McCarthy-Arnolds *et al* (n 193 above); IG Shivji *State and constitutionalism in Africa* (1996); M Mamdani *Citizen and subject: Contemporary Africa and the legacy of late colonialism* (1996); C Clapham *Africa and the international system* (1996) 249-256; J Sarkin 'The development of a human rights culture in South Africa' (1998) 20) *Human Rights Quarterly* 628; R Joseph *State, conflict and democratisation in Africa* (1999); Oloka-Onyango (n 351 above); An-Na'im (n 31 above). Much of this vast literature as well as other journal essays has been referred to in earlier chapters and will still be considered within the scope of their relevance to this work.

352 See M Sinjela 'Constitutionalism in Africa: Emerging trends' (1998) 60 *Review of the International Commission of Jurists* 23. Between 1990 and the end of 2001, elected regimes have emerged in the following African countries which were under one-party, apartheid or military regimes before 1990: Benin, Ethiopia, Ghana, Kenya, Malawi, Mozambique, Namibia, Nigeria, South Africa and Zambia, to mention a few. For a detailed discussion of multi-party democratisation in Africa in the 1990s, see L Rakner *et al Multi-party elections in Africa's new democracies report* (2002) 7. See also M Cowen *et al Multi-party elections in Africa* (2002), evaluating the series of national elections, local and bye-elections conducted in 14 African states throughout the 1990s.

353 African states currently in a constitutional reform/review process, or experiencing active civil society debates on reforms, include Angola, Burkina Faso, Central African Republic, Democratic Republic of the Congo, Egypt, Ghana, Guinea-Bissau, Kenya, Liberia, Malawi, Morocco, Mozambique, Nigeria, Rwanda, São Tomé and Principe, Sudan, Swaziland, Uganda, Zambia and Zimbabwe.

354 The outcomes of these intensive dialogues have been far-reaching, albeit only in the sense of agenda setting for democratisation in Africa. See B Ramcharan 'The evolving African constitutionalism: A constitutionalism of liberty and human rights' (1998) 60 *Review of the International Commission of Jurists* 7; A Ould-Abdallah 'The rule of law and political liberalisation in Africa' (1998) 60 *Review of the International Commission of Jurists* 29-39.

have facilitated a new African response to these ideals.[355] Thus, in present-day Africa, every country has a written constitution with varying elements of human rights provisions.[356]

3.1 Bills of rights

At the birth of the UN in 1945, and still in 1948 when the Universal Declaration was adopted as 'a common standard of achievement' for all human beings, only four African states – Egypt, Ethiopia, Liberia and apartheid South Africa – were free from colonial domination.[357] Eze has pointed out that, even though there were 'constitutions' within the respective jurisdictions of each colonial power in Africa, at that time, the only clear human right included was the right to property.[358] The value of the right to property was obviously to protect colonial economic interests. As Eze wrote much later:

> The imperatives of colonialism whether by direct or indirect rule were predominantly economic. The Europeans were no longer interested in dealing with the middlemen (rulers). It became necessary because of the demands and consequences of the industrial revolution and nascent capitalism to direct control. From then on, the capacity of the rulers to make laws for their own people passed into the hands of the colonialist who not only began to establish rudimentary dependent capitalist structures but imposed for their legitimation corresponding legal super-structures that increasingly emphasised private property and representative government even when the elites were belatedly incorporated into the machinery of government. *The foundation was already laid for the contradictory pre-eminence given to private property side by side with civil and political rights, even when the basic material and political inequality between colonials and locals ensured*

355 See Dore (n 315 above) 1301 1302; JM Mbaku 'Constitutional engineering and the transition to democracy in post-Cold War Africa' (1998) 2 *Independent Review* 501; M Ndulo 'The democratisation process and structural adjustment in Africa' (2003) 10 *Indian Journal of Global Legal Studies* 315.

356 Despite the desperate undercurrents of King Mswati's efforts to thwart popular agitation for a constitutional framework for Swaziland, the last bastion of absolute monarchy in Africa, the Swaziland Constitution of 2005 came into force in 2006. For an insight into the debates on Swazi constitutionalism, see C Okpaluba *Human rights in Swaziland: The legal response* (1997); JB Mzizi 'Constitutional developments in the Kingdom of Swaziland' (2001) 5 *The Human Rights Observer* 6; JB Mzizi 'The dominance of the Swazi monarchy and the moral dynamics of democratisation of the Swazi state' (2004) 3 *Journal of African Elections* 94; CM Fombad 'The Swaziland Constitution of 2005: Can absolutism be reconciled with modern constitutionalism?' (2007) 23 *South African Journal on Human Rights* 93.

357 See AA An-Na'im 'Introduction' in An-Naim *et al* (n 31 above) 9.

358 Eze (n 195 above) 20-21.

that there was discrimination in the manner in which the laws were applied.[359]

Apparently, since the inclusion of human rights in those colonial constitutions was originally conceived to give cold comfort to oppressed Africans, the core principles of *equality* and *non-discrimination* were practically absent.[360]

At the dawn of political independence, the preponderance of African states had adopted constitutional rights that fitted their respective colonial legal systems. Thus, while African states of the Anglo-American legal tradition had the bills of rights in their independence constitutions closely modelled after the European Convention for the Protection of Human Rights and Fundamental Freedoms (European Convention), 1950, as amended,[361] the Preambles of the constitutions in francophone African states simply refer to the French Constitution of 1958 as well as the Universal Declaration without further elaboration on the rights protected.[362]

I must call to mind that the European Convention only guaranteed civil and political rights while the French Constitution of 1958 only referred to the Declaration of the Rights of Man and the Citizen, 1789.[363] An instrument of 17 articles, the 1789 Declaration contains

359 Eze 'Human rights and social justice' (n 42 above) 31 (my emphasis). Supporting Eze's argument, Zambian human rights scholar Michelo Hansungule says: 'In the end, the colonialists decided to bequeath on the African people a written constitution complete with a bill of rights! Even though they had themselves denied the Africans the most elementary of human rights after more than 400 years of colonial rule, suddenly, on the eve of independence, constitutions hurriedly drawn in European capitals flooded the African continent. The Europeans were not being hypocritical. Quite contrary, they knew exactly what they were doing ... It was a clever device meant to perpetuate the dominance of the West on Africans even after the Europeans were gone.' See Hansungule (n 307 above) 6.

360 Hansungule (n 307 above).

361 213 UNTS 221 (1950), ETS 5, entered into force on 3 September 1953, amended by Protocol 13 of 2002 ETS 187 (2002).

362 n 361 above, 8. It must be noted that, at independence, the Constitutions of Malawi (1966) and Tanzania (1964) contained no bill of rights even though both were former British colonies. A typical francophone independence constitution was that of Senegal. The Preamble says: 'The people of Senegal solemnly proclaim their independence and their attachment to the fundamental rights as they are defined in the Declaration of the Rights of Man and the Citizen of 1789 and in the Universal Declaration of December 10, 1948.' See Constitution of the Republic of Senegal, Constitutional Law 63-22, 7 March 1963, amended by Constitutional Law 92-54 of 3 September 1992, reprinted in C Heyns *Human rights law in Africa* (1996) 301-304 (Heyns 1996).

363 The Preamble of the French Constitution, 1958, adopted 4 October 1958, says: 'The French people hereby solemnly proclaim their dedication to the Rights of Man and the principle of national sovereignty as defined by the Declaration of 1789, reaffirmed and complemented by the Preamble to the 1946 Constitution.' See Constitution of the Fifth French Republic 1958, reprinted in Wolf - Phillips (n 334 above) 13-23.

only civil and political rights.[364]

Obiagwu and Odinkalu succinctly describe the general outlook of African bills of rights at independence as follows:

> The bills of rights in the independence and subsequent constitutions contained only civil and political rights and, with a few insignificant modifications, was a *verbatim* transplantation of the substantive provisions of the European Convention on Human Rights. As was the case with the constitutions of most new African states at the time of Nigerian independence, economic, social, and cultural rights were excluded from judicially enforceable rights.[365]

Indeed, prior to the end of the Cold War, only the Constitutions of Libya, 1969,[366] Somalia, 1979,[367] Angola, 1980,[368] Egypt, 1980[369] and Algeria, 1989,[370] had contained any economic, social and cultural rights in justiciable language. All South African constitutions prior to the dethronement of apartheid structures in 1994 were devoid of any bill of rights.[371] The 1990s were to witness a radical change in the constitutionalisation of human rights as an increasing number of African countries began to incorporate economic, social and cultural rights as justiciable rights on equal footing with civil and political rights - a further negation of the idea that the constitutionalisation of economic, social and cultural rights was a communist fad.[372]

Contemporary African constitutions with economic, social and cultural rights provisions that are justiciable as civil and political

364 Declaration of the Rights of Man and of Citizens, 1789, adopted 26 August 1789, by the National Assembly of France, reprinted in DE Wheeler (ed) *Life and writings of Thomas Paine* (1908) 136-140.
365 Obiagwu & Odinkalu (n 31 above) 220.
366 Arts 14 & 15, Libya Constitution 11 December 1969, reprinted in Heyns (1996) (n 362 above) 208. For a critical evaluation of contemporary Libyan constitutional history, see D Vandewalle *Qadhafi's Libya 1969-1995* (1995) 3-46.
367 Arts 21, 23, 28, 51 & 52, Somali Constitution August 1979, reprinted in Heyns (1996) (n 362 above) 332.
368 Arts 26, 27 & 29, Angola Constitution 11 November 1975, revised 11 August 1980, reprinted in Heyns (1996) (n 362) 26.
369 Arts 7-39, Egypt Constitution 11 September 1971, amended 22 May 1980, reprinted in Heyns (1996) (n 362 above) 104.
370 Arts 37-38, 52-59, Algerian Constitution 23 February 1989, amended in 1996, reprinted in Heyns (1996) (n 362 above) 19.
371 See generally G Carpenter *Introduction to South African constitutional law* (1987) 100, admitting unequivocally that '[t]here [was] no constitutionally entrenched protection of fundamental rights in South Africa'.
372 Compare M Ssenyonjo 'The domestic protection and promotion of human rights under the 1995 Ugandan Constitution' (2002) 20 *Netherlands Quarterly of Human Rights* 445 467, suggesting, as some other African scholars are accustomed to do, that economic, social and cultural rights were rights 'which socialist governments emphasised in the early twentieth century'.

rights include those of Benin, 1990,[373] Burkina Faso, 1991,[374] Burundi, 1992,[375] Cape Verde, 1990,[376] Central African Republic, 1994,[377] Chad, 1993,[378] Comoros, 1992,[379] Congo, 1992,[380] Djibouti, 1992,[381] Ethiopia, 1994,[382] Gabon, 1991,[383] Guinea, 1990,[384] Guinea-Bissau, 1991,[385] Madagascar, 1992,[386] Mali, 1992,[387] Mauritania, 1991,[388] Morocco, 1992,[389] Mozambique, 1990,[390] Niger, 1992,[391] Rwanda, 1991,[392] São Toméand Principe, 1993,[393] Seychelles, 1993,[394] South Africa, 1996,[395] and Togo, 1992.[396]

373 Arts 9-13, 22, 27-29 & 30-31, Benin Constitution, Law No 90-32 11 December 1990 reprinted in Heyns (1996) (n 362 above) 29.

374 Arts 14-30, Burkina Faso Constitution, adopted 2 June 1991, promulgated 11 June 1991, reprinted in Heyns (1996) (n 362 above) 45.

375 Arts 27, 31-36, Burundi Constitution promulgated by Decree 1/06, 13 March 1992, reprinted in Heyns (1996) (n 362 above) 50.

376 Arts 58-64 Cape Verde Constitution, Law 01/IV/92, 25 September 1992, reprinted in Heyns (1996) (n 362 above) 60.

377 Arts 9, 10-11 & 14, Central African Republic Constitution, adopted 28 December 1994, promulgated 14 January 1995, reprinted in Heyns (1996) (n 362 above) 77.

378 Arts 20-22, 24, 27 & 35, Chad Constitution, adopted 5 April 1993, amended 4 April 1995, reprinted in Heyns (1996) (n 362 above) 83.

379 Preamble para 3, Comoros Constitution 8 April 1992, reprinted in Heyns (1996) (n 362 above) 62 87. For the avoidance of doubt as to the status of the Preamble, the Constitution says: 'This Preamble is an integral part of the Constitution' (para 4).

380 Arts 30-38, Congo Constitution 15 March 1992, reprinted in Heyns (1996) (n 362 above) 90.

381 Arts 14 & 15, Djibouti Constitution 4 September 1992, reprinted in Heyns (1996) (n 362 above) 100.

382 Arts 41-44, Ethiopian Constitution 8 December 1994, reprinted in Heyns (1996) (n 362 above) 118.

383 Arts 1, 7-20 Gabon Constitution, National Assembly Law 3/91, 26 March 1991, reprinted in Heyns (1996) (n 362 above) 130.

384 Arts 10, 15, 17-19 & 23, Guinea Constitution 23 December 1990, reprinted in Heyns (1996) (n 362 above) 163.

385 Arts 32, 36, 37, 39, 41 & 42, Guinea-Bissau Constitution, 11 May 1991, reprinted in Heyns (1996) (n 362 above) 168.

386 Arts 17-40, Madagascar Constitution 19 August 1992, reprinted in Heyns (1996) (n 362 above) 211.

387 Arts 8, 13 & 15-20, Mali Constitution 5 January 1992, reprinted in Heyns (1996) (n 362 above) 228.

388 Arts 10, 14-15 & 22, Mauritania Constitution 12 July 1991, reprinted in Heyns (1996) (n 362 above) 233.

389 Arts 12-15, Morocco Constitution, 4 September 1992, reprinted in Heyns, 1996 (n 362 above) 248.

390 Arts 86-95, Mozambican Constitution, 2 November 1990, reprinted in Heyns (1996) (n 362 above) 251.

391 Arts 15, 22 & 26-28, Niger Constitution, 26 December 1992, reprinted in Heyns (1996) (n 362 above) 270.

392 Arts 23, 24, 26-27 & 30-32, Rwanda Constitution, 30 May 1991, reprinted in Heyns1996 (n 362 above) 287.

393 Arts 40-55, São Tomé and Principe Constitution, Law 7/90, 10 September 1990, reprinted in Heyns (1996) (n 362 above) 292.

394 Arts 26-37, Seychelles Constitution, 18 June 1993, amended by Act No 14 of 1996, reprinted in Heyns (1999) (n 199 above) 230.

395 Arts 22-31, South African Constitution, 27 April 1994, amended by Act 200 of 1995, reprinted in Heyns (1999) (n 199 above) 253.

396 Arts 27, 34-41, Togo Constitution, 27 September 1992, reprinted in Heyns (1996) (n 362 above) 362.

There remain a number of African constitutions that exclusively retain the guarantee of traditional civil and political rights. Among these are the Constitutions of Cameroon, 1984,[397] Côte d'Ivoire, 1990,[398] Democratic Republic of Congo, 1990,[399] Equatorial Guinea, 1991,[400] Kenya, 1991,[401] Mauritius, 1994,[402] Senegal, 1992,[403] Sudan, 1987[404] and Tunisia, 1988.[405]

A common denominator in all bills of rights in African constitutions is the presence of enabling clauses that confer competence on regular courts to adjudicate them, through *judicial review*,[406] and since they are usually fundamental norms, any legislative, administrative or executive act that runs contrary to them can be declared invalid.

3.2 Fundamental objectives and directive principles

Although a preponderance of African states now have justiciable constitutional provisions on economic, social and cultural rights, the determination of the appropriate status of these rights has generated much conceptual disagreement among many human rights scholars. The controversy has been whether economic, social and cultural rights, since they are 'futuristic', 'aspirational', and 'dependent' on particular programmes and policies of the state, should ever be couched in the language of enforceable human rights.[407] This should impel some concern in Africa where profound constitutional changes are taking place simultaneously.

397 Cameroon Constitution, adopted 20 May 1972, promulgated 2 June 1972, amended by Law 84 - 1, 4 February 1984, reprinted in Heyns (1996) (n 362 above) 57.

398 Côte d'Ivoire Constitution, 3 November 1960, amended by Law 90-1529, 6 November 1990, reprinted in Heyns (1996) (n 362 above) 98.

399 Democratic Republic of Congo (Zaire) Constitution, 15 February 1978, amended by Law 90-002, 5 July 1990, reprinted in Heyns 1996 (n 362 above) 389.

400 Equatorial Guinea Constitution, 16 November 1991, reprinted in Heyns (1996) (n 362 above) 112. Note that the Constitution contains positive rights to education (art 23) and work (art 25).

401 Kenya Constitution, 1991, amended by Act No 6, 1992, reprinted in Heyns 1999 (n 199 above) 184.

402 Mauritius Constitution, 12 March 1968, amended by Mauritius (Amendment) Act 26, 1994, reprinted in Heyns 1996 (n 362 above) 237.

403 Heyns (1996) (n 362 above) 301-304.

404 Sudan Transitional Constitution, adopted 10 October 1985, amended by Sudan Transitional Amendment Act, 1987, reprinted in Heyns (1996) (n 362 above) 350.

405 Tunisia Constitution, 1 June 1959, amended by Constitutional Law 88-88, 25 July 1988, reprinted in Heyns (1996) (n 362 above) 368-370.

406 See generally A Mavcic *The constitutional review* (2001) 95-100.

407 See generally A Sachs *Protecting human rights in a new South Africa* (1990) 5-9, analysing the plenitude of the arguments confronted in the conceptualisation of a constitutional rights culture in the South African transition period. Even though his analysis was specifically on South Africa, it encapsulates some of the critical issues in the broader global context.

In the second wave of constitution making that swept across much of Africa in the post-independence era, at a time when many of the new states of Africa were still grappling with the formulation of coherent constitutional agenda for nation building as well as human and national development, a new idea began to surface in autochthonous African constitutions: the inclusion of national policy objectives which constitute core economic, social and cultural rights issues.[408]

Since these constitutional provisions, now variously known across Africa as Fundamental Objectives or Directive Principles, were not original to Africa, I must delve, even if tangentially, into their earliest frameworks for a proper understanding of the subject, in this instance, the Indian Constitution.[409]

Part III of the Indian Constitution of 1950[410] sets out 'fundamental rights' encompassing the right to equality,[411] the rights to freedom of speech, expression, assembly, association, movement and choice of work,[412] criminal procedural rights,[413] the right to life and personal liberty,[414] the right against exploitation,[415] the right to freedom of religion,[416] minority rights,[417] and the right to constitutional remedies.[418]

In Part IV of the Constitution, there is a cluster of Directive Principles of State Policy, dealing with such issues as an adequate means of livelihood; fair distribution of material resources; equal pay

408 See generally O Eze 'Human rights issues and violations: the African experience' in Shepherd Jr *et al* (n 196 above) 87 96, describing the failure of African post-independence constitutions to guarantee economic, social and cultural rights and their marginalisation as non-justiciable Directive Principles as betraying the pretensions of the ruling class about human rights and human development in Africa.

409 Even though such provisions had been included in Irish Constitution, 1937 (Directive Principles of Social Policy, art 45); Myanmar Constitution, 1947 (Directive Principles of State Policy, arts 32-44); Indonesian Constitution, 1951; Nepal Constitution, 1962 (Directive Principles and Policies of the State, pt IV, arts 24-26); and Sri Lanka Constitution, 1972 (Directive Principles of State Policy and Fundamental Duties, ch VI, arts 27-29), it was the Indian Constitution of 1950 that provided the model for their first African transplant: the Nigerian Constitution of 1979. See generally AD Yahaya 'The party system and the Nigerian polity' in S Kumo *et al* (eds) *Issues in the Nigerian Draft Constitution* (1977) 81, showing that the Indian Constitution entirely appealed to Nigeria because 'the spirit of the Constitution entrenched the notion of India's dignity and desire to assert its independence'.

410 India Constitution, adopted 26 November 1949, entered into force on 26 January 1950, amended by Constitution (Sixty-sixth) Amendment Act, 1990, 7 June 1990.

411 Arts 14-18.

412 Arts 19(a)-(g).

413 Arts 20 & 22.

414 Art 21.

415 Arts 23-24.

416 Arts 25-28.

417 Arts 29-30.

418 Arts 32-35.

for equal work; health and strength of all citizens; child development;[419] equal justice and free legal aid;[420] functional village arrangement;[421] the right to work, to education and to public assistance in certain cases;[422] the provision of just and humane conditions of work and maternity relief;[423] living wage and fair conditions of work for workers;[424] the participation of workers in industrial management;[425] a uniform civil code for citizens;[426] the provision of free and compulsory education for children;[427] the promotion of educational and economic interests of weaker sections of society;[428] the duty of the state to raise the level of nutrition and the standard of living;[429] organisation of agriculture and animal husbandry;[430] environmental protection and improvement;[431] protection of monuments, places and objects of national importance;[432] separation of the judiciary from the executive;[433] and the promotion of international peace and security.[434]

The summary of the provisions of Part IV can be found in article 38 that says:

> (1) The state shall strive to promote the welfare of the people by securing and protecting as effectively as it may a social order in which justice, social, economic and political, shall inform all the institutions of national life.
>
> (2) The state shall, in particular, strive to minimise the inequalities in income, and endeavour to eliminate inequalities in status, facilities and opportunities, not only amongst individuals but also amongst groups of people residing in different areas or engaged in different vocations.

Article 37, however, expresses the non-justiciable status of those provisions as follows:

> The provisions contained in this part shall not be enforceable by any court, but the principles therein laid down are nevertheless fundamental in the governance of the country and it shall be the duty of the state to apply these principles in making laws.

419 Art 39.
420 Art 39A.
421 Art 40.
422 Art 41.
423 Art 42.
424 Art 43.
425 Art 43A.
426 Art 44.
427 Art 45.
428 Art 46.
429 Art 47.
430 Art 48.
431 Art 48A.
432 Art 49.
433 Art 50.
434 Art 51.

The reduction of those provisions into non-justiciable claims had been the product of the protracted political intrigues that beleaguered India during its transition period. As constitutional historian Glanville Austin notes:

> Although the Fundamental Rights and Directive Principles appear in the Constitution as distinct entities, it was the [Constituent] Assembly that separated them; the leaders of the Independence Movement had drawn no distinction between the positive and negative obligations of the state. Both types of rights had developed as a common demand, products of the national and social revolutions, of their almost inseparable intertwining, and of the character of Indian politics itself.[435]

Austin is not alone in the assertion that those provisions were originally meant to be justiciable. As Indian human rights scholar, Narively writes:

> The prevailing sentiment in the [Indian national] Sub-Committee [on Fundamental Rights and to the Constituent Assembly] was in favour of formulating all rights, including those that later on became the directive principles of statepolicy, with legal enforceability.[436]

Another scholar of the Indian Constitution had explained the essence of the Directive Principles as follows:

> The principal object in enacting the directive principles was to set standards of achievement before the legislature and the executive, the local and other authorities, by which their success or failure could be judged. It was also hoped that those failing to implement the directives might receive a rude awakening at the polls.[437]

Austin's later statement lends unflinching credence to this assertion, and offers an insight into the philosophical basis of those provisions:

> The Directive Principles were a declaration of economic independence, a declaration that the privilege of the colonial era had ended, that the Indian people (through the democratic institutions of the Constitution) had assumed economic as well as political control of the country, and

435 G Austin *The Indian Constitution: Cornerstone of a nation* (1999) 52.
436 VZ Narively *Conflict: Right to property and directive principles of the Indian Constitution* (1988) 39.
437 HM Seervai *Constitutional law of India* (1967) 759. See also Narively (n 436 above) 43-46.

that Indian capitalists should not inherit the empire of British colonialists.[438]

The judicial interpretation of those directive principles at the earlier stages of the Indian constitutional experience demonstrated how the ossified letters of legal documents could assume a vibrant content. While the Supreme Court of India had in 1951 held, *inter alia*, that 'the Directive Principles have to conform to and run subsidiary to the chapter on fundamental rights',[439] in later years, particularly since the Indian emergency years (1975-1977), Indian courts were to adopt a new, radical and proactive approach to the interpretation of the scope and content of those directive principles.[440] Today, Indian courts have found a veritable juridical pedestal in the Directive Principles to address the plight of India's underprivileged masses, to challenge poverty and deprivation, and to question governmental acts that are capable of fettering the very life, capabilities and fulfilment of ordinary Indians.[441]

Ostensibly in its increasing effort to curtail the effect of the constitutional non-justiciability of Directive Principles, the Indian legislature has continually enacted a broad range of statutes that prioritise social issues, notable among which are the Plantation Labour Act, 1951; the Mines Act, 1952; the Employees Provident Fund Act, 1952; the Maternity Benefits Act, 1961; the Apprentices Act, 1961; the Contract Labour (Regulation and Abolition) Act, 1970; the Bonded Labour System (Abolition) Act, 1976; the Urban Land (Ceiling and Regulations) Act, 1976; and the Child Labour (Prohibition and Regulation) Act, 1986. It is significant to note that all these statutes resulted from the energetic activism put into the Directive

438 Austin (n 435 above) 61. The evolutionary processes of the Indian Constitution and the Directive Principles have been the subject of ample research and need not detain us any further. See eg P Sitaramayya *The history of the Indian National Congress* (1946) 463; Austin (n 435 above) 50-113; L Simon *et al* 'Fundamental rights: the constitutional context of human rights' in CJ Nirmal (ed) *Human rights in India* (2000) 41-71; B de Villiers 'Directive principles of state policy and fundamental rights: the Indian experience' (1992) 8 *South African Journal on Human Rights* 29; M Callahan 'Cultural relativism and the interpretation of constitutional texts' (1994) 30 *Willamette Law Review* 609; A Govindjee 'Lessons for South African social assistance law from India: Part 1 – The ties that bind: The Indian Constitution and reasons for comparing South Africa with India' (2005) 26 *Obiter* 575.

439 *State of Madras v Champakam Dorairajan* (1951) SCR 226 525.

440 See generally SB Shah 'Illuminating the possible in the developing world: Guaranteeing the right to health in India' (1999) 32 *Vanderbilt Journal of International Law* 435 462.

441 See De Villiers (n 438 above) 46-48. The tremendous impact of the Indian Constitution in the concerted efforts towards good governance and nation building since 1950, including particularly the emergency years 1975-1977 under Indira Ghandi's ill-fated regime, has been carefully analysed and documented in Austin (n 435 above) 293-390.

Principles.[442] The height of the sensitivity of the Indian political machinery to the vicissitudes of life confronting Indians was the enactment of the Legal Service Authority Act, 1995, that ensures *free* and *qualitative* legal aid to the most vulnerable of India's poor. In his overall assessment of the impact of Indian legislative initiatives in mitigating the vagaries of economic liberalisation in the era of globalisation, Rao says that 'other than making laws for the welfare of various segments of society, the government started programmes to enhance the quality of life, especially for marginalised groups such as the rural and urban poor'.[443] Posing the rhetorical question of whether the Directive Principles in the Indian Constitution have 'helped to bring Indian society closer to the Constitution's goal of social, economic, and political justice for all', Austin concludes thus: 'Briefly, the answer is yes.'[444]

The Indian constitutional design of directive principles had gained the attention of constitution drafters in Indonesia in 1951, Nepal in 1962, and Sri Lanka in 1972.[445] For Africa, Nigeria led the way in 1979 with its Second Republican Constitution.[446] That Constitution provided a litany of principles that would guide the administration of the Nigerian polity towards the general good (sections 13-22).[447]

442 See generally L Mishra 'Laws for the labour' in PK Ghandi (ed) *Social action through law* (1985) 107.

443 SNN Rao 'Human rights initiatives' in Nirmal (n 438 above) 52 60-61.

444 Austin (n 435 above) 114. In the next chapter, I consider in analytical detail the groundbreaking jurisprudential developments from Indian courts on this subject and their implications for galvanising a rights-based approach to human development in Africa.

445 For readings on the background to the adoption of Directive Principles in other jurisdictions, see the following: JAL Cooray *Constitutional and administrative law of Sri Lanka* (Ceylon) (1973); T Murphy *et al Ireland's evolving Constitution 1937-1997: Collected essays* (1999); R Stith 'Unconstitutional constitutional amendments: The extraordinary power of Nepal's Supreme Court' (1996) 11 *American University Journal of International Law and Policy* 47; P Nanakorn 'Re-making of the Constitution in Thailand' (2002) 6 *Singapore Journal of International and Comparative Law* 90 105-106; A Ellis 'The Indonesian constitutional transition: Conservativism or fundamental change?' (2002) 6 *Singapore Journal of International and Comparative Law* 116.

446 Fundamental Objectives and Directive Principles of State Policy, ch II (secs 13-22), Constitution of the Federal Republic of Nigeria (CFRN), promulgated into law by the CFRN Decree 104 of 1979, entered into force 1 October 1979. For a historical commentary on the CFRN 1979, see J Akande *Introduction to the Nigerian Constitution* (1982) i-xiv.

447 Sec 13 provides for the overarching duty of all organs and officials of government to apply the provisions of ch II; sec 14 proclaims sovereignty as being vested in the people of Nigeria; sec 15 entrenches the promotion of national loyalty as the cardinal political objective of Nigeria; sec 16 entrenches the establishment of a 'mixed economic system' as the fundamental objective, which was essentially an official proclamation of the existing free market ideology of the regime; sec 17 emphasises a system of welfare assistance; sec 18 declares the commitment of government to education and literacy among Nigerians; sec 19 asserts Nigeria's Afro-centric foreign policy; sec 20 directs the state to promote and preserve Nigerian cultures and values; sec 21 mandates the press and media to uphold the fundamental objectives and accountability; while sec 22 declares the ethics of

Those objectives and principles were essentially a set of guidelines designed to secure the 'national' targets of social well-being, social justice, political stability, and economic growth in accordance with the espoused vision of the Preamble to the Constitution.[448]

During the drafting stages of the Nigerian Constitution, 1979, Emovon, a Nigerian scholar, had justified the inclusion of these objectives as follows:

> Fundamental Objectives refer to a set of social ideals which are semi-justiciable and designed as targets towards which the country must aim. They define a goal for the Nation without which this country would drift as it appeared to have done in the past. In a country as vast and heterogeneous as Nigeria where we still have primacy of local interests and where the people have ... different historical, cultural and religious backgrounds, it has become necessary to spell out in detail the basic principles of the state for the guidance of government.[449]

While those Fundamental Objectives could have passed as one of the most innovative dimensions in the history of constitution making in Nigeria, they are prone to becoming worthless platitudes because of their emasculated constitutional status.[450] An overriding provision of the same Constitution nullifies their legal value:

> 6(1) The judicial powers of the Federation shall be vested in the courts to which this section relates, being courts established for the Federation.
>
> ...
>
> (6) The judicial powers vested in accordance with the foregoing provisions of this section
>
> ...
>
> (c) shall not, except as otherwise provided by this Constitution, extend to any issue or question as to whether any act or omission by any authority or person or as to whether any law or any judicial decision is in

the Nigerian state as 'discipline, self-reliance and patriotism'. Those same provisions were re-enacted *verbatim* as ch II (secs 13-24) in the 1999 version of the CFRN promulgated into law by the Constitution of the Federal Republic of Nigeria (Promulgation) Decree 24 of 5 May 1999, entered into force on 29 May 1999. For a robust critique of this constitutional model, see D Olowu 'Fundamental objectives and directive principles of state policy in Nigeria' in JA Sokefun (ed) *Issues in constitutional law and practice in Nigeria* (2002) 290.

448 Para 3 of the Preamble to the 1979 Constitution provided the basis of the constitution as 'to provide ... good government and welfare of all persons in our country on the principles of freedom, equality and justice, and for the purpose of consolidating the unity of our people'.

449 EU Emovon 'Fundamental objectives and directive principles and public accountability' in Kumo *et al* (n 409 above) 29.

450 See Akande (n 446 above) vi. See also Aguda (n 335 above) 77-78, describing those provisions as 'a white elephant ... attempt to introduce into the Constitution some ideals and concepts in the nature ... of a by-gone era'.

> conformity with the Fundamental Objectives and Directive Principles of State Policy set out in Chapter II of this Constitution ...[451]

It naturally follows, from the above ouster clause, that all the promises of the Objectives and Principles in Chapter II of the Nigerian Constitution serve no better purpose than the British coronation oath: mere moral appeal. The decisions of Nigerian courts, as far as the status of those provisions is concerned, were unequivocal in confining those provisions to the realm of principles that may only appeal to the morality of any government in power.[452]

The idea of *non-justiciable* constitutional provisions had indeed become Nigeria's legacy for constitutionalism in Africa. After the debut in 1979, political power brokers in other African countries had found a leeway out of rights-based accountability to their peoples. Thus, at independence, Zimbabwe (1980)[453] and Namibia (1990)[454] must have looked up to the Nigerian constitutional model of 1979 in drafting their versions of Fundamental Objectives that mirror the Nigerian model almost *verbatim*.[455] The constitutional model of Directive Principles was to fascinate many other African countries in the years that followed. Many African constitutions are now replete with provisions identical to the neo-Nigerian paradigm. These are

451 CFRN, 1979, sec 6(6)(c). This same section was re-enacted *verbatim* as sec 6(6)(c) in the CFRN, 1999.

452 I examine a number of relevant decisions in the next chapter. Comparative experience in India and Ireland shows that, although Directive Principles lack the force of positive law, they have nonetheless crystallised into political imperatives from which no 'responsible government' will openly derail. See Narively (n 436 above) 174-175. See also Austin (n 435 above) 74-75. As desirable as it would have been for the Directive Principles to become central political issues in Nigeria, the Nigerian political party system and post-election machinery for the implementation of campaign promises have remained problematic since independence. The notion of democratic auditing is yet to find its way into either intellectual debate or the Nigerian political arena. Nigerian electoral politics revolves more around cleavages and parochial interests rather than on political accountability. For readings on Nigerian politics and its long history of failure to yield tangible and sustainable democratic dividends, see A Fadahunsi 'The Constitution, parties and ideology: prospects for national unity and welfare' in Kumo *et al* (n 409 above) 103-108; PO Agbese 'The state versus human rights advocates in Africa: The case of Nigeria' in McCarthy-Arnolds *et al* (n 193 above) 147 159-167; D Olowu 'Centralisation, self-governance and development in Nigeria' in JS Wunsch *et al* (eds) *The failure of the centralised state: Institutions and self-governance in Africa* (1995).

453 Zimbabwe Constitution 18 April 1980, amended by Constitution of Zimbabwe (Amendment) Act 14, 1996, reprinted in Heyns (1999) (n 199 above) 318.

454 Principles of state policy (art 95), Namibian Constitution, 21 March 1990, Fundamental principles ch III (arts 12-14), reprinted in Heyns (1996) (n 362 above) 261.

455 See generally K Grundy 'The impact of regionalism on contemporary African politics' in GM Carter *et al* (eds) *African independence: the first twenty-five years* (1985) 97, highlighting Nigeria's frontline role in the decolonisation struggles of states in the Southern African sub-region. See also GO Olusanya 'Reflections on the first twenty-five years of the organisation of African Unity' (1988) 14 *Nigerian Journal of International Affairs* 67-72, commending Nigeria's yeoman role in the decolonisation and anti-apartheid agenda of the OAU.

Botswana, 1992,[456] Eritrea, 1997,[457] The Gambia, 1994,[458] Ghana, 1992,[459] Lesotho, 1993,[460] Liberia, 1984,[461] Malawi, 1995,[462] Sierra Leone, 1991,[463] Tanzania, 1984,[464] Uganda, 1995[465] and Zambia, 1991.[466] Common to all those constitutional provisions is their non-justiciability because of language similar to that found in section 6(6)(c) of the Nigerian model.[467]

It is important to note that the provisions usually couched as Directive Principles are often the exact spirit and letters of economic, social and cultural rights norms. I am perturbed that many African state parties that are obliged under article 2(1) of ICESCR 'to take steps ... by all appropriate means, including particularly the adoption

456 Botswana Constitution 30 September 1966, amended by Constitutional (Amendment) Act 27 of 9 October 1992, reprinted in Heyns (1996) (n 362 above) 35.

457 National Objectives and Directive Principles' ch II (arts 6-12) Eritrean Constitution 23 May 1997, reprinted in Heyns (1998) (n 128 above) 292.

458 Gambian Constitution, 24 April 1970, suspended July 1994, rewritten and approved on 8 August 1996, re-established January 1997, reprinted in Heyns (1996) (n 362 above) 135.

459 The Directive Principles of State Policy ch VI (arts 34-41), Ghanaian Constitution 28 April 1992, reprinted in Heyns (1996) (n 362 above) 146. Note that the Constitution recognises the right to work under satisfactory conditions (art 24); the right to 'equal educational opportunities' (art 25); and the right to social security (art 36) as justiciable rights.

460 Principles of State Policy ch III (arts 25-36), Lesotho Constitution, 25 March 1993, reprinted in Heyns (1996) (n 362 above) 186.

461 General Principles of National Policy, ch II (arts 1-10), Liberian Constitution, 27 January 1984, reprinted in Heyns (1996) (n 362 above) 201.

462 Fundamental Principles ch III (arts 12-14), Malawi Constitution, 16 May 1994, reprinted in Heyns (1996) (n 362 above) 216.

463 Fundamental Principles of State Policy ch II (arts 4-14), Sierra Leone Constitution 1 October 1991, reprinted in Heyns (1996) (n 362 above) 319.

464 Important Objectives and the Basic Structures of the Direction of Government Affairs sec 2 (arts 1-11), Tanzanian Constitution 1977, amended by Fifth Amendment of the State Constitution (Act 15) 1984, entered into force on 15 March 1988, reprinted in Heyns 1996 (n 362 above) 355. Note that art 22 recognises the right to work in positive language.

465 National Objectives and Directive Principles of State Policy' arts I-XXIX, Uganda Constitution, adopted 22 September 1995, reprinted in Heyns (1996) (n 362 above) 371.

466 Fundamental Objectives (art 16), Zambia Constitution, Act 1, 30 August 1991, amended by Constitution (Amendment) Act 18, 28 May 1996, reprinted in Heyns (1996) (n 362 above) 303.

467 See, eg, sec 34(1), Ghana Constitution: 'Directive Principles of State Policy contained in this chapter *shall guide* [not bind] all citizens, Parliament, the President, the Judiciary, the Council of State, the Cabinet, political parties and other bodies and persons in applying or interpreting this Constitution or any other law and in taking and implementing any policy decisions, for the establishment of a just and free society' (my emphasis); sec 25, Lesotho Constitution: 'These principles *shall not be enforceable* by any court but ... shall guide the authorities and agencies of Lesotho' (my emphasis); sec 14, Malawi Constitution: 'The principles of national policy contained in this Chapter *shall be directory* in nature' (my emphasis); sec 14, Sierra Leone Constitution: 'The provisions contained in this Chapter shall not confer legal rights and shall not be enforceable in any court of law'; art I, Uganda Constitution; and sec 111, Zambia Constitution. I shall be examining the case law on this subject from various jurisdictions in the next chapter.

of legislative measures' to secure economic, social and cultural rights provisions have generally shunned the inclusion of economic, social and cultural rights in the most fundamental of their domestic laws. The ESCR Committee would be acting in proper direction if it begins to admonish state parties to ICESCR to facilitate the consideration of economic, social and cultural rights in constitutional drafting and review processes.

3.3 National legislation

Since economic, social and cultural rights have been so retarded in much of Africa, can there be an identifiable juridical avenue to advance the interconnectedness principle of human rights without unnecessarily engaging the vexed subject of 'constitutional' non-justiciability? Alternatively, put in simpler form, can there be ways of situating the implementation of economic, social and cultural rights within conventional schemes of modern-day governance despite their traditionally weak constitutional status? I argue that against the background of the protracted historical and conceptual scepticism and reluctance toward the integrative human rights approach, it is reasonable for advocates of this idea to develop innovative strategies to secure the efficacy of all human rights at the domestic level. My careful survey of African domestic legal and political systems reveals that, apart from traditional constitutional constructs that may create direct basis for the adjudication of economic, social and cultural rights claims, these rights may also be subjects of statutes as well as legislation-based quasi-judicial mechanisms such as the institution of an ombudsman, national human rights bodies, or similar administrative complaints mechanisms.

The place of legislation in giving tangible meaning to basic social, economic and political priorities in any nation cannot be overemphasised. As Klaus observed in the year ICESCR was adopted:

> The *societas perfecta* cannot be achieved by [merely] acknowledging human rights and fundamental freedoms in fine-sounding words in the Constitution, yet failing to apply them in legislation and legal practice in a manner permitting man, as a rational being, freely to develop personality and exercise his right to order his own life.[468]

ICESCR obliges state parties thereto to 'take steps ... with a view to achieving progressively the full realisation of [economic, social and cultural rights] ... by all appropriate means, including *particularly the adoption of legislative measures*'.[469] The African Charter goes further

468 J Klaus 'Introduction' in Robertson (n 291 above) 2 (emphasis in the original).
469 Art 2(1) ICESCR (my emphasis).

to mandate state parties to '*adopt legislative or other measures* to give effect to [the provisions of the African Charter]'.[470]

Indeed, it has been argued that legislative implementation is the best guarantee for international human rights at domestic levels.[471] This is particularly so in societies having governments that value their responsibility to their people. Implementing human rights through legislative intervention only becomes problematic when either the legislature or the executive abdicates that responsibility.

The ESCR Committee itself has identified legislation made by competent bodies at the national level as a cardinal mechanism critical to the implementation of economic, social and cultural rights at the domestic level.[472] In General Comment No 9, the ESCR Committee unequivocally declared:

> The central obligation ... is for states parties to give effect to the rights recognised therein. By requiring governments to do so 'by all appropriate means', the Covenant adopts a broad and flexible approach which enables *the particularities of the legal and administrative systems of each state*, as well as other relevant considerations, *to be taken into account* ... In this respect, the fundamental requirements of international human rights law must be borne in mind. Thus the *Covenant norms must be recognised in appropriate ways within the domestic legal order, appropriate means of redress*, or remedies, must be available to any aggrieved individual or group, and appropriate means of ensuring governmental accountability must be put in place.[473]

There is hardly any other cogent interpretation to the above elaboration than the obligation to secure ICESCR provisions through all means, primarily legislation. Establishing a legislative basis for economic, social and cultural rights can be of immense benefit to circumvent the imprecision and indeterminacy that are allegedly inherent in economic, social and cultural rights as positive rights.[474]

It is commonplace all over Africa to find Acts of parliament making elaborate provisions pertaining to economic, social and cultural rights, often formulated as individual or subjective rights, and supported by the availability of remedies. The most notable drawback of this mechanism lies in the possibility of repeal especially where there is no political will to sustain goals envisioned in such statutes or

470 Art 1(my emphasis).
471 See IE Koch *et al* 'Judicialised protection of international human rights and the issue of power balance' in Scheinin (n 335 above) 175 177-179. See also Craven (n 69 above) 109.
472 See General Comment No 3 (n 91 above) paras 3 & 8.
473 General Comment No 9 (n 309 above) paras 1-2 (my emphasis).
474 See S Liebenberg 'Development of policy, plans and legislation to protect and promote ESC rights' in IHRIP (n 111 above) 407 412.

where there is instability in the national political climate. The ESCR Committee acknowledged the reluctance and ambivalence of many state parties in giving effect to the ICESCR provisions when it said:

> An analysis of state practice with respect to the Covenant shows that ... some states have failed to do anything specific at all. Of those that have taken measures, some states have *transformed* the Covenant into domestic law by supplementing or amending existing legislation, without invoking the specific terms of the Covenant. Others have *adopted* or *incorporated* it into domestic law, so that its terms are retained intact and given formal validity in the national legal order. This has often been done by means of constitutional provisions according priority to the provisions of international human rights treaties over any inconsistent domestic laws. The approach of states to the Covenant depends significantly upon the approach adopted to treaties in general in the domestic legal order.[475]

I have mentioned how India has exerted a conscious effort at protecting economic, social and cultural rights by deepening the interconnectedness of all human rights. The holistic Indian approach, coming from such a vast nation experiencing socio-economic challenges like those being experienced by many states of Africa, portends huge practical implications. In his provocative assessment of the Indian approach, Rao notes that

> India, which incorporated human rights in its Constitution, ranked civil and political rights higher than [economic, social and cultural rights]. Nevertheless, it passed much legislation and initiated various programmes to operationalise *economic rights without which civil and political rights would be meaningless* to the weaker sections of Indian society.[476]

Even though South Africa has only signed but not ratified ICESCR, its constitutional provisions on economic, social and cultural rights have been expressed in identical language as those in ICESCR.[477] The provisions of the South African Constitution on economic, social and cultural rights oblige the state to 'take reasonable legislative and other measures, within its available resources, to achieve the progressive realisation of each of these rights'.[478] In compliance with the broad economic, social and cultural rights provisions in the Constitution, a number of crucial legislation have been enacted. The Extension of Security of Tenure Act, 1997,[479] the Housing Act, 1997[480] and the Prevention of Illegal Eviction from and Unlawful Occupation

475 General Comment No 9 (n 309 above) para 6 (my emphasis).
476 Rao (n 443 above) 67 (my emphasis).
477 See De Waal *et al* (n 333 above) 437. See also Liebenberg (n 307 above) 371-372; K Yigen 'Enforcing social justice: Economic and social rights in South Africa' (2000) 4 *International Journal of Human Rights* 13 21.
478 Art 26(2) (housing) & art 27(2) (health care, food, water and social security).
479 Act 62, 4 February 1997.
480 Act 107, 19 December 1997.

of Land Act, 1998[481] were passed to add impetus to the right of access to adequate housing under the Constitution.[482] Similarly, the Employment Equity Act, 1998 ensures, *inter alia*, the prevention of discrimination in the enjoyment of the right of equal access to employment,[483] while the Promotion of Equality and Prevention of Unfair Discrimination Act, 2000 is aimed at the 'eradication of social and economic inequalities, especially those that are systemic in nature'.[484] In the same vein, the Labour Relations Act, 1995 is to ensure a legislative framework for the right of every worker to form and join trade unions, and the right to fair labour practices.[485] As I demonstrate in the next chapter, these statutes have played and are playing a positive role in advancing the integrative human rights approach to human development in South Africa.[486]

In Nigeria, elements of economic, social and cultural rights can be gleaned from several statutes.[487] The Labour Act, 1990[488] regulates the regime of employment rights; the Factories Act, 1990[489] and the Workmen's Compensation Act, 1990[490] regulate the health and safety, remuneration and compensatory rights of workers. The National Provident Fund Act, 1990[491] and the Pensions Act, 1990,[492] were enacted to cover a range of social security rights. The Environmental Impact Assessment Act, 1990;[493] the Federal Environmental Protection Agency Act, 1990;[494] the Petroleum Act, 1990;[495] the Oil in Navigable Rivers Act, 1990[496] as well as the Minerals and Mining Act, 1990,[497] were put in place to regulate the spoliation of the environment, and the effect of oil and mineral exploration on land tenure and environment. Particularly significant for our discourse is the fact that, despite the absence of a constitutional framework for the recognition of a specific right to

481 Act 19, 5 June 1998.
482 n 481 above, sec 26.
483 Act 55, 12 October 1998, sec 2.
484 Act 4, 2 February 2000 Preamble para 1.
485 Act 66, 11 November 1995, sec 1.
486 See L Seafield 'The interdependence of all human rights' in An-Na'im *et al* (eds) (n 31 above) 320.
487 There was a complete revision of the entire laws of the Federal Government of Nigeria in 1990, and so all federal Acts and Decrees which were not repealed as at 1 October 1990 were codified as 'Laws of the Federation of Nigeria, 1990' (LFN) as part of the abortive transitional processes to democratic rule under the defunct General Babangida-led regime. All these statutes were also designated 'Acts', even if they had originally been Decrees.
488 Ch 198 LFN 1990.
489 Ch 126 LFN 1990.
490 Ch 470 LFN 1990.
491 Ch 273 LFN 1990.
492 Ch 346 LFN 1990.
493 Ch 86 LFN 1990.
494 Ch 131 LFN 1990.
495 Ch 350 LFN 1990.
496 Ch 337 LFN 1990.
497 Ch 34 LFN 1990.

social security as envisaged in various international and regional standards, there exists a broad range of statutes regulating various schemes and policies designed to address social security issues.[498] The practical effect of these schemes is to afford some form of protection in cases of old age, death, invalidity, sickness, maternity and employment injury for certain classes of employees, but not for self-employed or unemployed people.[499]

However, apart from the failure of the present statutory schemes to provide for the larger population of the people, the protection afforded remains largely unknown to those who should benefit under them. It is also an area of undeveloped jurisprudence.[500] There is no doubt that if only these pieces of legislation are scrutinised and publicised with a view to bringing about their application and radical amendment as may be necessary, they could become viable platforms for the implementation of economic, social and cultural rights in Nigeria.[501]

One African state that has utilised, to a noticeable extent, the mechanism of legislation to implement economic, social and cultural rights, is Libya.[502] For instance, the Labour Act, 1970 as amended in 1975 and 1989, guarantees the right to employment and state assistance to find employment, which includes the provision of necessary vocational training.[503] Article 31 of the Labour Act prohibits remuneration below the minimum wage; forbids differentiation on

498 Notable among these are the Civil Service (Reorganisation) Act Cap 55 LFN 1990; Factories Act, ch 126, LFN, 1990; Labour Act, ch 198, LFN, 1990; National Provident Fund Act, ch 273, LFN, 1990; Pensions Act, ch 346, LFN, 1990; and Workmen's Compensation Act, ch 471, LFN, 1990. The social security envisaged by these schemes can be broadly classified into two categories, namely, social assistance and social insurance. See D Olowu 'The right to social security in Nigeria: Taking up the gauntlet' (2007) 1 *CALS Review of Nigerian Law and Practice* 91.

499 A leading Nigerian constitutional historian, Nwabueze, has asserted that the special protection for public servants in most African social security schemes is a legacy of colonialism, originally instituted as a preferential privilege for colonial expatriate officers, but later extended to African public servants under pressure from trade unions. See B O Nwabueze 'Social security in Nigeria' 45 (Nigerian Institute of Advanced Legal Studies, Lagos, Annual Lecture Series, 1989). This perhaps explains why those statutory schemes have remained dormant.

500 Olowu (n 93 above) 67 73; Olowu (n 498 above) 102.

501 In the isolated case of *Farrah v Shell Dev Corp* (1994) 3 NWLR (pt 264) 313, the Nigerian Court of Appeal granted compensation to a community whose environment was destroyed by oil production activities by the defendants. The plaintiffs, *inter alia*, relied on the Oil in Navigable Waters Act.

502 Libya is a state party to all the key human rights treaties, including ICESCR and the African Charter. The Libyan Bill of Rights, officially known as The Great Green Charter of Human Rights in the Jamahiriyan Era, proclaims a wide range of economic, social and cultural rights on the same justiciable footing as civil and political rights. See arts 11; 12; 14-17 & 19, the Great Green Charter, adopted 12 June 1988 http://www.qadhafi.org/THE_GREAT_GREEN_CHARTER.html (accessed 7 August 2008).

503 Al-Idarat al-Ammah lil-Qanoun [The Law on Labour], 1989, sec 14.

the ground of gender in terms of wages, promotion, bonus, paid vacations or compensation for sick leave. It also guarantees compensation for workplace injuries and the formation of labour and trade unions, within statutory limits.[504]

Again, beyond the guarantee of the right to education in the Great Green Charter,[505] the *Al-'ilmu Haqqun li-Kulli al-Muwatin* (The Law on Education), 1970 required all Libyan children to complete primary education. It emphasises compulsory education for boys and girls, as well as the children of nomadic families. This law was revised in 1992 to create the opportunity for all Libyans to study up to doctorate degree level at government expense.[506]

While it may be correct to criticise the Qhadhafi regime in terms of civil and political rights, its efforts in implementing economic, social and cultural rights should not be overlooked. The regime has consistently invested in improving socio-economic conditions and the process of advancing economic, social and cultural rights.[507] An Arab human rights scholar has asserted that through the effective use of legislation, Libya has advanced the frontiers of women's rights, children's rights and economic, social and cultural rights more than most other Islamic, Arab or North African states.[508] However, commendable as Libya's vigorous pursuit of human development schemes that enhance the dignity of Libyans may be,[509] the Qhadhafi regime must yield to other demands of twenty-first century genuinely representative democratic practices.

504 n 503 above, secs 3-11.

505 Great Green Charter (n 502 above). Art 15 provides that '[e]ducation and knowledge are natural rights for everyone. Any individual has the right to choose his education and the knowledge which suits him, without imposed constraint or orientation.'

506 See Vandewalle (n 366 above) 3-36. Indeed, the US Department of State Country Reports on Human Rights Practices, 2007, released by the Bureau of Democracy, Human Rights and Labour, Libya, 11 March 2008, http://www.state.gov/g/drl/rls/hrrpt/2007/100601.htm (accessed 12 June 2009) (US Libyan report 2007) even noted that '[t]he government subsidised education (which is compulsory until age 15) and medical care, and it has improved the welfare of children ...'.

507 This was noted in the Concluding Observations of the ESCR Committee at the review of the Initial Report of Libya in 1997. See ESCR Committee, Concluding Observations - Libyan Arab Jamahiriya UN Doc E/C.12/1/Add.15, 16 May 1997, paras 7 & 8, http://www.unhchr.ch (accessed 12 June 2009).

508 N Merheb 'Libya' in H Stokke *et al* (eds) *Human rights in developing countries yearbook* (1998) 258. It must be added, however, that the repressive nature of the Qhadhafi regime has stultified the independence of the Libyan judiciary and, invariably, the enforcement of these positive rights. For a critical but yet pertinent analysis of the positive impact of legislation on the subject of this discussion, see *US Libyan Report 2007* (n 506 above).

509 The UNDP *Human development report for 2007-2008* shows Libya as ranking highest, next only to Seychelles, among all 54 African states, with 73,4 years life expectancy at birth; 84,2% adult literacy rate; 94,1% combined primary, secondary and tertiary gross enrolment ratio; and US $10 335 GDP *per capita*. See *Human development report 2007-2008* (n 3 above) 230.

Within varying degrees, other African states also have vast spectra of statutes that contain elements of economic, social and cultural rights, although the weakness of such statutes lies in their class restrictions (for example, to workers, diplomats, security agents, etc) and the lack of publicity even when they are intended for unrestricted benefit.[510]

4 Other national human rights implementation mechanisms

Within the international arena, there has been a noticeable increase in awareness about the strategic value of quasi-governmental bodies in promoting and protecting economic, social and cultural rights and in advancing the interconnectedness of human rights. According to the UN:

> While the worldwide interest in national institutions is a relatively recent phenomenon, the original concern of the United Nations with such institutions dates back to 1946 when the issue was first addressed by the Economic and Social Council. The Council asked member states to consider *the desirability of establishing information groups or local human rights committees within their respective countries to collaborate with them in furthering the work of the Commission on Human Rights.*[511]

If the above statement indeed portrayed the eagerness of the world body in its early years, then it would mean that the pursuit of that agenda was largely isolated. It was not until 1993, following the recommendations of a large group of human rights activists and professionals convened by the UN Centre for Human Rights in October 1991, that the UN General Assembly first made an unequivocal effort at consolidating the role of national institutions in promoting and protecting human rights at the domestic level.[512] Those recommendations, officially known as The UN Principles Relating to the Status and Functioning of National Institutions for the Protection and Promotion of Human Rights, but more popularly as the Paris

510 See eg Disserted Wives and Children Protection Act, 1971 (Lesotho); Handicapped Persons Act 48 1972 (Malawi); Workers' and Farmers' Housing Development Fund, ch 20, 1974 (Tanzania); *Code de la Santé Publique* [Public Health Act], *Decret-Loi* No 1/16 1982 (Burundi); *Code de l'Eau* [Water Act] *Ordonnance* 85-144, 1985 (Mauritania); Education Act, 1989 (Sudan); Labour Law, 1992 (Liberia); *Loi* No 9-94 *sur la protection des naturelle végétales* [Law on the Protection of Natural Vegetation], 1994 (Morocco); Mines and Minerals Act, ch 21:05, 1996 (Zimbabwe); and Forestry Act, ch 57:01, 1997 (Malawi); Poor Persons Defence Act, ch 20, 2000 (Uganda).

511 United Nations Fact Sheet 19: 'National institutions for the promotion and protection of human rights', http://www.unhchr.ch (emphasis in the original).

512 n 511 above, analysing the human rights 'standard-setting' agenda that preoccupied the UN in the 1960s and 1970s.

Principles, were endorsed by the UN Commission on Human Rights in October 1992, and later adopted by the UN General Assembly in 1993.[513] The Paris Principles simply stressed the need for the creation of 'national human rights institutions' for the promotion and protection of human rights, without guidance on their outlook.[514]

The World Conference on Human Rights had in 1993, however, emphasised

> the important and constructive role played by national institutions for the promotion and protection of human rights, in particular in their advisory capacity to the competent authorities, their role in *remedying* human rights violations, in the *dissemination* of human rights information, and *education* in human rights.[515]

Later, in its General Comment No 10 in 1998, while acknowledging that despite the international promotion of the idea of creating national human rights institutions, the practice had neglected the interdependence principle, the ESCR Committee noted that:

> National institutions have a potentially crucial role to play in promoting and ensuring the indivisibility and interdependence of all human rights. Unfortunately, this role has too often either not been accorded to the institution or has been neglected or given a low priority by it. It is therefore essential that full attention be given to economic, social and cultural rights in all of the relevant activities of these institutions.[516]

However, while the phrase 'national human rights institutions' encompasses national human rights commissions, these alone do not constitute an exhaustive definition of the phrase. In addition, to be included in this catch phrase are ombudsman institutions, offices of public defenders, extra-ministerial agencies and parastatals, depending on the particular circumstances of and variations in each country.

513 UN Doc A/RES/48/134 (1993) 20 December 1993. See The Paris Principles UN Doc E/CN. 4/1992/54, Annex. See also 'Principles relating to the status and functioning of national institutions for protection and promotion of human rights' in Human rights Watch *Protectors or pretenders? Government Human Rights Commissions in Africa* (2001) 403, app IV.

514 Apart from provisions on the 'competence and responsibilities', 'composition and guarantees of independence and pluralism', 'methods of operation', and 'additional principles concerning the status of commissions with quasi-jurisdictional competence', the Paris Principles never stressed the inter-connectedness of human rights as a core mandate for such bodies.

515 Vienna Declaration (n 38 above) para 36 (my emphasis).

516 ESCR Committee 'The role of national human rights institutions in the protection of economic, social and cultural rights' General Comment No 10 UN Doc E/C12/ 1998/25 (General Comment 10) para 3, reprinted in *Compilation of general comments* (n 81 above) 49.

Even though international human rights scholars, activists and intergovernmental agencies generally recognise that these institutions do indeed occupy the strategic position of being purveyors of democracy, good governance as well as human rights promotion and protection,[517] virtually nothing has been said about their significance and possible role for the integrative human rights approach, particularly with respect to conceptualising a rights-based African human development agenda.

I posit that, if properly harnessed, there are formidable organs and agencies that can advance the application of economic, social and cultural rights in policy formulation and implementation, check malevolent governance and corruption, and help a government genuinely to keep focus on the well-being of its people.

4.1 National human rights commissions

Apart from the UN agenda for the establishment of national human rights institutions, all African states had placed themselves under an obligation to create and allow the creation of such bodies. The African Charter creates an obligation for state parties to establish and improve '*appropriate national institutions* entrusted with the promotion and protection of the rights and freedoms guaranteed by the present Charter'.[518] In elaborating this provision under its promotional mandate, the African Commission had requested the OAU Secretary-General in 1989 'to submit a detailed report on existing national [human rights] institutions'.[519] As a follow-up process later in 1996, the Commission called upon all African governments to establish national human rights commissions where none existed and to strengthen existing ones.[520] It became obvious that, just as the African Commission itself had shirked emphasising equal attention to all human rights, its call for the creation of national human rights

517 See United Nations Centre for Human Rights: *National human rights institutions: A handbook on the establishment and strengthening of national institutions for the promotion and protection of human rights* (1995) No 4 *Professional Training Series* 4-6, UN Doc HR/P/PT/4, UN Sales No E.95.XIV2 *(National human rights institutions: A handbook*); FS Azzam 'Update: the Palestinian Independent Commission for Citizens' Rights' (1998) 20 *Human Rights Quarterly* 338; I Bizjak 'The role and experience of an ombudsman in a new democracy' (1998) 2 *International Ombudsman Yearbook* 57; LC Reif 'Building democratic institutions: The role of national human rights institutions in good governance and human rights protection' (2000) 13 *Harvard Human Rights Journal* 1; S Cardenas 'National human rights commissions in Asia' (2002) 4 *Human Rights Review* 30.

518 Art 26 (my emphasis).

519 African Commission on Human and Peoples' Rights 'Resolution on the establishment of committees on human rights or other similar organs at national, regional or sub-regional level' 5th ordinary session, Benghazi, Libya, 3-14 April 1989 para 3, reprinted in Heyns 1999 (n 199 above) 197.

520 See 'The Mauritius Plan of Action 1996-2001', reprinted in (1996-1997) 6 *Review of the African Commission on Human and Peoples' Rights* 215 paras 64 & 66.

commissions was in tenuous language. In its elaborate Mauritius Plan of Action 1996-2001, the African Commission merely stated that

> [t]hese national institutions and associations could serve as a basis for initiatives for human rights in the respective countries and will help the Commission to disseminate the African Charter and to fulfil its educational mission on human and peoples' rights *in general*.[521]

Overall, the African Commission is yet to define a clear agenda for national human rights commissions in Africa either in pursuing an integrative human rights agenda or in identifying human development as a human rights problem.[522] Nevertheless, whether as a result of genuine concern for effective human rights monitoring, promotion and protection, or for the purposes of appeasing the curious international community, all that is certain is that the establishment of human rights commissions became a vogue in African countries in the 1990s. Such was the fascination of African governments, regardless of their legitimacy, structure, or democratic quality, that between 1987, when there was only one national human rights commission, and the end of 2000, such commissions and bodies had proliferated to 25.[523]

Quite ample literature exists on the criticisms of the legal basis, mandates, manner of appointing commissioners, government

521 n 520 above, para 67 (my emphasis).

522 So far, the African Commission has convened three conferences of African national human rights commissions (Yaoundé, Cameroon, February 1996; Durban, South Africa, July 1998; and Lomé, Togo, 2001), each time encouraging the creation of national [human rights] institutions and calling on African governments 'to provide their national [human rights] institutions with adequate human and financial resources and guarantee their independence'. See eg Lomé Declaration, Third Conference of African Human Rights Institutions held in Lomé, Togo 16 March 2001, para II. Similarly, the African Commission has adopted a standing resolution to confer 'special observer status [on] any national [human rights] institution established in Africa'. See African Commission on Human and Peoples' Rights 'Resolution on Granting Observer Status to National Human Rrights Institutions in Africa' 24th ordinary session, Banjul, The Gambia, 22-31 October 1998, para 4, reprinted in Heyns 1999 (n 199 above) 217 218.

523 See generally *Protectors or pretenders?* (n 513 above) 1, listing 24 national Human Rights Commissions in Africa comprising of Algeria, 1992; Benin, 1989; Cameroon, 1990; Central African Republic, 1999; Chad, 1994; Ethiopia, 1995; Ghana, 1993; Kenya, 1996; Liberia, 1997; Libya, 1989; Malawi, 1996; Mali, 1996; Mauritania, 1998; Morocco, 1990; Niger, 1999; Nigeria, 1995; Rwanda, 1999; Senegal, 1997; Sierra Leone, 1994; South Africa, 1994; Sudan; Togo, 1987; Tunisia, 1991; Uganda, 1995; and Zambia, 1996. The Libyan Arab Human Rights Committee was established in May 1989 pursuant to the *Al-lijna al-'arabiyya al-libiyya lihouqouq al-insan*, 1989 [Law on the Libyan Arab Human Rights Committee]. The UN Human Rights Committee has acknowledged the mandate of this body. See 'Concluding observations of the Human Rights Committee - Libya', UN Doc CCPR/C/28/Add.17, 2 March 1995 para 3. It is curious to note that the Human Rights Watch survey, as extensive and deep as it appears, excluded the Libyan experience. I feel it would have helped a broader and more objective perception and analysis of the African continent's struggles at promoting and protecting human rights if all existing indices for evaluation are fully considered. Human Rights Watch did not explain this omission.

interference, lack of publicity, inadequate funding, and low expertise of many of the national human rights commissions in Africa.[524] The details of issues covered in those analytical works remain largely accurate but heavily focused on civil and political rights. The trend towards an exclusive civil and political rights focus is by no means surprising. Out of all the 25 existing national human rights commissions in Africa, only two (those of Mauritania and South Africa) have an explicit economic, social and cultural rights mandate, while the stated mandates of other human rights commissions basically vest them with the responsibility to promote and protect human rights in general terms.

4.1.1 South Africa

The South African Human Rights Commission (SAHRC), created under the Human Rights Commission Act, 1994[525] is obliged, annually, to

> require relevant organs of state to provide the Commission with information on the measures that they have taken towards the realisation of the rights in the Bill of Rights concerning housing, health care, food, water, social security, education and the environment.[526]

Apart from its clear integrative human rights mandate, the SAHRC is empowered by the Constitution '(a) to investigate and to report on the observance of human rights; (b) to take steps to secure appropriate redress where human rights have been violated; (c) to carry out research; and (d) to educate'.[527]

This comprehensive legal framework has placed the SAHRC in a position to promote and protect in the usual nebulous diction, and also to confront acts and omissions of the government itself, state

524 See eg *Protectors or pretenders?* (n 513 above); K Hossain *et al* (eds) *Human rights commissions and ombudsman offices: National experiences throughout the world* (2000); NB Pityana 'The South African Human Rights Commission' in Hossain *et al* 627; R Carver *et al* 'National human rights institutions in Africa' in Hossain *et al* 733; FM Ssekandi *et al* 'Protection of fundamental rights in the Ugandan Constitution' (1994) 26 *Columbia Human Rights Law Review* 191; OC Okafor *et al* 'On legalism, popular agency and "voices of suffering": The Nigerian National Human Rights Commission in context' (2002) 24 *Human Rights Quarterly* 662; JO Kuye & U Kakumba 'The ombudsman institutions in the procurement of legal responsibilities in the Commonwealth: An overview of Canada, South Africa and Uganda' (2008) 43 *Journal of Public Administration* 156.

525 Act 54 of 1994. South African Constitution, 1996 conferred on the SAHRC constitutional recognition under schedule 6, item 20, that proclaims its continued existence with same functions and tenure as are found in Act 54 of 1994, subject to amendment or repeal. To date, the SAHRC continues to function undisturbed.

526 n 525 above, sec 184(3).

527 Sec 184(2). It must be borne in mind that sec 7(2) of the Constitution also stresses that '[t]he state *must* respect, protect, promote and fulfil the rights in the Bill of Rights' (my emphasis).

officials, corporate bodies and even private individuals that threaten or trample upon the dignity of human beings in South Africa.[528]

One area where the SAHRC has demonstrated its commitment and forthrightness is agenda setting. To the SAHRC's credit, in 1998, it collaborated with the South African NGOs Coalition (SANGOCO) and the Commission on Gender Equality (CGE) to convene a total of ten nationwide hearings over a period of 35 days on the question of poverty in South Africa. There were some 600 oral submissions, while well over 10 000 people participated.[529] Liebenberg and Pillay had captured the mindset of that joint initiative as follows:

> Through the Truth and Reconciliation Commission we've heard about the political and civil rights violations under apartheid. But what about the violations of social and economic rights? Understanding this legacy is critical to the success of strategies to eradicate poverty and inequality and secure a better life for South Africans. Speak Out on Poverty aimed to provide a platform to both understand the legacy of economic and social right violations and the extent to which our new Bill of Rights in the Constitution addresses this legacy.[530]

The Poverty Hearings not only exposed the unspoken hardships daily confronting millions of South Africans, but also helped the state in identifying the goals to pursue and the obstacles to overcome.[531] In pursuance of its information-gathering and investigative mandate, the SAHRC has developed a series of comprehensive monitoring questionnaires, popularly referred to as 'Protocols' on each economic, social and cultural right in the South African Bill of Rights and distributes these effectively to human rights NGOs, government departments and bodies, in compliance with its constitutional obligations. Deadlines are usually set for responses.[532]

The SAHRC, to an extent, has been able to hold the South African government to its human rights obligations. It achieves this through its investigation of state practices and by recommending remedial measures.[533] The SAHRC has also been able to censure some

528 See generally S Liebenberg 'Identifying violations of socio-economic rights: The role of the South African Human Rights Commission' (1997) 1 *Law, Democracy and Development* 161.

529 Liebenberg & Pillay (n 1 above) 2.

530 As above.

531 However, see M Seleoane *Socio-economic rights in the South African Constitution: Theory and practice* (2001) 67 70, criticising the 'measurement validity' of the poverty hearings. All the reports of the activities of the SAHRC can also be found at http://www.sahrc.org.za/ (accessed 12 June 2009).

532 See SAHRC *Economic and social rights Vol I* (1997-1998). See also SAHRC *Economic and social rights Vol 6* (2003-2008).

533 The SAHRC has kept a watchful eye over the incidences of forced evictions and 'land-grabbing' in the aftermath of the *Grootboom* case. See SAHRC *Third Report on Economic and Social Rights 1999-2000* (2000) 281-282.

government organs and agencies that were tardy in furnishing the required information under its Protocols.[534]

Beyond these efforts, the SAHRC has squarely positioned itself before the South African society as a key player in giving life and content to economic, social and cultural rights. In its judgment in *Grootboom*, the Constitutional Court had appointed the SAHRC 'to monitor and, if necessary, report in terms of ... the efforts made by the state to comply with its ... obligations in accordance with this judgment'.[535]

The juridical value of the SAHRC's work cannot be overemphasised. As Liebenberg points out, the SAHRC has also been effective in the formation of a 'co-operative relationship [with South African courts] in the enforcement of orders relating to economic and social rights'.[536]

Curiously, however, the SAHRC has never referred to the African Charter or to the jurisprudence arising under it in any of its deliberations, just like other national human rights commissions in Africa. Reproof for this shortfall may not be ascribed solely to the SAHRC or any other national mechanism, but to the African Commission as well. While the African Commission harps on the creation and funding of these bodies, it does not adequately stress the indispensable internalisation of the African Charter. National human rights commissions certainly occupy a position of great advantage to develop the core content of economic, social and cultural rights under the African Charter.

It is pertinent to note, however, that what the SAHRC has left out in developing its guidelines and jurisprudence because of the non-consideration of the African Charter, it has gained by its up-to-date engagement with the pronouncements of the ESCR Committee. In all its reports since 1997, the SAHRC has elaborated its mandate and the economic, social and cultural rights content of the South African Bill of Rights in concordance with the General Comments of the ESCR Committee.[537]

Even though the consequences of the apartheid system in South Africa have proven too deep and complex to be resolved in quick-fix fashion, the SAHRC is demonstrating its readiness to confront some of the more pronounced disparities and deprivations in the country. If

534 SAHRC *Fourth Report on Economic and Social Rights 2000-2002* (2002) 18.
535 *Grootboom* (n 144 above) para 97.
536 Liebenberg (n 31 above) 83.
537 See all the reports of the SAHRC on economic, social and cultural rights for the decade spanning 1998 to 2008 at http://www.sahrc.org.za/sahrc_cms/publish/cat_index_28.shtml (accessed 12 June 2009).

nothing else, the SAHRC is keeping the government and its officials conscious of their people-oriented obligations under the Constitution. One can only conjecture what the magnitude of social crises would have been in South Africa without an effective rights-based framework for legitimate social claims.[538] Having regard to the exercise of its broad but yet specific mandate and performance since 1994, there can be no gainsaying the fact that the SAHRC represents the most coherent national human rights institutional model in Africa.

4.1.2 Mauritania

While the right to strike 'is recognised' and the right to property 'shall be guaranteed' for citizens of Mauritania in accordance with the Constitution of 1991,[539] it was the mandate of the *Commissariat aux Droits de l'Homme a la Lutte contre la Pauvreté et a l'Insertion* (Commission on Human Rights, Poverty Alleviation and Integration), established in 1998, that had promised the hope of a better deal for ordinary Mauritanians.[540] Article 2 of the Decree expresses the mission of the Commission as 'the conception, promotion and implementation of a national policy on human rights, the fight against poverty, and social integration/inclusion'. The dual mandates of this Commission were stated as follows:

> Human Rights: Take all appropriate measures to promote and publicise human rights values and principles; strengthen dialogue and collaboration with national human rights associations; develop co-operation and exchange with regional and international organisations, as well as international human rights non-governmental organisations.
>
> Fighting Poverty and Promoting Social Integration: Promote, in collaboration with other departments, a national policy aimed at eradicating poverty by promoting the use and equitable distribution of basic social services; ensure the integration of vulnerable groups in the process of development and promote individual and collective development approaches, fully using their human and material resources.[541]

These promising mandates unfortunately conflict with the political realities of the Commission. As Human Rights Watch reports:

538 Compare G van Zyl & L Bonga-Bonga 'Economic growth, redistribution policy and fiscal policy in South Africa: An SVAR analysis' (2008) 38 *Africa Insight* 67-80, showing that the debate on appropriate budgetary allocation for social services has continued to be a source of tension between the government and civil society.

539 Arts 14 & 15 respectively.

540 *Commissariat aux Droits de l'Homme, a la Lutte contre la Pauvereté et a l'Insertion*, Prime Ministerial Decree 89/98, 2 July 1998.

541 n 540 above, art 3.

> The Prime Minister has complete control over the Commission, appoints its commissioner and adjunct commissioner, is represented on the supervisory council, and controls that council. When asked about this ... the commission's director of human rights promotion stated simply that such executive control was *a normal aspect of our constitutional system.*[542]

Although Human Rights Watch had enthusiastically noted in 2001 that '[n]ational human rights commissions rarely address poverty alleviation and social inequalities from a human rights perspective, and the Mauritanian Commission is breaking new ground',[543] that anticipated agenda has apparently become a matter for the back-burner under the Sid'Ahmed Taya regime. Apart from estranging human rights activists and the media, the Commission cannot be seen in any other light than being a *protégé* of the regime. Other than the infrequent rhetoric of poverty alleviation by the Commission's Chairperson, Abdessalam Ould Mohamed Saleh, there has been no report ever published on either the human rights situation in Mauritania or poverty alleviation efforts.[544]

While pursuing its real and imagined enemies, the government has abandoned the vision of poverty alleviation or social integration. Wages remain dismally low and trade unionists are under constant threat of arrests and detention.[545] Despite an international outcry against renewed slavery, Mauritania continues to be a frontline state in slavery-related practices.[546] It is a sad epitaph that the bright promise of the Mauritanian Human Rights Commission had indeed been destined for stillbirth.

542 *Protectors or pretenders?* (n 513 above) 224 (emphasis in the original).

543 As above.

544 See generally World Report, *Mauritania: Human Rights Commission fights to reduce poverty 25 November 2001*, http://www.worldreport-ind.com/mauritania/index.htm, reporting, among other analyses, the statement of AOM Saleh philosophising poverty as 'the biggest threat to human rights' in Mauritania.

545 See US Department of State 'Country reports on human rights practices, 2007' released by the Bureau of Democracy, Human rights and Labour: Mauritania, 11 March 2008, http://www.state.gov/g/drl/rls/hrrpt/2007/100493.htm (accessed 12 June 2009) (US Mauritanian Report 2003). As the last country to abolish slavery on earth, Mauritania officially abolished slavery in 1980 and ratified the Race Convention on 13 December 1988. See NJ Udombana 'Can the leopard change its spots? The African Union treaty and human rights' (2002) 17 *American University International Law Review* 1177 1225-1226 (emphasis in the original). See also press release, Media Foundation for West Africa, 'Newspapers seized by authorities' (29 September 2003).

546 See Amnesty International (AI), International Labour Organisation, Amnesty International's Concerns Relevant to the 91st Session of the International Labour Conference, 3-19 June 2003 (AI INDEX: IOR 42/003/2003 11 April 2003); D Gutnick 'Freedom's just another word: Contemporary slavery in Mauritania' 29 February 2008 http://www.cbc.ca/news/background/slavery/mauritania.html (accessed 22 November 2008).

4.1.3 Nigeria

The Nigerian National Human Rights Commission (NNHRC) was a product of pretentious foundations. The announcement by the infamous General Sani Abacha in late 1995 of his intention to establish the NNHRC came at a time when the regime was desperate to diffuse the spate of international opprobrium that had attended its brutal repression of democratic rights and the human rights community in Nigeria.[547]

The functions and powers of the NNHRC, as stated in the National Human Rights Commission Decree, 1995[548] are:

> (a) To deal with all matters relating to the promotion and protection of human rights as guaranteed by the Constitution of the Federal Republic of Nigeria 1979 as amended, the African Charter on Human and Peoples' Rights, the United Nations Charter and the Universal Declaration of Human Rights, and other international treaties on human rights to which Nigeria is a party;
>
> (b) To monitor and investigate all alleged cases of human rights violations in Nigeria and make appropriate recommendations to the Federal Military Government for the prosecution and such other actions as it may deem expedient in each circumstances;
>
> (c) To assist victims of human rights violations and seek appropriate redress and remedies on their behalf;
>
> (d) To undertake studies on all matters pertaining to human rights and assist the Federal Government in the formulation of appropriate policies on the guarantee of human rights;
>
> (e) To publish, from time to time, reports on the state of human rights protection in Nigeria;
>
> (f) To organise local and international seminars, workshops and conferences on human rights issues for public enlightenment;
>
> (g) To liaise and co-operate with local and international organisations on human rights with the purpose of advancing the promotion and protection of human rights;
>
> (h) To participate in all international activities relating to the promotion and protection of human rights;

[547] It will be remembered that on 10 November 1995, while the Commonwealth meeting was being held in Auckland, New Zealand, Ogoni environmental rights activist, Kenule Saro Wiwa, was executed as a sequel to a death sentence passed on him by an *ad hoc* tribunal, against all domestic and international protests prior to it. The massive outcry from within and outside Nigeria left the doomed Abacha-led regime to scamper for a means of whittling down the pressure being mounted. Nigeria was summarily suspended from the Commonwealth and a number of economic sanctions followed from Western nations.

[548] Decree 22 of 1995. This Decree has been renamed NNHRC 'Act' pursuant to sec 315 of the CFRN 1999, re-naming all existing laws that have not been repealed as at the commencement of the CFRN 1999 as subsisting statutes. All decrees thus became 'Acts'.

(i) To maintain a library, collect data and disseminate information and materials on human rights generally;

(j) *To carry out all such other functions as are necessary or expedient for the performance of its functions under this Decree.*[549]

A first-time observer of the above mandate would have anticipated a high human rights performance profile for a country with such an articulate and broad framework as this. The unfortunate reality is that the NNHRC statute was just one of the numerous policy documents in Nigeria designed for their rhetorical values rather than productivity.[550] With the intrigues surrounding the manner of establishing and constituting the NNHRC, the inevitable result was the virtual redundancy of the body throughout the remaining life of active military rule in Nigeria prior to 29 May 1999.[551]

In the atmosphere of the new dispensation of civilian rule in Nigeria, the NNHRC has hardly fared any better. Since the NNHRC is a government agency, the body has tragically been bogged down by the renowned Nigerian bureaucratic decay and corruption.

Despite its elaborate mandate, the NNHRC is yet to produce any agenda for addressing the massive economic, social and cultural rights violations in Nigeria. Apart from its few visits to prisons, the annual jamboree on International Human Rights Day at the Abuja City Centre and promotional activities involving seminars and workshops usually attended by the *crème de la crème* of Nigerian politics, there is nothing tangible to mention in terms of the NNHRC's protective mandate. In a country where the vast majority is illiterate and poor, the NNHRC's existence and activities have remained largely within the knowledge and engagement of elites. Almost a decade after transition to civilian rule, the NNHRC has not carried out any investigative

549 NNHRC Act sec 5 (my emphasis).

550 The Nigerian junta handpicked the Chairperson and the 15 other members of the NNHRC. For the period in which the military remained in power, the NNHRC was firmly under the control of the stooges and cronies of the Abacha-led regime as well as other members with doubtful credentials. See Okafor *et al* (n 524 above) 700 for a discussion of 'the extraordinarily high level of scepticism that has dogged the [NNHRC] and its work from its very beginning'. See generally AMO Obe 'Working with national human rights commissions: The Nigerian experience' paper presented at the Soochow University School of Law, Centre for the Study of Human Rights http://www.scu.edu.tw/hr/research_imgs/Ayo.pdf (accessed 12 June 2009), describing the circumstances surrounding the appointment of some of the members of the NNHRC that raised questions about the honesty of the body 'from the onset'.

551 For general discussions about the operations of the NNHRC and the abortive efforts of the human rights community to activate it during the Abacha and Abubakar years, the starvation and corruption of the body, and the question of its staffing system, see Obe (n 550 above); *Protectors or Pretenders?* (n 513 above) 233-234 238.

mission to any rural community and has no plan to do so in the near future.[552]

While 'lack of adequate resources' and 'insufficient funding from government' have become the *mantras* of successive Executive Secretaries of the Commission in explaining away the inefficacy of the NNHRC,[553] the Commission has never published how much it has received from donor organisations.[554]

In the Statutory Report of the NNHRC for 2002, one of the few ever published by the body, its Executive Secretary, at that time, Bukhari Bello, had catalogued what the NNHRC perceived as the 'formidable' impediments to NNHRC's effectiveness as follows:

> One of the major problems of the National Human Rights Commission is *the inadequacies contained in its enabling Act*. The Commission has, however, recommended some amendments to the Act ... The recommendations include, *inter alia*:
>
> (a) Granting the Commission power of access to all the information that it requires to deal with complaints of human rights violations;
>
> (b) Expressly empowering the Commission to resolve matters through arbitration, negotiation, mediation, and litigation;
>
> (c) Making express provision for the Commission's independence and autonomy;
>
> (d) Making it compulsory that inquiries or correspondence on human rights matters emanating from the Commission must be responded to within thirty (30) days as in the case of court summons;
>
> (e) Providing that the legal practitioners appointed in the Council be nominated by the national Executive Committee of the NBA; and
>
> (f) Entrenching the Commission in the Constitution.[555]

From the perspective of any conscientious observer of Nigeria's massive socio-political problems, the itemised 'inadequacies' betray a manifest lack of purpose and vision, and are detached from what an

552 Interview with 'TKO', Legal Officer, NNHRC [pleaded anonymity], in Abuja, Nigeria, 10 January 2008.

553 See M Tabiu 'National Human Rights Commission of Nigeria' in Hossain *et al* (eds) (n 524 above) 553 558; Excerpts from the statutory report of the National Human Rights Commission for the year 2002 presented by the Executive Secretary B Bello at the 2002 Annual Bar Conference of the Nigerian Bar Association held in Ibadan 26-30 August 2002 4(1) *NNHRC Human Rights Newsletter* January-March 2003 11 13.

554 The NNHRC had received US $250 000 and US $200 000, for years 2000 and 2002, respectively, from the MacArthur Foundation. In 2001, the NNHRC received a 'one-time grant' of US $170 000 from the same organisation. See e-mail from JS Richards on 10 October 2003. In the interview I conducted in January 2008, the designated official of the NNHRC declined to answer questions on 'institutional financing'.

555 n 554 above, 13-14 (my emphasis).

activist national human rights commission could do in the circumstances of the NNHRC.[556] Certainly, it was not those 'inadequacies' that had stopped the NNHRC from commenting on the prevalent culture of profligacy in public spending. They were also not the excuse for the NNHRC's failure to sensitise civil society's participation in budgetary processes at local, state and federal government levels. Despite brazen poverty and deprivation, the NNHRC is yet to identify poverty as a most horrendous human rights violation in twenty-first century Nigeria. Further, the NNHRC has not deemed it necessary to point to the seemingly intractable crisis of corruption as a human rights concern. I contend that the lack of an 'enabling Act' could neither have kept the NNHRC from realising its role in promoting international and regional human rights standards in Nigeria, nor of promoting the incorporation of human rights module into national educational curricula in post-military Nigeria. Years after the decision of the African Commission in *Ogoni*, the NNHRC has not exerted any perceivable effort at ensuring that the Nigerian government complies.

The above pointers denote that within its existing framework, the NNHRC can make itself more relevant to effective human rights monitoring, documentation and protection, to the development of economic, social and cultural rights jurisprudence and, ultimately, to the establishment of a rights-based approach to the challenges of human development in Nigeria. Such an agenda lies more in *the will to do* than in the means of doing.

4.1.4 Other African national human rights commissions

The problematic issues with African national human rights commissions have been examined in a number of works.[557] Human Rights Watch aptly pictures the general outlook of African national human rights commissions as follows:

> Africa's national human rights commissions are a mixed bag. *Given the needs of their societies, to date the performance of most has been disappointing*. Many have indeed been formed by governments with poor human rights records, weak state institutions, and little or no history of autonomous state bodies. Some appear largely designed to deflect international criticism of serious human rights abuses. Many have been formed with flawed mandates and weak powers that limit their ability to effectively investigate, monitor, or make public statements. Others have

556 See generally n 554 above 703, arguing that the NNHRC 'has a reasonably well-defined jurisdiction'. See also Carver *et al* (n 524 above) 754, concluding, after their independent assessments of national human rights commissions in Africa, that '[t]he problem [of funding] is a common one, although in some respects, the Nigerian [National Human Rights] Commission is well-endowed ...'.

557 See n 524 above and accompanying text.

> been undermined by the appointment of commissioners who are unwilling or unable to protest abuses from fear or hope of government favour. Other commissioners may be well-intentioned but have had little or no previous involvement in human rights work or training, and most commissions in Africa are under-funded and urban-based. Some commissions work almost entirely behind closed doors and do not make public statements or other documentation is not available or easily accessible.[558]

Against the backdrop of ongoing state practices, violations of economic, social and cultural rights with impunity, and unmitigated poverty among the mass of Africans, there is nothing to suggest that African national human rights commissions, save the South African version, have radically changed from that 2001 assessment and, thus, the integrative human rights approach to human development remains marginal in their respective agendas. The indices are overwhelming: The Togolese *Commission Nationale des Droits de l'Homme* (National Human Rights Commission) has become more efficient as a megaphone for legitimising the Eyadema dynasty;[559] the Libyan Arab Human Rights Committee, created in 1989, has never published any report;[560] the Cameroonian National Commission on Human Rights and Freedoms looks the other way as the Paul Biya government continues to repress human rights NGOs and labour union activists;[561] and despite the agitation by civil society groups against the patent mismanagement of the Highly Indebted Poor Countries (HIPC) funds while mass poverty intensifies,[562] the Zambian Human Rights Commission is yet to issue a statement.

Although only South Africa and Mauritania have national human rights commissions with a specific economic, social and cultural rights mandate, what is actually lacking among African national human rights commissions in giving attention to these rights along with civil and political rights is not necessarily the legal framework, but the unmistakable lack of *willingness* – a problem intertwined with age-long structural deficiencies in governance and complicated by increasing adverse social pressures.[563] As Human Rights Watch ob-

558 *Protectors or pretenders?* (n 513 above) 4 (my emphasis).
559 E Godwin 'Togo: After elections, what next?' (2003) 11 *The Ghanaian Chronicle* 4.
560 See 'US Libyan reports 2007' (n 506 above). See also Merheb (n 508 above) 230.
561 See US Department of State 'Country reports on human rights practices, 2007, released by the Bureau of Democracy, Human Rights and Labour: Cameroon' 11 March 2008 http://www.state.gov/g/drl/rls/hrrpt/2007/100470.htm (accessed 12 June 2009).
562 See M Chitendwe 'HIPC relief funds abused in Zambia' *African News Bulletin* 1 July 2003 Supp 459 8.
563 See generally DN Wai 'Human rights in sub-Saharan Africa' in A Pollis *et al* (eds) *Human rights: Cultural and ideological perspectives* (1979) 115; JCN Paul 'Participatory approaches to human rights in sub-Saharan Africa' in AA An-Na'im *et al* (eds) *Human rights in Africa: Cross-cultural perspectives* (1990) 213 257; JS Wunsch *et al* 'The failure of the centralised African state' in JS Wunsch *et al* (eds)

served, they all have the basic mandate to 'promote and protect' human rights,[564] and they all exist as state-established, government-funded organs.[565]

One concern that must continue to stimulate the mind is that with willingness, coupled with concerted efforts by civil society, national human rights commissions in Africa could structurally be disentangled from the apron strings of governments, and thus begin to interpret their mandates to cover the connective issues of economic, social and cultural rights and the broad interests of the mass of their peoples. The use of these bodies remains a viable strategy that African human rights NGO activists and researchers should extensively explore.

4.2 Ombudsmanship[566]

Another viable but more often ignored mechanism in the discourse on economic, social and cultural rights in Africa is the institution of ombudsmanship. A mechanism of great antiquity, its original nomenclature had been *justitieombudsman*, literally meaning 'a representative or agent of the people or a group of people, or procurator for civil affairs'.[567] The first ombudsman system was created in Sweden in 1809; Norway followed (initially for the armed forces) in 1952, as did Denmark in 1953.[568] Although traditionally a Scandinavian idea, it had attracted West Germany in 1957, New Zealand and Norway (for all civil affairs) in 1962, 'followed by a long wave of new offices in other ... countries around the world'.[569]

With the tremendous expansion of the sphere of governance after the process of independence, a lot of African states adopted institutions 'modelled' after the Swedish system, albeit with varying degrees of powers and functions and under different nomenclatures.[570] Explaining the antecedents of ombudsmen in Africa, Scott asserted that 'the origins of the office in underdeveloped

The failure of the centralised state: Institutions and self-governance in Africa (1995) 1-22; SBO Gutto *Peoples' rights for the oppressed* (1993) 55-72.

564 See *Protectors or pretenders?* (n 513 above) 14-15.

565 Carver *et al* (n 524 above) 733.

566 The use of this terminology is to encompass all such bodies as are conventionally created to serve as mediators between the public and the various branches of government. While not all of these usually have an explicit human rights mandate, I intend to examine their possible role in the integrative human rights discourse and human development in Africa.

567 G Sawyer *Ombudsman* (1969) 7.

568 RA Khan *An introduction to political science* (1972) 212.

569 Reif (n 517 above) 8. For a vivid historical account of 'how it all began', see W Gellhorn *Ombudsmen and others: Citizens' protectors in nine countries* (1966) 194-255.

570 See Carver *et al* (n 524 above) 734. In Botswana, Ethiopia, Lesotho, Malawi, Mauritius, Namibia, Seychelles, Swaziland and Zimbabwe, it is known as Ombudsman. In Burkina Faso, Djibouti, Gabon, Mauritania, Senegal and Tunisia, it

countries may well be a response to political problems facing the country rather than a particular concern with citizen's rights'.[571]

Having regard to the background of the ombudsmanship in many African countries, Scott's assertion may not be unfounded. There is an argument that most African governments in the 1960s and 1970s had considered the ombudsman system to be an effective mechanism to curb corruption, racial discrimination and colonial orientation, and to curtail other bureaucratic misdemeanours that may adversely affect the public image of those governments.[572]

While scholarly discourse about the ombudsman institution is not a recent development, the discourse has theoretically been limited to its administrative implications for bureaucracies in Africa.[573] Until very recently, ombudsmanship has not been considered a platform for rigorous human rights engagement in Africa, and where such is identified, it had conceptually been more restricted to the Southern African sub-region.[574] More importantly, ombudsmanship is yet to be explored as a potential instrumentality for integrative human rights, the protection of economic, social and cultural rights and human development in Africa.[575]

is known as *Mediateur.* In Ghana, it is known as Commissioner for Human Rights and Administrative Justice. In Madagascar, it is known as *Defenseur du Peuple.* In Nigeria, it is Public Complaints Commission. In South Africa, it is known as Public Protector. In Tanzania, it is known as Permanent Commission of Enquiry. In Uganda, it is known as Inspector-General of Government. In Zambia, it is known as Investigator-General.

571 I Scott 'The ombudsman, the executive and collective rights in underdeveloped countries' (1979) 13 *Quarterly Journal of Administration* 101 102.

572 n 571 above, 105; Reif (n 517 above) 61; Carver *et al* (n 524 above) 736; ST Akindele 'Judicial review and ombudsman system: Examination of their efficacy as means of citizens' redress' (1992) 1 *Journal of Nigerian Public Administration and Management* 55.

573 See VO Ayeni 'Evolution of and prospects for the ombudsman in Southern Africa' (1997) 63 *International Review of Administration Sciences* 543 547; N Steytler 'The judicialisation of Namibian politics' (1993) 9 *South African Journal on Human Rights* 477.

574 Some of the literature that illuminates the ombudsman institution's significance for human rights generally include J Sarkin 'The drafting of South Africa's final Constitution from a human rights perspective' (1999) 47 *American Journal of Comparative Law* 67; SAM Baqwa 'The role of the Public Prosecutor *vis-à-vis* other institutions that redress grievances in South Africa' in LC Reif (ed) *International Ombudsman yearbook* (1999)129; M Maree 'The institution of ombudsman in the Republic of Namibia' in LC Reif (ed) *International Ombudsman yearbook* (1999) 141; SM Hatteea 'The ombudsman in Mauritius - Thirty years on' in LC Reif (ed) *International Ombudsman yearbook* (1999) 11; and J Sarkin 'The role of national human rights institutions in post-apartheid South Africa' in J Sarkin *et al* (eds) *Human rights, the citizen and the state: South African and Irish approaches* (2001) 13 35-38.

575 As a pointer, among all 15 scholarly articles contained in the Special Issue of the *Review of the International Commission of Jurists* on 'The evolving African constitutionalism', a collection of intellectual contributions drawn from every sub-region of Africa, only the piece by J Sarkin 'Innovations in the interim and 1996 South African Constitutions' 57 66 alluded to ombudsmanship.

Nevertheless, I contend that there should be, and there is indeed, a close nexus between ombudsmanship and the promotion of an integrative human rights approach to human development in Africa. While not all African ombudsmen have an explicit human rights mandate, the general mandates of these bodies for *investigating* maladministration and the abuse of power are broad enough to accommodate their crucial involvement in economic, social and cultural rights monitoring.

For example, the Ombudsman of Mauritius is empowered to investigate any case 'in which *a member of the public* claims, or appears to the Ombudsman, to have sustained injustice in consequence of maladministration'.[576] The Constitution of Malawi provides:

> The office of the Ombudsman may investigate *any and all cases* where it is alleged that a person has suffered injustice and it does not appear that there is any remedy reasonably available by way of proceedings in a court or by way of appeal from a court or where there is no other practicable remedy.[577]

The Ugandan Constitution vests in the Inspector-General the power:

> (a) ...
>
> (b) to eliminate and foster the elimination of corruption, abuse of authority and of public office;
>
> (c) to promote fair, efficient and good governance in public offices;
>
> (d) ...
>
> (e) to investigate *any act, omission, advice, decision or recommendation by a public officer or any other authority* to which this article applies, taken, *made, given or done in exercise of administrative functions*; and
>
> (f) to *stimulate public awareness* about the values of constitutionalism in general and the activities of its office, in particular, through any media and other means it considers appropriate.[578]

In its own unique outlook, the Namibian Constitution confers on the Ombudsman:

> (a) ...
>
> (b) the duty to investigate complaints concerning the functioning of the Public Service Commission, administrative organs of the state, the defence force, the police force and the prison service in so far as such complaints relate to the failure to achieve a balanced structuring of

576 Mauritius Constitution (n 402 above) sec 96 (my emphasis).
577 Malawi Constitution (n 462 above) sec 123(1) (my emphasis).
578 Uganda Constitution (n 465 above) sec 225(1) (my emphasis).

> such services or equal access by all to the recruitment of such services or fair administration in relation to such services;
>
> (c) the duty to investigate complaints concerning the over-utilisation of living *natural resources*, the *irrational exploitation of non-renewable resources*, the *degradation and destruction of ecosystems* and failure to protect the beauty and character of Namibia.[579]

The South African Constitution empowers the Public Protector, *inter alia*:

> (a) to investigate *any conduct in state affairs*, or in the public administration in any sphere of government, that is alleged or suspected to be improper or to result in any impropriety or prejudice;
>
> (b) to report on that conduct; and
>
> (c) to *take appropriate remedial action*.[580]

On the performance of the South African Public Protector within the scope of this tripartite mandate, Sarkin observes: 'He has investigated many issues relating to government departments, nepotism, roles of cabinet ministers and other issues ... the Public Protector's office has recently been asserting greater independence.'[581]

Some other African states have the enabling statutes for the ombudsman in instruments outside their constitutions. The Nigerian model is instructive here. The Public Complaints Commission (PCC) Act mandates the body:

> [T]o investigate ... complaints lodged ... by any other person [against] *any administrative action* taken by:
>
> (a) *any Department* or Ministry of the federal or any state government;
>
> (b) any department of *any local government authority* (howsoever designated) set up in any state in the federation;
>
> (c) *any statutory corporation or public institution* set up by any government in Nigeria;
>
> (d) ...
>
> (e) *any officer or servant of any of the aforementioned*.[582]

The normative framework of an ombudsman institution could hardly have been drafted in any more effective language. But beyond the issue of mandates, the mode of constituting the ombudsmen in Africa

579 Namibian Constitution (n 454 above) sec 91 (my emphasis).

580 South African Constitution (n 395 above) sec 182(1) (my emphasis).

581 Sarkin (n 574 above) 36-37. See also S Liebenberg 'Human development and human rights: South African country study', UNDP 'Human development report 2000: Background paper 15' (2000).

582 Sec 4(2), Public Complaints Commission Decree 31, 16 October 1975, re-enacted Public Complaints Commission Act ch 377, LFN 1990 (my emphasis).

has been a matter of concern. Arguments are rife, for instance, that because almost in all cases, African ombudsmen are constituted by 'executive branch appointments', the 'independence and impartiality' of these bodies are inherently questionable.[583] Much more than that, however, because those who constitute the institution of ombudsmanship in Africa, like other governmental political establishments, are products of the prevailing political dynamics (possibly with very rare exceptions), their efficacy in using their mandates to promote human rights, good governance and human development is often stunted or virtually non-existent.[584]

Notwithstanding the inherent or artificial normative and structural inadequacies of ombudsmen in Africa, the human rights community also has a vital role to play in making the institutions relevant. In Nigeria, for instance, even though the mandate of the PCC under its enabling statute confers on the body broad investigative powers, the activities of the body since 1975 have revolved around complaints of wrongful dismissal and non-payment of salaries.[585] Nigerian human rights groups should begin to stimulate the PCC towards human rights monitoring and investigation. As promising as the Ugandan model appears, it has been mired in questions of transparency and credibility.[586]

In her lucid analysis of the capacity of national human rights institutions to serve as viable purveyors of good governance, democratisation and human rights, Reif is correct to stress that '[t]he fact that a national human rights institution has been established does not automatically lead to the conclusion that it will be effective in building good governance and protecting human rights'.[587] Nonetheless, ombudsmanship can become a veritable platform for addressing economic, social and cultural rights and the core issues affecting millions of Africans.

583 Reif (n 517 above) 61. *Contra* MGJ Kimweri 'The effectiveness of an Executive Ombudsman' in LC Reif (ed) *The international ombudsman anthology: Selected writings from the international ombudsman institute* (1999) 379.

584 See generally M Okoye 'The African context of human rights: Development, equality and justice' in Shepherd Jr *et al* (n 196 above) 163 178-179; JM Mbaku 'Preparing Africa for the twenty-first century: Lessons from constitutional economics' (1995) 6 *Constitutional Political Economy* 139 145.

585 See generally L Adamolekun *et al Nigeria's ombudsman system* (1982) 50-71.

586 See Ssenyonjo (n 372 above) 479-480.

587 Reif (n 517 above) 23.

5 Concluding remarks

I have analysed the sub-themes of this chapter with a view to identifying the existence of normative and institutional frameworks that are critical to the enhancement of the place of economic, social and cultural rights and, invariably, of a holistic rights-based approach to some of the most pronounced human development challenges in Africa.

I argued that the constitution of any African country should guarantee and secure *all human rights* for the individual. Human rights here, referring not just to the right to vote or to speak, to assemble or to worship, important as they are; but also *all* rights that would secure the *equal* and non-discriminatory *access* of all Africans to the basic necessities that enhance human freedoms, choices and capabilities.

My arguments underscore the point that the functions of modern governments are no longer confined to defence, foreign affairs, maintenance of law and order and other similar matters mentioned by jurists and thinkers of the age of enlightenment. It should now be the duty of the state also to promote economic democracy and social justice.

With regard to Directive Principles, notwithstanding that these principles are, in 'strict' legal terms, non-justiciable, they should nevertheless be accorded their interpretative values. It is no longer acceptable, in the light of the grave socio-economic conditions of the vast majority of Africans wallowing in naked squalor and deprivation, for African governments, jurists, constitutionalists, and even human rights activists, to ignore the path of proactive approach to these principles in meeting some of the most profound challenges for human beings in Africa.

I have also emphasised the importance of legislation in meeting one of the *basic* requirements of ICESCR and the African Charter: the adoption of measures. Even where certain statutes were not purposely adopted pursuant to ICESCR or African Charter obligations or where subsisting legislation is simply revised versions of earlier legislation, such enactments do not cease to hold implications for the approach envisaged in this discourse. It is now a challenge for all Africans to begin to activate all legislation that would improve the plight of the most vulnerable.

The insight I have provided here, thus far, is that, while there are indeed broad provisions for institutional intervention in the day-to-day challenges confronting many Africans, these mechanisms have largely remained under-utilised. A need therefore arises for a change in perceptions. African human rights scholars and activists should begin to explore the various dynamics that would make these mechanisms more responsive to the issues highlighted in this book.

4

Comparative Law and Jurisprudence

[W]hile interpreting and applying ... human rights ... we can certainly take into account economic and social rights and interpret and apply the specifically enumerated human rights in such a manner as to advance and achieve economic and social rights. The scope and ambit of the specifically enumerated human rights can and must receive colour from economic and social rights ... which can be spelt out from the specifically enumerated human rights and thus become enforceable by the judiciary. *Everything depends on the creativity, valour and activism of the judge deciding the particular case.*[588]

1 The implementation of economic, social and cultural rights: The justiciability question

As I have highlighted in previous chapters, the implementation of economic, social and cultural rights has for long been enmeshed in the obstructionist debate on their *justiciability*,[589] not the least in Africa.

588 PN Bhagwati 'Fundamental rights in their economic, social and cultural context' in *Developing human rights jurisprudence Vol ii* (1989) 79 82.

589 The use of the term 'justiciability' in this chapter and in any part of this work does not assume any technical meaning. It only connotes the ability of judicial, quasi-judicial and non-judicial bodies to examine any of the elements or issues involved in promoting or protecting human rights. Contrary to the general assumption among many scholars to equate the justiciability of economic, social and cultural rights narrowly with their remedial enforceability in the law courts, my use of the term is centrally to advance economic, social and cultural rights not as isolated rights, but as intrinsic values and claims within the whole body of *all* human rights. For some of the different scholarly perceptions on the connotations of this term, see HV Conde *A handbook of international human rights terminology* (1999) 79; MK Addo 'The justiciability of economic, social and cultural rights' (1988) 10 *Commonwealth Bulletin* 1415; JK Mapulanga-Hulston 'Examining the justiciability of economic, social and cultural rights' (2002) 6 *International Journal of Human Rights* 29 36-37; and VA Leary 'Justiciability and beyond: Complaint procedures and the right to health' (1995) 55 *Review of International Commission of Jurists* 105 110-112. Warning us about the misconceptualisation of the term 'justiciability', Scott & Macklem contend the impression that what is or is not justiciable inheres in the judicial function and is written in stone. In fact, the reverse is true: Not only is justiciability variable from context to context, but its content varies over time.' See C Scott & P Macklem 'Constitutional ropes of sand or justiciable guarantees? Social rights in

I consider it crucial in a pioneering work of this nature critically to address this question and to diffuse prevalent misgivings about the substance of economic, social and cultural rights as norms incapable of juridical application. To evade the issue of justiciability in our present discourse will amount to sustaining the devaluation of economic, social and cultural rights as *legal* rights in Africa. From my experience of the general weakness of legislation to ensure the adequate implementation of economic, social and cultural rights in African states, ascertaining their juridical parameters becomes an inevitable option if these rights are ever to be efficacious as legal entitlements. While there has been an impressive discourse on the recognition of economic, social and cultural rights within the international legal arena, the question of the justiciability of these rights is far from being resolved within many national legal domains.[590] African states are no exception.

Apart from the institutions already highlighted, however, there exists a central role for the judiciary (or court system) in every country as well as the quasi-judicial, non-judicial and inquisitorial bodies that are replete in the structures of supra-national inter-governmental entities. Within the contemplation of this discourse, examining the scope of judicial involvement *vis-à-vis* adjudicating, protecting or promoting economic, social and cultural rights will allow us to calibrate and define the potential role and responsibility of national courts in giving content to these rights. My evaluation of the juridical element of the implementation of economic, social and cultural rights does not connote a tendency towards the bandwagon of conceptualising these rights as claims whose validity absolutely depends on *enforceability* or litigability.[591] Rather, the essence of this chapter is to demonstrate that economic, social and cultural rights are rights capable of juridical application; that these rights

a new South African Constitution' (1992) 141 *University of Pennsylvania Law Review* 1 17.

590 See Tomaševski (n 42 above) 206. Bruno Simma, a long-time member of the ESCR Committee, had lamented that 'there hardly exists another human rights treaty which has been more frequently misinterpreted, downplayed or intentionally abused than the [I]ICESCR'. See B Simma 'The implementation of the International Covenant on Economic and Social Rights' in E Verlag *et al* (eds) *The implementation of economic and social rights: National, international and comparative aspects* (1991) 75 79. Beyond high-level rhetoricisation, there is hardly any plausible indication of a radical departure from that 1991 assessment.

591 See generally Scott & Macklem (n 589 above) 6. Compare Vierdag (n 36 above) 73; GJH van Hoof 'The legal nature of economic, social and cultural rights' in P Alston *et al* (eds) *The right to food* (1984) 100-101; A Sachs *Affirmative action and good government* (1991) 28; CR Sunstein 'Three civil rights fallacies' (1991) 79 *California Law Review* 765-769; M Cappelletti 'The future of legal education: A comparative perspective' (1992) 8 *South African Journal on Human Rights* 1 10; S Holmes & CR Sunstein *The cost of rights: Why liberty depends on taxes* (1999) 15 118-121. See also UE Effeh 'A case study on how not to realise economic, social and cultural rights, and a proposal for change (2005) 3 *Northwestern University Journal of International Human Rights* 2.

have been interpreted substantially with helpful decisions and outcomes that are both politically feasible and practically sustainable. While this chapter serves as both a descriptive precursor to the next chapter on remedial implementation, its thrust towards accentuating the cross-cultural appreciation of economic, social and cultural rights as tangible legal rights is unmistakable.

Central to the debate on the justiciability of *all* human rights has been the underpinning need to demarcate the extent to which a court should intervene in matters that fall within the spheres of the executive and legislative arms of government. The arguments of advocates of a restrictive judicial role are firmly rooted in the classical principles of the separation of powers propounded by Baron de Montesquieu in 1748 as well as the rule of law postulated by Dicey in 1885.[592] The thrust of these arguments, as advanced by many scholars in contemporary times, has been the need to maintain checks and balances on the three traditional spheres of government because, according to some of the 'puritan' advocates of these doctrines, 'an activist government, let alone an activist judiciary, is anathema to the rule of law and its libertarian foundations'.[593]

While it would be erroneous to confine the subject of justiciability of human rights to the dimension of 'judicialism', as some scholars are wont to do, without adequate reflection on the constitutive element of advancing economic, social and cultural rights beyond the formalised terrain of courts,[594] the notion of justiciability fundamentally imports the concept of *judicial review* through which ordinary law courts exercise their supervisory functions in law ordered societies.[595]

592 See generally C Secondat in AM Cohler *et al* (eds) Baron de Montesquieu *The spirit of the laws xi* (1992) 6; AV Dicey in E Wade (ed) *The law of the constitution* (1965) 188-203.

593 AC Hutchinson *et al The rule of law: Ideal or ideology* (1987) 97. See also F Hayek *The road to serfdom* (1946) 54. See also AF Bayefsky 'The judicial function under the Canadian Charter of Rights and Freedoms' (1987) 32 *McGill Law Journal* 791 815-827.

594 See Mapulanga-Hulston (n 589 above) 36-37.

595 For a historical account of the development of the concept of judicial review from ancient Athenian times to the present time, see Mavcic (n 406 above) 18-22. Much as I recognise the strong connection between judicial review and the protection of human rights, it is not my intention either to provide theoretical justification for the doctrine or to engage on either side of scholarly debates on the subject. Suffice to state that the law and practice of constitutional judicial review has grown tremendously over the last one hundred years and has generated a wealth of literature in a variety of jurisdictional contexts. See eg C Platto *Trial and court procedures worldwide* (1990); OH Phillips *Constitutional and administrative law* (1967); Lord Woolf *et al De Smith, Woolf and Jowell's principles of judicial review* (1999); M Cappelletti *Judicial review in the contemporary world* 45-68; JH Ely *Democracy and distrust* (1980); TO *Elias Judicial process in the newer Commonwealth* (1990) 179-193; M Demerieux *Fundamental rights in Commonwealth Caribbean Constitutions* (1992) 485-499; R Clayton *et al* 'The role of judicial review in curing breaches of article 6' (2003) 8

More significant for our discourse are the extrapolations being generated about the role of the judiciary or, rather, the judicial process, in social welfarism and, indeed, economic, social and cultural rights advocacy in many countries.[596] From the perspective of strict legal constructionists (positivists), human rights only 'exist when one party can effectively insist that another deliver goods, services or protection and third parties will act to reinforce (or at least not hinder) their delivery'.[597] However, even among liberal scholars and jurists who insist on the criterion of adjudication, the overarching message has been one of caution in judicial intervention in policy matters.[598]

Since the very nature of human rights entails a complex matrix of jural relations (claims and obligations as well as rights and duties),[599] the debate among scholars and jurists in respect of the adjudication of economic, social and cultural rights has been whether or not bringing these contestations into the purview of judicial evaluation would amount to 'judicialising' the realm of politics.[600] In the words of Russell, '[t]he principal impact ... [of judicial involvement] on the process of government can be neatly summarised as a tendency to judicialise politics and politicise the judiciary'.[601]

Judicial Review 90-96; R Dworkin *A matter of principle* (1985) 71; P Monahan *Politics and the constitution: The Charter, federalism and the Supreme Court of Canada* (1987); RJ Sharpe *et al The Charter of Rights and Freedoms* (1998) 18-29.

596 See eg P Lenaghan 'Implications of the Trade and Development Co-operation Agreement with specific reference to the justiciability of economic rights in a municipal framework: The South African and European position' in Sarkin *et al* (eds) (n 574 above) 208; E Mureinik 'Beyond a charter of luxuries: Economic rights in the Constitution' (1992) 8 *South African Journal on Human Rights* 464 471-472; T Buck *Judicial review and social welfare* (1998); G Hogan 'Judicial review and socio-economic rights' in Sarkin *et al* (eds) (n 574 above) 1; WF Pratt 'A new vocabulary for a new constitutional law: *United States v Carolene Products*' in EO Dell (ed) *Leading cases of the twentieth century* (2000) 125; J de Ville 'The rule of law and judicial review: Re-reading Dicey: The constitutional context' (2006) *Acta Juridica* 62.

597 A Eide 'Article 25' in A Eide *et al* (eds) *The Universal Declaration of Human Rights: A commentary* (1992) 385 386. See also R Nozick *Anarchy, state and Utopia* (1971) 238.

598 See AP le Sueur 'Justifying judicial caution: Jurisdiction, justiciability and policy' in B Hadfield (ed) *Judicial review: A thematic approach* (1995) 228 229; L Patrick 'Judicial restraint and overreach' (2004) 20 *South African Journal on Human Rights* 544.

599 For a scholarly analysis and critique of some philosophical ideas about rights as jural relations, see J Finnis 'Some professorial fallacies about rights' (1972) 4 *Adelaide Law Review* 377.

600 See eg Cranston (n 36 above) 66; FG Jacobs 'The extension of the European Convention on Human Rights to include economic, social and cultural rights' (1978) 3 *Human Rights Review* 172; Mureinik (n 596 above) 471-472; Haysom (n 350 above) 457-458; W Sadurski 'Economic rights and basic needs' in C Sampford *et al* (eds) *Law, rights and the welfare state* (1986) 57.

601 P Russell 'The political purposes of the Canadian Charter of Rights and Freedoms' (1983) 61 *Canadian Bar Review* 30 51-52.

As a result of the fledgling or virtually non-existent profile of economic, social and cultural rights in the constitutional law and human rights jurisprudence of many countries, therefore, there seems to be an emerging consensus among many human rights scholars and jurists in various parts of the world that the most potent machinery through which judiciaries can give substance to economic, social and cultural rights is by adopting an 'activist' approach: a pseudonym for *judicial activism*.[602] While so much scholarly work exists on both sides of the debate on judicial activism, what is central to my interest here is the invaluable and strategic relevance of the doctrine to strengthening economic, social and cultural rights in Africa and, perhaps, elsewhere.[603]

What has become evident and pronounced in states where judiciaries have adopted proactive approach in their understanding and interpretation of human rights is the relatively enhanced capacity of such judiciaries to uphold the expectations of liberty and equality, to strive to intervene in times of national crisis or, as would be seen in the next chapter, to be able to fashion an appropriate remedial stance where the factors that sustain human life and livelihood are at stake.[604]

602 See eg PN Bhagwati 'Fundamental rights in their economic, social and cultural context' *Developing human rights jurisprudence Vol i* 57 62 63, pointing to 'how human freedom and dignity can be promoted and protected at all without realisation of both categories of human rights' and stressing that, to make them meaningful, judiciaries must adopt 'an activist goal-oriented approach'; KM Holland *Judicial activism in comparative perspective* (1991) 1.

603 For diverse perspectives on the controversy relating to whether a judiciary should be 'passive', 'activist' or 'dynamic', see R Cooke 'Empowerment and accountability: The quest for administrative justice' in *Developing human rights jurisprudence Vol v* (1992) 81 84; R McCracken *et al* 'Standing and fundamental rights: A South Asian perspective' (2002) 7 *Judicial Review* 172 173; FL Morton 'Judicial activism in France' in Holland (n 602 above) 133 134-135; TJ Peretti *In defence of a political court* (1999) 186-188; AS Miller *Toward increased judicial activism: The political role of the Supreme Court* (1982) 306-307; MC Miller 'A comparison of the judicial role in the United States and in Canada' (1998) 22 *Suffolk Transnational Law Review* 1 8; PL Joshi 'Judicial activism - A critique' (2001) 4 *Journal of the Institute for Human Rights*.; Bhagwati (n 588 above) 81; P Lenta 'Democracy, rights disagreements and judicial review (2004) 20 *South African Journal on Human Rights* 1-31; D Bilchitz 'Judicial remedies and socio-economic rights: A response to Christopher Mbazira' (2008) 9 *ESR Review: Economic and social rights in South Africa* 9-12.

604 See generally C Wolfe *Judicial activism: Bulwark of freedom or precarious security?* (1997) 69-78.

One country outside the industrialised nations of the West that has achieved phenomenal development of a liberal approach to judicial activism through 'public interest litigation' is India.[605] Although the idea of public interest litigation is not peculiar to India, its judiciary inevitably holds the credit for the innovative evolution of a process that has torn its courts away from the restrictive, conservative and hardship-working doctrine of *locus standi* and legalistic pleadings.[606]

Having discarded the legal technicalities usually attached to the institution of a suit (for example, filing a writ in prescribed statutory form, and often by engaging a counsel), Indian courts now consider as sufficient even mere letters addressed to a court or judge to assume the commencement of public interest suits.[607]

What had been the momentous query of critical observers of the Indian approach was the likelihood of the abuse of the process: opening the floodgates of frivolous and vexatious litigation.[608] The Indian experience has, however, shown that, rather than encouraging unbridled litigation, it may indeed reduce litigation.[609] Since the purport of public interest litigation is to expose and redress social deprivations, once the court pronounces on the aggregated humiliating, dehumanising or undignifying conditions of a class or

605 See CD Cunningham 'Public interest litigation in the Indian Supreme Court: A study in the light of American experiment' (1987) 29 *Indian Journal of International Law* 505; V Langer 'Public interest in civil law, socialist law, and common law systems: The role of the public prosecutor' (1988) 36 *American Journal of Comparative Law* 279; DP Lalwani 'Public interest litigation - Offshoot of judicial activism' (2001) 4 *Journal of the Institute for Human Rights* 86 90; U Baxi 'Taking suffering seriously: Social action litigation in the Supreme Court of India' in R Dhavan *et al* (eds) *Judges and the judicial power: Essays in honour of Justice VRK Iyer* (1995) 289-305.

606 More than a decade ago, in describing the posture of the Indian judiciary towards activism, Bhagwati had said: 'We in India are moving away from formalism and to use judicial activism for achieving social or distributive justice and in this expression, I include basic human rights. We firmly believe that *the modern judiciary cannot afford to hide behind notions of legal justice when social justice issues are addressed to it*. It can no longer obtain social and political legitimacy without making a substantial contribution to issues of social justice.' See PN Bhagwati 'The role of the judiciary in the democratic process: Balancing activism and judicial restraint' in *Developing human rights jurisprudence Vol v* (n 603 above) 10 14 (myemphasis).

607 See CV Das 'Accountability mechanism: Judicial checks on government' paper presented at the Commonwealth workshop on accountability, scrutiny and oversight, 23-25 May 2001, Canberra, Australia; Lalwan (n 605 above) 100. See also PN Bhagwati 'Liberty and security of the person in India with particular emphasis on access to courts' in *Developing human rights jurisprudence Vol vii* (1998) 203 212, referring to the origins of what he termed 'epistolary jurisdiction', where the court can be moved by just addressing a letter on behalf of the vulnerable class of persons; SV Manohar 'The Indian judiciary and human rights' in V Iyer (ed) *Democracy, human rights and the rule of law* (2000) 150.

608 See RR Vadodaria 'Constitutional crises and judicial activism' (2001) 4 *Journal of the Institute for Human Rights* 46 50.

609 Lalwani (n 605 above) 105.

group, the need for further judicial intervention on behalf of each particular member of such a class or group diminishes. The decision in *Bandhua Mukti Morcha v Union of India* [610] vividly illustrates the argument: The petition had originated from a letter written by the *Bandhua Mukti Morcha*, an organisation representing hundreds of bonded labourers across India who had been working in stone quarries for many years. Although the petition had actually named only 32 of the victims, the decision declaring their bondage work unlawful had led to nationwide freedom for all such workers. The two commissioners appointed by the court to monitor compliance and to report had a nationwide mandate. The task then becomes how to monitor the response(s) of the concerned executive or administrative agencies or officials.

Apart from adding impetus to the clamour for access to justice, the result-oriented activist approach of the Indian judiciary to the interpretation of 'fundamental' human rights has been described as marking the unique transition of the institution from being a 'traditional captive agency with low social visibility into a liberated agency with high socio-political feasibility'.[611] The adoption of an activist approach by Indian courts has led to a broadening of the scope of the rule of *locus standi* to afford the marginalised and poorer sections of the Indian society the opportunity to seek judicial intervention in matters affecting their lives and dignity.[612]

Through the expansive interpretation of article 21 of the Indian Constitution,[613] the judiciary has been able to circumvent the non-justiciability of the Directive Principles in the Constitution and to apply economic, social and cultural rights norms in domestic situations. Much more, it has garnered enablement to grant reliefs

610 AIR 1984 SC 802. For an analysis of other cases where Indian courts intervened in class actions, see SLA Khan *Justice Bhagwati on fundamental rights and directive principles* (1996) 97-112. It is apt to note that in a slew of cases, the Indian judiciary has been very cautious in ensuring that petitions that are frivolous, vexatious and filed in bad faith are not entertained. Similarly, an action calculated to placate an individual is readily declined. See eg *Samiti v State of Andhra Pradesh*, AIR (1990) SC 1473; *Prasad v State of Bihar* (1993) 4 SCC 547; *Kumar v Shivraj Patil* (1993) 1 SCC 47. For a scholarly critical evaluation of the public interest litigation paradigm in India, see AH Desai *et al* 'Public interest litigation: Potentials and problems' in BN Kirpal *et al* (eds) *Supreme but not infallible: Essays in honour of the Supreme Court of India* (2000) 159-191.

611 Bhagwati (n 602 above) 63.

612 See Bhagwati (n 588 above) 83. Compare P Hunt *Reclaiming social rights: International and comparative perspectives* (1996) 171. Even though Hunt appreciates the immense burden the Indian paradigm may entail over time, he was quick to emphasise that the fact-finding powers of the courts, their capacity to issue detailed orders of remedy as well as their capacity for monitoring sustains the desirability of that activist approach.

613 Art 21 provides that '[n]o person shall be deprived of his life or personal liberty except according to procedure established by law'.

and remedies that would ordinarily have been inconceivable in the legal formalism of a writ system.[614]

In the face of the helplessness, poverty and deprivation confronting the vast majority of ordinary Africans, the Indian judicial approach towards poverty alleviation, human development and social justice offers a promising model for economic, social and cultural rights activism in Africa. Despite huge challenges to constitutionalism in Africa, it is noteworthy that the power of judicial review is known in virtually all the existing domestic legal systems.[615]

Regrettably, however, the process of engaging the protection of human rights and fundamental freedoms through the judicial process has been a chequered, slow, and arduous experience. Dumbutshena, late Chief Justice of Zimbabwe and Justice of Appeal in Namibia, had described the African reality as follows:

> In Africa, people have seen judges who have sold their souls to dictatorships and abandoned the hopes of the people ... there are judges who believe that human rights play no part in the doing of justice and that those judges who support and put into practice international human rights norms are sheer agitators ... Some judges are executive minded. They believe in governments. And if they support the [political] party in power, which they ought not to do, and that party is for various reasons against human rights, they too will be against human rights.[616]

Some years later, another African jurist and President of the World Association of Judges had admonished African judicial systems in the following words:

> We as African judges must firmly uphold our constitutions and the rights of all our citizens ... If we should fail in our duty, society may not take our judgments seriously and posterity may not forgive us. Confidence in the judiciary could vanish. Respect for law and order may diminish and even break down. If it should, anarchy would take over. People may ... take the law into their own hands and violence would be the order of the day.[617]

614 See Lalwani (n 605 above) 102. Shortly, I shall be analysing some of the remarkable Indian decisions that portend implications for the theme of this book. In the next chapter, I explore the remedial significance of these decisions.

615 In his extensive survey of African constitutions, alongside those of other regions, Mavcic discovered that '[a]ll the systems feature the principle of the independence of judges who exercise constitutional review ... These systems adopted the constitutional review of statutes. Some systems also adopted the preventive review of statutes and/or the so-called consultative function of bodies exercising constitutional review concerning the drafting of statutes, executive regulations or presidential acts.' See Mavcic (n 406 above) 99.

616 E Dumbutshena 'Role of the judge in advancing human rights' in *Developing human rights jurisprudence Vol v* (n 603 above) 49.

617 Justice B Ajibola 'Welcoming addresses' in B Ajibola & D van Zyl (eds) *The Judiciary in Africa* (1998) xv.

It would therefore appear, at least as far as rhetorical commitment would show, that some African judges are being sensitised to the social dimensions of their oversight responsibilities. At the high-level Second Judicial Colloquium on the Domestic Application of International Human Rights Norms, held in Harare, Zimbabwe, in April 1989, leaders of African judiciaries acknowledged that:

> There is a close inter-linkage between civil and political rights and economic and social rights: Neither category of human rights can be fully realised without the enjoyment of the other ... Indeed ... the denial of human rights and fundamental freedoms is not only an individual tragedy, but also creates conditions of social and political unrest, sowing seeds of violence and conflict within and between societies.[618]

Contrary to the noble visions expressed at such fora, however, the output of judicial work as regards the integrative human rights approach has remained unmistakably paltry.[619] Since most African judiciaries are still having difficulty in grappling with human rights adjudication generally, it should be discernible why economic, social and cultural rights jurisprudence has been such a neglected and negligible subject in much of Africa.

Tumwine-Mukubwa had rightly identified the anachronistic relic of imperial constitutionalism as being a formidable obstacle to judicial intervention in matters of 'political questions' in Africa.[620] While some jurists and scholars of the Anglo-American tradition would contend that any matter with political colouration is beyond the

618 *The Harare Declaration of Human Rights*, Concluding Statement of the Judicial Colloquium held in Harare, Zimbabwe, 19-22 April 1989, reprinted in 60 *Review of the International Commission of Jurists* (1998) 251 252-253, Preamble paras 7-8. This landmark statement reverberated at subsequent editions of the African judicial colloquium. See 'The Banjul Affirmation' Concluding Statement of the Judicial Colloquium held in Banjul, The Gambia, 7-9 November 1990, reprinted in *Developing human rights jurisprudence Vol VII* (n 607 above) 223-225 para 8; 'The Abuja Confirmation' Concluding Statement of the Judicial Colloquium held in Abuja, Nigeria, 9-12 December 1991, reprinted in *Developing human rights jurisprudence Vol VII* 215-231 para 14; 'The Balliol Statement' Concluding Statement of the Judicial Colloquium held in Balliol College, Oxford, United Kingdom, 21-23 September 1992, reprinted in *Developing human rights jurisprudence Vol VII* 232-234 para 5; 'The Bloemfontein Statement', Concluding Statement of the Judicial Colloquium held in Bloemfontein, South Africa, 3-5 September 1993, reprinted in (1998) 60 *Review of the International Commission of Jurists* 151 paras 10-11.

619 See D Olowu 'Human development challenges in Africa: A rights-based approach' (2004) 5 *San Diego International Law Journal* 179 191.

620 See GP Tumwine-Mukubwa 'Ruled from the grave: Challenging antiquated constitutional doctrines and values in Commonwealth Africa' in Oloka-Onyango (n 351 above) 287 297-299. See generally M Kirby 'The judge in the new world order: A role in advancing human rights?' in *Developing human rights jurisprudence Vol iv* 207 210-211.

purview of adjudication and, therefore, non-justiciable,[621] that line of orientation is unsupportable in the newer states of Africa that are still grappling with huge challenges of nation building and development that implicate a necessary nexus between governmental accountability and good governance.

2 Imperative of economic, social and cultural rights jurisprudence

Although a significant measure of apparatuses exists for monitoring, promoting and applying economic, social and cultural rights as normative values at various international, regional and national levels, establishing these rights as efficacious norms has nonetheless been generally problematic at all levels. The reason for this scenario is traceable to the late emergence of economic, social and cultural rights as 'universal' values, the global paradigm shift towards trade liberalisation, and a decrease in governmental social controls.[622] It therefore appeals to both logic and expediency, flowing from the depth of the global discourse on the integrative human rights approach, that every human right — civil, political, economic, social or cultural — must be made legitimate and operational if all the efforts at human advancement since 1945 are to have any meaning at all.

While so much effort has been devoted to understanding the twin crisis of maladministration and underdevelopment in Africa,[623] a rights-based approach to these challenges remains unidentified and undefined. An urgent need therefore arises for the formulation of appropriate human rights responses. It is arguable, for instance, that the establishment of a comprehensive economic, social and cultural rights culture will facilitate a cogent platform for checking the tendency towards profligacy in governance.[624] The task, however, goes beyond monitoring state responsibility.

621 See eg R Berger *Government by judiciary: The transformation of the 14th Amendment* (1977) 298; W Whitford 'The rule of law: New reflections on an old doctrine' (2000) 6 *East African Journal of Peace and Human Rights* 34; Bayefsky (n 593 above) 794.

622 See S Maxwell, Overseas Development Institute (ODI) 'What can we do with a rights-based approach to development?' 2 (ODI Briefing Paper 3, September 1999).

623 See eg KR Hope Sr *et al Corruption and development in Africa: Lessons from country case studies* (2000); T Martin 'Corruption and improper payments: Global trends and applicable laws' (1998) 36 *Alberta Law Review* 416.

624 See generally Agbakwa (n 46 above) 190, contemplating that an effective human rights culture may present an 'opportunity to challenge the government's priorities and to hold it accountable for the expenditure of international loans'.

As a case in point, it has become evident from the extensive works of human rights and development NGOs, scholars and activists that the broad range of human rights abuses is not always unavoidable or natural, but that most of such abuses arise from calculated policy decisions and actions, at the levels of states as well as non-state actors, particularly international financial institutions (IFIs), transnational corporations (TNCs) and multinational enterprises (MNEs). The imperative therefore is that all identifiable violators, sponsors and purveyors of violations must be rendered accountable.[625]

In an age of legal positivism such as ours, the most appropriate and competent platform to inquire into human rights abuses will be the judicial, quasi-judicial and inquisitorial fora that have been established at the tripartite levels of human rights regimes that converge in Africa.[626] Even while I acknowledge the problematic dynamics involved in excessive reliance on adjudicatory methods for securing the protection of economic, social and cultural rights, the foreseeable effect of the convergence of all methodical approaches towards establishing 'a culture of compliance' is nevertheless critical.[627]

It must always be borne in mind that most economic, social and cultural rights, whether in international, regional or national instruments, merely require that the state should adopt appropriate policies as well as legislative measures to give substance to their contents. The kernel of the question for national courts to determine should therefore, in the first instance, lie in whether a state has taken reasonable steps towards this *policy* obligation.

All international, regional and domestic instruments recognising economic, social and cultural rights emphasise the need for states to ensure that these rights are protected and secured from illegitimate encroachment by direct and indirect agencies of the state. It

625 See generally G Russell 'All rights must be guaranteed, all actors must be held accountable' (2002) 17 *Fletcher Journal of Developmental Studies* 1 3, asserting that '[a]ddressing all rights, in terms of their economic, political and social context, and holding all actors accountable, constitute critical steps towards challenging the conditions that create and tolerate poverty'.

626 While I must acknowledge that the UN human rights treaty-monitoring bodies as well as many other regional and national human rights institutions (eg the African Commission and the Inter-American Commission) do not assume adjudicatory roles, the juridical values of their inquisitorial functions in the course of monitoring and promoting human rights cannot be ignored. For an insight into how the various human rights treaty-monitoring bodies have become very significant in developing economic, social and cultural rights jurisprudence through their Concluding Observations, General Comments, Recommendations and other supervisory activities, see Maxwell (n 622 above) 3-4; Scott & Macklem (n 589 above) 88-93.

627 See Maxwell (n 622 above) 3-4.

therefore becomes immanent that whenever a violation or encroachment of rights occurs, there should be a praxis for evaluation and possible redress. While the debates about the scope and content of economic, social and cultural rights, the specific obligation(s) of states for each right, and the responsibility of non-state actors may continue to elicit critical thinking around the globe, efforts should nonetheless be channelled into establishing a convergence of responses that will facilitate valid and practical assumptions upon which all these elements will be assessed. 'All human rights for all'[628] will end up being a vain homily if we do not begin to examine *how* and on *what* premises economic, social and cultural rights claims and duties are to be founded. I contend that the solution to the harmonisation of human rights lies not in evading or estranging their 'problematic parts', but in subjecting identifiable problems to rigorous, frank and objective scrutiny.

In the face of the growing menace of HIV/AIDS, internal displacements and refugee problems together with the domestic implications of globalisation, national courts will certainly have no way of avoiding adjudicating the economic and social dimensions of human rights.[629] I conjecture that addressing economic, social and cultural rights as essential components of a rights-based approach to national growth and human development in Africa will engender a conscious movement towards the adoption of appropriate *remedies* to 'violations' as well-reasoned, deepened and carefully analysed jurisprudence increasingly crystallises.

By virtue of their unique quality of independence and the advantage of balanced reasoning, judiciaries are most well placed and capable to match the demands of economic, social and cultural rights as *legal* rights with the dynamics of social and political pressures at the national level. This line of reasoning validates the legitimacy of the power of judicial review.

If properly exercised, judicial review offers the promise of charting the path towards the evolution of a tangible body of jurisprudence on economic, social and cultural rights in Africa. With the varying dismal experiences of maladministration and deep-rooted

628 This was the popular slogan adopted by the World Social Forum in challenging the multifarious socio-economic issues that have been brought into focus by civil society groups in the advent of globalisation. For an insight into the moral appeal and force of this slogan, see Press Release, Amnesty International, 'World social and economic fora: All human rights for all, everyone's responsibility' 23 January 2003 AI INDEX: ACT 79/002/2003.

629 See generally M Kirby 'AIDS and the law: A new challenge for human rights' (1994) 20 *Commonwealth Law Bulletin* 1457-1473; B Toebes 'Towards an improved understanding of the international human right to health' (1999) 21 *Human Rights Quarterly* 661 671 673-674. See also N Sanajaoba *Human rights in the new millennium* (2000) 85- 01.

kleptomaniac governance in many African states, juxtaposed with the increasingly parlous socio-economic realities, the primary thrust of my argument here is the need to establish accountability for decisions taken by state and non-state actors where such lead, directly or indirectly, to human deprivation and suffering; and for the justification of public spending *vis-à-vis* the prioritisation of a qualitative life for Africans.

An effective way to begin the process of evolving a coherent corpus of economic, social and cultural rights jurisprudence in Africa, therefore, will be to consider the trends in relevant national and supranational institutions, the body of jurisprudence emerging from such institutions, and to delineate their marked significance in serving as basis for understanding salient issues of conceptualisation as well as for charting the path towards the progressive development of an economic, social and cultural rights jurisprudence in Africa. I proceed to examine the plenitude of these indices in sequence.[630]

3 Economic, social and cultural rights jurisprudence in the United Nations human rights treaty system

While current discussions on an integrative human rights approach would seem to suggest that economic, social and cultural rights has been an engaging aspect for the treaty-monitoring bodies of the UN human rights system,[631] only the ESCR Committee has an unequivocal and explicit mandate for the protection and promotion of economic, social and cultural rights. Despite this weakness, I argue that the other treaty-monitoring bodies for ICCPR, CERD, CEDAW, CAT, CRC and the Convention on the Rignts of Persons with Disabilities (CRPD) possess mandates that can become vehicles for advancing the interconnectedness principle in Africa.[632] This segment therefore

630 It must be borne in mind that, in respect of all the human rights regimes discussed hereafter in this chapter, I deliberately avoided whatever doctrinal, procedural or philosophical debates that abound in such regimes where engaging therein will take this discourse outside its focus. The only purpose a discussion of 'emerging' jurisprudence will serve is to highlight *how* economic, social and cultural rights have been made justiciable human rights, *how* these species of human rights can become enlivened through the efforts of stakeholders and purveyors, and *how* otherwise reluctant national and intergovernmental judicial and quasi-judicial bodies in Africa can begin to contemplate and evolve pragmatic approaches to securing the protection of economic, social and cultural rights within their respective systems.

631 See Sepulveda (n 80 above) 52.

632 For other views on the 'derivative relations' among UN human rights treaties, see C Scott 'The interdependence and permeability of human rights norms: Towards a partial fusion of the international covenants on human rights' (1989) 27 *Osgoode Hall Law Journal* 769 851-878; C Scott 'Reaching beyond (without abandoning)

considers the integrative currents of UN human rights treaty-monitoring bodies through their salient 'decisions',[633] General Comments, Concluding Observations and Recommendations *only* as far as they provide guidance for understanding stereotyped elements of human rights and in interpreting them in a holistic manner.

3.1 The Committee on Economic, Social and Cultural Rights

The far-reaching efforts of the ESCR Committee in defining the scope and content of economic, social and cultural rights have been considered in many scholarly writings.[634] It will therefore suffice for the present analysis to explore the significance of these efforts for the evolution of a rights-based praxis for human development in Africa.

Notwithstanding its structural constraints, the ESCR Committee has been able to elaborate the terse provisions of ICESCR through its General Comments and Concluding Observations. The ESCR Committee specifically placed a primary duty for the implementation of the provisions of ICESCR on national judiciaries when it asserted:

> Within the limits of the appropriate exercise of their functions of judicial review, courts should take account of Covenant rights ... to ensure that the state's conduct is consistent with its obligations under the Covenant. *Neglect by the courts of this responsibility is incompatible with the principle of the rule of law, which must always be taken to include respect for international human rights obligations.*[635]

In a world still struggling to evolve juridical standards for measuring compliance with economic, social and cultural rights, the ESCR Committee's General Comments have set the tone for identifying the 'minimum core content' of each of the rights so far elaborated, and from which no state or persons should derogate. For instance, General Comment No 14 outlines the four scales of measuring the right to

the category of "economic, social and cultural rights"' (1999) 21 *Human Rights Quarterly* 633 650-651.

633 Although the HRC readily declines to acknowledge that its 'views' under art 5(4) of the first Optional Protocol to ICCPR are 'decisions' as to connote enforcement, some scholars have argued that, since all state parties voluntary subjected themselves to the procedure of the HRC, the outcomes of its deliberations are to be 'treated as the authoritative interpretation of the Covenant under international law'. See Hanski & Scheinin (n 62 above) 21-22.

634 Few among the literature reviewing the interpretive efforts of the ESCR Committee include Craven (n 73 above) 68-93; Sepulveda (n 80 above) 311-378; Scott (n 632 above) 639-640; Leckie (n 114 above) 129-144; KG Young 'The minimum core of economic and social rights: A concept in search of content' (2008) 33 *Yale Journal of International Law* 113.

635 ESCR Committee, General Comment No 9 (n 309 above) para 14 (my emphasis).

health as 'availability, accessibility, acceptability, and quality'.[636] Arbitrary interference by the state with the expectations of individuals to receive medical attention will constitute non-observance of that right. For the right to education, as elaborated in General Comment No 13, the non-negotiable standards are access, facilities and choice.[637] It follows that any act or policy (or omission) of the state that lowers the quality of education in the country breaches the standard. For the right to food, as explained in General Comment No 12, any act or omission of the state that results in the *denial of access* to 'the dietary needs of individuals' breaches that right.[638] In respect of the right to water, the obligation includes 'adopting the necessary and effective legislative and other measures to restrain, for example, third parties from denying equal access to adequate water; and polluting and inequitably extracting from water resources, including natural sources, wells and other water distribution systems'.[639] These illuminating guides are helpful for any conscientious national judiciary to apply in 'reviewing' states' actions or inactions.

In similar vein, at various regional and national levels, the ESCR Committee's General Comments have been taken up, considered and applied in determining diverse cases.[640] Likewise, through its Concluding Observations, the ESCR Committee has been able to establish the parameters of conduct that would constitute violations of ICESCR provisions. A particularly significant aspect is its recognition of a strong linkage between the policies of IFIs and the conditions that impede the full enjoyment of economic, social and cultural rights in borrowing states.[641] Thus, in its Concluding Observations on Egypt, the ESCR Committee had recommended:

> [t]hat Egypt's obligations under the covenant should be taken into account in all aspects of its negotiations with international financial institutions, like the international monetary fund, world bank and the world trade organisation, to ensure that economic, social and cultural

636 General Comment No 14 (n 80 above) 88-89 para 12. See A Chapman 'Core obligations related to the right to health' in *Core obligations* (n 101 above) 185 195.

637 ESCR Committee 'The right to education (art 13)', General Comment No 13, UN Doc E/C12/1999/10, 8 December 1999, in *Compilation of general comments* (n 81 above) 70, 72 para 6. See F Coomans 'In search of the core content of the right to education' in *Core obligations* (n 101 above) 217 225 229-230.

638 ESCR Committee, General Comment No 12 'The right to adequate food (art 11)', UN Doc E/C 12/2000/22 in *Compilation of general comments* (n 81 above) 65 para 8.

639 ESCR Committee, General Comment No 15 (n 81 above) para 23.

640 See cases cited in texts accompanying nn 143-146. Those cases and more are discussed in parts IV and V of this chapter.

641 See ESCR Committee, General Comment No 2 para 6; General Comment No 4, para 19, in *Compilation of general comments* (n 81 above) 12 19.

> rights, particularly of the most vulnerable groups, are not undermined.[642]

In consistent fashion, the ESCR Committee has also emphasised the obligation of 'developed states' to abstain from any policy that may obstruct or violate the implementation and full enjoyment of economic, social and cultural rights in other countries. In its Concluding Observations on Belgium, as an illustration, the ESCR Committee called upon Belgium:

> [a]s a member of international organisations, in particular the International Monetary Fund and the World Bank, to do all it can to ensure that the policies and decisions of those organisations are in conformity with the obligations of states parties to the Covenant, in particular the obligations contained in article 2.1 concerning international assistance and co-operation.[643]

The ESCR Committee has expressed the same position, in identical wording, regarding some other developed states.[644] On the strength of this stance, it is arguable that the obligation in article 2(1) of ICESCR thus entails the duty of states to abstain from supporting or implementing the decisions and policies of bodies such as IFIs that could foreseeably impede the effective realisation of economic, social and cultural rights within national domains. While it has indeed been problematic to ensure the compliance of states, IFIs, TNCs and MNEs with these pronouncements,[645] it is yet possible and practicable for national courts to consider and pronounce on some of these obligations in specific cases where states and their agencies would customarily plead economic incapacity as excuse for the non-implementation of economic, social and cultural rights.

As I mentioned in chapter II, even though the ESCR Committee lacks an explicit adjudicatory mandate, the extensive interpretive activities of the body since its advent in 1985 have helped in giving

642 ESCR Committee 'Consideration of reports submitted by state parties under articles 6 and 17, Egypt' (2000) para 28.

643 ESCR Committee 'Consideration of reports submitted by state parties under articles 6 and 17, Belgium' (2000) para 31.

644 See eg ESCR Committee 'Consideration of reports submitted by state parties under articles 16 and 17, Italy' (2000) para 20; ESCR Committee, Consideration of reports submitted by state parties under articles 16 and 17, Germany (2001) para 31; ESCR Committee 'Consideration of reports submitted by state parties under articles 16 and 17, Japan' (2001).

645 I examine in fuller detail the impact of IFIs, TNCs, MNEs, and other 'non-state actors' on economic, social and cultural rights in ch VI of this book.

content to economic, social and cultural rights and making them less problematic.[646]

3.2 The Human Rights Committee

Since the Human Rights Committee (HRC) issued its General Comment No 6 in 1982, the body has evinced the willingness to read and interpret ICCPR provisions to cover economic, social and cultural rights elements. Apart from the *Zwaan-De Vries* and *Broeks* decisions discussed earlier in chapter II, the HRC has demonstrated this posture in a number of other instances, most of which also relate to social security. The strength of the HRC's engagement with economic, social and cultural rights has been particularly felt in the area of discrimination.[647]

In *Nahlik v Austria*,[648] the HRC had signalled its stance on discriminatory practices when it declared:

> [U]nder articles 2 and 26 of the Covenant the state party is under an obligation to ensure that all individuals within its territory and subject to its jurisdiction are free from discrimination, and consequently the courts of state parties are under an obligation to protect individuals against discrimination, whether this occurs within the public sphere or among private parties in the quasi-public sector of, for example, employment.[649]

Thus, in *Vos v The Netherlands*,[650] where the petitioner was challenging the stoppage of a disability allowance to her on the ground of discrimination under article 26 of ICCPR, although the HRC took the view that 'the facts as submitted do not disclose a violation',[651] it nonetheless seized the opportunity to declare its

646 See text accompanying nn 138-141. For a further discussion of the immense contribution of the ESCR Committee to the development of jurisprudence through its 'quasi-judicial role', see M Craven 'Towards an unofficial petition procedure: A review of the role of the UN Committee on Economic, Social and Cultural Rights' in Drzewicki *et al* (n 311 above) 91 102-103.

647 See eg Communication 180/1984 *Danning v The Netherlands* (9 April 1987), UN Doc Supp 40 (A/42/40) (1987) 151, alleging discrimination in the changes envisaged by two statutes on disability benefits; Communication 196/1983 *Gueye v France* (3 April 1989) UN Doc Supp 40 (A/44/40) (1989) 189, concerning the suspension of pension and life disability annuity due to retired soldiers who were formerly of Senegalese nationality; Communication 786/1997 *Vos v The Netherlands* (29 July 1999) UN Doc CCPR/C/66/D/786/1997, involving a complaint against discriminatory calculation of civil service pension; Communication 716/1996 *Pauger v Austria* (30 April 1999) UN Doc CCPR/C/65/D/716/1996, a complaint about sex-based discrimination in the payment of pensions.

648 Communication 608/1995 (15 July 1996) UN Doc CCPR/C/57/D/608/1995, involving the allegation of discrimination in the income of some retirees.

649 n 648 above, para 8.2.

650 Communication 218/1986, UN Doc A/44/40 (29 March 1989), 232.

651 n 650 above, para 13.

readiness to read the provisions of ICCPR in conjunction with other UN human rights treaties.[652]

In *Pons v Spain,*[653] where the petitioner alleged discrimination in access to public service as well as the denial of his unemployment benefits, the HRC asserted that 'although the right to social security is not protected, as such, in the [CCPR], issues under the Covenant may nonetheless arise if the principle of equality contained in articles 14 and 26 of the Covenant is violated'.[654]

Furthermore, in *Lantsova v The Russian Federation,*[655] where the HRC found that a prisoner had died as a result of overcrowding and other inhuman conditions regarding food and hygiene, the HRC interpreted article 6 of ICCPR on the right to life to encompass the provision of adequate medical assistance. The HRC further held that inhuman conditions of detention violated the provision of article 10 of ICCPR on the right to respect the inherent dignity of detainees.[656]

While the HRC might have been able to exert a stronger output, its proactive contribution to defining some of the *de lege ferenda* contents of economic, social and cultural rights in the face of negative pressure by the states concerned to deny their justiciability deserves commendation. Certainly, the jurisprudence emanating from the HRC can be of great assistance to national judiciaries in the interpretation of non-discriminatory clauses in their respective constitutions and in extending these to define the social and economic dimensions of other human rights. The work of the HRC helps tremendously to demonstrate that in the analysis of any human right, judicial and quasi-judicial bodies can pronounce on the indispensable equality and non-discrimination content of such rights.[657]

652 n 650 above, para 11(2).

653 Communication 454/1991 (30 October 1995), UN Doc CCPR/C/55/D/454/1991.

654 n 653 above, para 9.3. See also Communication 941/2000, *Young v Australia*, UNHR Committee (12 August 2003), UN Doc CCPR/C/78/D/941/2000, involving discrimination in the payment of a war veteran's dependant pension.

655 Communication 763/1997 (15 March 2002), UN Doc CCPR/C/74/D/763/1997.

656 n 655 above, paras 10-11. For similar reasoning on an earlier occasion, see Communication No 458/1991, *Mukong v Cameroon* (21 July 1994), UN Doc CCPR/C/51/D/458/1991.

657 For a comprehensive study of how UN human rights treaty-monitoring bodies have grappled with the subject of discrimination, see Sepulveda (n 80 above) 53-58. See also S Leckie 'Violations of economic, social and cultural rights' in TC van Boven *et al* (eds) *The Maastricht Guidelines on violations of economic, social and cultural rights SIM Special* No 20 (1998) 37 67.

3.3 Other United Nations human rights treaty-monitoring bodies

Although two other key UN human rights treaty-monitoring bodies – the CERD Committee, the CAT Committee and, lately, the CEDAW Committee – do have complaint mandates, their contributions to the development of an integrative human rights approach have usually been considered marginal. The limited scholarly attention to those bodies' approach should, however, not be a ground for dismissing the significance of their mandates in the innovative development of the cross-cutting integration of all human rights.[658]

Contrary to the pessimism usually expressed about the willingness of UN human rights treaty-monitoring bodies to address economic, social and cultural rights, I contend that there exists a sizeable number of decisions confirming their willingness to do so. In one of its most remarkable decisions, *Ylimaz-Dogan v The Netherlands*,[659] the CERD Committee held that both a letter terminating the petitioner's employment on the ground that foreign working mothers were more likely absentees from work and the Cantonal Court's endorsement of the action violated article 5(e)(i) of CERD. The Committee consequently directed that the state party should secure for the petitioner alternative gainful employment.[660]

Also in *Koptova v Slovak Republic*,[661] after the petitioner lost her job along with others who were of Romany roots, their official accommodation was revoked on the ground of what she alleged to be their racial background. The same Committee found for the petitioner and asserted that the right to housing of all minorities must be respected regardless of their 'gender, race', and so on.[662] Further, in *Lacko v Slovak Republic*,[663] where the petitioner challenged a

658 See generally Arambulo (n 123 above) 183; Sepulveda (n 80 above) 54 and text accompanying n 54; Arambulo (n 123 above) 194-195; V Leary 'Lessons from the experience of the ILO' in P Alston (ed) *The United Nations and human rights: A critical appraisal* (1992) 580. See the CEDAW decision in Communication 4/2004, *Andrea Szijjarto v Hungary* (29 August 2006), UN Doc CEDAW/C/36/D/4/2004, asserting the reproductive health rights of the complainant and ordering compensation for violations.

659 Communication 1/1984 (29 September 1998), UN Doc CERD/C/36/D/1/1984.

660 It is extremely important to note that the Committee founded its recommendation on the right to work (art 5(e)(i) CERD). See above para 10.

661 Communication 13/1998 (8 August 2000).

662 n 661 above, para 4. For other cases where the Committee dealt with housing rights, see *LK v The Netherlands* Communication 4/1991 (16 March 1993) UN Doc A/48/18 131; Communication 18/2000, *FA v Norway* (12 April 2001) UN Doc A/56/18 125.

663 Communication 11/1998 (9 August 2001) UN Doc CERD/C/59/D/11/1998. See also Communication 31/2003, *LR* et al *v Slovakia* (10 March 2005), UN Doc CERD/C/66/D/31/ 2003 (2005), asserting the right to equality in the enjoyment of the right to housing for the Roma population.

racially-motivated policy that regulates access to a restaurant, the Committee recommended that the state should immediately adopt legislation to guarantee the right of access to public places to all persons and to sanction refusal of such access.

Apart from those resplendent opinions of the CERD Committee, the effort of the CAT Committee is also instructive. In one of its most significant decisions, *Dzemajl v Yugoslavia*,[664] the Committee found that racial resentment had led to the destruction by fire of a Roma settlement and rendered the 65 petitioners homeless – an implicit breach of the right to housing. The investigations thereafter were shoddy and the state made no effort to alleviate the suffering of the victims. In its decision, the Committee held:

> The positive obligations that flow from the first sentence of article 16 of the Convention include an obligation to grant redress and compensate the victims of an act in breach of that provision. The Committee is therefore of the view that the state party has failed to observe its obligations under article 16 of the Convention by failing to enable the complainants to obtain redress and to provide them with fair and adequate compensation.[665]

What becomes discernible from all the above is that within the scope of their normative mandates, each UN human rights treaty body possesses the capacity to adopt an integrative approach to human rights, even if it would be a gradual effort as seen under the HRC. It would be helpful to the advancement of *all* human rights when scholars and jurists begin to perceive these bodies as strategic instrumentalities toward that end. It is plausible to anticipate that national judicial and quasi-judicial organs would gain tremendous insight from the increasing efforts of these UN human rights treaty-monitoring bodies in grappling with the challenges of implementing economic, social and cultural rights.

4 Economic, social and cultural rights jurisprudence in regional human rights systems

4.1 The European regional human rights system

Whereas the outstanding hallmark of the integrative approach in the work of the HRC is in the principle of non-discrimination, the highpoint of the approach in the European regional human rights

664 Communication 161/2000 (21 November 2002) UN Doc CAT/C/29/D/161/2000.
665 n 664 above, para 9.6.

system is located in the fair trial clause of article 6(1) of the European Convention.[666] The European Court of Human Rights has applied this clause in its broadest terms in a long line of cases, demonstrating how economic, social and cultural rights can receive juridical protection through other human rights norms.

In *Airey v Ireland*,[667] the applicant wanted to obtain an order of judicial separation against her violent husband, but was too indigent to retain the services of a lawyer. The applicant had alleged that her inability to gain access to the determination of her civil rights was contrary to article 6(1). The court upheld her claim, recognising that, since it would be futile for the applicant to conduct her own case successfully through the technicalities of Irish legal procedure, a right to legal assistance arises to give her effective access to court. In its memorable pronouncement acknowledging the socio-economic dimensions of civil and political rights, the European Court said:

> The Court is aware that the further realisation of social and economic rights is largely dependent on the situation - notably financial - reigning in the state in question. On the other hand, the Convention must be interpreted in the light of present-day conditions ... and it is designed to safeguard the individual in a real and practical way as regards those areas with which it deals ... *Whilst the Convention sets forth what are essentially civil and political rights, many of them have implications of a social and economic nature.* The Court therefore considers ... that the mere fact that interpretation of the Convention may extend into the sphere of social and economic rights should not be a decisive factor against such an interpretation; there is no water-tight division separating that sphere from the field covered by the Convention.[668]

This decision is an outstanding landmark symbolising the capability of intergovernmental juridical organs to address the otherwise 'latent' challenges of poverty, social justice as well as human development and livelihood in the course of administering 'legal' justice.[669] Although Scott and Macklem had suggested that the *Airey* decision had become 'unscrupulously absent ... from subsequent case law' of

666 For expositions on the numerous developments that have emerged from this provision in the European regional human rights experience, see P van Dijk *et al* *Theory and practice of the European Convention on Human Rights* (1998) 391-458; LG Loucaides *The European Convention on Human Rights: Collected essays* (2007).

667 *Airey*, 32 Eur Ct HR (9 October 1979) in Series A, Application 6289/73, reprinted in RA Lawson & HG Schemers (eds) *Leading cases of the European Court of Human Rights* (1999) 85.

668 n 667 above, 88 para 15 (my emphasis).

669 See generally K Reid *A practitioner's guide to the European Convention on Human Rights* (1998) 389-393, analysing through the case law of the European Court the 'welfare benefits' dimensions of art 6(1). For a comparative analysis of the cases decided by the European Court prior to 1979, see HC Yourow *The margin of appreciation doctrine in the dynamics of European human rights jurisprudence* (1996) 25-54.

the European Court,[670] the philosophy behind the decision has resonated in many cases thereafter.

In *Benthem v The Netherlands,*[671] the licence granted to the applicant for the installation of a liquid petroleum gas (LPG) storage tank was quashed by higher state authorities. The applicant claimed his right under article 6(1) had been violated as he had no access to an independent tribunal. While this decision would appear to be a purely administrative law matter, the court brought out its economic, social and cultural rights connotations when it held, *inter alia*, that:

> The grant of a licence to which the applicant claimed to be entitled was one of the conditions for the exercise of part of his activities as a businessman. It was closely associated with the right to use one's possessions in conformity with the law's requirements ... a licence of this kind has a proprietary character ... According to the government, Mr Benthem ... could have obtained a licence for another locality. The court is not persuaded by this argument: a change of this kind ... might have had adverse effects on the value of the business and of the goodwill and ... Mr Benthem's contractual relations with his customers and his suppliers.[672]

Moreover, in *Feldbrugge v The Netherlands,*[673] the sickness allowances due to the applicant had been stopped because the *Raad van Beroep* (Appeals Board) had consulted some medical doctors who judged her fit to resume active duties. The applicant claimed that she had not received a fair trial. Taking into cognisance 'the personal and economic nature of the right', the court held that there was a violation of article 6(1).[674]

Apart from the fair trial principle of article 6, the Court has also developed considerable jurisprudence on housing and environmental rights through other provisions of the European Convention. Thus, in *Asker v Turkey,*[675] the applicants had claimed that the demolition of their homes by the Turkish military violated their right to freedom from torture, inhuman or degrading punishment under article 3 of the European Convention.

670 Scott & Macklem (n 589 above) 99.
671 97 ECHR (23 October 1985) in Series A, reprinted in Lawson & Schemers (n 667 above) 178.
672 n 671 above, para 36.
673 99 ECHR in Series A, Application 8562/79 (29 May 1996) reprinted in Lawson & Schemers (n 667 above) 186.
674 n 673 above, n 23. For other cases involving social benefits where the court upheld a violation of art 6(1), see *Deumeland v Germany,* 100 ECHR in Series A (29 May 1986) Application 9384/81, reprinted in Lawson & Schemers (n 667 above) 510; *Salesi v Italy,* 257 ECHR in Series A (15 February 1993), where the court held that 'today the general rule is that article 6(1) does apply in the field of social insurance, including even welfare assistance'. See above 511, sec 19, *Schuler-Zgraggen v Switzerland,* 153 ECHR in Series A (24 June 1993).
675 Application 23185/94 (24 April 1998).

In holding that the manner of demolition violated the applicants' rights to peaceful enjoyment of their property and to respect for their homes, the court emphasised that under article 3, no such violation is justifiable, even during national emergencies.[676]

The court has also examined the perspective of balancing the tension between the demands of development and human rights in other cases. For instance, in *Lopez Ostra v Spain*,[677] where the applicant had alleged that the failure of the state to regulate the pollution-emitting project of a private tannery company resulted in serious health problems for her, the court held that the state had failed to balance the interests of economic development and an individual's right to respect for her home and her private and family life. The court held that there was a violation of article 8.[678]

While the European Court of Human Rights has indeed been active in the integrative human rights approach, the body primarily vested with the responsibility for monitoring economic, social and cultural rights under the (Revised) European Social Charter (ESC) is the European Committee of Social Rights.[679]

Although its mandate was originally limited to the examination of reports of state parties, the Committee has over the years been able to develop a body of economic, social and cultural rights jurisprudence on many of the provisions in the ESC through its consistent interpretative activities.[680] For instance, in assessing the compliance of Denmark, Ireland, Malta, Spain and the United Kingdom with the right of workers to bargain collectively under article 6(1) of

676 See also *Akkus v Turkey*, Application 19153/92 (24 June 1997), where the state's delay in paying compensation to the applicant, whose land had been expropriated for development purposes, was held to have constituted a violation of the right to property under art 1 of Protocol 1 to the European Convention.

677 303 ECHR in Series A (5 December 1994) Application 16798/90.

678 See also *Guerra v Italy* (19 February 1998) Application 14967/89. Compare *Hatton v The United Kingdom* (8 July 2003) Application 36022/97. See J Hyam '*Hatton v United Kingdom* in the Grand Chamber: One step forward, two steps back?' (2003) 6 *European Human Rights Law Review* (2003) 631-640.

679 Art 25, European Social Charter, ETS 35 (1961), entered into force on 26 February 1965 revised by ETS 163 (1996). See the Revised European Social Charter, reprinted in (1996) 14 *Netherlands Quarterly of Human Rights* 343. See Samuel (n 68 above) 461-463; Scott (n 632 above) 656-659; Scheinin (n 175 above) 42-43.

680 Scheinin (n 175 above) 44. See AW Heringa 'The European Social Charter: New initiatives for the improvement of basic social rights protection within the framework of the Council of Europe' in APM Coomans *et al* (eds) *The increasing importance of economic, social and cultural rights* (1994) 30, adopted on 9 November 1995. There is a collective complaint mechanism that would allow complaints to be submitted by employers' organisations, NGOs and trade unions. For a critical analysis of the economic, social and cultural rights profile envisaged under this procedure, see A Hendriks 'Revised European Social Charter' (1996) 14 *Netherlands Quarterly of Human Rights* 341-342; MA Toth 'The right to dignity at work: Reflections on article 26 of the Revised European Social Charter' (2008) 29 *Comparative Labour Law and Policy Journal* 275.

the ESC, the Committee struck down certain restrictive statutes in those states because they were enacted without workers' participation.[681] Since 1999, when the 1995 Protocol to the Revised ESC came into force, the procedure allowing NGOs to submit 'collective complaints' is being perceived as a channel for further development of economic, social and cultural rights jurisprudence at the European regional level.[682]

In *International Commission of Jurists v Portugal*,[683] the applicant INGO had petitioned against the poor and unhealthy working conditions of a large number of children in Portugal, alleging that the state had violated article 7(1) of the European Social Charter for its failure to provide adequate supervision for child labour. The Committee found that there were indeed thousands of children performing heavy-duty tasks, frequently for long hours, and since this was not within the exception recognised under the Charter, it held the state was in violation.[684]

From the foregoing consideration of the developments within the European arrangement, the prospect is manifest that the value of the protection available for economic, social and cultural rights as rights capable of implementation would further appreciate with time.[685]

4.2 The Inter-American regional human rights system

The elaborate structures for human rights implementation monitoring within the Inter-American regional human rights system have quite been active in the promotion and protection of economic, social and cultural rights.[686] It is worthy of mention, however, that, apart from the abounding regional human rights instruments that have become helpful in the remarkable movement of the Inter-American regional

681 Samuel (n 68 above) 140-148.

682 n 681 above. See also Harris *et al* (n 68 above) 366.

683 Complaint 1/1998, CM Res ChS (99) 4.

684 See also *European Roma Rights Centre (ERRC) v Italy*, Complaint 27/2004 (21 December 2005) and *European Roma Rights Centre (ERRC) v Greece*, Complaint 15/2003, involving the systemic violation of the right to housing of the Roma population through evictions; *Autism Europe v France*, Complaint 13/2002, asserting children's rights and the right to education notwithstanding disability.

685 See generally HP Graver 'Welfare state and constitutionalism under the EEA Agreement' in Scheinin (n 335 above) 95; K Fuchs 'The European Social Charter: Its role in present-day Europe and its reform' in Drzewicki *et al* (n 311 above) 151-152 156; O de Schutter 'The protection of social rights by the European Court of Human Rights' in Van der Auweraert *et al* (n 46 above) 207-239.

686 See Baspineiro (n 68 above) 99-110; B Thiele 'Litigating against forced evictions under the American Convention on Human Rights' (2003) 21 *Netherlands Quarterly of Human Rights* 463; J M Pasqualucci 'The right to a dignified life (*vida digna*): The integration of economic and social rights with civil and political rights in the Inter-American human rights system' (2008) 31 *Hastings International and Comparative Law Review* 1.

system towards the protection of economic, social and cultural rights, the consistent stance of the monitoring bodies has been much more the result of the sensitivity of these bodies to the stark and harsh realities of mass poverty and the grim social conditions across the Latin American region.[687]

The positive trend towards an effective protection of economic, social and cultural rights in the Inter-American regional system is primarily anchored on the workings of the Inter-American Commission on Human Rights (Inter-American Commission) as well as the Inter-American Court on Human Rights (Inter-American Court).[688]

The Inter-American Commission had set itself on the path of commitment to the integrative human rights approach at the turn of the 1980s when it asserted that:

> When examining the situation of human rights in various countries, the Commission has had to establish the organic relationship between the violation of the rights to physical safety on the one hand, and the neglect of economic and social rights and suppression of political participation, on the other. That relationship ... is in large measure one of cause and effect ... *The essence of the legal obligation incurred by any government in this area is to strive to attain the economic and social aspirations of its people, by following an order that assigns priority to the basic needs of health, nutrition and education.* The priority of the 'rights of survival' and 'basic needs' is a natural consequence of the right to personal security.[689]

Later, in the face of the environmental pollution resulting from oil industry activities in the Oriente region of Ecuador, the Inter-American Commission unequivocally asserted that the state was not only obliged to prevent oil-related pollution that could threaten the lives and health of people, but is also obliged 'to promote the inclusion of all social sectors ... and transparency' in all the processes

687 See Baspineiro (n 68 above) 101-103. See also J Gideon 'Economic and social rights: Eploring gender differences in a Central American context' in M Molyneux *et al* (eds) *Gender justice, development, and rights* (2002) 173, 186-192.

688 See generally Sepulveda (n 80 above) 50-51, observing that, while the Inter-American Commission has consistently addressed 'the realisation of [economic, social and cultural rights] in its country reports, and takes into consideration the [economic, social and cultural rights] contained in the Declaration when dealing with individual cases, the Inter-American Court has adopted a gradualist approach.

689 Annual report of the Inter-American Commission on Human Rights (1979-1980), IAm Comm of HR, OEA/Ser.L/V/II.50, Doc 13 Rev 1 (1980) 2.

pertaining to energy and other development activities.[690]

Although the body of jurisprudence emerging from the Inter-American regional system is not as elaborate and dynamic as one would have anticipated following the entry into force of the Additional Protocol to the American Convention on Human Rights in the Area of Economic, Social and Cultural Rights (Protocol of San Salvador), 1988,[691] there are positive indications that the individual complaints procedure thereunder will galvanise greater economic, social and cultural rights attention in a short while.[692] Nevertheless, some juridical developments in the Inter-American regional system portend unmistakable implications for economic, social and cultural rights protection in other regional systems.

In one of the most exceptional decisions by the Inter-American Court, *Tingni v Nicaragua*,[693] the applicants alleged that Nicaragua had violated their right to property by failing to demarcate and secure indigenous lands and by approving destructive logging licences to private companies. The Court held that article 21 of the American Convention on Human Rights[694] guaranteed the rights of indigenous peoples to communal property and that for failing to take effective measures to ensure those rights, Nicaragua was in violation of article 21. The Court ordered the payment of compensation to the victims. This is a particularly instructive decision for the African regional system. Even though the right to property is not explicit in ICESCR, article 21 of the African Charter makes it a plain legal entitlement for individuals and communities.

Also of remarkable significance is the Court's decision in *Ricardo v Panama*.[695] Two hundred and seventy government workers who took part in a labour protest had been accused of complicity in a consequent military take-over and were summarily dismissed under a retroactive law. The workers claimed that their rights to due process of law and judicial protection had been violated. Although the Court acknowledged that the Protocol of San Salvador was not applicable in

690 See Inter-American Commission Report of the situation of human rights in Ecuador (1997) OEA/Ser.L/V/II.96, Doc 10 Rev 1, 24 April 1997 81-82. The Commission reaffirmed its position in its follow-up report in 1998. See Inter-American Commission, Follow-up report on compliance by the Republic of Ecuador with the recommendations offered by the Inter-American Commission on Human Rights in its 1997 report on the situation of human rights in Ecuador OEA/Ser.L/V/II.102, Doc 6 Rev 16 April 1999.

691 OASTS 69 (1988), entered into force in 1999.

692 See generally Sepulveda (n 80 above) 51, indicating the increasing focus of human rights NGOs in the Inter-American region on economic, social and cultural rights at the regional level of protection.

693 IACHR (31 August 2001) Series C No 79.

694 (Pact of San Jose), 22 November 1969, OEA/Ser.C/II.5, OASTS 36 (1969), entered into force 18 July 1978.

695 IACHR (2 February 2001) Series C No 72.

the case,[696] it nonetheless held that the state of Panama had violated the fundamental principle of non-retroactivity under article 9, the rights to judicial guarantees and judicial protection provided for in articles 8(1), 8(2) and 25, and the right to freedom of association enshrined in article 16 of the American Convention. The Court ordered the state to reinstate the workers and settle their unpaid salaries, and even awarded the payment of 'moral damages' to each of the 270 workers.[697] This is an epochal decision on economic, social and cultural rights by any intergovernmental juridical body as they affect human survival and livelihood, and is worthy of wholesale emulation.

More recently, in Cinco Pensionistas (Five Retired Persons) v Peru,[698] the Court sustained its proactive approach. The pensions of five workers, who had worked for over 20 years in a governmental agency responsible for supervising banks and insurance companies, were reduced without prior notification. In its judgment, the Court held that pension rights are property rights under article 21 of the Inter-American Convention because they form part of assets and that the reduction without notice to the pensioners was a deprivation of those rights.[699]

The Inter-American Commission has equally made its own mark in the field of economic, social and cultural rights. In Commission v Brazil (Yanomami case),[700] the applicants, who were Yanomami Indians, alleged that in the course of a road construction project, the government of Brazil had displaced them from their ancestral home and exposed them to various epidemics without any effort towards relief. The Commission found that the government of Brazil had violated the right of the applicants under articles VIII and XI of the American Declaration of the Rights and Duties of Man for failing to protect them against deforestation, to provide them with facilities to preserve their heritage, and to protect them from adverse health effects of the forest exploitation.[701]

696 n 695 above, paras 95-96.
697 n 695 above, para 8.
698 *Cinco Pensionistas* (unreported) reprinted in (2003) 21 *Netherlands Quarterly of Human Rights* 540-545.
699 See similar reasoning and conclusion in *Robles v Peru* Case 2.035, Report 75/02 of 13 December 2002 http://www.cidh.oas.org/annualrep/2002eng/Peru.12035.htm (accessed 12 June 2009).
700 *Yanomami*, Case 7615, IAm Comm of HR 12/85 (1985).
701 See also *Commission v Paraguay*, Case 1802, IAm Comm of HR 1802/77 (1977), where the Commission regarded the persecution of the Ache Tribe and the withholding of medical assistance during epidemics as not only violations of civil and political rights, but also of the rights to the protection of the family; to the preservation of health and well-being; and to work.

The *Yanomami* decision has aptly been described as an emphatic illustration of 'the fact that [economic, social and cultural rights] can be adjudicated by quasi-judicial bodies' when they could otherwise have kept themselves under constraints.[702] It is also particularly instructive that through its various decisions, the Inter-American system has opened new vistas to the practicability of remedying abuses of economic, social and cultural rights when they do occur.

Notwithstanding the commendable foray of the Inter-American Court and Commission into the promotion and protection of economic, social and cultural rights, the efforts of these bodies would greatly appreciate when the Protocol of San Salvador eventually obtains overwhelming accession by states in the region.[703]

4.3 The African regional human rights system

The development of a coherent economic, social and cultural rights jurisprudence in the African regional human rights system is still at a formative stage. Although the African Charter abounds with affirmative economic, social and cultural rights provisions, there has been scanty jurisprudence arising therefrom.

Apart from the three cases already mentioned,[704] there is hardly any other noteworthy decision in which the African Commission alluded to specific economic, social and cultural rights in the African Charter.[705] The integrative human rights approach has remained an estranged idea in the African regional human rights system.

It is striking to note that prior to the *Ogoni* decision in 2001, in none of the decisions of the African Commission had the Commission explored the possibility of expanding the content of any of the 'settled' civil and political rights in its broader context to accommodate an economic, social and cultural rights provision of the African Charter. Yet, there is no gainsaying the fact that in virtually all the cases where the African Commission found a violation of a civil

702 Scott & Macklem (n 589 above) 111.

703 See generally GG Giraldo 'Latin America: Challenges in economic, social and cultural rights' (1995) 55 *Review of the International Commission of Jurists* 65-69; Pasqualucci (n 686 above) 15.

704 *Malawi African Association* (n 256 above), *Free Legal Assistance* (n 257 above) and *Ogoni* (n 143 above).

705 See eg *Pagnoulle (on behalf of Mazou) v Cameroon* (2000) AHRLR 57 (ACHPR 1997), where the African Commission found that the victim had not been reinstated to his office of magistracy despite the provision of an Amnesty Law that guaranteed that persons in his category were to be so reinstated. The Commission, *inter alia*, declared the failure of the government to reinstate him to be a violation of the right to work under art 15.

and political right, there was an undertone of economic, social and cultural rights.[706]

While the 'radical' turn-around in the approach of the African Commission to economic, social and cultural rights, as seen in *Ogoni*, is thus to be viewed as a healthy development, the euphoria would have to be tempered with some degree of circumspection.[707] *Ogoni* requires scrutiny by virtue of its potential manifestation as a model, not only for African Commission jurisprudence, but also for that of the emerging regional court system. It is indeed foreseeable that *Ogoni* might most probably become the standard for economic, social and cultural rights implementation in the African regional system for some time to come.[708]

It is therefore apposite, at this juncture, to reflect on some of the salient issues in that decision. The first relates to the normative interpretation of the African Charter's economic, social and cultural rights provisions as rendered by the African Commission. In the wisdom of the African Commission:

> Although the right to housing or shelter is not explicitly provided for under the African Charter, the corollary of the combination of the provisions protecting the right to enjoy the best attainable state of mental and physical health ... under article 16 ... the right to property, and the protection accorded to the family forbids the wanton destruction of shelter because when housing is destroyed, property, health, and family life are adversely affected. *It is thus noted that the combined effect of articles 14, 16 and 18(1) reads into the Charter a right to shelter or housing which the Nigerian government has apparently violated.*[709]

706 See eg *Amnesty International v Zambia* (2000) AHRLR 325 (ACHPR 1999), where the African Commission established that, in deporting the victim, he was 'blindfolded, drugged and dumped across the border', an obvious violation of the right to enjoy the best attainable state of physical and mental health under art 16. See also *Union Interafricaine des Droits de l'Homme v Angola* (2000) AHRLR 18 (ACHPR 1997), where the allegation had primarily been against the deportation of the victims who were West African citizens, contrary to art 12 of the African Charter, the African Commission itself acknowledged that that 'this type of deportations calls into question a whole series of rights ... such as the right to property ... the right to work ... the right to education ...'. The African Commission, in characteristic manner, ended with a mere declaration of 'a violation'. See generally Ouguergouz (n 42 above) 201.

707 See generally J Oloka-Onyango 'Reinforcing marginalised rights in an age of globalisation: International mechanisms, non-state actors, and the struggle for peoples' rights in Africa' (2003) 18 *American University International Law Review* 851 883.

708 See Oloka-Onyango (n 707 above) 866, contending that 'although [*Ogoni*] was not the first case on economic, social and cultural rights handled by the Commission, it certainly is the most prominent'; (n 707 above) 873, noting that, since *Ogoni* 'is well-reasoned and broadly expansive of some of the most critical elements in the conceptualisation of the African Charter ... the decision may represent a coming of age for the [African] Commission'.

709 *Ogoni* (n 143 above) para 60 (my emphasis).

Continuing in the same reasoning, the African Commission asserted that:

> The Communication argues that the right to food is implicit in the African Charter, in such provisions as the right to life (article 4), the right to health (article 16) and the right to economic, social and cultural development (article 22). By its violation of these rights, *the Nigerian government trampled upon not only the explicitly protected rights, but also upon the right to food implicitly guaranteed.*[710]

The petitioners' communication had specifically alleged violations of the right to enjoy the best attainable state of physical and mental health (article 16), the right of all peoples freely to dispose of their wealth and natural resources (article 21), and the right of all peoples to a general satisfactory environment favourable to their development (article 24).[711] As a dynamic petition, it also alleged the violation of the right to adequate housing and the right to food.

However, the reading of the right to food and the right to housing into the contents of the provisions of the African Charter would have served more than purpose of mere impression if only the Commission had seized that opportunity to define and assert the *peculiar* nature of the obligations of states under the African Charter. It is disquieting that the Commission could not mention, even if only in passing, that the obligations created for state parties under the African Charter are *immediate* and are devoid of ICESCR's 'progressive realisation' typology. While the African Commission had found it comfortable to rely extensively on the interpretive efforts of the ESCR Committee in developing the *rationes decidendi* in that case against the government of Nigeria, would there have been credible and justifiable basis for the Commission to apply that same approach were it to have involved a state that is not party to ICESCR? In essence, to what extent can the African Commission's 'exotic' jurisprudence establish an economic, social and cultural rights standard for *all* African states — including Botswana, Comoros, Mauritania, Mozambique and Swaziland — that are neither signatories nor state parties to ICESCR? The African Charter certainly envisages a higher threshold than ICESCR proffers and the Commission will have to reconsider its approach at the earliest opportunity.

It is also particularly regrettable that in reaching its decision in *Ogoni*, the African Commission deftly avoided addressing the

710 *Ogoni* (n 143 above) para 64. See also above paras 65-66 (my emphasis).
711 *Ogoni* (n 143 above) para 10.

controversial issue of what constitutes 'peoples' in article 21.[712] Apart from declaring that Nigeria was in violation of article 21, the Commission could add nothing of jurisprudential value other than to ascribe the origins of that provision 'to colonialism' and the foreign exploitation of a bygone era.[713] Perhaps the African Commission chose to play the ostrich game, once again.[714]

It is not clear whether the African Commission was, by this pronouncement, suggesting that the provision of this African regional human rights treaty adopted in 1981 has become so obsolete that it holds no relevance for the deep and complex geo-political imbalances that are ubiquitous across the states of twenty-first century Africa.[715]

It is equally strange how the entire Commission was led into confusing the Niger Delta with 'Ogoniland'.[716] International scholarship has laboured persistently under this misconception and misrepresentation. Furthermore, just as the African Commission was culpable in abdicating the necessity of defining or analysing the status of the 'Ogoni communities' within the Nigerian context as to qualify them for being 'peoples' under the African Charter, so were the two NGOs that brought the communication equally indictable for subterfuge activism. Beyond merely listing article 21 as one of the rights allegedly violated, the communication presenters neither raised a head of argument particularising the violation nor canvassed

712 See generally P Alston 'Peoples' rights: their rise and fall' in Alston (n 259 above) 286, identifying the ominous lack of description of 'peoples' in the African Charter as one of the main problems in evolving a body of jurisprudence on peoples' rights in Africa. See also P Jones 'Human rights, group rights, and peoples' rights' (1999) 21 *Human Rights Quarterly* 80 99 n 33; RE Howard 'Group versus individual identity in the African debate on human rights' in An-Na'im *et al* (n 563 above) 159 178-179.

713 *Ogoni* (n 143 above) para 56.

714 The history of the African Commission since 1987 shows that it has always avoided pronouncing on the right of peoples to self-determination. See eg *Katangese Peoples' Congress v Zaire* (2000) AHRLR 72 (ACHPR 1995), where the African Commission had declared the communication admissible but eventually evaded the question of defining 'peoples' by simply holding that there was 'no evidence of violations'. See generally Oloka-Onyango (n 707 above) 893, observing that '[t]he African Commission is generally coy about addressing issues that relate to the question of self-determination, and ... prior to the *Ogoni* case, the Commission had only declared admissible one communication concerning the right to self-determination'.

715 See generally P Esterhuysen (ed) *Africa A-Z continental profiles* (1998) 41 45; CO Uroh 'Beyond ethnicity: The crisis of the state and regime legitimation in Africa' in O Oladipo (ed) *Remaking Africa: Challenges of the twenty-first century* (1998) 94 95-105.

716 It is apparent that the African Commission failed to note that in all the correspondence from the Nigerian government during the proceedings, the government consistently referred to 'the Niger-Delta'. See *Ogoni* (n 143 above) para 30. For purposes of records and further empirical studies, the 'Ogoni Communities' constitute a mere fraction of the Niger-Delta region of Nigeria that traverses some eight coastal states of the Nigerian federation. See the decision of the Supreme Court of Nigeria in *Attorney-General of the Federation v Attorney-General of Abia State & 35 Others* (2002) 6 Nigerian Supreme Court Monthly 20

oral arguments to establish that the 'Ogoni communities' were so distinct and particularly affected as to be entitled to the 'exclusive interest' emphasised in article 21(1).[717]

With all the outcomes that many activists, scholars and NGOs had anticipated at the commencement of Ogoni,[718] the remedies afforded by Ogoni have grossly failed to meet the dire circumstances of the victims. I shall reflect more on the remedial dimension of the case in the next chapter.

In the more recent decision of *Purohit and Another v The Gambia*,[719] the complainants had submitted the petition on behalf of inmates of a mental health facility alleging that the conditions of detainees were deplorable and, thus, violated, *inter alia*, articles 16 and 18(4) of the African Charter. The African Commission upheld the allegations without elucidating the rationale for its finding.

Unlike its European and Inter-American counterparts, the African Commission is yet to embrace the culture of defining the core content and minimum obligations of the rights *in the African Charter* - objective standards to apply in subjective cases. Beyond merely holding that violations have actually occurred, the African Commission has the responsibility to elaborate on the right-duty components of each right in the African Charter. That is how coherent jurisprudence would emerge rather than the present system of *ad hoc* fact-finding. I propose that, since the concept of 'progressive realisation' is alien to the African regional human rights system, the obligation of a state party to the African Charter should be assessed based on its *positive* acts and *negative* omissions.[720] It is only when the African Commission demonstrates its willingness and readiness to

186, where the apex Nigerian court deliberated, *inter alia*, on the revenue allocation distribution as it affects the 'eight littoral states of Nigeria'. For an analysis of that decision, see D Olowu 'Re-enacting fiscal federalism in Nigeria: A review of the Supreme Court Decision in *Attorney-General of the Federation v Attorney-General of Abia State & 35 Others*' (2002) 9 *Nigerian Supreme Court Monthly* 172. See also I Okonta *et al Where vultures feast: 40 years of Shell in the Niger-Delta* (2001) 147 178-179, identifying the various 'oil communities' comprising 'twenty-eight ethnic groups in all' in the Niger-Delta region of Nigeria. See also C Quaker-Dokubo 'Ethnic minority problems in the Niger Delta' (2000) 1 *African Journal of Conflict and Resolution* 69 73; D Olowu 'Federalism, the national question and sustainable democracy in Nigeria' in SA Adesina *et al* (eds) *Perspectives on sustainable democratic governance in Nigeria in the new millennium* (2000) 9, analysing the age-long geo-political imbalances in Nigeria and the debates on the 'national question'.

717 See J Bisina 'Conflict and conflict resolution in the Niger Delta: The Bayelsa experience' (2001) 9 *Ife Psychologia* 95 96 103-110; Olowu (n 262 above) 41.

718 See generally D Buhl *Ripple in still water: Reflections by activists on local and national level work on economic, social and cultural rights* (1997) 65-66, expressing the anticipated remedial outcomes of *Ogoni* through 'the use of complaints procedure'.

719 (2003) AHRLR 96 (ACHPR 2003).

720 See Olowu (n 619 above) 197 for my analytical discussion of this theory.

characterise the subsets of rights in the African Charter that national judicial systems would find the regional body relevant.

5 Economic, social and cultural rights jurisprudence in national jurisdictions

Generally, the development of economic, social and cultural rights jurisprudence at national levels reflects an incipient experience. Even in states where there are constitutional guarantees for economic, social and cultural rights, including African states, judiciaries still require inspiration for what should be the objective standards of the involvement required in ensuring the efficacy of such rights.[721]

In this segment, I shall be examining some of the most notable decisions and pronouncements of courts in diverse national jurisdictions.[722] By so doing, I shall be identifying the significance of the reasoning in such cases and accentuate their implications for a new judicial approach to economic, social and cultural rights in Africa. While this dimension of my analysis is not intended to be an exhaustive exposition on every available piece of national judicial decision on the subject, my effort here is aimed at demonstrating that, contrary to the general assumption that economic, social and cultural rights cannot be the subjects of judicial review, there is an emerging body of judicial opinions from which to assess the scope of converging economic, social and cultural rights jurisprudence at national levels.

721 F Piovesan 'Implementation of economic, social and cultural rights: Practices and experiences' in Carbonari (n 40 above) 116 120-121; R Wieruszewski 'Some comments concerning the concept of economic and social rights' in Drzewicki *et al* (n 311 above) 67 71; S Leckie 'Where it matters most: Making international housing rights meaningful at the national level' in S Leckie (ed) *National perspectives on housing rights* (2003) 3 5.

722 Apart from the specific countries from which I have juxtaposed case law here, there remain others in respect of which, although case law were not readily available or the available materials were negligible, there have been quite insightful scholarship on certain positive developments in jurisprudence. See eg S Bouckaert *et al* 'The growing impact of human rights standards on the socio-economic status of undocumented migrants in Belgium: A few illustrations' in Van der Auweraert *et al* (n 46 above) 289, analysing the impact of case law on the right to work and the right to social security in Belgium; G Russell 'Housing rights in Honduras: No housing' in Drzewicki *et al* (n 46 above) 163, reflecting on judicial and civil society efforts in checking the violations of housing rights by the Honduran government. See also DP Kommers *The constitutional jurisprudence of the Federal Republic of Germany* (1997) 241-297, examining the impact of judicial review, *inter alia*, on the protection of the economic, social and cultural rights elements recognised under the German basic law.

5.1 Europe

5.1.1 Nordic countries

The domestic protection of economic, social and cultural rights in the Nordic states of Denmark, Finland, Norway and Sweden and the jurisprudence emanating from those states signify a practicable model of how economic, social and cultural rights can effectively be realised within national jurisdictions.[723] Whereas the justiciability of these rights has for long been mired in the allegation of imprecision in many other domestic contexts, the Nordic states have had the long-standing practice of establishing economic, social and cultural rights as legal entitlements through legislation.[724] Apart from the traditional use of legislation, the role of the courts has been quite significant as they consistently emphasise that the 'principles of indivisibility, interdependence and interrelation contradict the assumption that [economic, social and cultural rights], for instance, health services, are beyond judicial control ...'.[725] Such has been the efficacy of the judicial protection of economic, social and cultural rights in these states (practically denouncing the judicial restraint rhetoric) that Koch and Vedsted-Hansen say:

> There is hardly any clear distinction between law and politics, and *national jurisprudence and human rights jurisprudence show several examples of administration of social welfare which are obliged to respect certain rules and requirements.*[726]

A consideration of some of the judicial decisions lends credence to that assertion. In the *Employment Act* case,[727] the complaint had been that the defendant municipal authority had refused to comply with a statutory obligation to arrange a short-term working chance for a person who had been unemployed for a long time. The Supreme Court of Finland held that the responsibility of the municipality goes beyond simply promoting employment generally, but denotes an express duty to facilitate a six-month job for a qualified person under

723 See generally P Gynther 'The conditions of education for young immigrants in the Nordic welfare states' in Scheinin (n 335 above) 381 388-415, describing how, since the end of World War II, 'all the Nordic countries have gradually developed into more and more matured [rights-based] welfare states'.

724 See Koch *et al* (n 471 above) 195-198.

725 n 724 above, 199.

726 n 724 above, 200 (my emphasis). See also P Ilveskivi 'Fundamental social rights in the Finnish Constitution, with special reference to their enforcement by the administration' in Scheinin (n 335 above) 219 230 235, describing the conceptualisation of social welfare rights in Finnish constitutional jurisprudence as 'fundamental' obligations addressed to 'public authority' and which must be accorded 'direct application'.

727 Judgment of the Supreme Court of Finland, KKO 1997 (1997) No 141 *Yearbook of the Supreme Court* http://www.nordichumanrights.net/tema/tema3/caselaw (accessed 22 November 2008).

the Employment Act. For failing to so provide, the Court ordered the payment of compensation to the affected petitioner.

In another case involving the interpretation of the positive aspect of the constitutional guarantees of economic, social and cultural rights, the *Child Care Services* case,[728] the Finnish Supreme Court followed the same reasoning. Here, under both section 15a(3) of the Constitution of Finland, 1995, and the Act on Child Day Care, 1973,[729] parents had subjective rights to have their school-age children assigned to municipal day care centres provided they submit their application within a prescribed time limit. The Vantaa City authorities delayed in arranging a day care centre for the child of the petitioner, as a result of which the parents had to stay at home and, thus, incurred a loss of income. The Court held that the City was liable to pay damages 'equivalent to the income the family had lost'.[730]

In Norway, in the *Fusa Municipality* judgment,[731] the Norwegian Supreme Court had cause to examine the validity of an administrative decision limiting the monetary benefits due to a disabled elderly Norwegian citizen under statute. Although it acknowledged the wide discretionary powers of the municipality, the Court invalidated the decision because it did not respect the 'minimum core' of the right created thereunder.[732] The stance of the Norwegian Supreme Court on cases involving human survival and livelihood has resonated in many subsequent cases.[733]

728 Case S 98/225, Judgment of the Supreme Court of Finland, KKO 2001 (2001) No 93 *Yearbook of the Supreme Court* http://www.nordichumanrights.net/tema/tema3/ caselaw (accessed 12 June 2009).

729 Act on Day Care, Act 36, 1973, *amended by* Act 630, 1991.

730 As above. See also the *Medical Aids* case, Case 3118, judgment of the Supreme Administrative Court, 27 November 2000 http://www.nordichumanrights.net/tema/tema3/caselaw (accessed 12 June 2009), where the Court held that it was an integral component of the right to medical rehabilitation for the health department of a municipality to provide sufficient shoes for women with special shoe needs. For further discussion on economic, social and cultural rights in Finland generally, and with particular reference to housing rights, see M Scheinin 'Protection of the right to housing in Finland' in S Leckie (n 721 above) 241.

731 Judgment of the Supreme Court of Norway, 25 September 1990, reprinted in *Rettstidende* (Norway Legal Magazine) (1990) 874.

732 n 731 above, 876. See also Koch *et al* (n 471 above) 200-203.

733 See eg the *Borthen* judgment, judgment of the Supreme Court of Norway, 8 November 1996, reprinted in *Rettstidende* (Norway Legal Magazine) (1996) 1415, and the *Thunheim* judgment, judgment of the Supreme Court of Norway, 8 November 1996, reprinted in *Rettstidende* (1996) 1440, in both of which the Court held that, while the legislature was free to make and amend its statutes, any unreasonable retroactive changes, as purported under the legislation in these cases – to reduce spousal supplement and supplementary pension, respectively – will be unconstitutional and void under art 97 of the Constitution of Norway, 1995.

5.1.2 Hungary

The Constitutional Court of Hungary's decision in the *Benefits* case[734] manifested a plausible channel of compromise in what the attitude of a domestic court could be when addressing the 'political' dimension of economic, social and cultural rights. The maternity and child welfare benefits ordinarily made available to citizens applying for it were to become limited to only those people considered as being in need of such benefits under the Economic Stabilisation Act, 1995. Upon challenge by some litigants who claimed that the legislation would violate their social security right as guaranteed under the Hungarian Constitution, the Constitutional Court acknowledged the discretion of the executive in policy making, but emphasised that welfare support benefits could not be lowered beyond a minimum threshold.

5.1.3 Germany

The preservation of the fundamental principles of equality and non-discrimination, which are often in question in the protection of economic, social and cultural rights, was pivotal in the German Constitutional Court's decision in the *Numerus Clausus I* case.[735] Several German universities, including Hamburg and Bavaria, had imposed restrictions on the number of students that would be admitted annually. Many students who could not secure admission to medical schools instituted an action claming that the restrictions were arbitrary and had violated their rights freely to choose their occupation as well as their right to equality as guaranteed under articles 12(1), 20 and 28 of the German Basic Law. In its judgment, the Court held that the state was obliged to establish that the restrictions were necessary and that the available spaces were equitably distributed. The Court therefore upheld the claim of the complainants.[736]

The German Constitutional Court has remained unwavering in upholding equality and non-discrimination as cardinal values in German constitutionalism. Twenty years after the *Numerus* case, in the *Nocturnal Employment* case,[737] a supervisor who had been convicted for engaging women as night workers in a confectionery factory challenged the statute on the ground that it violated the rights to the equality of men and women and freedom from

734 Constitutional Court of Hungary, Judgment 43/1995 (*trans* S Obesk).
735 *Numerus* (1972) 33 BVerfGE 303. See E de Wet *The constitutional enforceability of economic and social rights: The meaning of the German constitutional model for South Africa* (1998) 43-47 56 98.
736 See also De Wet (n 735 above) 37 48-49 54-70.
737 (1992) 85 BVerfGE 191.

discrimination on grounds including sex under article 3 of the German Basic Law. The Court held that both the prohibition against the employment of women as night workers as well as the fine imposed were incompatible with the Basic Law and were thus void.[738]

5.2 Latin America

Despite the formidable social, economic and political challenges confronting most states of Latin America, the courts in a number of those countries have made a significant contribution to the development of jurisprudence on various aspects of economic, social and cultural rights.[739]

5.2.1 Argentina

The Argentine judiciary in *Viceconti v Ministry of Health and Social Welfare*[740] aptly demonstrated the capability of national courts to define the core obligations of economic, social and cultural rights as 'legal' rights. The suit was instituted to obtain a court order compelling the government of Argentina to protect the health rights of people living in an area seriously affected by hemorrhagic fever and, particularly, to provide the required vaccines. According to the court, the right to health, as guaranteed under the Universal Declaration, ICESCR and the American Declaration, is capable of giving rise to an action by an individual by virtue of the Argentine Constitution, 1998. The court upheld the claims of the applicants and ordered ancillary reliefs to secure the manner of executing the judgment.[741]

5.2.2 Colombia

The menacing upsurge in the HIV/AIDS pandemic has presented the Constitutional Court of Colombia with its most notable engagement with the direct protection of economic, social and cultural rights. In

738 See a detailed analysis of this decision in *Kommers* (n 722 above) 291.

739 See generally Giraldo (n 703 above) 61; J Gideon 'Economic and social rights: Exploring gender differences in a central American context' in N Craske *et al* (eds) *Gender and the politics of rights and democracy in Latin America* (2002) 173; Pasqualucci (n 686 above) 18; C Fairstein 'Positive remedies: The Argentine experience' in J Squires *et al* (eds) *The road to a remedy: Current issues in the litigation of economic, social and cultural rights* (2005) 139.

740 Causa No 31.777/96, *Poder Judicial de la Nacion*, 2 June 1998.

741 See also *Defensoria de Menores Nro 3 v Poder Ejecutivo Municipal*, Tribunal Superior de Justicia (Superior Justice Court), Neuquen, 2 March 1999, upholding the decision of the lower court that had ordered the provision of drinkable water to the families living in a rural colony. The court relied on CRC in its judgments.

the case of *Gomez v Hospital Universitario del Valle Evaristo Garcia*,[742] the complainant had claimed that under articles 13, 23, 49 and 86 of the Colombian Constitution, he was entitled, as 'an indigent person suffering from the serious illness known as AIDS [to be] supplied with the necessary medical services and specialised tests, free of charge'.[743] In its well-reasoned judgment, the Court declared:

> The fundamental right to equal protection, in its modality of special protection for persons in circumstances of manifest vulnerability, is a right of immediate application ... AIDS is a fatal illness. *The delivery of health services to AIDS patients is an imperative which arises from the solidarity and respect for human dignity which our judicial system proclaims and seeks to make effective.*[744]

The Court therefore held that the refusal of the hospital to provide the complainant with the relief services guaranteed by law was a violation of the Constitution that guarantees equal 'special protection' to all persons who are in position of 'manifest vulnerability'.[745]

5.2.3 *Venezuela*

In the face of the HIV/AIDS epidemic in Venezuela, its judiciary is putting up a commendable effort in assuaging the plight of the mass of victims. In the landmark judgment in *Cruz Bermudez v Ministerio de Sanidad y Asistencia Social* (Ministry of Health and Social Assistance),[746] the Supreme Court adopted a liberal interpretation of the rights to life (article 58 of the Venezuelan Constitution, 1961), the right to health (article 76) in ordering the Ministry of Health and Social Assistance to provide HIV/AIDS medication for the 170 petitioners.

It is significant to note that in granting this *amparo* relief, the Court extended its coverage to all Venezuelans. Apart from the right to health, however, the same court has also intervened in securing

742 See *Tutela* (Proceedings) No T-505/92 Constitutional Court of Colombia, 22 August 1992.

743 n 742 above, para 1.

744 n 742 above, para 7 (my emphasis).

745 n 742 above, para 8. See also *Mora v Bogota District Education Secretary*, Decision T-170/03, Colombian Constitutional Court, 28 February 2003, where the Court invalidated the location of a pupil to a public school not of that in which she resides with her parents. The Court declared that the positive obligation to provide education must be construed as implying effective access to education. The Court held that the costs of transportation would not secure the right of the child and, consequently, it ordered her relocation.

746 Case 15.789, Supreme Court of Venezuela Judgment 916 (15 July 1999). For a scholarly analysis of this decision, see MA Torres 'The human right to health, national courts, and access to HIV/AIDS treatment: A case study from Venezuela' (2002) 3 *Chicago Journal of International Law* 105; J George 'HIV-AIDS' http://www.lawyerscollective.org/lc-hiv-aids/magazine_articles/june_2002.htm (accessed 12 June 2009).

the protection and implementation of the right to education. In *Iván José Sánchez v Universidad Simón Bolivar,*[747] the petitioners had claimed that the introduction of tuition fees at the Simón Bolivar University violated both the constitutional provision on the right to education and ICESCR. In granting an *amparo* relief to the aggrieved students, the court held that the introduction of compulsory tuition fees violated article 78 of the Venezuelan Constitution, 1961, as amended in 1999, that obligates the state to guarantee ace to education for all individuals.

5.3 Asia-Pacific

5.3.1 India

In his assessment of the Indian judiciary's efforts at giving life to the otherwise non-justiciable provisions on Directive Principles in the Indian Constitution, Rao says: 'From ... a restrictive and narrow definition of human rights, the Supreme Court has expanded the scope of enforceable rights such as the right to life and liberty'.[748] It is particularly striking to note that the pivot of the Indian judicial approach to the expansive and proactive interpretation of fundamental rights have been the Directive Principles, which, technically speaking, are non-justiciable. The Supreme Court has resoundingly reaffirmed the status of the Directive Principles as being the non-negotiable corollary of fundamental human rights.[749] This reconceptualisation has meant a sustained commitment to the integrative approach to all human rights in Indian courts. A long line of cases demonstrates this assertion.

In the groundbreaking case of *Maneka Ghandi v Union of India,*[750] the applicant's passport had been seized by the authorities pursuant to the Emergency Orders of that period and, thus, she had been denied the opportunity to travel abroad. Observing that any procedure affecting any human rights must not be 'arbitrary, fanciful

747 *Sanchéz*, Supreme Court of Venezuela judgment http://www.escr-net.org/EngGeneral/ CaseLawSearchResult.asp (accessed 28 June 2008).

748 Rao (n 443 above) 64. Art 21 of the Indian Constitution provides: 'No person shall be deprived of his life or personal liberty except according to procedure established by law.' For an insight into how the National Human Rights Commission of India, in partnership with civil society, has been of tremendous assistance in monitoring the implementation of the Supreme Court's decisions on human rights, see SC Jain 'The Commonwealth and human rights: An Indian perspective' (1999) 25 *Commonwealth Law Bulletin* 117 128-132.

749 In *Minerva Mills Ltd v Union of India* AIR 1980 SC 1789, the Supreme Court declared that '[t]hose [fundamental human] rights are not an end in themselves but are the means to an end. The end is specified in Part IV [Directive Principles].' See *Minerva Mills* (above) 1806-1807, *per* Chief Justice Chandrachud. See also *Bharati v State of Kerala* AIR 1973 SC 14611641.

750 *Ghandi*, AIR 1978 SC 597.

or oppressive',[751] the Indian Supreme Court seized the opportunity of *Ghandi* to affirm that the right to life entrenched in article 21 of the Indian Constitution also covered the right to travel abroad.

This case was to mark a historic defining moment for the Indian judiciary as well as human rights protection in years to follow.[752] While *Ghandi* had arisen as an action in defence of the right to personal liberty, its broader effects have been felt in the areas of criminal justice, judicial review, contracts, ecology, fundamental rights as well as other 'implied fundamental rights', including education, legal aid, pollution-free environment, livelihood and human dignity.[753] The proactive approach of the Indian judiciary to many questions involving social justice, individual liberty, human development, labour rights and poverty alleviation has been the offshoot of the judiciary's commitment to this 'creative interpretative process' that considers a fundamental human right to 'mean merely animal existence [when it is bereft of] human dignity'.[754]

Thus, in *Olga Tellis v Bombay Municipal Corporation*,[755] the petitioners, who were slum dwellers, had petitioned against their forcible eviction by the defendant corporation, alleging a violation of their right to life under article 21. The Supreme Court held that the right to life conferred by article 21 of the Indian Constitution

751 n 750 above, 24.

752 See *Antulay v Naik*, AIR 1992 SC 1701 1717, where the Supreme Court described the transformative influence of the provision of art 21 in Indian constitutionalism as follows: 'Article 21 got unshackled from the restrictive meaning placed upon it ... It came to acquire a force and vitality hitherto unimagined. A burst of creative decisions of this Court fast on the heels of *Maneka Ghandi* gave a new meaning to the article and expanded its content and connotation.'

753 MP Jain 'The Supreme Court and fundamental rights' in SK Verma *et al* (eds) *Fifty years of the Supreme Court of India: Its grasp and reach* (2000) 1 43 51-52. See, eg, *Vellore Citizens' Welfare Forum v Union of India*, AIR 1996 SC 3399, where the Supreme Court laid down the fundamental rule that precautionary measures must be taken by the state and other authorities in the anticipation and prevention of causes of environmental degradation; *Vishaka v State of Rajasthan* AIR 1997 SC 3011, where the Supreme Court held the workplace sexual harassment of a woman to be a violation of her rights to equality, life and liberty under arts 14, 15 & 21; *Krishnan v State of Andhra Pradesh*, AIR 1993 SC 2178, where the Supreme Court acknowledged that the provision of education depended on the economic capacity of the state. It held that the commercialisation of education could not be permitted. The Court further established that, under art 21, the right to education until the age of 14 is a fundamental right; *Shetty v The International Airport Authority of India* AIR 1979 SC 259, where the Supreme Court established the rule that, although the discretion of awarding contracts for state projects vested in the government, such discretion must be rational, relevant and non-discriminatory'. See above 157; and *Hoskot v State of Maharashtra*, AIR 1978 SC 1548, where the Supreme Court declared that the right to legal aid and speedy trial was an integral part of art 21.

754 n 742 above, 43 30.

755 *Tellis* AIR 1986 SC 180.

extended to the right to livelihood, and that, in this particular instance, the eviction of the slum dwellers would deprive them of livelihood and, invariably, life. Even though the applicants had failed to demand that the corporation allowed the slum dwellers to show why they should not be evicted, the Court ordered that further evictions must cease until the end of the prevailing monsoon season, to mitigate their hardship.[756] The Court explained the basis of its decision as follows:

> The sweep of the right to life conferred by article 21 is wide and far-reaching. It does not mean merely that life cannot be extinguished or taken away as, for example, by the imposition and execution of the death sentence, except according to procedure established by law ... An equally important facet of that right is the right to livelihood because, no person can live without the means of living, that is, the means of livelihood. *If the right to livelihood is not treated as a part of the constitutional right to life, the easiest way of depriving a person of his right to life would be to deprive him of his means of livelihood to the point of abrogation.* Such deprivation would not only denude the life of its effective content and meaningfulness but it would make life impossible to live. Yet, such deprivation would not have to be in accordance with the procedure established by law, if the right to livelihood is not regarded as a part of the right to life. That, which alone makes it possible to live, leave aside what makes life livable, must be deemed to be an integral component of the right to life.[757]

The Indian judiciary has consistently shown in many other instances that it will not abandon the helpless to the vicissitudes of life. In *Samity v State of West Bengal*,[758] involving a petitioner who had suffered serious cerebral injuries occasioned by a train accident, the

[756] 'Monsoon' refers to the volatile climatic torrents that sweep sporadically and unpredictably across India and the South Asian region annually, creating adverse weather conditions.

[757] n 755 above, paras 79F-H & 80A-B (my emphasis). This reasoning was applied in the more recent case of *Anthony v Bihar Gold Mines Ltd* AIR 1999 SC 1416, where a government worker had his employment and salary suspended while disciplinary action was being considered. The court held that he must be paid subsistence allowance' notwithstanding the interdiction. In the court's words, '[n]on-payment of subsistence allowance is an inhuman act which has an unpropitious effect on the life of an employee'; see 1423. See also *Coralie v Union Territory of Delhi* AIR 1981 SC 746 753, where the same court declared: 'We think that the right to life includes the right to live with human dignity and all that goes along with it, namely, the bare necessities of life such as adequate nutrition, clothing and shelter over the head and facilities for reading, writing and expressing oneself in diverse forms, freely moving about and mixing and commingling with fellow human beings.'

[758] AIR 1996 SC 2415.

Supreme Court held that, under article 21, he had a right to 'timely medical treatment'.[759]

The effect of the proactive stance of the Indian judiciary has also been felt in the fields of industrial, labour and trade practices.[760] In a slew of cases, for instance, the Supreme Court has held that the 'equal pay for equal work' principle in article 39(d) of the Indian Constitution was within the expanded scope of articles 14 and 21.[761]

In addition, in *Randhirin Shri Literam Sugar Co Ltd v Union of India*,[762] citing the Directive Principles, the Supreme Court held that the price control on foodstuffs was in the public interest.[763]

The manner of consistency and clarity with which the Indian Supreme Court has been administering social justice through its efficacious protection of the 'implied' economic, social and cultural rights in the Indian Constitution has led a scholar to proclaim that 'after *Maneka Ghandi*'s case, the Court began to apply the fair and reasonable requirements of law, not only to deprivation of life, but also to the well-ordered concept of human dignity and life'.[764] The Indian approach to human rights certainly portends strategic implications for other countries of the developing world.

759 n 758 above, 2429. See also *Panikulangara v India* AIR 1987 SC 990, laying the precedent for the judicial principle that access to medical treatment is an integral part of the right to life under art 21); *Kataria v Union of India* AIR 1989 SC 2039, upholding the claim of the victim to the right to assistance by a medical doctor. For an extensive analysis of concerted efforts of various cadres of the Indian judiciary to incorporate the right to health into the fundamental right to life, see Shah (n 440 above) 475-484.

760 See generally MR Jois 'The Supreme Court on service law governing employees of state' in Verma *et al* (n 753 above)127-155; B de Villiers 'The socio-economic consequences of directive principles of state policy: Limitations on fundamental rights' (1992) 8 *South African Journal on Human Rights* 188-199. See also *Bandhua Mukti Morcha* (n 610 above), where the Supreme Court read art 21 in conjunction with the directive principles in arts 39(e)(f), 41 and 42, to hold that bonded labour was unconstitutional, constituting a 'gross and revolting violation of constitutional values', *per* Justice Bhagwati, above 811. For an analysis of other judicial decisions on these issues, see Rao (n 443 above) 66-67.

761 See eg *Singh v Union of India* AIR 1982 SC 879; *Singh v J & K*, AIR 1986 SC 584; *Federation of Stenographers v Union of India*, AIR 1988 SC 1291.

762 (1990) I SCR 909.

763 See *Khandsari v State of Uttar Pradesh* (1981) SC 873, for an earlier decision on an identical point. See also *Shantistar Builders v Totane* AIR 1990 SC 630, 633, where the Supreme Court held that the right to life included the right to 'food, clothing, shelter and a decent environment'.

764 TR Andhyarujina 'The evolution of due process of law by the Supreme Court' in Kirpal *et al* (n 610 above) 193 204. For an assessment of the proactive drive of the Indian Supreme Court between 1950 and 2000, see V Sripati 'Towards fifty years of constitutionalism and fundamental rights in India: Looking back to see ahead' (1998) 14 *American University International Law Review* 413 439-452.

5.3.2 *The Philippines*

The Supreme Court of the Philippines added its own forward-looking dimension to the integrative human rights approach in the celebrated case of *Minors Oposa v Department of Environment and Natural Resources*.[765] The petitioners had instituted the action complaining that the continuous issuance of timber logging licenses was a violation of 'the right of the people to a balanced and healthful ecology in accord with the rhythm and harmony of nature' as guaranteed by Section 16 of the Philippines Constitution, 1987. The petitioners contended that the incessant tree felling led to deforestation and would not only impair the rights of the present generation of human beings but also their succeeding generations.

In its judgment, the learned Court declared:

> It must ... be emphasised that the political question doctrine is no longer the insurmountable obstacle to the exercise of judicial power or the impenetrable shield that protects executive and legislative actions from judicial inquiry or review.[766]

The Court held that the government of the Philippines must cease the provision of logging licences to the corporate body in order to preserve the health of present and future generations of Filipinos.

5.3.3 *Australia*

Although a conservative institution, the judiciary in Australia has had to contend with the impact of the HIV/AIDS pandemic as it relates to family matters, discrimination, employment, and even issues involving the rights of accused persons during trial.[767]

In *R v McDonald*,[768] an accused person had been aware of his positive HIV status at the time of his sentencing, but had not disclosed that fact. It was shown on appeal that, because of his HIV status, he had been transferred to a special section of the prison where there were more restrictive health conditions. The Court of Criminal Appeal held, *inter alia*, that that treatment was discriminatory. According to the Court:

> The very nature of the confinement in the assessment unit imposes hardships, including the lack of opportunity that would exist in other sections of the prison for the appellant to determine who his associates

765 *Minors Oposa* 33 ILM 173 (1994).
766 n 765 above, para 3, *per* Hon Eriberto U Rosario, presiding judge.
767 See MD Kirby 'AIDS legislation – Turning up the heat?' (1985) 60 *Australian Law Journal* 324.
768 (1988) 38 A Crim R 470 (CCA NSW).

> would be ... While so confined, the appellant would have reduced opportunities for courses of education ... A further consequence of confinement ... is the loss of opportunity for remissions.[769]

There are positive indications that the Australian judiciary will progressively continue to respond to the HIV dimension in future cases in increasing measure.[770]

5.4 Africa

5.4.1 South Africa

Although South Africa is yet to ratify ICESCR, over the years, the ESCR Committee's interpretations of ICESCR and its General Comments have proven to be veritable tools in developing South African jurisprudence on economic, social and cultural rights. Rather than being evasive, the South African judiciary had, very early in its post-apartheid life, courageously engaged the question of the fiscal implications of *all* human rights. In *In Re: Certification of the Constitution of the Republic of South Africa,*[771] the Constitutional Court of South Africa had declared:

> [M]any of the civil and political rights entrenched ... will give rise to similar budgetary implications without compromising their justiciability. The fact that socio-economic rights will almost inevitably give rise to such implications does not seem to be a bar to their justiciability. At the very minimum, socio-economic rights can be negatively protected from improper invasion.[772]

Through a plethora of judicial decisions of the Constitutional Court, constitutional provisions on economic, social and cultural rights have received pronouncements that recognise their justiciability while at the same time demonstrating that it will not perfunctorily interfere with the budgetary commitments of the state and its agencies. The *locus classicus* was the case of *Soobramoney v Minister of Health, KwaZulu*-Natal,[773] where the Court was called upon, *inter alia,* to decide on whether the applicant's claim to renal dialysis treatment at

769 n 768 above, 490-491. See also RT Andrias 'Shed your roles – Three reasons for aggressive judicial leadership in coping with the HIV epidemic' (1990) 29 *Judges Journal* 2 7.

770 See generally RT Andrias 'Urban criminal justice: Has the response to the HIV epidemic been fair?' (1993) 20 *Fordham Urban Law Journal* 497-12; M Kirby 'Courts and justice in the era of HIV/AIDS' (2000) 15 *Commonwealth Law Bulletin* 1277 1281; EA Reid 'Re-thinking human rights and the HIV epidemic: A reflection on power and goodness' in N Stephenson *et al* (eds) *Testing, trials and re-thinking human rights: Reflections from the HIV pPandemic* (2005) 20-23.

771 1996 4 SA 744 (CC).

772 n 771 above, para 78.

773 1998 1 SA 765 (CC).

a state hospital fell within the scope of 'emergency treatment' under section 27(3) as envisaged in sections 26(2) and 27(2) of the 1996 Constitution (the right of access to health care). In its judgment, the Court had established the philosophical foundations of its approach to socio-economic conditions in South Africa when it stated:

> We live in a society in which there are great disparities in wealth. Millions of people are living in deplorable conditions and in great poverty. There is a high level of unemployment, inadequate social security, and many do not have access to clean water or to adequate health services. These conditions already existed when the Constitution was adopted and a commitment to address them, and to transform our society into one in which there will be human dignity, freedom and equality, lies at the heart of our new constitutional order. For as long as these conditions continue to exist that aspiration will have a hollow ring.[774]

In its wisdom, the Court went on to interpret the rights in question in their broader constitutional context as follows:

> What is apparent from these provisions is that the obligations imposed on the state by sections 26 and 27 concerning access to housing, health care, food, water and social security are dependent upon the resources available for such purposes, and that the corresponding rights themselves are limited by reason of the lack of resources. Given this lack of resources and the significant demands on them that have already been referred to, an unqualified obligation to meet these needs would not presently be capable of being fulfilled.[775]

Another landmark decision on economic, social and cultural rights is the later decision of the South African Constitutional Court in *Grootboom*,[776] where the apex Court made the following reverberating pronouncement:

> [The 1996] Constitution entrenches both civil and political rights and social and economic rights. All the rights in our Bill of Rights are inter-related and mutually supporting. *There can be no doubt that human dignity, freedom and equality, the foundational values of our society, are denied those who have no food, clothing or shelter.* Affording socio-economic rights to all people therefore enables them to enjoy the other

774 n 773 above, para 8.

775 n 733 above, para 11. Although the claimant's relief was not granted, the court asserted that, while the state has a margin of discretion in determining which measures it will implement and how it will utilise its resources, it must show that it is exercising its discretion rationally and in good faith. For a dialectical analysis of this case, see De Waal *et al* (n 333 above) 431-454. For a decision where the Constitutional Court of South Africa accentuated the positive obligations of civil and political rights and the budgetary connotations therein, see *August v Electoral Commission* 1999 3 SA 1 (CC), upholding the right of prisoners to participate in general elections.

776 *Grootboom* (n 144 above).

> rights enshrined in chapter 2. The realisation of these rights is also key to...race and gender equality and the evolution of a society in which men and women are equally able to achieve their full potentials.[777]

In that case, the Court considered the legality of the conduct of a local authority in evicting a group of squatters who had moved onto land that had been earmarked for low-cost housing. A magistrate's court had ordered the squatters to vacate the land by a certain date or face eviction. However, the eviction, under the control of the municipality, took place a day earlier and in circumstances that got the squatters' homes bulldozed, their building materials and many of their possessions deliberately destroyed. This was, according to the Court, a violation of the obligations in the constitutional guarantees. In its analysis of section 26, which guarantees the right of access to adequate housing, the Court re-asserted the international obligation that the state must not only restrain itself from interfering in the enjoyment of economic, social and cultural rights, but also specifically that the state has a duty to 'create the conditions for access to adequate housing for people at all economic levels' of society, 'including those who cannot provide themselves with housing'.[778]

In considering whether the housing policies and programmes of the state and its agencies met the obligations in section 26(2), the Court held that those programmes adopted by the state fell short of the requirements of that section in that no provision was made for relief to the categories of people identified as being in desperate need.[779]

777 n 144 above, paras 23 & 35 (my emphasis).

778 n 144 above, paras 35-36.

779 n 144 above, paras 67-69.The *Grootboom* decision has become a radiant guiding force in many subsequent economic, social and cultural rights cases in South Africa. See eg *Port Elizabeth Municipality v Various Occupiers* 2004 12 BCLR 1268 (CC); *Khosa v Minister of Social Development* 2004 6 SA 505 (CC); *President of the Republic of South Africa & Another v Modderklip Boerdery (Pty) Ltd & Others* 2005 8 BCLR 786 (CC); *Occupiers of 51 Olivia Road, Berea Township & 197 Main Street, Johannesburg v City of Johannesburg & Others* 2008 5 BCLR 475 (CC). See also *Hoffman v South African Airways* 2000 11 BCLR 1211 (CC), where the refusal of the airline to employ the applicant solely because of his HIV-positive status was declared to be unfair discrimination and unconstitutional. All the cases mentioned here have received unmistakable scholarly attention from within and outside South Africa. Revisiting the wealth of literature here will add no value than perhaps to becloud the thrust of our discussion. For some of the scholarly efforts on these cases, see S Khosa 'Reducing mother-to-child transmission of HIV' (2004) 3 *ESR Review* 2; K Iles 'Limiting socio-economic rights: Beyond the internal limitations clauses' (2004) 20 *South African Journal on Human Rights* 448; DM Davis 'Adjudicating the socio-economic rights in the South African Constitution: Towards "deference lite"' (2006) 22 *South African Journal on Human Rights* 301; D Brand 'Socio-economic rights and courts in South Africa: Justiciability on a sliding scale' in F Coomans (ed) *Justiciability of economic and social rights: Experiences from domestic systems* (2006) 207-236; C Mbazira 'Confronting the problem of polycentricity in enforcing the socio-economic rights in the South African Constitution' (2008) 23 *SA Public Law* 30.

The implications of *Grootboom* for African states in developing a coherent economic, social and cultural rights jurisprudence cannot be overemphasised. *Grootboom* is a radiant testimony to the capacity of national courts to declare that a government policy fails the standard of reasonableness particularly where the basic needs of the most vulnerable are involved.

In yet another celebrated case, Minister of Health v Treatment Action Campaign,[780] the applicants, a coalition of South African HIV/AIDS NGOs, had sought, *inter alia*, orders for the provision of Nevirapine drugs and the establishment of a comprehensive national programme for the prevention of mother-to-child HIV transmission. It is significant, for our present purposes, to note that in asserting the justiciability of the right in article 27, and indeed every socio-economic right in the Bill of Rights, the Constitutional Court proclaimed:

> The Constitution contemplates rather a restrained and focused role for the courts, namely, to require the state to take measures to meet its constitutional obligations and to subject the reasonableness of these measures to evaluation. Such determinations of reasonableness may in fact have budgetary implications, but are not in themselves directed at rearranging budgets. In this way the judicial, legislative and executive functions achieve appropriate constitutional balance.[781]

Apart from holding that the subsisting programme was inflexible, unreasonable and amounted to 'a breach of the state's obligations under section 27(2) read with section 27(1) of the Constitution', the apex Court ordered the government to 'remove the restrictions' that prevent the use of Nevirapine, without delay to 'permit and facilitate' its use, and to

> take reasonable measures to extend the testing and counselling facilities at hospitals and clinics throughout the public health sector to facilitate and expedite the use of Nevirapine for the purpose of reducing the risk of mother-to-child transmission of HIV.[782]

It was clear from the specific orders sought by the applicants that they had learnt so much from the weaknesses of Grootboom.[783] But beyond the purview of state obligations under the South African Constitution, scholarly efforts are now focusing at the possibilities of

780 2002 5 SA 721 (CC); 2002 10 BCLR 1033 (CC).
781 n 780 above, para 38.
782 n 780 above, para 135.
783 For a scholarly insight into the impressive progress made in economic, social and cultural rights advocacy in South Africa between the *Grootboom* and *Treatment Action Campaign* decisions, see J Fitzpatrick *et al* '*Republic of South Africa v Grootboom* and *Minister of Health v Treatment Action Campaign*' (2003) 97 *American Journal of International Law* 669 677-680.

giving these provisions horizontal application through the expansive interpretation of section 8 of the 1996 Constitution, such that would make the negative components of these obligations have effect in the private domain as well as making them directly relevant in government policy strategies.[784]

As regards accessibility by citizens to economic, social and cultural rights, the South African Constitution contains generous provisions relating to legal standing, allowing a broad range of individuals and groups to apply for the enforcement of any of the rights in the Constitution.[785]

While it may be reasonable to posit that formal access to court does not guarantee access to substantial justice, it is nonetheless important for the effective protection of human rights, especially in jurisdictions with little legal guarantee for economic, social and cultural rights, to achieve liberal and wider access to court for social action and public interest litigation. The South African paradigm has considerably secured that end.

5.4.2 Nigeria

Since 1979, when the Fundamental Objectives and Directive Principles of State Policy debuted in Nigerian constitutionalism, the entrenched non-justiciability clause has remained a veritable bulwark against their appreciation in Nigerian courts. The non-justiciability of these provisions has received judicial pronouncement in a series of cases, chief among which was *Okogie v Attorney-General Lagos State*.[786] Here, the plaintiff had sued as the trustee of Roman Catholic schools challenging the abolition of private primary schools on the ground that it was contrary, *inter alia*, to freedom of expression guaranteed in the Nigerian Constitution of 1979. The government had

784 See S Liebenberg 'The right to social assistance: The implications of *Grootboom* for policy reform in South Africa' (2001) 17 *South African Journal on Human Rights* 232; DG Newman 'Institutional monitoring of social and economic rights: A South African case study and a new research agenda' (2003) 19 *South African Journal on Human Rights* 189; M Pieterse 'Indirect horizontal application of the right to have access to health care services' (2007) 23 *South African Journal on Human Rights* 157.

785 See Seafield (n 486 above) 305; Liebenberg (n 784 above) 8. Sec 38 of the 1996 Constitution empowers anyone in any of these categories to sue for the enforcement of the human rights contained in the Constitution: '(a) Anyone acting in their own interest; (b) anyone acting on behalf of another person who cannot act in their own name; (c) anyone acting as a member of, or in the interest of, a group or class of persons; (d) anyone acting in the public interest; and (e) an association acting in the interest of its members.' The liberal approach to the issue of 'standing' in South Africa received exhaustive consideration in *Ngxusa v Secretary, Department of Welfare Eastern Cape*, 2000 12 BCLR 1322 (E) 1327, *per* Froneman J.

786 (1981) 1 NCLR 218.

argued that the operation of private schools was inconsistent with the obligation of the state to give 'equal and adequate educational opportunities' under section 18(1) of the Constitution. The court also held that, while the phrase 'equal and adequate educational opportunities' did not necessarily restrict the right of private institutions or other persons to provide similar or different educational facilities at their own expense, taste and preference, the Directive Principles have to conform to and run subsidiary to the fundamental human rights provisions.[787]

The reasoning in that decision found wholesale affirmation in *Adewole v Jakande, Governor of Lagos State.*[788] It had become evident that the economic, social and cultural rights elements in the Directive Principles were to remain cosmetic constitutional provisions in Nigeria. Indeed, the first time those provisions were ever referred to as 'rights' was in the 1991 decision of the Nigerian Court of Appeal in *Uzuokwu v Ezeonu II,*[789] where the Court held, *inter alia*, that

> [t]here are other *rights* which may pertain to a person which are neither fundamental nor justiciable in the court. These may include *rights* given by the Constitution as under the Fundamental Objectives and Directive Principles of State Policy under Chapter II of the Constitution.[790]

For a very long period, therefore, as far as economic, social and cultural rights were concerned, Nigerian courts had declined to assume jurisdiction. It is worthy to note, however, that since the era of the repressive military regimes that ruled Nigeria between 1984 and 1999, efforts had been made by human rights NGOs and activists to explore the application of the African Charter in national courts in view of its domestication.[791] Thus, in a long line of cases, Nigerian courts have been called upon to adjudicate on the domestic legal status of the African Charter. In *Ogugu v State,*[792] the Supreme Court of Nigeria held that all rights provisions in the African Charter are applicable and enforceable in Nigeria through the ordinary rules of court in the same manner as those fundamental rights set out in

787 Sec 18(1) CFRN 1979 provided that '[g]overnment shall direct its policy towards ensuring that there are equal and adequate educational opportunities at all levels'. Sec 18(1) CFRN 1999 retains the provision in its exact wording.

788 (1981) 1 NCLR 152.

789 (1991) 6 NWLR (pt 200) 708.

790 n 789 above, 761-762 (my emphasis).

791 By virtue of the African Charter on Human and Peoples' Rights (Enforcement and Ratification) Act, Ch 10 LFN 1990, the African Charter was incorporated into the municipal laws of Nigeria. In *Oshevire v British Caledonian Airways* (1990) 7 NWLR (pt 163) 507, the Court of Appeal held that international treaties incorporated into municipal laws were superior to other municipal laws.

792 (1994) 9 NWLR (pt 366) 1.

chapter IV of the Constitution. This position has been affirmed by the later decision of the apex court in *Abacha v Fawehinmi*.[793]

Notwithstanding the fact that the scanty Nigerian jurisprudence on the African Charter has exclusively been on civil and political rights, it is plausible to argue that, *a priori*, the economic, social and cultural rights provisions in the African Charter are domestically enforceable although further development of jurisprudence in this direction will still be required to make this thinking resonant.[794] In this regard, I conjecture a re-awakening of the Nigerian judiciary to its responsibility in nation building in the light of the Supreme Court's decision in *Attorney-General, Ondo State v Attorney-General, Federation*.[795] The Ondo State government had brought an action challenging the constitutional validity of the Corrupt Practices and Other Related Offences Act, 2000 as well as the Independent Corrupt Practices and Other Related Offences Commission set up under it to initiate criminal proceedings in any court in Nigeria.[796]

In what may be considered a new judicial perception about the status of the Fundamental Objectives in Nigeria, the Supreme Court added:

> As to the non-justiciability of the Fundamental Objectives and Directive Principles of State Policy, section 6(6)(c) ... says so. While they remain mere declarations, they cannot be enforced by legal process but would be seen as a failure of duty and responsibility of state organs if they

793 (2000) *Federation Weekly Law Reports* (pt 4) 533. Compare *Fawehinmi v Abacha* (1996) 9 NWLR (pt 475) 710, where the Court of Appeal opined that the African Charter was superior to any other municipal law in Nigeria.

794 It would appear that the new 'democratic' dispensation has added impetus to economic, social and cultural rights activism in Nigeria going by the number of cases relating to them. In *Eze Amadi v Attorney-General, Federation*, Suit ID/ 231/99, the plaintiffs sought to enforce the right to accessible and qualitative education as guaranteed under the African Charter. Similarly, in *Ilemobayo v Nigerian National Petroleum Corporation*, Suit FHC/L/593/97, a Lagos Federal High Court was asked to hold that the right to work under a favourable environment under the African Charter was enforceable despite sec 6(6)(c) of the Constitution. It is certain that the outcomes of these cases would go a long way in boosting economic, social and cultural rights jurisprudence in Nigeria.

795 (2002) 9 *Supreme Court Monthly* 1.

796 In holding that the statute and the commission set up under it were constitutional and valid, the apex court referred extensively to the Fundamental Principles in ch II of the CFRN 1999. According to the court, '[i]t is incidental or supplementary for the National Assembly to enact the law that will enable the ICPC to enforce the observance of the Fundamental Objectives and Directive Principles of State Policy ... The ICPC was established to enforce the observance of the Directive Principle set out in section 15 subsection (5) of Chapter II.' See above 38-39, 79. Sec 15(5) CFRN 1999 provides that '[t]he state shall abolish all corrupt practices and abuse of power'.

> acted in clear disregard of them ... the Directive Principles can be made justiciable by legislation.[797]

From the tone of the *Ondo State* decision, it would appear that the Nigerian Supreme Court might become favourably disposed to economic, social and cultural rights adjudication in the future, particularly where there are appropriate statutes to fortify rights-based claims.

While one might be prone to ascribe the parlous state of economic, social and cultural rights adjudication in Nigeria to substantive issues of the legal framework, perhaps the most formidable impediment to the effective protection of such rights remains the common law procedural doctrine of *locus standi*. Nigerian courts still interpret the rule on the right to sue very strictly, that is, only the person who shows the court that he or she has *personal* interest in the subject matter of the litigation or that the violation complained of affects him or her *directly* and personally, has the 'standing' to institute an action. This has always been particularly difficult to establish in public interest litigation cases as few of such actions ever scale the hurdle.[798]

The leading decision on the question of *locus standi* in Nigeria is *Adesanya v President of the Federal Republic of Nigeria*,[799] where the appellant had commenced an action challenging the appointment of the Chairperson of the Federal Electoral Commission on the ground that it would violate some constitutional provisions. After a protracted process of appeals, the Supreme Court of Nigeria held that the appellant lacked *locus standi* to institute the action. In laying the foundation of what was to become Nigeria's 'strict constructionist approach' to *locus standi*, the apex court had preoccupied itself with the imprecise task of keeping 'vexatious litigants or frivolous claims' at bay.[800] Regrettably, despite rigorous attempts by Nigerian lawyers to whittle down the conservative rule of *locus standi*, *Adesanya* has

797 n 796 above, 96-97. Also notable was the decision of the Nigerian Federal High Court in *Gbemre v Shell Petroleum Development Company Nigeria Limited & Others* (2005) AHRLR 151 (NgHC 2005) 155, where the Court read the provisions of the African Charter into the CFRN 1999 in holding that the defendants had violated the plaintiffs' right to a clean, poison-free, pollution-free and healthy environment.

798 For general discussions on the operation of the doctrine of *locus standi* in Nigerian courts, see MAA Ozekhome *The Nigerian law on locus standi* (1998) 82-90; EA Taiwo '*Locus standi* in Nigeria' in Sokefun (n 447 above) 242-153.

799 *Adesanya* (1981) 2 NCLR 358.

800 n 799 above, 373 *per* Fatayi-Williams, Chief Justice of Nigeria.

continued to reverberate on the Nigerian legal terrain since 1981.[801]

It is my contention that, based upon the dynamic trends on the doctrine in England as well as in many common law jurisdictions, the test of 'interest' in Nigerian courts should be based on liberal rules of *genuine concern* and *legitimate expectation*.[802] This argument has received isolated judicial approval in *Ezezoobo v The Provisional Ruling Council*,[803] where the Federal High Court held that in public law, *locus standi* should not deprive citizens' access to court for remedies.

Once this proposition gains acceptance in the higher courts and becomes settled, the question of the extent of state obligations would follow, but for now, the economic, social and cultural rights struggle must advance towards achieving basic recognition for these rights and their beneficiaries in Nigerian courts.[804]

5.4.3 *Other African countries*

The non-domestication of international human rights treaties, conservatism, the lack of knowledge about global trends, the virtual non-availability of economic, social and cultural rights precedents,

801 See eg *Irene Thomas v Olufosoye* (1986) 2 Supreme Court 325; *Adefulu v Oyesile*(1989) 5 NWLR (pt 122) 377; *Okoye v Lagos State Government* (1990) 3 NWLR (pt 136) 115; *Obaba v Military Governor of Kwara State* (1994) 4 NWLR (pt 336) 15; *Ezeafulukwe v John Holt Ltd* (1996) 2 NWLR (pt 432) 511; *HURILAWS v Government of Zamfara State of Nigeria* unreported Suit ZMS/GS/17/2000, judgment of the High Court of Zamfara State 4 May 2001. But see *Fawehinmi v Akilu* (1987) 4 NWLR (pt 67) 797, where the Supreme Court, in an unusual manner, held that the appellant had *locus standi* to commence private criminal proceedings against two suspected military officers in the light of the state's reluctance and unwillingness to prosecute them for the murder of a frontline Nigerian journalist. Note, however, that the decision was rendered practically useless as the military government retroactively amended the criminal procedure law that guaranteed the right of private prosecution.

802 This is an alchemy of the reasoning that prevailed in cases like *Inland Revenue Commissioners v National Federation of Self-Employed and Small Businesses Ltd* [1982] AC 617 (British House of Lords); *Kajing Tubek v Ekran BAD* (1995) Saman Remula 55-27-66 (Supreme Court of Pakistan).

803 Unreported Suit FHC/CS/640/95.

804 For other decisions relating to *locus standi* in public law matters in Nigeria, see *Akinpelu v Attorney-General, Oyo State* (1984) 5 NCLR 557, and *Ejeh v Attorney-General, Imo State* (1985) 6 NCLR 390, in both of which the court held that where the cause of action involves the validity or constitutionality of any enactment, the litigant is relieved of the requirement of *locus standi*. See also *Kokoro-Owo v Lagos State Government* (1998) Human Rights Law Reports 322, and *Olatoye v Governor of Lagos State*, unreported Suit FHC/CS/144/99, where the High Court of Lagos State and the Federal High Court, respectively, held that the established practice of forced evictions from homes was inhuman. *Contra Thomas v Olufosoye* (n 801 above) 352-353, where the Supreme Court declared, *per* Obaseki JSC, that '[a]s the law stands, there is no room for the adoption of the modern views on *locus standi* being followed by England and Australia. The adoption of those views in England has found support in the statute law of England.' This might very well be an unmistakable omen of the apex court's unwillingness to adapt itself to change.

and an inadequately-equipped civil society have been the combined factors for the stunted development of an economic, social and cultural rights jurisprudence by most judiciaries in Africa.[805] A survey of the judicial terrain across Africa reveals that pronouncements relevant for an economic, social and cultural rights jurisprudence are to be gleaned mainly from decisions on other tangential issues.[806] Thus, while it will not be preposterous to assert that the growth of human rights jurisprudence is generally stunted in much of Africa because of deep and complex inherent and structural problems,[807] many African judicial institutions function under limitations that have reduced human rights to abstract ideas, stultifying their appreciation as legal imperatives.

Some scholars have painted the reality of how societal perceptions about the Ugandan judiciary have negatively affected the promotion and protection of economic, social and cultural rights.[808] Indeed, a notable Ugandan human rights NGO described the dysfunction of the Ugandan judiciary as follows:

> [T]he judicial processes are poorly managed, funded, poorly co-ordinated and susceptible to corrupting influences. As a result, public

805 See generally Adjami (n 304 above) 124, identifying what he referred to as the 'insurmountable obstacles in developing a domestic human rights jurisprudence' in African courts. Although the context of that discussion is civil and political rights, it nonetheless finds relevance in the present discourse.

806 See eg *Minister of Home Affairs v Bickle* 1983 2 Zimbabwe Law Reports 400 (SC), where the Supreme Court of Zimbabwe struck down an emergency law that automatically forfeited the properties of perceived 'enemies' of the state; *Katekwe v Muchabaiwa* 1984 2 Zimbabwe Law Reports 112 (SC), where the Zimbabwean Supreme Court literally abolished the age-long customary rule that exclusively entitled fathers to sue for seduction damages when their daughters were not yet married; *Ephrahim v Pastory* (1990) LRC (Const) 757, where the Tanzanian High Court declared as invalid a rule of Haya customary law that denies a woman the power to sell land. The Court had held the customary law rule to be unconstitutionally discriminatory; as above 764; *Dow v Attorney-General Botswana* (1991) RC (Const) 574, where the Botswana Court of Appeal held that a statute that purported to deny citizenship to children of female citizens married to alien fathers was discriminatory and therefore unconstitutional; *New Patriotic Party v Inspector-General of Police* [1992-1993] Ghana Law Reports 87, where the Supreme Court of Ghana held the Public Order Decree, 1972 to be inconsistent with the constitutional freedoms of assembly and association. The Court had referred to the African Charter as follows: 'Ghana is a signatory [*sic*] to this African Charter. I do not think that because Ghana has not passed specific legislation to give effect to the Charter, the Charter cannot be relied upon' (as above, *per* Archer, 87); *Longwe v Intercontinental Hotels* (1993) LRC 221, where the Zambian High Court declared that the denial of access to the plaintiff into the bar of the hotel, on the ground that she was female, amounted to the unconstitutional violation of the non-discrimination and equality provisions of the Zambian Constitution. See generally Tumwine-Mukubwa (n 620 above) 301-302, analysing the impact of judicial activism on the domestic application of international human rights norms through cases from Southern Africa.

807 See generally EJSE Opolot *A discourse on just and unjust legal institutions in African English-speaking countries* (2002) 25-91 108-144 203.

808 S Dicklitch & D Lwanga 'The politics of being non-political: human rights organisations and the creation of a positive human rights culture in Uganda' (2003) 25 *Human Rights Quarterly* 482 495.

> confidence in the justice system is undermined. Economic, social and political conditions render the justice system irrelevant to the peoples' needs who are ignorant of their rights, formal laws and procedures of the systems.[809]

In their careful scrutiny of housing rights and related litigation in Kenya, Bodewes and Kwinga had described the judicial landscape as follows:

> In Kenya, politics play a much more important role than the rule of law in the area of housing and land disputes. The adjudication process, which was intended to provide the necessary safety valve to protect the rights ... has totally collapsed under the massive weight of corruption. As a result, the courts have ignored both the unlawful and forced evictions of residents ... and have sanctioned the rabid land grabbing that is endemic in Kenya today. In Kenya, there is a dearth of jurisprudence in the area of housing rights.[810]

There can hardly be any realistic disputation that the above assessment broadly epitomises the stunted evolution of an economic, social and cultural rights jurisprudence in Africa.

6 Implications for economic, social and cultural rights in Africa

The aim of my extensive foray into the descriptive dimensions of an economic, social and cultural rights jurisprudence in this discourse is to identify trajectories upon which a stronger economic, social and cultural rights jurisprudence and, invariably, a rights-based approach to human development can be built in Africa. From the decisions examined, an inevitable inference emerges: that African juridical entities can no longer afford to be complacent in the delivery of social justice whatever their legal traditions might be. The path to that lofty goal lies in the integrative approach to *all* human rights.[811]

809 Foundation for Human Rights Initiatives *Striving for justice* (2000) 8. See also J Oloka-Onyango *The problematique of economic, social and cultural right in globalised Uganda: A conceptual review* (2007) 57.

810 C Bodewes & N Kwinga 'The Kenyan perspective on housing rights' in Leckie (n 721 above) 221 236. See also O Odindo 'Litigation and housing rights in Kenya' in J Squires *et al* (eds) *The road to a remedy: Current issues in the litigation of economic, social and cultural rights* (2005) 155 162.

811 As Bhagwati strongly admonished: 'It is now being increasingly realised that civil and political rights have no meaning and value unless they are accompanied by economic and social rights. This is particularly important in Third World countries. We in the Third World countries have unique problems, totally different from those in the Western countries ... we in the Third World are trying to bring about change in the social and economic conditions of the large masses of people with a view to uplifting them from the quagmire of poverty and ignorance and so making basic human rights meaningful for them.' See Bhagwati (n 588 above) 80.

The consciousness would need to be strengthened among jurists and other stakeholders in the administration of justice in Africa that, in the whirlpool of the dynamic social, economic, legal and policy complexities of contemporary Africa, their role as interpreters and arbiters must be underpinned by a constant watch on the products of democratisation and governance. It can no longer be the norm that the judiciary should insulate itself from social realities, more so when it has become axiomatic that a considerable number of human groups and minorities – the homeless, HIV/AIDS patients and orphans, disabled persons, the unemployed, the illiterate, rural dwellers, refugees, children, the aged, people of 'different' sexual orientations – are often marginalised even in a democratic set-up.[812]

As I already demonstrated, proactive national judicial institutions and supranational human rights bodies have jettisoned the notion of the non-justiciability of economic, social and cultural rights. In many of the jurisdictions cited, the bulwark of opposition to judicial activism is crumbling, giving way to efforts at rendering substantial (distributive) justice to vast populations. Little wonder that Peretti argues:

> Judicial activism and decision making based on personal political preference or calculations of political acceptability do not pose a great threat to the court's power and independence. What does pose such a threat is extreme judicial restraint or, alternatively, judicial activism accompanied by political insensitivity and carelessness.[813]

Reflecting on the Indian judiciary's legendary breakaway from its earlier conservatism to respond to the demands of social pressure and its implications for Africa, the now late Zimbabwean jurist, Dumbutshena, had argued:

> India has many more problems of poverty, ignorance and illiteracy than we have in ... Africa. Yet it is in India that judicial activism has changed the face of justice ... *The question of delivery of justice to the disadvantaged was paramount in the minds of Supreme Court judges.* They reformed its procedures and jurisdictional rules relating to constitutional and legal rights of the poor classes who could not approach the court for redress of their grievances ... This was judicial activism at its best.[814]

812 See generally M Kirby 'The role of the judge in advancing human rights by reference to international human rights norms' in Bhagwati (n 602 above) 81. See also M Foscarinis 'Downward spiral: Homelessness and criminalisation' (1996) 14 *Yale Law and Development Policy Review* 1.

813 Peretti (n 603 above) 184.

814 E Dumbutshena 'Judicial activism in the quest for justice and equity' in Ajibola & Van Zyl (n 617 above) 185 191-192 (my emphasis).

If, therefore, by any figment of imagination, the responses of European and American courts are considered peculiar to former colonialist/imperialist legal traditions and thus objectionable, can the Indian approach be equally so assailed by African scholars, jurists and activists? By no means.

Without doubt, the gains of global economic, social and cultural rights advocacy through the jurisprudence of the South African courts cannot but be a veritable pointer to the capacity of other African states to achieve tangible accomplishment in social justice delivery and rights-based human development if they are so willing.[815] Herein lies the very heart of any credible human rights and development agenda in Africa. The outcome of decisions like *Magaya v Magaya*[816] clearly demonstrates the tragic consequences that non-activist judiciaries portend for Africa and Africans.[817]

It now behoves African judges, courts and lawyers, as well as human rights activists, to take up the challenge of building a socially relevant and responsive rule-based human rights system on the domestic fronts. For preliminaries, it will be most appropriate for African judges, lawyers as well as human rights scholars and activists to ask themselves the same question as Indian judges had asked themselves since the dark emergency years until the present time:

> Can judges really escape addressing themselves to substantial questions of social justice? Can they simply turn round to litigants who come to them for justice and the general public that accords them power, status and respect and tell them that they simply follow the legal text, when they are aware that their actions will perpetuate inequity and injustice? Can they restrict their inquiry into law and life within the narrow confines of a narrowly defined rule of law? Does the requirement of constitutionalism not make greater demands on the judicial function?[818]

815 It is noteworthy that since South Africa acceded to the African Charter, no individual or inter-state complaint has been brought against it before the African Commission. There is no gainsaying that this situation demonstrates the robust output of the institutional structures, particularly the judiciary, in tackling the legal and constitutional challenges for human rights in the relatively 'new' state.

816 [1999] 3 LRC 35 (Zimbabwe) (SC).

817 In this case, the Zimbabwean Supreme Court upheld a rule of customary law that denies a woman heirship to her father's estate. In this particular instance, the heirship passed to the appellant's half-brother, son of the late father's second wife. In its outrageous decision, the Supreme Court held that customary inheritance rules override the constitutional right to non-discrimination. For a critique of this decision, see DM Bigge *et al* 'Conflict in Zimbabwean courts: Women's rights and indigenous self-determination in *Magaya v Magaya*' (2000) 13 *Harvard Human Rights Journal* 289. Equally outrageous was the refusal of a Lagos State High Court in Nigeria to allow an HIV-positive litigant to enter the courtroom to give evidence in her own case challenging her dismissal from employment on the ground of her HIV status. The judge declined to listen to all arguments that HIV could not be transmitted by the litigant's entry into the courtroom.

818 Bhagwati (n 602 above) 61.

Even courts that were traditionally conservative are finding it no longer problematic to identify discriminatory practices where there are any. Strikingly, discrimination coupled with the denial of access to the necessities of life constitutes the most problematic obstacle to meeting the goals of economic, social and cultural rights in Africa.

Apart from normative standardisation, critical engagement with the integrative human rights approach will facilitate the opportunity for judiciaries as well as quasi-judicial bodies in Africa to develop appropriate remedies for non-compliance with economic, social and cultural rights obligations. Since many economic, social and cultural rights issues are most likely to be fluid and dynamic, national courts in Africa would be able to respond, much like the Indian judiciary,[819] in rendering purposive justice to the aggrieved, marginalised and oppressed, taking cognisance of peculiar circumstances.

7 Concluding remarks

The discourse in this chapter raises no suggestion that the judiciary should replace government in the prioritisation of socio-economic policies and budgetary commitments. Rather, my contention is that the law courts can exert a tremendous influence in the evolution of accountable and responsible governance in Africa when they become emphatic in the application of the tenets of *all* human rights and the rule of law.

A clear message from my analysis in this chapter is that there is adequate room for any national or regional human rights body, irrespective of geopolitical or cultural orientation, to uphold and secure the implementation of economic, social and cultural rights, if there is a willingness to do so. Even where a national constitution does not explicitly recognise economic, social and cultural rights, or where there is a dearth of precedents, a court can still apply international human rights standards in holding that governmental justification for human rights limitations must comply with international legal norms. By so doing, an evolutionary process for effectively assessing the proportionality between governmental acts or policies and protection of human entitlements would emerge.

In pursuing a credible agenda for rights-based human development in Africa, therefore, the notion that budgetary processes and decisions of 'political colour' are the exclusive preserve of the executive and legislature will have to be consigned to the scrap heap of anachronistic legal traditions.

[819] In the next chapter, I shall examine in detail how the Indian courts have met the challenge of remedies in their efforts at social justice through the protection of elements of economic, social and cultural rights.

5

Human Rights: Remedial Implementation and its Paradigms

Impunity for violations of basic rights compromises the ... obligation of states to guarantee [economic, social and cultural rights] and to punish failure to respect them. What is the point of proclaiming rights if they can be violated with impunity and disregarded? In this connection, it should be remembered that *the efficacy of ... protecting the human rights of the individual is based on the right to an effective remedy*, yet the various mechanisms which produce impunity make this right completely inoperative.[820]

1 Remedial implementation in human rights discourse

The quest for an understanding of *remedies* in the context of international human rights law is an endeavour that has not attracted as much intensive scholarly attention as other theoretical and normative aspects of the subject have done. Except for very few and isolated examples,[821] most of the contributions by writers have addressed the subject from the perspective of historically symptomatic 'gross' violations of human rights, for example, slavery, apartheid, colonialism, aboriginal displacement, and in the post-World War II era, other 'massive' violations of international

[820] *Final report on the question of the impunity of perpetrators of human rights violations (economic, social and cultural rights)* prepared by Mr El Hadji Guissé, Special Rapporteur on Impunity, pursuant to Sub-Commission Res 1996/24, UN Doc E/CN.4/Sub.2/1997/8 (27 June 1997) para 30 (my emphasis).

[821] Some of the most outstanding treatises on the subject include M Evans *Remedies in international law: The institutional dilemma* (1998); S Davidson *The Inter-American human rights system* 214-231; D Shelton *Remedies in international human rights law* (2001); N Jayawickrama *The judicial application of human rights law: national, regional and international jurisprudence* (2002); G Sharma *Human rights and legal remedies* (2003); S Djajic 'Victims and promise of remedies: International law fairytale gone bad' (2008) 9 *San Diego International Law Journal* 329.

humanitarian law, especially of the civil and political rights genre.[822] The reasons for this state of affairs are not arcane.

Despite the recognition of the right to an 'effective remedy' in a number of international and regional human rights instruments,[823] substantial scholarly engagement with the subject within global human rights discourse has generally been a recent experience.[824] Within the UN human rights system, there have been noticeable efforts toward the development of standard guidelines on remedial responses to 'gross' violations of human rights, as exemplified, for instance, by the appointment of a special rapporteur on the subject.[825] Commendable as those efforts might have been, however, it would have conformed to overall UN human rights vision if this thematic mandate had covered the subject of human rights remedies

822 Some of the notable works in this regard include NJ Kritz *Transitional justice: How emerging democracies reckon with former regimes* (1995); N Roht-Arriaza *Impunity and human rights in international law and practice* (1995); SR Ratner *et al Accountability for human rights atrocities in international law: Beyond the Nuremberg legacy* (1997); M Minow *Between vengeance and forgiveness: Facing history after genocide and mass violence* (1998); RL Brooks *When sorry isn't enough: The controversy over apologies and reparations for human injustice* (1999); E Barkan *The guilt of nations: Restitution and negotiating historical injustices* (2000); M Ratner 'Civil remedies for gross human rights violations' in D Barnhizer (ed) *Effective strategies for protecting human rights: Economic sanctions, use of national courts and international fora and coercive power* (2001) 249-262; J Torpey 'Making whole what has been smashed: Reflections on reparations (2001) 73 *Journal of Modern History* 333-358; S Bachman *Civil responsibility for gross human rights violations: The need for a global instrument* (2007).

823 See art 8 Universal Declaration; arts 2(3) & 9(5) ICCPR; art 6 CERD; art 5(5) European Convention; art 14(1) CAT; art 19 UN Declaration on the Protection of All Persons from Enforced Disappearances, UN Doc A/RES/47/133 (1992), 18 December 1992; arts 63(1) & 68 American Convention on Human Rights. See Shelton (n 821 above) 14-37.

824 See generally RL Maddex *International encyclopaedia of human rights: Freedoms, abuses and remedies* (2000) 293, indicating that remedies only appeared in global human rights discourse after World War II.

825 Pursuant to its Res 1989/13 (31 August 1989), the UN Sub-Commission on the Prevention of Discrimination and Protection of Minorities appointed Prof T van Boven as Special Rapporteur to consider the right to restitution, compensation and rehabilitation of 'gross' violations of human rights and fundamental freedoms and to produce appropriate draft guidelines on the subject. The outcome of that study was titled 'Study concerning the right to restitution, compensation and rehabilitation for victims of gross violations of human rights and fundamental freedoms: Final report submitted by Mr T van Boven, Special Rapporteur' UN Doc E/CN.4/Sub.2/1993/8 (2 July 1993). For a detailed analysis and discussions of this thematic mandate, see Shelton (n 821 above) 19-22 and accompanying nn 47-60. For an insight into the current position of the new mandate of Professors T van Boven and C Bassiouni as 'independent experts' on the preparation of the 'Basic principles and guidelines on the right to a remedy and reparation for victims of violations of international human rights and humanitarian law', see UN Commission on Human Rights, Res 2003/34, UN Doc E/CN.4/2003/L.11/Add.4 (23 April 2003). All the resolutions and reports relevant to these mandates are available at http://www.unhchr.ch/.

in general rather than its strict confinement to 'gross' violations.[826] This conceivably explains why the defunct UN Commission on Human Rights had only been calling 'upon the international community to give due attention to the right to restitution, compensation and rehabilitation for victims of *grave violations* of human rights',[827] without more. An understanding that 'grave' or 'gross' violations of human rights could encompass *all* human rights beyond civil and political rights is yet to emerge clearly.[828]

Even though the Vienna Declaration acknowledged the paucity of remedies for human rights in various countries when it proclaimed that '[e]very state should provide an effective framework of remedies to redress human rights grievances or violations',[829] that clarion call is yet to generate the anticipated global attention, more than a decade later.[830]

The experience with domestic arrangements for the redress of human rights 'violations' has not been very encouraging either. Decrying the attitude of most states towards remedying human rights violations, Humphrey more than three decades ago argued that

> the matter of implementation will continue to be one of frustration and lost opportunities, and governments will continue to manoeuvre pretty

826 Prof Van Boven seemed to have subjected his mandate to a rather narrow definition when, in his final report, he described the 'gross violations' covered by his mandate as including 'murder; torture ... slavery; servitude or forced labour; persecution ... in a systematic manner or on a mass scale; deportation or forcible transfer of population'. See Van Boven (n 825 above) para 9.

827 See UN Commission on Human Rights, Res 1998/43, ESCOR Suppl 3, 'The right to restitution, compensation and rehabilitation for victims of grave violations of human rights and fundamental freedoms' UN Doc E/CN.4/1998/43 (1998), para 1 (my emphasis). This has become a common thread running through every resolution of this UN human rights body on this subject. See Res 2003/34 (n 825 above) Preamble paras 4-5.

828 It is worthy to note, however, that the phenomenon of forced evictions has lately, but assuredly, crept onto the international human rights agenda, where, among others, it is being treated as a 'gross' violation of the right to adequate housing. See UN Commission on Human Rights, Forced Evictions, Res 1993/77, paras 1 & 4 (10 March 1993); Van Boven (n 825 above) para 21; ESCR Committee 'The right to adequate housing (art 11(1) of the Covenant): Forced evictions' General Comment No 7, UN Doc E/C.12/1997/4 (20 May 1997) in *Compilation of general comments* (n 81 above) 45 para 2. see also Leckie (n 657 above) 11.

829 Vienna Declaration (n 38 above) para 27.

830 See generally eg Shelton (n 821 above) 14-15; Starke (n 822 above) 125; KN Wuerffel 'Discrimination among rights?: A nation's legislating a hierarchy of human rights in the context of international human rights customary law' (1998) 33 *Valparaiso University Law Review* 369 411; SP Marks *et al* 'International human rights at fifty: A foreword' (1998) 8 *Iowa Journal of Transnational and Contemporary Problems* 113 119. See also NH Afran 'International human rights law in the twenty-first century: Effective municipal implementation or paean to platitudes' (1995) 18 *Fordham International Law Journal* 1756.

much as they like and so prevent the effective development of any machinery which might expose them to criticism.[831]

The question of remedies is of vital importance to any aspect of human rights discourse because, as Shelton argues, '[a]ppropriate remedies can have a dissuasive effect on those who would commit violations, as well as serving to redress the wrongs done to victims. Remedies are thus a significant aspect of ensuring the rule of law.'[832]

Addressing the question of remedies at the national level is also important because virtually every international and regional human rights treaty makes the exhaustion of domestic remedies a condition precedent to the admissibility of complaints against violations before the applicable supervisory organs.[833] The regime of remedies for human rights violations is evident in the diverse frameworks from country to country and from region to region.[834] In most legal systems of the world where there exist human rights norms, whether by virtue of treaties or municipal law, there is a concomitant imperative that a violation of an individual or group's human rights entails remedial intervention.[835] According to Alston and Quinn, 'a requirement that judicial remedies for violations be provided in national law is a characteristic of the great majority of international human rights treaties'.[836] However, the question of remedies in the field of human

831 JP Humphrey 'The international law of human rights in the middle twentieth century' in M Bos (ed) *The present state of international law and other essays* (1973) 75 95. See also T van Boven 'The future codification of human rights status of deliberations – A critical analysis' (1989) 10 *Human Rights Law Journal* 1 3; C Lasco 'Repairing the irreparable: Current and future approaches to reparations' (2003) 10 *Human Rights Brief* 18.

832 Shelton (n 821 above) 14. See also JJ Shestack 'The legal profession and human rights: Globalisation of human rights law' (1997) 21 *Fordham International Law Journal* 558 560.

833 For scholarly discussions and analysis of the doctrine of exhaustion of domestic remedies, see CF Amerasinghe *Local remedies in international law* (1990) 1 45-51; MN Shaw *International law*(1997) 509-511; M Scheinin 'International mechanisms and procedures for implementation' in Hanski *et al* (n 37 above) 429 438. See generally NJ Udombana 'So far, so fair: The local remedies rule in the jurisprudence of the African Commission on Human and People's Rights' (2003) 97 *American Journal of International Law* 1 3-6.

834 See eg sec 32 Indian Constitution; art 13 European Convention; sec 172(1) South African Constitution; sec 42 CFRN 1979; R English 'Remedies' in R English *et al* (eds) *An introduction to human rights and the common law* (2000) 71-87; S Grosz *Human rights: The 1998 Act and the European Convention* (2000) 133 138-146. Compare M Shaw *et al* 'Right to an effective remedy' in Lord Lester of Herne Hill *et al* (eds) *Human rights law and practice* (1999) 217; Z Kędzia 'The implementation of social and economic rights in Central and Eastern European countries' in F Matscher (ed) *The implementation of social and economic rights: National, international and comparative aspects* (1991) 237; De Waal *et al* (n 333 above) 166-196.

835 See PN Drost *Human rights as legal rights: The realisation of individual human rights in positive international law* (1951) 56-57. See also Van Boven (n 825 above) para 46.

836 P Alston & G Quinn 'The nature and scope of state parties' obligations under the International Covenant on Economic, Social and Cultural Rights' (1987) 9 *Human Rights Quarterly* 156 169.

rights has been as problematic at national levels as it has been in the UN and regional human rights systems.[837] Even the European regional human rights arrangement, reputed to be the most progressive in terms of structures for remedial implementation, has not been free from procedural delay and other bottlenecks that have often left many victims without remedy.[838]

Despite the spate of human rights violations that occur with little or no remedy in Africa at both the regional and national levels, scholars have generally avoided the subject of remedial implementation under the African Charter. As the *Ogoni* decision demonstrates, for instance, African human rights institutions, scholars, activists and NGOs are still grappling with the best approach to the issue of remedies under the African Charter.[839] The degree of pessimism about the subject of remedies in the African regional human rights setting is so deeply rooted that the African Charter

837 See generally CRL Fairweather 'Obstacles to enforcing international human rights law in domestic courts' (1998) 4 *UC Davis Journal of International Law and Policy* 119 120-122; D Kennedy 'Boundaries in the field of human rights: The international human rights movement: Part of the problem?' (2002) 15 *Harvard Human Rights Journal* 99 107 116; M Scaperlanda 'Polishing the tarnished golden door' 1993 *Wisconsin Law Review* 965; B Conforti *Enforcing international human rights in domestic courts* (1997); E Benvenisti 'Judicial misgivings regarding the application of international law: An analysis of attitudes of national courts' (1993) 4 *European Journal of International Law* 159; K Knop 'Here and there: International law in domestic courts' (2000) 32 *International Law and Policy* 501-535; N Roht-Arriaza 'Reparations decisions and dilemmas' (2004) 27 *Hastings College of the Law* 157; TM Antkowiak 'Remedial approaches to human rights violations: The Inter-American Court of Human Rights and beyond' (2008) 46 *Columbia Journal of Transnational Law* 351; SB Starr 'Rethinking "effective remedies": Remedial deterrence in international courts' (2008) 83 *New York University Law Review* 83.

838 See AAC Trindade 'The consolidation of the procedural capacity of individuals in the evolution of the international protection of human rights: Present state and perspectives at the turn of the century' (1998) 30 *Columbia Human Rights Law Review* 1 7 12 17 24. It is worthy to note that Trindade's analysis covered the procedural problems within all the three existing regional human rights system. See also Starke (n 822 above) 127; JG Merrills 'Promotion and protection of human rights within the European arrangements' in Hanski *et al* (n 37 above) 275 279; L Clements *et al European human rights: Taking a case under the Convention* (1999) 32-38.

839 See eg GW Mugwanya 'Realising universal human rights norms through regional human rights mechanisms: Reinvigorating the African system' (1999) 10 *India International and Comparative Law Review* 35 43 49. Even though a renowned work containing the essays of diverse African scholars and activists edited by An-Na'im and published in 1999 carried a title that suggests a focus on human rights 'remedies' in Africa, the work contained no chapter on remedies. See AA An-Na'im *Universal rights, local remedies: Implementing human rights in the legal systems of Africa* (1999).

appears to some to be essentially bereft of any framework for remedies.[840]

I argue that *all* human rights applicable within the African region as well as within the domestic legal systems that constitute it are capable of implementation with appropriate and effective remedies. The identification of appropriate remedies for human rights 'violations' will enhance the purpose and essence of every human right. My approach to this subject, therefore, not only conceives of the provision of juridical relief to victims of violations but also contemplates the nuanced dimension of *preventive* implementation. If proper modalities for human rights implementation are put in place at the domestic level – in this context, for economic, social and cultural rights as much as have been the case for civil and political rights – they can lessen or remove the burden of remedying massive, sporadic and egregious abuses at much more enormous human and monetary costs.

2 Economic, social and cultural rights and the dilemma of implementation

From the perspective of the UN human rights regime, the ultimate effectiveness of any human rights instrument is contingent on the measures taken by national governments to give actual effect to them. The ESCR Committee has thus recognised the critical importance of the adoption by states of appropriate legislative measures and the provision of judicial remedies, demonstrating the legal nature of economic, social and cultural rights. Regarding the possibility of these rights being subjected to judicial remedies, the ESCR Committee stated that '[a]mong the measures which might be considered appropriate, in addition to legislation, is the provision of judicial remedies with respect to rights which may, in accordance

840 According to Benedek, under the African Charter, 'a remedy is provided only for "special cases" which reveal the existence of a series of serious and massive violations of human and peoples' rights'. See W Benedek 'The African Charter and Commission on Human and Peoples' Rights: How to make it more effective' (1993) 11 *Netherlands Quarterly of Human Rights* 25 31. See also CA Odinkalu 'The individual complaints procedures of the African Commission on Human and Peoples' Rights: A preliminary assessment' (1998) 8 *Iowa Journal of Transnational and Contemporary Problems* 359 372-374; CE Welch Jr 'The African Charter and freedom of expression in Africa' (1998) 4 *Buffalo Human Rights Law Review* 103; Mutua (n 221 above) 349.

with the national legal system, be considered justiciable'.[841] Over the course of time, the ESCR Committee has added more vigour to the discourse on remedies as it has declared that specific economic, social and cultural rights can be open to 'judicial or other appropriate remedies'.[842]

In its General Comment No 9, the ESCR Committee further advanced the critical value of remedies when it interpreted the phrase 'by all appropriate means, including particularly the adoption of legislative measures' in article 2(1) of ICESCR as denoting that

> the Covenant norms must be recognised in appropriate ways within the domestic legal order, *appropriate means of redress, or remedies, must be available to any aggrieved individual or group,* and appropriate means of ensuring governmental accountability must be put in place.[843]

The output of the ESCR Committee's concern about the evolution of a regime of remedies for economic, social and cultural rights builds on the earlier work of experts and has contributed to the emergence of various schools of thought on best approaches to the protection and remedial implementation of economic, social and cultural rights.[844] For instance, according to the Limburg Principles:

> In reporting on legal steps taken to give effect to the Covenant, states parties should not merely describe any relevant legislative provisions. They should specify, as appropriate, the judicial remedies,

841 General Comment No 3 (n 91 above) para 5. The ESCR Committee had emphatically indicated that a number of provisions in ICESCR are capable of immediate implementation, including the rights covered in arts 3 (equality); 7(a)(i) (equal remuneration for work of equal value); 13(2)(a) (free and compulsory primary education); 13(3) & (4) (choice of education); and 15(3) (scientific research and creative activity). See M Craven 'The domestic application of the International Covenant on Economic, Social and Cultural Rights' (1993) 40 *Netherlands International Law Review* 360 367.

842 See, eg, General Comment No 12 (n 638 above) para 32, where the ESCR Committee emphasised that '[a]ny person or group who is a victim of a violation of the right to adequate food should have access to effective judicial or other appropriate remedies at both national and international levels. All victims of such violations are entitled to adequate reparation, which may take the form of restitution, compensation, satisfaction or guarantees of non-repetition.' See also General Comment No 14 (n 80 above) para 59, where the ESCR Committee stressed that '[a]ny person or group victim of a violation of the right to health should have access to effective judicial or other appropriate remedies at both national and international levels. All victims of such violations should be entitled to adequate reparation, which may take the form of restitution, compensation, satisfaction or guarantees of non-repetition.'

843 General Comment No 9 (n 309 above) paras 1-2 (my emphasis).

844 For a comprehensive view of various shades of understanding among scholars relating to the implementation of economic, social and cultural rights under the UN human rights system, see Symposium 'The implementation of economic, social and cultural rights' (1987) 9 *Human Rights Quarterly* 121-273. See also A Rosas *et al* 'Implementation mechanisms and remedies' in Eide (n 29 above) 425. Compare Craven (n 73 above) 27; C Puta-Chekwe *et al* 'From division to integration: Economic, social and cultural rights as basic human rights' in Merali & Oosterveld (n 37 above) 39 44; Nmehielle (n 220 above) 121-122.

> administrative procedures and other measures they have adopted for enforcing those rights and the practice under those remedies and procedures.[845]

Similarly, the Maastricht Guidelines assert that

> it is the duty of the state to set up procedures, structures and other modes by which victims of the violations [of economic, social and cultural rights] can have redress and remedies. If the mechanisms for obtaining redress do not exist, the ultimate responsibility for the violation lies with the state.[846]

So critical to the authors of these Guidelines was the question of remedies that they emphasised that 'without remedies and other responses to violations, the labour of respecting, protecting and fulfilling economic, social and cultural rights would be in vain'.[847]

Since the primary focus of my discourse is economic, social and cultural rights in the African context, I proceed to highlight the arguments, strengths and weaknesses engendered by some of the current approaches to the implementation of economic, social and cultural rights, particularly as they could negatively or positively influence a rights-based approach to human development in Africa.

In order to properly conceptualise the subject of remedial implementation of economic, social and cultural rights within African regional and national human rights systems, I place particular emphasis on the dynamics of these rights in the UN human rights system. This is because, as decided cases demonstrate,[848] there has been a noticeable tendency among judicial and quasi-judicial organs at both the regional and domestic human rights fora in Africa to follow the reasoning of the ESCR Committee as well as the extrapolations of scholars and activists based on that paradigm. While I do not advocate that theoretical and practical interpretations of economic, social and cultural rights in Africa should jettison the jurisprudence of the ESCR Committee and scholarly inferences therefrom, I nonetheless contend that such extrapolations should be applied with caution. I stress caution here because of the need to eliminate the espousal of either a model that will create a leeway for African governments to evade their economic, social and cultural rights responsibilities or one that will reinforce the protracted scepticism that has for long beleaguered the economic, social and cultural rights discourse.

845 Limburg Principles (n 48 above) para 78.
846 Maastricht Guidelines (n 49 above) para 16.
847 Maastricht Guidelines (n 49 above) para 21.
848 The 'celebrated' decision of the African Commission in *Ogoni* as well as most of the prominent economic, social and cultural rights decisions in South African courts already discussed in ch IV are instructive here.

2.1 Current approaches to standards of implementation

Scholarly and other informed responses to the demand of asserting economic, social and cultural rights as legal rights and of ascertaining modalities for their *effective* implementation have produced a divergent range of formulae and methods. It is therefore important in asserting economic, social and cultural rights as 'real' rights that overt effort be directed at evaluating current approaches and perceptions about these rights. For the purposes of this discourse, I classify these as (1) the 'obligations' approach (encompassing the 'minimum threshold approach' and a hybrid variant that I tag the 'resource-based obligations' approach) and (2) the 'violations' approach.

2.1.1 The 'obligations' approach

For a very long time, the attitude of the ESCR Committee, many scholars and NGO activists had been one of defining economic, social and cultural rights entitlements primarily from the perspective of *who* owes *what* 'duty'.[849] To many of the protagonists of this approach, including the ESCR Committee, the starting point in the process of making economic, social and cultural rights effective begins with clarifying and fine-tuning the 'positive' and 'negative' obligations imposed by ICESCR.[850] This approach is both a systematic response to the controversial conceptualisations about economic, social and cultural rights and a desire to evolve a rapprochement between the norms of these rights and their enforcement in practical terms.[851]

To substantiate and refine economic, social and cultural rights as legal rights capable of implementation, and 'to redress the problem of normative ambiguity that could serve as a subterfuge for states' inaction in realising [economic, social and cultural rights entitlements]',[852] a shift had occurred in the obligations discourse

849 As Sepulveda notes, '[f]rom the time of the adoption of the [ICESCR] to the present day, commentators have repeatedly noted the necessity of determining the scope and content of the Covenant obligations in order to enhance the protection of economic, social and cultural rights'. See Sepulveda (n 80 above) 3.

850 n 849 above, 4. Understandably, the ESCR Committee has actively been promoting the obligations approach. The overarching concern in all the General Comments it has issued to date reflects its unmistakable emphasis on clarifying the nature and scope of the obligations of state parties in respect of each economic, social and cultural right. Moreover, as a matter of custom, the ESCR Committee opens its concluding observations by reiterating the obligations of concerned states. See P Alston 'The Committee on Economic, Social and Cultural Rights' in P Alston (ed) *The United Nations and human rights: A critical appraisal* (1992) 473; Craven (n 73 above) 182-184.

851 See generally Alston & Quinn (n 836 above) 158; Sepulveda (n 80 above) 5.

852 G Handl 'Human rights and protection of the environment' in Eide (n 29 above) 303 314.

towards identifying the *core* of the obligations of states for each economic, social and cultural right.[853] It is now taken for granted that a state is in violation of its obligations when it goes below the minimum essential elements of an economic, social and cultural right.[854] This is the kernel of the notion variously referred to as the 'minimum core content' or 'minimum core obligations' or 'minimum essential level'.[855]Capturing the nexus among these terminologies, Sepulveda says that '[t]hese elements constitute the 'minimum core content' of each right and the 'minimum core obligations' are those obligations necessary to satisfy [the] minimum essential levels'.[856]

To facilitate coherent argument and understanding of my analysis and critique, and in conforming to the original scholarly expression of this innovative approach, I address this aspect of the 'obligations' approach as the 'minimum threshold approach'.

The 'minimum threshold approach'

Although this approach has gained eloquent support in the work of the ESCR Committee,[857] its conceptualisation, development and prominence had been the result of ample scholarly patronage. The original proponents of this approach were Nordic human rights scholars Bård-Anders Andreassen, Tor Skåines, Alan Smith and Hugo Stokke.[858] According to the proposition of these distinguished scholars, because there are marked differences in the economic situations of states, minimum thresholds should be established based on country-specific indices such as infant mortality, prevalence of disease, life expectancy, income, unemployment, underemployment, food consumption, and so on. Once these specific thresholds are set up in every country, each state would then be able to aggregate local needs and apply its resources towards ensuring the minimum level of

853 In 1987, Alston had proposed that the 'core content' of each economic, social and cultural right should be identified, making it the minimum entitlement for beneficiaries and the minimum obligation of state parties under ICESCR. See P Alston 'Out of the abyss: The challenges confronting the new UN Committee on Economic, Social and Cultural Rights' (1987) 9 *Human Rights Quarterly* 332-381. See also F Coomans 'Economic, social and cultural rights' (1998) 16 *SIM Special* 11.

854 See Alston (n 352 above) for the proposition that under this approach, each economic, social and cultural right gives rise 'to an absolute minimum entitlement, in the absence of which a state party is to be in violation of its obligations'.

855 See Sepulveda (n 80 above) 366-367.

856 As above. See also F Coomans 'Clarifying the core elements of the right to education' in Van Boven (n 657 above).

857 See generally Craven (n 73 above) 141-144.

858 B Andreassen *et al* 'Assessing human rights performance in developing countries: The case for a minimum threshold approach' in B Andreassen *et al* (eds) *Human rights in developing countries 1987/88* (1988) 333-356. See B Toebes 'The right to health' in Eide *et al* (n 29 above) 169 185.

subsistence for its most vulnerable population groups.[859] Elaborating the essence and thrust of this approach, Eide stated:

> The minimum threshold approach calls on the identification of the most deprived groups, not only according to conventional definitions of distinctions, such as ethnic-cultural, racial, regional, and gender, but also distinctions defined by the control over assets eg the distinction between land owners on the one hand and landless labourers or small-holding share croppers on the other.[860]

This approach has received considerable endorsement by the ESCR Committee, other UN human rights mechanisms, regional human rights bodies and scholars across geo-cultural boundaries.[861] In 1990, the ESCR Committee adopted the approach in the following manner:

> On the basis of the extensive experience gained by the Committee ... over a period of more than a decade of examining states parties' reports *the Committee is of the view that a minimum core obligation to ensure the satisfaction of, at the very least, minimum essential levels of each of the rights is incumbent upon every state party.* Thus ... a state party in which any significant number of individuals is deprived of essential foodstuffs, of essential primary health care, of basic shelter and housing, or of the most basic forms of education is, *prima facie*, failing to discharge its obligations under the [ICESCR]. If the [ICESCR] were to be read in such a way as not to establish such a minimum core obligation, it would be largely deprived of its *raison d'être*.[862]

In his Second Progress Report, Danilo Türk, UN Special Rapporteur on Economic, Social and Cultural Rights, asserted that '[s]tates are obliged, regardless of the level of economic development, to ensure respect for minimum subsistence right for all'.[863]

In adopting this approach, the Inter-American Commission stressed that

859 Andreassen *et al* (n 858 above) 341-342. For an extensive analysis of how these authors have sought to apply this 'groundbreaking' approach to the rights to food, health, work and education, see Andreassen *et al* 'Compliance with economic and social human rights: Realistic evaluations and monitoring in the light of immediate obligations' in A Eide *et al* (eds) *Human rights in perspective: A global assessment* (1992) 252-267.

860 A Eide 'Realisation of social and economic rights and the minimum threshold approach' (1989) 10 *Human Rights Law Journal* 35 47.

861 See eg M Craven 'The protection of economic, social and cultural rights under the Inter-American system of human rights' in D Harris *et al* (eds) *The Inter-American system of human rights* (1998) 289 317-319, discussing the minimum threshold approach in the Inter-American human rights system; Handl (n 852 above) 303 314. See also Leckie (n 657 above) 63.

862 General Comment No 3 (n 91 above) para 10 (my emphasis).

863 'Realisation of economic, social and cultural rights' second report prepared by Mr Danilo Türk, Special Rapporteur, UN Doc E/CN.4/Sub.2/1991/17, 18 para 10. See also UN Commission on Human Rights Res 1993/14, UN Doc E/CN.4/Sub.2/ 1993/14 (28 July 1993).

> the obligation of member states to observe and defend the human rights of individuals within their jurisdictions, as set forth in both the American Declaration and the American Convention, obligates them, regardless of the level of economic development, to guarantee a minimum threshold of these rights.[864]

The first reference to this approach within the African regional human rights system occurred in *Ogoni* where the petitioners alleged that the Nigerian government had failed to fulfil the 'minimum duties' imposed by the rights to health and a healthy environment; the right to housing; and the right to food.[865] In respect of the rights to health and a healthy environment, the communication alleged that the Nigerian government had failed 'to fulfil all three minimum duties required';[866] with regard to the right to housing, the communication alleged that the Nigerian government had failed to fulfil the 'two minimum obligations', namely, 'not to destroy the housing of its citizens; and not to obstruct efforts by individuals or communities to rebuild lost homes'.[867] It also alleged that the Nigerian government violated 'all three minimum duties of the right to food', namely, 'not [to] destroy or contaminate food sources; not [to] allow private parties to destroy or contaminate food sources; and not [to] prevent peoples' efforts to feed themselves'.[868] It is interesting to note that the African Commission adopted all these 'minimums' as formulated by the petitioners,[869] without scrutiny. But more curious, however, was the failure of both the petitioners and the African Commission either to identify the legal basis for these 'minimum duties' or to explicitly refer to any of the ample international jurisprudence on 'minimum core' to ground its legal basis in that context.[870]

864 Inter-American Commission on Human Rights *Annual report of the inter-American Commission on Human Rights* (1994) 524.

865 See 'Petition to the African Commission on violations of the Ogoni people's rights in Nigeria' submitted March 1996 by the Social and Economic Rights Action Centre (Lagos, Nigeria) and the Centre for Economic and Social Rights, reprinted in Buhl (n 718 above) 113.

866 According to the petitioners, these were: 'to take reasonable precautions to avoid contaminating the environment in a manner that threatens the physical, mental and environmental health of its citizens; to ensure that private parties do not systematically threaten peoples' health and environment; to provide citizens with information regarding environmental health risks, and with meaningful opportunities to participate in development decisions'; n 866 above, 7.

867 n 866 above, 9.

868 n 866 above, 10.

869 See *Ogoni* (n 143 above) paras 50, 57-58, 61 & 65.

870 Rather than examining or mentioning any specific General Comment from the ESCR Committee or any other UN human rights treaty-monitoring body, the African Commission deftly stated that '[i]n accordance with articles 60 and 61 of the African Charter, this communication is examined in the light of the provisions of the African Charter and the relevant international and regional human rights instruments and principles'. See *Ogoni* (n 143 above) para 49. The African Commission is yet to ascertain what constitutes the 'minimum core' of each human right in the African Charter.

Although this approach is yet to attract active debate among African human rights scholars, Agbakwa has suggested an indication of its abstract implications for the implementation of economic, social and cultural rights in Africa. In his words:

> Using the minimum threshold approach, the African Commission or the African Court could set up country-specific thresholds (or minimum core obligations) measured by indicators to determine what amounts to 'the best attainable state of physical and mental health' or 'necessary measures to protect the health of their people' [under the African Charter]. In this way, what the government can or cannot afford can be independently verified and juxtaposed with other competing national priorities. This baseline approach could also be used to set up satisfactory working conditions ... it would [thus] be easier to monitor when a state fails to fulfil its obligations.[871]

Conceptualising a basis for the applicability of this approach in South African economic, social and cultural rights jurisprudence, Bollyky argues that '[t]he absence of a predetermined minimum standard reduces the likelihood of obtaining redress by increasing the perceived complexity of the budgetary and policy implications of remedying violations'.[872]

As plausible and attractive as the theoretical assumptions of the minimum threshold approach might seem, the approach has not been free from criticism and controversy. On one side of the debate has been the 'question as to whether or not a universal (minimum) core content or country-based (minimum) type of core content should be established'.[873] The other dimension to the debate concerns the 'question as to whether such minimums apply primarily to the individual enjoyment of a right or to society-wide levels of enjoyment'.[874] Even though the purveyors of this approach also emphasise that it makes for easier development of subjective and objective indicators and benchmarks for monitoring the implementation of economic, social and cultural rights at national

871 Agbakwa (n 46 above) 213-214.

872 T Bollyky 'R if C > P + B: A paradigm for judicial remedies of socio-economic rights violations' (2002) 18 *South African Journal on Human Rights* 161 184. However, see *Grootboom* (n 144 above) paras 27-33, where the Constitutional Court of South Africa declined to adopt the minimum threshold approach as postulated in international instruments on housing, but chose to adopt a case-by-case approach. Contrast the recent decision of the Witwatersrand High Court in *Lindiwe Mazibuko & Others v The City of Johannesburg & Others* 2008, Case 06/13865 (W).

873 Toebes (n 858 above) 184.

874 Leckie (n 657 above) 64.

and international levels,[875] there are more critical issues yet unresolved.

From the expositions of writers on this subject, it is apparent that the minimum threshold approach at best only offers a platform for implementing economic, social and cultural rights as aggregated interests and claims.[876] How then, I ask, would those minimum essentials be assessed in respect of an individual's economic, social and cultural rights claim, and implemented or remedied such that his or her legitimate expectations will be met? Or, are these rights necessarily rights of such nature that cannot sustain claims by individuals within national schemes? Since the minimum threshold approach debuted in 1988, how much consideration has it received before regional and national juridical bodies outside the industrialised world, particularly in Africa? Its relevance has been limited to economic, social and cultural rights discourses within the UN system.

The minimum threshold approach also presents itself as a minimalist strategy and lends itself to escapist interpretations as it suggests that nothing more may be required of a state once it demonstrates its compliance with the minimum standards. Since the socio-economic conditions of countries are not static, how this approach that relies heavily on long-term collation of statistical data can effectively respond to the dynamic changes that could occur within a country within short periods remains an open question. It could become possible for states experiencing a boost in their economies to keep their standards of economic, social and cultural rights implementation at the level of otherwise obsolete 'minimum' benchmarks.[877]

Beyond being mere abstract guides, it is difficult to see how much promise this approach holds for rendering recalcitrant regimes pliable

875 For a comprehensive analysis of the place of indicators and benchmarks in global economic, social and cultural rights discourse, see K Tomaševski 'Indicators' in Eide *et al* (n 29 above) 531-543; A Eide 'The use of indicators in the practice of the Committee on Economic, Social and Cultural Rights' in Eide *et al* (n 29 above) 545-551. See also M Nowak 'The right to education' in Eide *et al* (n 29 above) 245 257; P Hunt 'State obligations, indicators, benchmarks and the right to education' Background Paper submitted to the ESCR Committee, UN Doc E/C.12/1998/11 (16 July 1998), 3-9, reprinted in *Human Rights Law and Practice* (1998) 109-115.

876 See Coomans (n 853 above) 12; Eide (n 860 above) 46.

877 As far back as 1988, a special committee of INGOs working in the field of economic, social and cultural rights had discovered the futility of the minimum threshold approach as 'a more radical attempt to arrive at distributive justice as a means of achieving all such rights in a process of rapid equalisation'. According to that body, '[t]ragic examples of failures in implementing such a process have led to a growing realisation that this is an unrealisable alternative in the light of contemporary realities'. See D Lack 'Human rights and the disadvantaged' (1989) 10 *Human Rights Law Journal* 53 55.

to adopting those indicators and benchmarks that would facilitate the effective monitoring of their compliance.

Proponents of this approach do not seem to have addressed their minds to the stand-by excuses of otherwise unwilling governments as regards the resource-intensive implications and statistical complexities involved in such a venture. Since 1991 when the ESCR Committee issued its Reporting Guidelines requiring state parties to furnish details of the indicators and national benchmarks developed to measure the achievement of ICESCR provisions,[878] how many African state parties have effectively complied with that directive?[879] None. With the tremendous difficulties already acknowledged and anticipated in the formulation of country-specific benchmarks,[880] and the collation of statistical data over several years, I wonder how long the marginalised, homeless, oppressed, deprived, AIDS-orphaned children and HIV sufferers in Africa will have to wait for their governments to respond to those indicators and benchmarks. It becomes inevitable to conclude that the inherent weaknesses and difficulties of the minimum threshold approach will not enhance the effective implementation of economic, social and cultural rights in Africa.

'Resource-based obligations'

This is an offshoot of the obligations approach. It flows from the language of article 2(1) of ICESCR which obligates states to 'take steps ... to the maximum limit of available resources'. There seems to be a consensus among economic, social and cultural rights scholars that 'available resources' refers not only to those located within a state, but also includes all resources available to a state from the international community through 'international assistance and co-operation' as envisaged by article 2(1) of ICESCR.[881] There is also agreement that, while a state is obliged to apply the maximum of its available resources to secure the fulfilment of ICESCR, it is not

878 See 'Revised Guidelines' (n 117 above).

879 Rather than showing in their periodic reports the extent to which the various rights are, or are not being enjoyed by all individuals within their territories by giving 'special attention' to 'specific groups or sub-groups which appear to be particularly vulnerable or disadvantaged', as contemplated by ESCR Committee General Comment No 1, most states simply prepare and submit general national development statistics or estimates.

880 See generally Toebes (n 858 above) 185, observing that '[s]tates ... would not easily set their own benchmarks, because they are not inclined to make themselves accountable voluntarily'.

881 See Sepulveda (n 80 above) 315; Limburg Principles (n 48 above) para 26; Tomaševski (n 875 above) 548.

substantially fettered in its liberty to allocate resources according to its priorities.[882] What is, however, problematic is the tendency towards considering the requirement of article 2(1) as a subjective test based on the economic strength of a state. Setting out what constitutes the crux of this understanding, Eide posits:

> The immediate obligations of states under article 2 imply that *countries with more resources have a higher level of core content or immediate duties than those with more limited resources*. Objectively this should be possible to determine on the basis of GNP *per capita*. The question is not what resources are in the hands of the government as compared to privately owned resources – that is a political question which cannot be used as an excuse – but on the total resources of the country as a whole. *How the implementation is to be carried out*, either by reliance on what people manage themselves when income distribution is relatively equal, or by redistribution through the government when resources are unevenly distributed, *depends on the conditions which will vary in the different countries*.[883]

This interpretation has found acceptance in other scholarly works. In their intuitive suggestion that the obligation of a state under ICESCR is contingent on the availability of its resources, Alston and Quinn stated that 'it is the state of a country's economy that most vitally determines the level of its obligations as they relate to any of the enumerated rights under the Covenant'.[884] In his own interpretation of the identical phrase 'to the maximum extent of their available resources' in CRC, Hammarberg asserted that:

> The sentence ... asks all states parties to give priority within their means to the implementation of the [CRC]. This has interesting implications. One is that *countries with more resources should offer services to children on a higher absolute level than is possible for poor countries ... This makes the Convention more relevant in the affluent countries*.[885]

On the question of what then becomes of the responsibility of 'poorer' states, Hammarberg advocates that 'poor countries should at least endeavour to fulfil the minimum core obligations'.[886] Despite its

882 See Sepulveda (n 80 above); P Alston 'International law and the human right to food' in P Alston et al (eds) *The right to food* (1984) 9 38; RE Robertson 'Measuring state compliance with the obligation to devote the maximum available resources to realising economic, social and cultural rights' (1994) 16 *Human Rights Quarterly* 693. See also Alston & Quinn (n 836 above) 177, observing that '[i]n ascertaining the quantum of resources to be set aside to promote the realisation of [ESCR], the state is ... entitled to a wide measure of discretion'.

883 Eide (n 108 above) 27 (my emphasis).

884 Alston & Quinn (n 836 above) 156 169.

885 T Hammarberg 'Children' in Eide *et al* (n 29 above) 353 366 (my emphasis). See also 'World declaration and plan of action from the world summit for children, United Nations' Children Fund (UNICEF)' 1990 point 10; SA Hewlett *Child neglect in rich nations* (1993) 1-10, for a similar reasoning.

886 As above.

scholarly support, the 'resource-based' understanding within the global economic, social and cultural rights discourse has some limitations in deepening the relevance of economic, social and cultural rights in the states that make up Africa. It is indeed a flawed approach in many ways. For one, it complicates the fragile status of economic, social and cultural rights by relativising them. If these rights are to attract universal reckoning as civil and political rights have done, fracturing the standards of measuring state capacities in terms of resources will only lead to variegated responses and destroy the hope of translating economic, social and cultural rights into universal norms. Further, this approach is capable of defeating concerted efforts aimed at negating the earlier-day notion that the fulfilment of economic, social and cultural rights is contingent on the fiscal ability of a state.[887] The Maastricht Guidelines, for instance, stipulate that 'resource scarcity does not relieve states of certain minimum obligations in respect of the implementation of economic, social and cultural rights'.[888] The Limburg Principles also stress that the obligation to implement economic, social and cultural rights in every state exists 'regardless of the level of economic development, to ensure respect for minimum subsistence rights for all'.[889] Similarly, in its General Comment No 3, the ESCR Committee had underscored

> the fact that even in times of severe resources constraints whether caused by a process of adjustment, of economic recession, or by other factors, the vulnerable members of society can and indeed must be protected by the adoption of relatively low-cost targeted programmes.[890]

As I have argued at various points in this book, it will be unhelpful to the economic, social and cultural rights struggle to define the obligations of states strictly in terms of their resource ability.[891] Rather than creating divergent human rights responsibilities among states by overgeneralising the problem of national poverty, efforts

887 See generally Goldewijk *et al* (n 45 above) 37, warning that, because the 'available resources' for some states are very limited in comparison to those of others ... this formula [must not] easily be misconstrued as suggesting that they thus have few if any obligations and responsibilities'.

888 Maastricht Guidelines (n 49 above) para 10. For an analysis of this guideline as a de-emphasis of resources as precondition for economic, social and cultural rights fulfilment, see V Dankwa *et al* 'Commentary on the Maastricht Guidelines on violations of economic, social and cultural rights' (1987) 20 *Human Rights Quarterly* 705 717.

889 Limburg Principles (n 48 above) para 25.

890 General Comment No 3 (n 91 above) para 12. See ESCR Committee 'Concluding observations - Iraq' UN Doc E/1998/22, para 253, where the ESCR Committee asserted that 'while being aware that the embargo imposed on Iraq creates extremely difficult conditions with respect to the availability of food, medicines and medical articles, the [ESCR Committee] recommends that the government take all necessary measures, to the maximum extent of its available resources, to address the needs of the ... most vulnerable groups'.

891 See, eg, 87-91 above where I discussed this as a thematic concern in this book.

should be directed more at emphasising the fiscal accountability of the so-called poorer states for the disbursement of their scarce resources. This is the kind of 'resource-based' approach that will boost the implementation of economic, social and cultural rights in Africa and reinforce the path towards good governance, human development and the alleviation of the adversities of the African masses.

From all the works so far cited on the obligations approach, the approach is overly state-centric because it predicates the realisation of economic, social and cultural rights entirely on states - what a state is obliged to do, to what extent, and in what manner. That in itself presents a potent shortfall as it may offer little or no assistance to individuals and NGOs directly seeking a remedy against non-state actors (for example, IFIs, MNEs, TNCs and private persons) who, by experience, have been prominent in the infringement of economic, social and cultural rights in Africa.[892]

2.1.2 The 'violations' approach

Much scepticism had surrounded the question as to whether or not there can be 'violations' of economic, social and cultural rights as one would have in the field of civil and political rights.[893] This scepticism

892 On the impact of IMF and World Bank activities on economic, social and cultural rights, livelihood and human development in Africa, see L Tshuma 'The impact of IMF/World Bank dictated economic structural adjustment programmemes on human rights: erosion of empowerment rights' in P Nherere *et al* (eds) *The institutionalisation of human rights in Southern Africa* (1993); A Adepoju *The impact of structural adjustments on the population of Africa* (1993); Y Osinbajo *et al* 'Human rights and economic development in developing countries' (1994) 28 *International Law* 727; SP Schatz 'Structural adjustment in Africa: A failing grade so far' (1994) 32 *Journal of Modern African Studies* 679; B Sadasivam 'The impact of structural adjustment on women: A governance and human rights agenda' (1996) 19 *Human Rights Quarterly* 630; PJ Kaiser 'Structural adjustment and the fragile nation: The demise of social unity in Tanzania' (1996) 34 *Journal of Modern African Studies* 679; J Oloka-Onyango 'Poverty, human rights and quest for sustainable human development in structurally-adjusted Uganda' (2000) 18 *Netherlands Quarterly of Human Rights* 23.

893 The Limburg Principles was the first instrument to define the 'failure by a state party to comply with an obligation contained in the [ICESCR to be] ... under international law, a violation of the Covenant'. See Limburg Principles (n 48 above) paras 70-73. Under para 72, a state would have committed a 'violation' in any of the following seven circumstances: if 'it fails to take a step which it is required to take by the Covenant; it fails to remove promptly obstacles which it is under a duty to remove to permit the immediate fulfilment of a right; it fails to implement without delay a right which it is required by the Covenant to provide immediately; it wilfully fails to meet a generally accepted international minimum standard of achievement, which is within its powers to meet; it applies a limitation to a right recognised in the Covenant other than in accordance with the Covenant; it deliberately retards or halts the progressive realisation of a right, unless it is acting within a limitation permitted by the Covenant or it does so due to a lack of available resources or *force majeure*; it fails to submit reports as required under the Covenant'. For a scholarly analysis of these elements, see EVO Dankwa *et al* 'Commentary by the Rapporteurs on the nature and scope of

has simply not been the product of the complacency of states and powerful intergovernmental institutions, but also of the cynicism of some human rights traditionalists.[894] From the early 1990s, however, more critical understanding was directed at the connotations of the 'progressive realisation' concept of ICESCR, prompting a rigorous inquiry into what would constitute the 'violations' of economic, social and cultural rights.[895]

The most articulate version of the 'violations approach' was propounded by Audrey Chapman at the International Commission of Jurists Conference on Economic, Social and Cultural Rights and the Role of Lawyers held in Bangalore, India, in October 1995 as 'a new approach' to monitoring the implementation of ICESCR.[896] Contending that focusing on the evaluation of 'progressive realisation' within the context of 'the maximum of available resources' leads to complicated methodologies, Chapman advocated that 'it seems more fruitful and significant to focus on monitoring violations'.[897]

In Chapman's reasoning, since the preconditions required for the methodical monitoring of economic, social and cultural rights were non-existent at the levels of states,[898] the 'violations approach' provides the most viable alternative means of monitoring economic,

state parties' obligations' (1987) 9 *Human Rights Quarterly* 136 145-146. The Maastricht Guidelines also enumerate seven 'acts of commission' and ten 'acts of omission' that would constitute 'violations' of economic, social and cultural rights. See Maastricht Guidelines (n 49 above) paras 14 & 15, respectively. For a scholarly discussion of these violations, see Dankwa *et al* (n 49 above) 721-723.

894 See generally Leckie (n 657 above) 37-39.

895 See Dankwa *et al* (n 49 above) 706; Leckie (n 657 above) 57. See also *Report of UN Seminar on appropriate indicators to measure achievements in the progressive realisation of economic, social and cultural rights* UN Doc A/CONF.157/PC/73 (1993).

896 See A Chapman 'A new approach to monitoring the International Covenant on Economic, Social and Cultural Rights' (1995) 55 *Review of the International Commission of Jurists* 23 30-32. Chapman advanced her theory in a 1996 article titled 'A "violations approach" for monitoring the International Covenant on Economic, Social and Cultural Rights' (1996) 18 *Human Rights Quarterly* 23-66. See Sepulveda (n 80 above) 20. Other literature by Chapman promoting the same approach includes 'Monitoring socio-economic rights: A violations approach' (1998) 1 *Economics and Social Rights Review* 3; 'Background paper on violations of the right to education' UN Doc E/C.12/1998/19 (14 October 1998); 'Violations of the right to health' in *SIM Special* No 20 (n 657 above) 87-112.

897 Chapman (n 896 above) 30.

898 The five preconditions identified by Chapman were: '(1) conceptualisation of the specific components of each enumerated right and the concomitant obligations of state parties; (2) delineation of performance standards related to each of these components, including the identification of potential major violations; (3) collection of relevant data, appropriately disaggregated by sex and a variety of other variables; (4) development of an information management system for these data to facilitate analysis of trends over time and comparisons of the status of groups within a country; and (5) the ability to analyse these data in order to determine patterns and trends'. Chapman (n 896 above) 29.

social and cultural rights.[899] Ostensibly to evade the theoretical difficulties about the exact nature and scope of the obligations of states under ICESCR, as experienced in the work of the ESCR Committee,[900] Chapman essentially proposes that, rather than defining obligations simply in terms of what states *must do*, it will be more helpful to first identify violations in terms of what states *must not do*.[901]

While the debate continues on whether or not the non-performance of economic, social and cultural rights obligations amounts to a 'violation',[902] the terminology has continued to be employed in human rights literature.[903] As vital as this approach may be to the understanding of economic, social and cultural rights, I find some inherent conceptual weaknesses in it. In the first instance, this approach over-generalises the elements that would constitute 'violations'.[904] This is particularly grave, considering the fact that the ESCR Committee itself has adroitly avoided the use of the 'violation' terminology in its Concluding Observations and General Comments.[905]

On another ground, since the 'violations approach' is essentially predicated on the goal of avoiding the complexities of the 'progressive realisation' concept of ICESCR, it is difficult to perceive how much assistance it portends for the implementation of economic, social and cultural rights in regional and national human rights

899 Chapman (n 896 above) 36.

900 See n 896 above 39, where Chapman relied extensively on the official records of the ESCR Committee from the 6th session in 1991 to the 11th session in 1994.

901 See Chapman (n 28 above) 34-35. See also Leckie (n 657 above) 58, analysing the 'three categories' of violations based on Chapman's theory as '(1) violations deriving from governmental actions, laws and policies; (2) violations based on acts or policies reflecting discrimination; and (3) violations resulting from the failure to implement a core minimum'.

902 See eg F van Hoof Explanatory note on the Utrecht Draft Optional Protocol 'The right to complain about economic, social and cultural rights' (1995) 18 *SIM Special* 147. Compare Leckie (n 657 above) 57.

903 Some of the relevant literature in which this approach was considered and applied includes the Maastricht Guidelines (n 49 above); Leckie (n 657 above) ch 4; S Leckie 'Another step towards indivisibility: Identifying the key features of violations of economic, social and cultural rights' (1998) 20 *Human Rights Quarterly* 81; VA Leary 'A violations approach to the rights to work (labour rights)' in *SIM Special* No 20 (n 657 above) ch 5; F Coomans 'Identifying violations of the right to education' in *SIM Special* No 20 (n 657 above) ch 6; I Westerndorp 'The feasibility of a violations approach of women's economic, social and cultural rights' in *SIM Special* 20 (n 657 above) ch 7; R Künnemann 'Violations of the right to food' in *SIM Special* No 20 (n 657 above) ch 8; R Künnemann 'The right to adequate food: Violations related to its minimum core content' in Chapman et al (n 101 above) 32-36; M Nowak 'The right to education' in Eide *et al* (n 29 above) 245 256-257; Toebes (n 858 above) 180-181.

904 According to Leckie, eg, 'this approach defines violations very loosely by considering virtually all critical comments by the [ESCR Committee] as *prima facie* violations of the [ICESCR], whether or not this body (the only authoritative body legally competent to make such pronouncements) viewed a particular act or omission as a violation or not'. See Leckie (n 657 above) 58-59.

905 As above and accompanying n 49.

regimes where that concept is unknown. A critical danger that lies in the importation of this approach into a human rights system such as exists in the African region would mean a diminution of the quest for a stronger and more efficient accountability of states for economic, social and cultural rights.

Another critical issue is that the employment of 'violations' in the economic, social and cultural rights discourse imports the notion that there must be *victims* of such violations.[906] At this fledgling stage of economic, social and cultural rights jurisprudence in most countries, it is doubtful if one can argue that victims of economic, social and cultural rights violations are so invariable and so ascertainable that they can individually seek a remedy in their national courts or even before intergovernmental juridical bodies based on the statistical methodology propounded by Chapman. Even where economic, social and cultural rights are established as positive legal rights, national judiciaries have not sufficiently grasped the definitive and normative complexities of these rights so well as to be adequately equipped to redress every individual 'violation'.

The approach also amounts to putting the cart before the horse as far as its applicability is concerned at the domestic level. Chapman stresses that the advantage of the violations approach lies in identifying violations 'without having first to conceptualise the full scope of the right in question'.[907] This in itself is an antithesis to the basic philosophical understanding of rights-duties dynamics that seek first to determine the legal basis of every claim by a right-holder against a duty-bearer.[908]

A basic understanding that emerges from the foregoing analysis is that attempts at establishing a coherent and universal paradigm for the remedial implementation of economic, social and cultural rights are still evolving. The analysis of current approaches highlights their strong points and weaknesses and exposes the need to re-conceptualise their significance and relevance for the effective implementation of economic, social and cultural rights in Africa.

906 See *Guissé Final Report* 1997 (n 820 above) paras 13-137, for an unhelpful attempt by the UN Special Rapporteur on Impunity at establishing a basis for the identification of 'victims' of economic, social and cultural rights. See generally Leckie (n 657 above) 59-60 and accompanying nn 50-51. For a discussion of 'victim' in international human rights law, see Shelton (n 821 above) 183-189.

907 Chapman (n 896 above) 4.

908 See generally Leckie (n 657 above) 37 67.

2.2 An African response to the dilemma

No matter how active the discourse within the international arena might be, it remains a matter of critical importance that economic, social and cultural rights must acquire active legal, juridical and popular recognition at the regional and domestic levels. Moreover, in formulating approaches through which global economic, social and cultural rights understanding would crystallise, contextual normative and structural peculiarities should be taken into account. By this I mean that any human rights approach that would be helpful to the ultimate goals of development in Africa should always consider the dynamics of continental human rights frameworks and experiences. Current approaches do not seem to consider these and their human development enhancing capacities are also yet to be adequately explored. While these approaches overstress the role of economic, social and cultural rights players at the international level, and the role of 'willing' states at the domestic level, they largely ignore the question of *how* to pursue and *who* will pursue the task of implementing them in states under recalcitrant regimes. By Chapman's violations approach, for example, the implementation of economic, social and cultural rights 'necessitates the development of a *multiplicity of performance standards for each enumerated right* in relationship to the varied social, developmental, and resources contexts of specific countries.[909] However, in the impecunious circumstances of the African Union (AU), the African regional human rights system cannot afford the enormous cost of such 'multiplicity of [country-specific] performance standards'.[910] A wholesale adoption of the violations approach in the African regional system would create unnecessary and unhelpful conceptual debates and may invariably defeat or blunt the entire struggle for economic, social and cultural rights at that level.

I contend that the African Charter already sufficiently equips the African Commission (and the emergent African Court) with both the statutory mandate and the moral authority to address economic, social and cultural rights claims, and to implement these rights through case-by-case situations and through its reporting mechanisms – without unnecessarily beclouding this institutional capacity with a complex and hypothetical 'violationist' methodology.

909 Chapman (n 45 above) 31 (my emphasis).

910 See generally D Olowu 'Regional integration, development and the African Union agenda: Challenges, gaps and opportunities' (2004) 13 *Journal of Transnational Law and Contemporary Problems* 211 244, noting the 'financial kwashiorkor' of the AU, a carried-over feature of the defunct Organisation of African Unity, as a formidable impediment to the good intentions of the AU human rights agenda. Chapman herself acknowledged the unwillingness of states to disseminate the type of statistical data she envisages with supranational organs. See Chapman (n 45 above) 34.

Save for the question of her methodology that is centrally predicated on the 'progressive realisation' concept, and its outright rejection of the obligations approach, Chapman's violations approach would have been suitable for an African regional understanding of economic, social and cultural rights. The African Charter is an instrument squarely founded on the obligations of state parties. There can therefore be no conceivable basis for rendering states accountable under the Charter without identifying what wrongful act or omission a state has committed.[911] However, that again accentuates a low side to the minimum threshold approach.

Rather than attempting to create supposedly 'objective' indicators that might either turn out to be problematic or even futile, I argue that the regional and national human rights organs saddled with oversight responsibilities should be left to determine what states' responsibilities are in each *specific* situation (whether on individual or collective claims), prescribing the *most appropriate remedies* for such situations, and thus engender a process that would crystallise economic, social and cultural rights standards of implementation across the board. By virtue of their natural and historical role as dispassionate arbiters, juridical organs are generally better placed to administer specifically framed remedies to meet the demands of each case rather than formulating broad rules of general application that may turn out to be impracticable or to occasion hardship. This will not prevent such organs from adopting predictable responses to easily recognised economic, social and cultural rights violations like inequality and discriminatory practices. This proposal seems to me to be the most viable in the present African circumstances as it serves both the demands of the immediate and long-term implementation of economic, social and cultural rights in Africa.

It is remarkable to note that both the Cape High Court and the Constitutional Court of South Africa declined to consider the minimum threshold approach in their interpretation of article 26 of the South African Constitution in *Grootboom*[912] and article 27 in *Treatment*

911 It has become an entrenched rule of practice within the African regional human rights system that for a communication to be admissible, it must set out the '[p]rovision(s) of the [African] Charter allegedly violated', supported by the 'facts of the claim'. See Rule 103, Rules of Procedure of the African Commission on Human and Peoples' Rights, adopted 6 October 1995.

912 See *Grootboom* (n 144 above) paras 30-33. See K Pillay *et al* 'Case review: *Grootboom v Oostenberg Municipality* (2000) 2 *Economics and Social Rights Review* 6; K Young 'Conceptualising minimalism in socio-economic rights' (2008) 9 *ESR Review: Economic and Social Rights in South Africa* 6-11.

Action Campaign.[913] The near-absolute silence of economic, social and cultural rights commentators and scholars on this incident is ominous.[914]

As far as the resource dimension to the implementation of economic, social and cultural rights is concerned in Africa, scholars often over-generalise the poverty of African states. While many African states are indeed shackled by the adverse conditionalities of IFIs, the bigger crisis of their incapacity lies in corruption and malevolent governance exemplified by skewed policy prioritisation.[915] As an illustration, in an extensive consultative research on Africa in November 1999, it was discovered that 'more than 50% of the annual budget of [Burundi, the Democratic Republic of Congo and Rwanda] is spent on war efforts, and less than 3% on social issues such as food security, health and education'.[916] Similarly, between 1983, when the Nigerian military took over political control and suspended constitutional democracy, and 1999, when civil rule re-emerged, the defence budget (military and security expenditure) consistently exceeded the combined sub-total for education, health and rural development. In the nascent Nigerian civil rule, there has been no noteworthy shift in budgetary priorities.[917] Despite Angola's enviable position of being the second largest crude oil exporting country in Africa, colossal sums of public funds continue to be squandered through gigantic corruption and mismanagement, a phenomenon that has perpetuated malnutrition, humanitarian crises, and the devaluation of the economic, social and cultural rights of ordinary Angolans.[918]

913 *Treatment Action Campaign* (n 780 above) para 37, where the Constitutional Court stressed that 'the courts are not institutionally equipped to make the wide-ranging factual and political enquiries necessary for determining what the minimum-core standards called for by the first and second amici should be'.

914 For an extensive analysis of the refusal of the Constitutional Court to uphold the 'minimum core obligation' concept in *Treatment Action Campaign* and its indication of the court's 'retreat from its position in *Grootboom*', see Fitzpatrick (n 783 above) 677-679. See also S Yeshanew 'Combining the "minimum core" and "reasonableness" models of reviewing socio-economic rights' (2008) 9 *ESR Review* 8.

915 See generally G Scott 'Who has failed Africa? IMF measures or the African leadership?' (1998) 33 *Journal of Asian AND African Studies* 265; N Kofele-Kale 'Change or the illusion of change: The war against official corruption in Africa' (2006) 38 *George Washington International Law Review* 697.

916 See A Benoit *et al* 'Development and economic, social and cultural rights: An NGO challenge' May 2000 http://www.11.be/standpunten/internationaal/esc_paper2000.htm (accessed 12 June 2009).

917 See generally Department for International Development (DFID) *Governance, development and democratic politics: DFID's work in building more effective states* (2007).

918 See 'Angola: Account for missing oil revenues: Disappearance of $4,2 billion undermines fundamental rights' http://www.hrw.org/english/docs/2004/01/12/angola6925.htm (accessed 22 November 2008).

Commentators are yet to emphasise that in the ordinary exercise of their constitutional functions, national judiciaries have rendered judgments that essentially shape policies or that directly implicate budgetary expenditure. African judiciaries have not been left out of this phenomenon, albeit mainly in the civil and political rights field. A long line of cases from diverse jurisdictions vindicates this assertion.[919]

Against the backdrop of the tangled conceptual state of economic, social and cultural rights at the international level and the marginalisation of these rights in much of Africa, compounded by their threatened atrophy at regional and national fora, from what standpoint can Africa begin to evolve its approach to the implementation of economic, social and cultural rights? I strongly propose an evolution of economic, social and cultural rights implementation at national levels drawing on lessons from salient comparative human rights experiences. By this I mean the overarching necessity to understand the basic interpretative elements and remedial implementation techniques that have been adopted and applied in strikingly similar or familiar contexts and subjecting their viable elements to local specificities. With particular regard to this discourse, the Indian and South African contexts provide the best examples for the same reasons as I had highlighted in previous chapters.[920] While not deviating from my permeating concern for

919 See eg *Shugaba v The Federal Minister of Internal Affairs* (1981) 2 NCLR 459, where, in a case involving the violation of the right of immunity from deportation, apart from the declaratory and injunctive reliefs, the court granted the deported Nigerian citizen compensatory and exemplary damages; *August* (n 775 above), where the South African Constitutional Court ordered the state to ensure that prisoners who are not statutorily barred from voting are allowed to vote in the South African general elections; *Strydom v Minister of Correctional Services* 1993 3 BCLR 342 (W), where Schwartzman J, of the High Court of the Western Cape, South Africa, held that maximum-security prisoners at the Johannesburg prisons had a right to electricity in their cells, and thus ordered the respondents to report to court with a cogent timetable setting out the period within which the electrical upgrading of the affected section of the prisons would be completed. The Court found out that the respondents had no explanation for the delay. Also, in *Blanchard v Minister of Justice, Legal and Parliamentary Affairs* 1999 10 BCLR 1169 (Zimbabwean Supreme Court), the Court expressed its displeasure with the inhuman and degrading treatment of prisoners and granted them an order for costs against the state.

920 Apart from the appeal of contextual similarities, I have chosen these two as models to accentuate the active *follow-up* mechanisms adopted and applied by the juridical bodies in these two states. An analysis of the pragmatism of the judiciaries in these two states will be helpful to the understanding and development of economic, social and cultural rights jurisprudence and implementation through the proposed individual complaints mechanism in the ESCR Committee, the emerging African Court, and of course, other national judicial institutions, particularly in states where institutional economic, social and cultural rights protection is weak. Although the European and Inter-American regional human rights arrangements have recorded notable juridical efforts in pronouncing justiciable aspects of economic, social and cultural rights, they have not exerted the use of *supervisory jurisdiction* as the courts in India and South Africa have done in the implementation of remedies.

asserting economic, social and cultural rights as *legal* rights, I am emphasising those elements that underscore the role of other national juridical bodies in adopting innovative approaches to remedial implementation.

At the regional level, I contend that within the purview of available normative frameworks, what remains to enliven economic, social and cultural rights is the adoption of creative and innovative implementation strategies by regional monitoring bodies as well as the organised civil society and other stakeholders. It is simply neither enough for the African Commission to declare that a state is in violation without identifying ways by which such a state might remedy its violation(s), nor to be selective in the remedial implementation of economic, social and cultural rights.[921]

This will be a litmus test for the new-fangled African Court also.[922] Rather than hoisting itself like a lame duck institution in the remedial implementation of economic, social and cultural rights, the African Commission can begin to assert its under-utilised interpretive and monitoring mandates to enhance the appreciation of economic, social and cultural rights in Africa.

921 There were a number of cases where the African Commission should have prescribed appropriate remedies for established 'violations.' Eg, in *Pagnoulle* (n 705 above), even though the African Commission had found that the failure of Cameroon to reinstate the applicant was a violation of the right to work, it declined to recommend his reinstatement. Similarly, in *Free Legal Assistance* (n 257 above), where the African Commission established that the arbitrary closure of universities for two years and the non-payment of teachers' salaries as a result of egregious corruption violated the right to education under the African Charter, a recommendation that such schools be re-opened, that arrears of salaries be paid and that the government should desist from such acts in the future would have been appropriate. In *Ogoni*, once the African Commission had found a violation of the rights to housing, food and of people to freely dispose of their wealth and natural resources, the body should have proceeded to recommend compensation to be paid to those who lost shelter and livelihood, and that any effort by government to remedy the age-long spoliation activities should fashion out viable participatory role for Niger-Delta peoples in the distribution of the wealth and resources of their natural environment. In all these decisions, it would have been appropriate for the African Commission to have directed the affected states to submit in their next periodic reports, or within the scope of a period prescribed by the African Commission, measures taken to comply with the recommendations. Compare *Moore v The Gambia* (n 719 above), where the African Commission established, *inter alia*, a violation of the right to health of the complainants under a Lunatics Detention Act. The African Commission called on the government of The Gambia to effect the following recommendations: (a) repeal the Act and replace it with one compatible with the African Charter and international standards; (b) create an expert body to review all cases of detention under the Act and to make recommendations for release; and (c) to provide medical and material care for all mental health patients in the country. The Commission added that the government should submit in its next periodic reports measures taken to comply with the Commission's recommendations.

922 Art 27 of the African Court Protocol provides: 'If the Court finds that there has been a violation of a human or peoples' right, it shall make appropriate orders to remedy the violation, including the payment of fair compensation or reparation'.

It might also become helpful that, in considering some of the real-life situations where national judiciaries have positively intervened in remedying human rights violations of socio-economic and cultural nature, the African human rights community should begin to view the remedial implementation of economic, social and cultural rights at regional and national levels, not merely as a subject of possibility, but also of inevitable reality. To this end, I contend that a pragmatic approach to the effective implementation of economic, social and cultural rights in Africa should focus more on prevention of the circumstances that engender economic, social and cultural rights 'violations' rather than on *ex post facto* remedial responses as are traditionally attached to human rights abuses generally.[923]

3 Paradigms of remedial implementation: Two case studies

How have national courts confronted the challenge of providing a remedy for economic, social and cultural rights claims? How have international and regional juridical bodies responded to the task of holding governments and institutions accountable for human rights violations? In these circumstances, how have these bodies interpreted the *substantive provisions* of human rights instruments to secure the implementation of economic, social and cultural rights either as direct or indirect legal claims? This plethora of questions is worthy of examination.

In a comparative regional context, the most detailed regime for the remedial implementation of economic, social and cultural rights should ordinarily be the European Social Charter.[924] However, because the work of its supervisory organs has essentially dealt more with the consideration of states' reports, in particular, the textual conformity of national legislation to Charter provisions, the European system

923 See generally the *Velazquez Rodriguez* case, IACHR Series C No 4 (29 July 1988) para 134, where the Inter-American Court stressed that '[t]he objective of international human rights law is ... to protect the victims and to provide for the reparation of damages resulting from the acts of the states responsible'. See also Drost (n 835 above) 56-57, analysing how the occurrence of 'the violation of a human right' gives rise to an obligation of a state 'to make amends, to give compensation and to adjust or correct the illegal condition, act or omission'.

924 I have considerably analysed the framework of economic, social and cultural rights implementation under the European regional human rights system in ch IV.

offers little remedial exemplar as I contemplate in this discourse.[925] The implication is to look elsewhere for helpful paradigms.

It is, however, not my intention in this segment to explore the details of *all* jurisprudence emanating from international, regional and national judicial, quasi-judicial and non-judicial organs on economic, social and cultural rights protection as these have been covered elsewhere, to the extent of their relevance.[926] I merely intend to examine how judicial bodies in two model states approached the implementation of human rights generally as to give effect to economic, social and cultural rights, and how, in other cases, they approached the subject of *remedial* implementation where these rights were concerned. By so doing, my discourse will accentuate essential elements that would inform the formulation of a practical trajectory towards the effective implementation of economic, social and cultural rights in Africa.

3.1 India

In the exercise of its 'epistolary jurisdiction',[927] the Indian judiciary not only created innovative procedural mechanisms as I discussed in chapter IV, but it has also evolved dynamic remedial approaches where traditional Anglo-Saxon judicial remedies would otherwise have been inadequate or belated.[928] For instance, in *Bandhua Mukti*

925 As of 12 June 2009, 51 collective complaints had been filed before the European Committee on Social Rights. Since the *International Commission Jurists v Portugal* decision, already discussed in ch IV above, numerous other complaints have received the adoption of a Resolution by the Committee of Ministers. See European Social Charter, list of complaints and advancement of the procedure (as of 12 June 2009)' http://www.coe.int/t/e/human_rights/esc/4_collective_complaints/List_of_collective_complaints/default.asp#TopOfPage (accessed 12 June 2009). See Council of Europe *European Social Charter: Collected texts* (2003) 211-224.

926 See my earlier discussion of that subject in ch IV. It is pertinent to note, however, that, while Shelton's leading work in this area extensively examined human rights remedies from diverse perspectives (international, regional and national), the economic, social and cultural rights dimension was less explored. The heads of remedies discussed in Shelton's work are 'declaratory judgments'; 'compensation'; 'punitive or exemplary damages'; and 'non-monetary remedies'. See Shelton (n 821 above) 68-92 199-357. Contrast W Trengrove 'Judicial remedies for violations of socio-economic rights' (1999) 1 *Economics and Social Rights Review* 8; C Steinberg 'Can reasonableness protect the poor? A review of South Africa's socio-economic rights jurisprudence' (2006) 123 *South African Law Journal* 264-284; C Mbazira 'Confronting the problem of polycentricity in enforcing the socio-economic rights in the South African Constitution' (2008) 23 *SA Public Law* 30-49; C Mbazira 'Appropriate, just and equitable relief in socio-economic rights litigation: The tension between corrective and distributive forms of justice' (2008) *South African Law Journal* 71.

927 See n 607 above and accompanying text.

928 See generally Lalwani (n 605 above) 91-93, discussing the 'collaborative' and 'investigative' components that have become the hallmark of remedial implementation through the public interest litigation system in India.

Morcha,[929] an order was made issuing various directives for identifying, releasing and rehabilitating bonded labourers, ensuring the payment of minimum wages, the observance of labour laws, the provision of hygienic water, and the setting up of dust-sucking equipment in the affected stone quarries. The court backed its pronouncements up with the creation of an agency to monitor and report on the progress of implementation.

Similarly, in *Khatri v State of Bihar* (the *Bhagalpur Blinding* case),[930] where the police had allegedly tortured and inflicted blindness on pre-trial detainees, the court directed the government of the state of Bihar to provide medical and rehabilitative services to the injured detainees even before it went into the determination of criminal liability for the wrong. In that instance, the court sought the reports of independent assessors on the level of compliance with its order.

The Supreme Court's role in *Mehta v Union of India* (the *Sri Ram Fertiliser Gas Leak* case)[931] is also of particular interest. An emission of noxious fumes from a private factory had caused serious injuries to a number of persons. Upon the filing of an action against the factory, the Court first ordered the closure of the plant and the setting up of a victims' compensation fund. The Court had deferred the question of whether or not it had jurisdiction under article 32 of the Indian Constitution to provide relief against a private entity. As part of its final decision, the Court recommended that the government set up special courts consisting of a professional judge and two environmental experts to deal with environmental matters.[932]

The Indian judiciary has also shown that the implementation of human rights may not always require conventional judicial decrees but, rather, a redirection of administrative priorities. In *Narayan v State of Bihar*,[933] a case involving complaints against the inhuman and life-threatening conditions in an Indian mental institution, the court directed the infirmary's management to remove the limitations it imposed on inmates' drugs and to revise its expenditure for meals and

929 *Morcha* (n 610 above).

930 AIR 1981 SC 928. For a scholarly commentary on the 'compensatory' jurisdiction exercised by the court in *Khatri* and many other cases, see PS Jaswal 'Public accountability for violation of human rights and judicial activism in India: Some observations' (2002) 3 *SCC* (Journal) 6 http://www.ebc-india.com/lawyer/articles/2002v3a2.htm (accessed 12 June 2009).

931 AIR 1987 SC 965.

932 It is noteworthy that in 1997, the Indian government eventually set up a National Environmental Appellate Authority to handle matters on the environment. The body is headed by a retired justice of the Supreme Court of India and exercises quasi-judicial powers. See Ministry of Environments and Forests, Annual Report of the Government of India http://envfor.nic.in/report/9798/legis.html#lis_neaa (accessed 12 June 2009).

933 *Narayan* AIR 1989 SC 348.

medicines.[934] Similarly, in *State of Himachal Pradesh v Umed Ram Sharmas*,[935] the Supreme Court declined to reverse the decision of the High Court ordering the state to fulfil a constitutional obligation of a positive nature. Some residents of the state of Himachal Pradesh who were all poor *harijans* (untouchables) had applied for an order of the High Court compelling the state to complete the construction of a road to their village. The Court established that the construction of the road had formed part of the state budget, that funds had been allocated for the project, and that some parts of the road had been constructed before the abrupt stoppage. The High Court therefore ordered the Public Works Department to proceed with the road construction and to report to the Court the progress being made. The Supreme Court reiterated its cautious exercise of judicial review, asserting that it would only intervene in cases where there is proven administrative inaction.[936]

It is crucial to note that, in spite of this extensive intervention in *Narayan* and *Umed Ram Sharmas*, the court's orders did not require an increase in financial resources, but a judicious and effective use of what was already available.

In administering social justice through the law, the Indian judiciary has not simply evolved appropriate remedies, but has established a pattern of accompanying them with detailed implementation processes. Thus, in the celebrated case of *Mehta v State of Tamil Nadu*,[937] which served as the springboard for the governmental clampdown on child labour in India, the court directed the state to complete its survey of child labour within six months of the ruling, to create a Child Labour Rehabilitation/Welfare Fund, and to provide education for children.[938] Similar to *Mehta* was the case in *Laxmi Kant v Union of India*.[939] Here there was an action complaining about the failure of the Child Aid Society (CAS) – a governmental parastatal set up to regulate child adoption and to promote the interests of children – to stop the illicit trading in babies to foreigners. In determining the obligation of CAS, the court declared that the body was not only bound by its enabling statute, but also by

934 n 933 above, 352-353.

935 *Umed Ram Sharmas* AIR 1986 SC 817.

936 n 935 above, 831. See also *Manubhai Pragaji Vashi v State of Maharashtra*, AIR 1989 (Bombay) 296, where the High Court interpreted art 14 (equality before the law) and art 41 (directive principle on education) in ordering the government to continue its financial support for a private institution. The college was the only one providing legal education in the state and the state had been funding other colleges - of commerce, engineering and physics. The Court viewed the stoppage of the assistance to the college of law as an infringement of the right to equal treatment in the provision of education.

937 (1996) 6 SCC 756.

938 n 937 above, 760.

939 (1987) 1 SCC 67.

articles 21 and 39(f) of the Indian Constitution to protect the rights of children to life, livelihood and protection against emotional and material neglect. Beyond this declaration, the court went on to issue a set of regulations to guide CAS in fulfilling its constitutional obligations and in dealing with the adoption of children, particularly by foreigners.[940] The court ordered the state to implement these regulations and it monitored their implementation.

In the more recent case of *People's Union for Civil Liberties v Union of India*,[941] the Supreme Court of India laid the foundation of what might become a reference point in a structured approach towards fulfilling the positive aspects of economic, social and cultural rights – in this instance, the right to food, despite the absence of such a right in the Indian Constitution. In response to a public interest action instituted for state intervention in the severe famine that had affected the *Antyodaya* population (the poorest of the poor, comprising approximately 4% of the population), the Court delivered a judgment that has been regarded as a 'landmark' in the evolution of economic, social and cultural rights and 'the battle for the right to food'.[942] In unequivocal fashion, the Court affirmed that once people were shown to be unable to feed themselves in a manner that would ensure their right to life under article 21, the state had an obligation to provide for them, at the very least, what will ensure that they are not exposed to malnourishment, starvation and other related problems. Beyond this normative development, however, the interim orders issued by the Court are significant. Through a series of directive orders, the Court had directed the Indian government to (1) introduce midday meals in all primary schools; (2) provide 35 kilograms of grain per month at highly subsidised prices to 15 million destitute households; and (3) double resource allocations for *Sampoorna Grameen Rozgar Yojana*, India's largest rural employment programme. To monitor the effective implementation of all its orders, the Supreme Court appointed two independent commissioners who were to identify violations of those orders and to demand their redress under the full authority of the Supreme Court. They also had the duty of reporting to the court on implementation.[943]

940 These rules are set out in the Judgment Report 70-79.

941 *PUCL* case (2001) 7 SC 484 (2001).

942 See 'Right to food: The Indian experience' http://www.hrdc.net/sahrdc/hrfeatures/HRF58.htm (accessed 12 June 2009).

943 The appointment of commissioners has been of immense benefit in the fact-finding and implementation activities of the Indian judiciary in public interest litigation cases. See generally Desai *et al* (n 610 above) 166 and accompanying nn 46-58.

3.2 South Africa

South African courts have consistently shown that human rights cases that implicate fiscal disbursement and governmental policies are not automatically beyond judicial consideration. In *August*, having established that the applicant was not within the category of persons to be lawfully deprived of the right to vote under the Electoral Act of 1993,[944] the Constitutional Court embarked on the quest for an 'appropriate remedy' for all prisoners who suffered the same fate.[945] In its judgment, the Court set forth certain structured orders that not only met the justice of the case, but also held promise for future remedial potentials. In the words of the Court:

> 3.1 ... *all persons who were prisoners during each and every period of registration ... and who are not excluded from voting by the provisions of section 8(2) of the Electoral Act 73 of 1998, are entitled to register as voters on the national common voters' rolls*;
>
> ....
>
> 3.4 *The respondents are to make all reasonable arrangements necessary to enable the applicants and other prisoners referred to ... above to vote at the forthcoming general election*;
>
> 3.5 The first respondent is required ... [within 14 days] to serve on the applicants and the third and fourth respondents, and lodge with the Registrar of this Court, an affidavit setting out the manner in which it will comply with ... this order. Any interested person may inspect this affidavit at the registrar's office once it has been lodged.[946]

The *August* decision has quite far-reaching implications. Although the respondents had vehemently contended that remedying the violation as sought by the applicant 'would present the respondents and the electoral process with immense logistical, financial and administrative difficulties ... [with the propensity of being] enormously costly and time consuming',[947] the Court nonetheless proceeded to order a remedy that impelled a shift in the prevailing government policy.

In *Grootboom v Oostenberg Municipality*,[948] the High Court had established a violation of section 28(1)(c) of the South African Constitution which creates a right to shelter for children and consequently granted some extensive remedies that required structured implementation. While holding that the right was not absolute, the Court nonetheless held that, in that particular case, the

944 Sec 16 Electoral Act 202 of 1993.
945 See *August* (n 775 above) para 37.
946 *August* (n 775 above) para 42 (my emphasis).
947 n 946 above, para 13.
948 2000 3 BCLR 277 (C).

state was obliged to provide the applicant children, and by derivation, their accompanying parents, with appropriate shelter until the parents were able to provide for their children. The Court further directed the respondents to present sworn report(s) to the Court on the implementation of the order within three months from the date of that order. It is remarkable that the High Court also ordered that the applicants should file a 'commentary' in response to the reports while the respondents were given an opportunity to reply to that 'commentary'.[949] Even though the Constitutional Court eventually set most of this decision of Davis J aside,[950] the lower court had exhibited a significant level of flexibility and pragmatic understanding in the remedial implementation of economic, social and cultural rights.[951]

In Grootboom, on appeal, the nub of the Court's scrutiny of the state's performance of the right of access to adequate housing (section 26) had been reasonableness. In the finding of the Court, the state had 'failed to make reasonable provision for those living in the Cape metropolitan area with no access to land, no roof over their heads, and who were living in intolerable conditions or crisis situations'.[952] To ensure that its declaratory relief in terms of section 26 did not become ineffective, the Constitutional Court appointed the SAHRC to monitor and report on the compliance by the state with the orders in the judgment.[953]

Later, in Treatment Action Campaign,[954] having established that the South African government's health policy, which confined the distribution of the anti-retroviral drug Nevirapine to certain research and training sites, breached section 27 of the Constitution,[955] the Constitutional Court not only ordered the state to remove restrictions on the distribution of Nevirapine in the prevention of mother-to-child

949 The specific orders of the Court are found at 293H-294C. For a review of the judgment of the High Court, see C Scott *et al* 'Adjudicating constitutional priorities in a transnational context: A comment on Soobramoney's legacy and Grootboom's promise' (2000) 16 *South African Journal on Human Rights* 206 211 256-257.

950 The crux of the Constitutional Court's rejection of the High Court's order was that 'neither sec 26 nor sec 28 entitles the respondents to claim shelter ... immediately upon demand. The High Court order ought therefore not to have been made.' See *Grootboom* (n 144 above) para 95.

951 See generally Scott *et al* (n 949 above) 211, stating that '[t]he order is both deferential to government in terms of fashioning a remedial plan and demanding of government ...'.

952 *Grootboom* (n 144 above) para 99(c).

953 *Grootboom* (n 144 above) para 97. The Court ordered the state to devise and implement measures that would provide relief for desperately homeless people. See also *EN & Others v Government of the Republic of South Africa & Others* 2007 1 BCLR 84 (D), implicating the use of structured orders by the the High Court in ensuring compliance with its ruling on the implementation of treatment for some prison inmates suffering from HIV/AIDS.

954 See *Treatment Action Campaign* (n 780 above).

955 *Treatment Action Campaign* (n 780 above) para 80.

HIV transmission, but ordered the government to make provision for the training of adequate personnel to expedite the availability of the drug in the prevention of HIV transmission.[956]

The robust efforts of the Indian and South African courts, as demonstrated in the foregoing cases, demonstrate the commendable capacity that those courts exerted to adjudicate economic, social and cultural rights claims and, where appropriate, to evolve interactive modalities for their implementation. While I acknowledge that the historical, socio-economic and political contexts of countries may never be exactly the same, and that these factors may result in dissimilar obstacles to adopting similar approaches, yet, the possibility remains for African national courts to adopt proactive approaches to the implementation of economic, social and cultural rights.

With the ample theoretical and interpretive jurisprudence on economic, social and cultural rights so far considered, and against the backdrop of the largely weak and incoherent African approach to economic, social and cultural rights, the lessons learnt portend the need for a holistic approach to the protection and implementation of economic, social and cultural rights that would exude rays of viability within African regional and domestic human rights schemes.

4 Proposal for an integrative approach

If human rights are to retain their essence and relevance in today's Africa, it necessarily demands that no violation should go without a remedy. Correlative to this assertion is that all human rights will appreciate in their value in the African experience when their implementation is not restrictively defined in terms of adjudicatory competencies, but considered also within the broader framework of well-articulated and multidimensional approaches. However, critical to the formulation of a feasible approach to the remedial implementation of economic, social and cultural rights in Africa is the need to identify what I consider to be the essential elements of such an exercise. My preceding exposition on the problems inherent in the

956 *Treatment Action Campaign* (n 780 above) paras 135(3)(c)-(d). For a critique of the Court's 'failure to exercise supervisory jurisdiction in this matter', see D Bilchitz 'Towards a reasonable approach to the minimum core: Laying the foundations for future socio-economic rights jurisprudence' (1993) 19 *South African Journal on Human Rights* 1 23-24. It is gratifying to note that less that six months after the judgment in *Treatment Action Campaign* was handed down, the South African government issued a 'Comprehensive plan for treatment and care of people living with HIV and AIDS'. See 'Cabinet decision on the operational plan for a comprehensive plan for treatment and care of people living with HIV and AIDS' http://www.govza/issues/hiv/cabinetaidsqa19nov03.htm (accessed 12 June 2009).

current theoretical approaches to the implementation of economic, social and cultural rights underscores the need to develop a more pragmatic method for assessing the validity of what would constitute a 'violation' of an individual's rights and for formulating the indices of how duty-holders should demonstrate compliance with applicable standards.

As Mureinik convincingly argued:

> No one can fashion a remedy [for economic, social and cultural rights] without choosing among the alternatives ... it is the manner of enforcement that is complex, and the complexity is one that judges are unqualified to resolve [alone].[957]

On my part, I am proposing an integrative approach that will mitigate the shortcomings of the prevalent approaches to the remedial implementation of economic, social and cultural rights. The approach canvassed here is at one and the same time multidimensional as it is inclusionary, requiring a combination of some elements of current hypotheses as well as an interdisciplinary understanding of novel ideas.

My approach represents an integration or 'amalgamation' of a trilogy of concepts: performance evaluation, basic human needs and administrative justice, and it underscores the overarching cognisable concerns on which they converge. Because my approach does not isolate the interplay of the UN and African regional human rights regimen pertaining to economic, social and cultural rights, it elicits certain innate justifications. One, it seeks to diffuse the conceptual conundrum currently associated with the programmatic understanding of economic, social and cultural rights. Second, because my approach is predicated on collaborative strategies and preventive methods of implementation, it aims at presenting a platform that could promote the monitoring and adjudication of economic, social and cultural rights in respect of every African state. Rather than diminishing the vital dimension of the continuing discourse on normative conceptualisation of economic, social and cultural rights in Africa, my approach offers a practical agenda from which further initiatives can be extracted.

4.1 Performance evaluation

Although diverse factors make it inevitable to formulate a distinct theoretical basis for measuring the compliance of African states with

957 Mureinik (n 596 above) 468. Although Mureinik's analysis was limited to the South African constitutional experience, it is nonetheless equally important and instructive to our present discourse.

their economic, social and cultural rights obligations, two of these constitute major factors. First, under both the African Charter and ICESCR, the obligation to take 'legislative or other measures' makes the *actual* adoption or amendment of relevant statutes and the formulation of appropriate policies the most basic and fundamental question to be addressed in assessing a state's performance of its obligations. Second, since all African states are singularly and collectively state parties to the African Charter, more so when a preponderance of them are also states parties to ICESCR, none of these states can plausibly plead incapacity for failure to enact laws or to amend its laws or to formulate policies that would facilitate the opportunity to scrutinise its willingness to fulfil its economic, social and cultural rights obligations *vis-à-vis* the level of the protection of these rights within its territory.

While the tendency among scholars to assimilate the economic, social and cultural rights provisions in the African Charter into the interpretive standards of ICESCR may seem inevitable, it is my contention that the absence of the 'progressive realisation' phraseology in the African Charter presupposes and impels the identification of a higher threshold of performance. However, rather than suggesting a disharmonious outlook to economic, social and cultural rights implementation, the convergence of global and regional human rights instruments in Africa creates an auspicious environment for these instruments to be harnessed and promoted in ways that would enhance their purpose, effect and significance in African states.

Therefore, a pragmatic approach that will facilitate an objective basis for assessing economic, social and cultural rights in Africa primarily lies in evaluating what a state *has done* to fulfil its economic, social and cultural rights obligations and what a state *has not done* in fulfilling these obligations. The strength of such an approach lies in destructing, at the very onset of examination, the prevailing attitude towards assessing *how much* fiscal resource a state has committed or is able to commit to the fulfilment of its economic, social and cultural rights obligations.

The failure, neglect or refusal by an African state to take positive steps in providing a legislative and policy framework for the protection of, and non-retrogression from matters pertaining to, economic, social and cultural rights should be sufficient ground for judicial and quasi-judicial organs at international, regional and national levels to find whether a state is in breach.[958] The remedy for this sort of finding lies in the establishment by the state of appropriate legislative and policy frameworks to the satisfaction of the relevant international, regional or national human rights monitoring or implementation organs.

Similarly, failure by any African state to hold private actors accountable for economic, social and cultural rights violations presupposes condoning impunity and should in itself be considered non-performance.[959] Thus, at regional and national fora, when a state has neglected, refused or failed to perform its basic economic, social and cultural rights obligations, appropriate supervisory organs should so proclaim and issue appropriate remedial directives. While subjecting states to scrutiny in this way may not in itself be a remedy in the short term, the weight of popular opprobrium and political costs against governments cannot be undermined.

The African Commission has not been considering communications before it against the background of this sort of approach. In *Ogoni*, for instance, even though it was a fact before the Commission that there was a Niger Delta Development Commission (NDDC) Act enacted by the respondent government 'to address the environmental and social related problems of the Niger Delta area and other oil producing areas of Nigeria',[960] the Commission never requested to see the statute for the purpose of establishing the *efficacy* of the remedies alleged by the state.[961]

My approach does not exclude national judiciaries. A coherent culture of economic, social and cultural rights will only materialise as domestic courts engage in interpreting and applying them to real-life situations. If nothing at all, in the process of adjudicating economic, social and cultural rights, national judiciaries assume a vantage position to make the executive or legislature justify the

958 This perception strikes concordance with Limburg Principle No 37 which says: 'Upon becoming a party to the Covenant, states shall eliminate *de jure* discrimination by abolishing without delay any discriminatory laws, regulations and practices, including acts of omission as well as commission affecting the enjoyment of economic, social and cultural rights.' See Limburg Principles (n 48 above).

959 See generally Maastricht Guidelines (n 49 above) para 27.

960 See *Ogoni* (n 143 above) para 30.

961 Relying entirely on the *note verbale* filed by the Nigerian government, the African Commission merely noted 'the efforts of the present civilian administration to redress the atrocities that were committed by the previous military administration'. *Ogoni* (n 143 above) para 69. Under sec 2(1) of the NDDC Act, 2000, as amended, out of the 11 members that constitute the Governing Board, *only one* is statutorily required to represent the nine oil-producing states of Nigeria, and that person must be appointed by the President. The oil companies in the Niger-Delta area also have one representative. Votes carry equal weight and all persons on the board are appointed by the President.

reasonableness of a legislation or policy, and yet leave enough margin of discretion for policy choices.[962]

A demonstration of the capacity of courts to keep a balanced view in this regard was *Soobramoney*, where the South African Constitutional Court held that the guidelines adopted by hospital authorities, and which were applied in disqualifying the applicant for dialysis treatment, were fair and rational and that there was no suggestion that those guidelines were 'unreasonable'.[963] Despite the growing relevance of public interest litigation, Indian courts have meticulously refused to meddle unnecessarily with policy matters unless they are manifestly in breach of constitutional provisions.[964]

I acknowledge that, while some conventional judicial remedies such as declaration, *certiorari*, prohibition, *mandamus* and injunction may be appropriate in some cases, they may be inadequate or impracticable in others. In such instances, national courts will be expected to adopt reformatory remedies through *inquisitorial methods*, as the Indian and South African courts have demonstrated in many of the cases already discussed. Through collaborative adjudication and follow-up implementation initiatives, courts can promote the goals of structural and institutional reforms and thus eliminate or drastically reduce endemic violations of economic, social and cultural rights in a body politic.[965] Extrapolating from the foregoing, it therefore follows that the relevant intergovernmental and national juridical bodies should begin the scrutiny of economic, social and cultural rights in Africa by examining the efficacy of a state's framework of 'legislative or other measures' in terms of the quality of remedial implementation it facilitates. I am of the opinion that, through sustained methodical interpretation and implementation in real life situations, economic, social and cultural rights will appreciate in their value. This approach will, however, only work effectively where state institutions are co-operative and where adequately mobilised civil society activism and vibrant media culture

962 See generally Scott & Macklem (n 589 above) 146-147. For a discussion of how Indian courts have shown their 'readiness to step in where the legislature had not' and how they have refused to intervene in matters that 'are not within the judicial ambit of capacity', see Desai *et al* (n 610 above) 176-178.

963 *Soobramoney* (n 773 above) para 25.

964 In *Jain v Union of India* (1993) 4 SCC 177, the Supreme Court declared that it is not for an aggrieved third party to challenge the appointment of another person into public office through public interest litigation where there is unfettered constitutional discretionary power vested in the appointing body.

965 See generally C Scott 'Social rights: Towards a principled, pragmatic judicial role' (1999) 1 *Economics and Social Rights Review* 4; S Liebenberg 'Enforcing positive socio-economic rights claims: The South African model of reasonableness review' in J Squires *et al* (eds) *The road to a remedy: current issues in the litigation of economic, social and cultural rights* (2005) 73; K Roach & G Budlender 'Mandatory relief and supervisory jurisdiction: When is it appropriate, just and equitable?' (2005) 122 *South African Law Journal* 325.

thrive. African regional human rights bodies, particularly the emerging African Court, and national courts will have to realise the potential that lies in this approach.

4.2 Basic 'human' needs[966]

Even though there are theoretical difficulties among scholars in agreeing on precise yardsticks for measuring the indices of poverty and human underdevelopment, there has been an increasing consensus on its assessment through 'unfulfilled [basic] needs or capability shortfalls'.[967] Despite the conceptual debates about what constitutes the basic needs of human beings, certain core elements – food, shelter and health – have emerged as invariable considerations.[968]

The 'basic needs' strategy to human development arose in response to the failure of the economic growth recorded in many nations in the late 1970s to alleviate poverty.[969] It was aimed at evolving effective strategies that would ensure just and fair distribution of basic needs and services that will enable all members of the society to meet their basic requirements for a satisfactory life, even at the lowest measure.[970] In the light of the deprivation of millions of people whose basic needs were never fulfilled despite the economic prosperity in the years that followed World War II, Stewart argues that, when expressed in 'the language of rights', the basic needs approach will ensure the recognition of what the priorities of a

966 While all available literature on this subject refers to the phraseology of 'basic needs', there is every reason to aver that no other connotations are intended by writers other than human needs. However, to be consistent with references, I retain the popular phrase 'basic needs', but my emphasis on its particular attachment to *human beings* must not be overlooked. This approach is referred to in some Asian countries as the 'human security approach'. See A Woodiwiss *Making human rights work globally* (2003) 111, quoting a definition of the term by Japanese Prime Minister Koizumi in the *Japan Times*, 16 December 2001, as saying: 'Human security is an approach aimed at reinforcing measures to attach importance to the viewpoints of each individual so as to protect people from threats against subsistence, life and dignity and to realise the rich potential of each individual.'

967 See J May 'An elusive consensus: Definitions, measurements and analysis of poverty' in A Grinspun (ed) *Choices for the poor: Lessons from national poverty strategies* (2001) 23 32 36. See also JF Weeks *et al* 'Basic needs: Journey of a concept' in ME Crahan (ed) *Human rights and basic needs in the Americas* 131 132.

968 See generally D Braybrooke *Meeting needs* (1987) 34-36. Compare JC Espada *Social citizenship rights: A critique of FA Hayek and R Plant* (1996) 186.

969 See F Stewart 'Basic needs strategies, human rights and the right to development' (1989) 11 *Human Rights Quarterly* 347; Weeks *et al* (n 967 above) 131 132.

970 Stewart (n 969 above) 351-356.

state should be and increase the 'moral weight' and 'political commitment' required for the fulfilment of such priorities.[971]

In June 1976, The World Employment Conference defined 'basic needs' and highlighted the principles to which all nations should be committed. These included (i) the minimal consumption requirements needed for a physically healthy population (for example, food, shelter, clothing); (ii) access to essential services and amenities (for example, safe drinking water, sanitation, health and education); (iii) access of all to adequately remunerated employment opportunities; and (iv) the satisfaction of needs of a more qualitative nature: a healthy, humane environment, and popular participation in making decisions that affect the lives and livelihood of the people and their individual freedoms.[972]

The basic needs theory is thus founded on the philosophical assumption that the sanctity of human dignity finds expression in the material and non-material conditions of life required for human survival and happiness. [973] Correlative to this is the idea that to have a right vested in one person constitutes the basis for legitimate claims against another person, group, or organisation (and with regard to this discourse, states and institutions of state).[974]

To analytical jurists, rights are widely characterised as legitimate claims that give rise to correlative duties or obligations. In this sort of jural relations, the state, as duty-bearer, fulfils its obligation by ensuring or assisting the right-bearer to secure the right involved.[975] Hohfeld had described this right-duty formula as follows: 'X has a right against Y in relation to Z', where X is the right-bearer, Y is the duty-bearer, and Z is the object or end of that right.[976] The underpinning concourse of jural opposites and jural correlatives presented by the Hohfeldian theory has engaged ample scholarship in clarifying the nature of liberties and rights. While the semiotics and

971 Stewart (n 969 above) 350.

972 ILO 'Employment, growth and basic needs: A one-world problem' (1978) 7. See also D Hunt *Economic theories of development: An analysis of competing paradigms* (1989) 76.

973 Stewart (n 969 above) 350-351. See also VP Nanda 'Development and human rights: The role of international law and organisations' in GW Shepherd *et al* (eds) *Human rights and world development* (1995) 297, analysing the essentials of the basic needs concept as being country-specific and, more importantly, as connoting the framework for 'the dignity of individuals and peoples and their *freedom to chart their destiny without hindrance*' (my emphasis).

974 See McMorrow (n 291 above) 54-55. See also A Sen 'The ends and means of sustainability' keynote address at the International Conference on Transition to Sustainability, http://www.iisd.org/pdf/sen_paper.pdf (accessed 12 June 2009). Compare Howard (n 294 above) 477-478.

975 See generally MDA Freeman 'R Dworkin' in *Lloyd's introduction to jurisprudence* (2001) 1429-1434.

976 This is otherwise referred to as the 'Hohfeldian analysis of rights'. See *Hohfeld's analysis of rights* (1919), reprinted in Freeman (n 975 above) 355-358.

other fine details of the right-duty theory need not detain us here,[977] it suffices to argue that the basic needs concept presents a meeting point between legalism and the demands of social justice.

Drawing stimulation from the growing consensus on the interconnectedness of all human rights, especially in the post-Cold War era, scholars are becoming more involved in theorising a rights-based development paradigm that finds its premise on the dynamic of basic human needs.[978] Without doubt, the day-to-day realities of increasing numbers of people all over the world who are chronically malnourished, unhealthy, homeless and illiterate constitute a huge cutback in whatever progress the world has recorded since the 1990s. Certainly, the world cannot celebrate its advancement in fundamental freedoms as long as there are overwhelming populations who lack the basic essentials for human survival.[979]

Applying the basic human needs paradigm to the quest for effective economic, social and cultural rights implementation in Africa therefore presents governments and policy makers with a viable alternative strategy for meeting most of the obligations implicated by these rights. I propose that in policy-making and budgetary disbursements, African states should prioritise the basic 'human' needs of their peoples, namely, health, equality of access to housing, education and fair conditions of work, to the extent that their non-fulfilment threatens the lives and dignity of human beings within national territories. These are the non-negotiable indicators against which a state's implementation of economic, social and cultural rights should be measured at domestic, regional and international fora.[980]

977 For the legal and conceptual rationalisations that have ensued from Hohfeld's analysis of rights, see the following expository works: JW Singer 'The legal rights debate in analytical jurisprudence from Bentham to Hohfeld' (1982) *Wisconsin Law Review* 975-1059; JM Balkin 'The Hohfeldian approach to law and semiotics' (1990) 44 *University of Miami Law Review* 1119-1142.

978 See eg McMorrow (n 291 above) 37-38; Braybrooke (n 968 above) 131. For scholarly expositions on the marked linkages between human rights and 'basic needs', see P Alston 'Human rights and basic needs: A critical assessment' (1979) 12 *Human Rights Law Journal* 19; A McChesney 'Promoting the general welfare in a democratic society: Balancing human rights and development' (1980) 27 *Netherlands International Law Review* 283; Craven (n 73 above) 141.

979 To put this discourse in proper perspective, it is crucial to mention that the basic needs concept had attracted the attention of African leaders as a core human rights subject as far back as 1991. See 'Draft final document of the tenth conference of the Heads of State and Government of the non-aligned countries' reprinted in *Beijing Review* 4-10 November 1991 9.

980 It is pertinent to note that, to a considerable extent, the South African judiciary has recognised, adopted and applied this approach in some of the most prominent economic, social and cultural rights cases. In determining the 'reasonableness' of the affected government policies in *Grootboom* and *Treatment Action Campaign*, the Constitutional Court explicitly had regard to the needs of the vulnerable. See *Grootboom* (n 144 above) para 44, where the Court held that '[t]o be reasonable, measures cannot leave out of account the degree and extent of the denial of the

Although I acknowledge that there could be a vigorous debate over methods of meeting the basic needs of the most vulnerable in Africa, the primary challenge should be to entrench this concept in the philosophy and psychology of African human rights discourses generally. While there is no magical path to El Dorado, the implications of my proposal are for a strengthened and widened scope of strategies within African socio-political systems, a pursuit that must begin with deepening intellectual exchanges.[981]

4.3 Administrative justice

Are economic, social and cultural rights necessarily to be subjected to conventional human rights implementation to make them 'real' rights? Is the protection of economic, social and cultural rights to be exclusively defined in terms of juridical interpretation to make them 'legal' rights? To what extent can unconventional juridical measures be galvanised to evolve innovative responses to the implementation of economic, social and cultural rights? Within the purview of the global economic, social and cultural rights discourse, it is no longer difficult to find a basis for a critical consideration of informal mechanisms that would strengthen the remedial implementation of economic, social and cultural rights. At the Vienna Conference in 1993, for instance, participants had perceived that most breaches of economic, social and cultural rights could be remedied with or without recourse to the courts. The Vienna Declaration thus proclaimed that 'to strengthen the enjoyment of economic, social and cultural rights, *additional approaches* should be examined ...'.[982]

Similarly, in one of its General Comments, the ESCR Committee had asserted that

> [t]he right to an effective remedy need not be interpreted as always requiring a judicial remedy. *Administrative remedies will, in many cases, be adequate* and those living within the jurisdiction of a state

right they endeavour to realise. *Those whose needs are the most urgent* and whose ability to enjoy all rights therefore is most in peril, must not be ignored by the measures aimed at achieving realisation of the right'. (my emphasis). See also *Treatment Action Campaign* (n 780 above) para 78, where the Court declared that '[t]he *provision of a single dose of [N]evirapine to mother and child for the purpose of protecting the child against the transmission of HIV is, as far as the children are concerned, [most] essential. Their needs are "most urgent" and their inability to have access to [N]evirapine profoundly affects their ability to enjoy all rights to which they are entitled.* Their rights are "most in peril" as a result of the policy that has been adopted and are most affected by a rigid and inflexible policy that excludes them from having access to [N]evirapine' (my emphasis).

981 For a commendable but narrow effort in this direction, see D Bilchitz 'Placing basic needs at the centre of socio-economic rights jurisprudence' (2003) 4 *Economic and Social Rights Review* 3.

982 Vienna Declaration (n 38 above) para 98 (my emphasis).

> party have a *legitimate expectation*, based on the principle of good faith, that all administrative authorities will take account of the requirements of the Covenant in their decision making. Any such administrative remedies should be accessible, affordable, timely and effective.[983]

The growing awareness that constitutional frameworks alone cannot secure the protection of economic, social and cultural rights and governmental accountability impels the identification of other platforms beyond established judicialism that would further enhance the realisation of economic, social and cultural rights. One platform that I have thus identified is the *administrative justice process*.

In many states of the modern world, administrative law has evolved as that branch of public law dealing with the scrutiny of the discretionary powers of bureaucratic organs and agencies of the state as they affect the liberties and *legitimate expectations* of individuals.[984] From this evolution has emerged a strong formalised culture that views every exercise of statutory or other public law power that implicates policy choices or decisions affecting an individual's pecuniary, proprietary or other personal rights and interests as being liable to review by a higher authority.[985] This body of state-citizen administrative ethos is what is commonly referred to as administrative justice.

Firmly rooted in the classical notions of democracy, administrative justice represents

> [a] rights-based conception of public law, which is openly and unashamedly concerned with the imposition of certain standards of legality and which is designed to prevent the abuse of power both by

983 General Comment No 9 (n 309 above) para 9 (my emphasis).

984 Although the origin of the concept of legitimate expectation is readily traced to the evolutionary process of English administrative law, it has attracted attention in other jurisdictions. See eg E Schmidt-Aßmann 'Basic principles of German administrative law' (1993) 35 *Journal of Indian Law Institute* 65; E Sharpston 'European Community law and the doctrine of legitimate expectations: How legitimate, and for whom?' (1990) 11 *North Western Journal of International Law and Business* 87; G Quinot 'Substantive legitimate expectations in South African and European administrative law' (2004) 5 *German Law Journal* 1; C Eversley 'Legitimate expectation and the creation of procedural and substantive legal rights in commonwealth Caribbean public law' (2004) 33 *Common Law World Review* 332-351.

985 See C Lewis *Judicial remedies in public law* (2000) 112-125; Woolf *et al* (n 595 above) 3-22 245-273; LN Brown *et al French administrative law* (1993) 5; J Bell *French constitutional law* (1992); LH Tribe *American constitutional law* (2000); J Alder *General principles of constitutional and administrative law* (2002) 403-454; H Corder (ed) *Comparing administrative justice across the Commonwealth* (2007).

> public bodies *stricto sensu*, and by a range of other quasi-public or private bodies which possess a certain degree of power.[986]

One of the most outstanding purveyors of the administrative justice approach to democratic governance, Hugh Corder, explains the whole essence of the approach this way:

> The core values of this approach to democracy and the functioning of the state are openness of action, participation in decision making, justification for decisions made, and accountability for administrative action. The importance of the constitutional requirements of lawfulness, procedural fairness, reason-giving and justification for administrative action to such a conception of democracy is self-evident.[987]

Extending the frontiers of the democratic governance values of administrative law to the realm of social justice and human development, therefore, I contend that it should be possible, with the tremendous developments that are being witnessed in the irresistible intercourse between administrative law and modern day governance, and it is indeed practicable, to extract a praxis for rights-based application of administrative law to the remedial implementation of implicated economic, social and cultural rights. Against the background of the increasing incursions of institutionalised bureaucracies into more spheres of human endeavours in Africa, as elsewhere,[988] I conceive of a significant potential in the responses available in administrative law to prevent, remedy or mitigate some of the most pronounced challenges to economic, social and cultural rights, poverty alleviation, social justice and human development —basically charting a practical and purposive path to the fulfilment of individuals' legitimate expectations.[989]

986 PP Craig *Administrative law* (1994) 17. For the argument that the attainment of genuine democracy will depend 'upon administrative law: upon the legal forces which pull or fail to pull - government decision making towards democratic decision making', see E Mureinik 'Reconsidering review: Participation and accountability' (1993) *Acta Juridica* 35, quoted in H Corder 'Administrative justice: A cornerstone of South Africa's democracy' (1998) 14 *South African Journal on Human Rights* 38.

987 Corder (n 986 above) 41. See further comparative elaboration in R Grote 'The scope of judicial review of administrative action and the changing rule of law: Some comparative reflections' (2004) 19 *SA Public Law* 513.

988 See generally Lord Hewart of Bury *The new despotism* (1945) 9-22; Grote (n 987 above) 514.

989 The approach I contemplate here is akin to the concerted efforts of the 1960s and 1970s in the United States towards addressing the problem of widespread poverty through the instrumentality of social rights. For scholarly insights into that historic process, see MR Sosin *et al* 'Legal rights and welfare change 1960-1980' in SH Danziger *et al* (eds) *Fighting poverty: What works and what doesn't* (1996) 260-286; CV Hamilton *et al* 'Social policies, civil rights, and poverty' in Danziger (above) 287-311; ML Gillette *Launching the war on poverty: An oral history* (1996) 279-298. See also DA Richie 'Foreword' in Gillette (above) ix, observing that even though 'the "war on poverty" did not eradicate poverty in the United States, it had a profound influence on many people's lives and significantly shaped the social and economic commitments of the federal government'.

One of the distinguishing features of the South African Constitution is its emphatic commitment to administrative justice. Article 33 of the Constitution provides as follows:

> (1) Everyone has the right to administrative action that is lawful, reasonable and procedurally fair.
>
> (2) Everyone whose rights have been adversely affected by administrative action has the right to be given written reasons.
>
> (3) National legislation must be enacted to give effects to these rights, and must -
>
> (a) provide for the review of administrative action by a court or, where appropriate, an independent and impartial tribunal;
>
> (b) impose a duty on the state to give effect to the rights in subsections (1) and (2); and
>
> (c) promote an efficient administration.[990]

Even though there has been some notable references to administrative remedies as being significant for the protection of human rights,[991] the implications of this approach for the remedial implementation of economic, social and cultural rights has not been adequately explored.[992]

In both practical and purposive ways, the administrative justice method holds tremendous potential for the effective implementation for economic, social and cultural rights in Africa, going by the spate of bureaucratic corruption and decay that has continually and negatively affected the rights of individuals.[993]

Even though jurisprudence exhibiting this method is scanty, a decision of the Supreme Court of South Africa commends it for appreciation. In *Applicant v Administrator, Transvaal and Others*, the applicant, an HIV/AIDS sufferer, challenged the refusal of the respondents to continue providing him with medication for his disease. The respondents' contended, among others, that the drug in question was expensive. The Supreme Court held that, although the respondents had a discretion to allow the use of a non-registered

990 For a comprehensive exposition on these provisions as a basis for 'just administrative action' under South African constitutionalism, see De Waal *et al* (n 333 above). For an insight into the philosophy of administrative justice in South African constitutionalism, see Corder (n 986 above) 39-45.

991 See n 780 above; n 995 and accompanying texts. See also C Hoexter 'Judicial policy revisited: Transformative adjudication in administrative law' (2008) 24 *South African Journal on Human Rights* 281 287-291.

992 Particularly important here is Trengrove's work (n 926 above) as well as H Corder 'Administrative justice' in D Van Wyk *et al Rights and constitutionalism: The new South African legal order* (1994) 387 398.

993 See generally G Hyden 'Reciprocity and governance in Africa' in JS Wunsch *et al* (eds) *The failure of the centralised state: Institutions and self-governance in Africa* (1995) 245 262-263; Emery (n 919 above) 22.

drug, in the present case, they had failed to consider all of the relevant factors as required by law.[994]

Removed from the trappings of contemporary human rights debates, therefore, I submit that the administrative justice paradigm will facilitate effective and more accessible platforms for the affective communities of the disadvantaged, deprived, marginalised and vulnerable in Africa to challenge untoward administrative choices and decisions that threaten their legitimate expectations.

This third component of my 'amalgamated' approach, therefore, contemplates that through vigilant scrutiny of procedural rules, a transparent and unbiased oversight of the activities of administrative agencies and institutions, together with proactive citizens' participation in decision-making processes, many violations of economic, social and cultural rights that encroach or threaten to encroach on the legitimate expectations of individuals and collectives can be exposed, and thus become amenable to remedy and the prevention of future occurrences. This prospect has been vindicated in diverse national contexts.[995]

I contend that adopting the administrative justice approach as a platform for the remedial implementation of economic, social and cultural rights in Africa will help in circumventing the problematic question of justiciability and dispense with other controversies that have arisen out of the legalistic conceptualisations around economic, social and cultural rights as human rights. In adjudicating economic, social and cultural rights-related complaints against administrative agencies, rather than dragging the court or superior tribunal or administrator onto a collision path with the executive or legislative arm over policies, what will be set down for determination will be such questions as the reasonableness, legality, proportionality, substantive error and procedural fairness of acts (or omissions) of administrative officials or agencies occurring under *enabling*

[994] 1993 4 SA 733 (W).

[995] See eg De Waal *et al* (n 333 above) 488-524 and accompanying nn 3, 14, 35, 38 & 50, highlighting salient instances in which South African courts were called upon to determine the scope of administrative justice; *Australian National University v Burns* (1982) 40 *Australian Law Review* 707, where the Federal Court of Australia held that the decision to dismiss a professor on grounds of incapacity due to ill-health was of an administrative character; Sharma (n 821 above) 654-698, analysing the effect of administrative justice in Indian courts as manifest in diverse cases involving 'due process', 'natural justice', and 'fundamental justice'; F Donson 'Civil liberties and judicial review: Can the common law really protect rights?' in P Leyland *et al* (eds) *Administrative law facing the future: Old constraints and new horizons* (1997) 347-373, analysing a plethora of cases where British courts subjected administrative actions to the rigors of judicial review to the extent of their encroachment on individual liberties.

instruments.[996] An advantage of this method is that, in remedying the potential adversities of an impending exercise of discretionary powers, the reviewing body or administrator would have had the opportunity of issuing such directives as would meet the demands and 'legitimate expectations' of the situation in question.[997] Explaining the *raison d'être* of the concept of legitimate expectations, Thomas states:

> The principle means that expectations raised as a result of administrative conduct may have legal consequences. Either the administration must respect those expectations or provide compelling reasons why the public interest must take priority. The principle therefore concerns the degree to which an individual's expectations may be safeguarded in the face of a change of policy which tends to undermine them. The role of the ... court ... [will therefore be] to determine the extent to which the individual's expectation can be accommodated within changing policy objectives.[998]

The purport of the concept of administrative justice is therefore to hold a government accountable to its people on its *policies* understandably because most governmental actions that directly affect individuals' rights usually manifest through policies. This is of significant importance in forging a praxis for an African rights-based human development agenda. On a continent where institutionalised cleavages and a culture of appeasement commonly define equations of governance and balance of political power,[999] it will be most helpful to adopt this concept that could turn economic, social and cultural rights claims into viable platforms for curbing warped and insensate policies that adversely affect the day-to-day lives of human beings in African states. Applying this approach in deserving cases will also afford the courts a basis for, and the advantage of, assuming *supervisory jurisdiction* to monitor the accountability of the administration.

996 For some of the diverse grounds upon which the courts will found a review of administrative actions, and the possible remedies, see Emery (n 919 above) 77-141.

997 See generally R Thomas *Legitimate expectations and proportionality in administrative law* (2000) 41-75. For another perspective on the import of 'legitimate expectation' to administrative justice as seen through case law, see H Iyengar 'Legitimate expectation: Promises by a different public authority' (2003) 8 *Judicial Review* 215-220.

998 Thomas (n 997 above) 41.

999 See generally DL Gordon 'African politics' in Gordon *et al* (n 299 above) 55 79-82; JS Wunsch 'Centralisation and development in post-independence Africa' in Wunsch *et al* (n 993 above) 43 57-58; S Wunsch 'Beyond the failure of the centralised state: Toward self-governance and alternative institutional paradigm' in Wunsch *et al* (n 993 above). See also An-Na'im (n 31 above) 1 13.

The adoption of supervisory jurisdiction in complaints involving economic, social and cultural rights is capable of lessening the necessity of judicial involvement in policy and fiscal expenditure.[1000] Once a court pronounces on the quality and quantity of implementation programmes or acts that would satisfy the purport of an economic, social and cultural right, it might then specify an appropriate organ or agency of state that would finalise and implement the fine details of such programmes. In such a scenario, the judiciary assumes the dynamic role of both a facilitator and enforcer.[1001] The decisions in *Grootboom, Treatment Action Campaign, August* and *Occupiers of 51 Olivia Road* present a real-life application of this paradigm.[1002]

It may then be pertinent to ask: Does the supervisory approach not reinforce the conceptual perception of economic, social and cultural rights being programmatic rights? By no means. Two points need to be stressed here. First, because of the historical exclusion of economic, social and cultural rights from the human rights discourse and development in Africa, systemic violations of these rights have continued unabated for a very long time, so much so that, for the current manifestations of those violations to be remedied, only a combination of methods and processes will be desirable and viable in most cases, if not all. Second, if every effort aimed at clarifying the scope and content of each economic, social and cultural right is perceived as a further justification for the chequered 'programmatic' stereotype of the debate, virtually every human right will be liable to the charge of being programmatic because, under closer analysis, there will be an element of 'programming' in the implementation of every right.[1003]

5 Concluding remarks

The authors of the Limburg Principles acknowledged the critical importance of effective remedies when they proclaimed that 'state parties shall provide for effective remedies including, where appropriate, judicial remedies'.[1004] The ESCR Committee also

1000 See Trengrove (n 926 above) 9-10.
1001 See generally Bollyky (n 872 above) 184-186.
1002 For an extensive scholarly critique of the attitude of the courts in many of these and similar cases, see Liebenberg (n 965 above) 76-81. Compare M Heywood 'Contempt or compliance? The *TAC* case after the Constitutional Court judgment' (2003) 4 *Economics and Social Rights Review* 3; RJ de Beer & S Vettori 'The enforcement of socio-economic rights' (2007) 3 *Potchefstroom Electronic Law Journal* 2.
1003 An illustration of the 'programmematic' content of the right to vote, eg, is found in *August* (n 775 above).
1004 Limburg Principles (n 48 above) para 19.

emphasised that 'remedies should be accessible, affordable, timely and effective'.[1005]

The interactive web of international, regional and domestic human rights standards, instruments and institutions that converge within the African human rights context presents such an abundant array of platforms for the protection of economic, social and cultural rights, the enrichment of a rights-based approach to human development and the actualisation of the legitimate expectations of individuals.

African regional human rights bodies will be taking this matter seriously when they begin to critically examine the possibility of developing viable and objective standards of performance based on the African Charter specificity. I have attempted to identify some of the key platforms that I consider essential to result-oriented economic, social and cultural rights advocacy. The challenge is to advance them on multidimensional fronts.

Even though a prevalent positivist paradigm strictly constructs economic, social and cultural rights as rights-duties structures, I have demonstrated in this chapter that such an approach is not sacrosanct or exhaustive and should not be considered exclusive. The strength of the trilogy in my conceptual approach lies in its inclusionary and interdisciplinary outlook to the diagnosis of the complex issues at stake in the tangible delivery of the promises of economic, social and cultural rights in Africa. My approach also reveals the possibility and practicability of cross-pollinating its methodical elements at the UN, regional and national human rights fora, thereby negating any anachronistic appeal to relativism.

An added advantage of this approach is that, in fashioning the most appropriate methods for remedying violations and for preventing a systematic encroachment of economic, social and cultural rights, in a manner devoid of the adversarial trappings of conventional adjudication, national, regional and international juridical entities will be at liberty to seek, *in proprio motu*, the input of relevant experts, professionals, bureaucrats, interest groups and private persons in matters implicating policy and fiscal disbursement. By so doing, they will be promoting popular participation in governance and nation building.

While I do not discard the importance of legalism, I contend that, rather than preoccupying ourselves with the question of *what* constitutes the 'positive' or 'negative' aspects of each economic,

[1005] See General Comment No 9 (n 309 above) para 4.

social and cultural right, analytical efforts should begin to examine the question of *how* to implement each of these rights beyond the narrow language of subjective legal rights. This is what will ensure the effective delivery of economic, social and cultural rights to their human beneficiaries.

6

Non-State Actors: Roles and Responsibilities

All persons are entitled to full respect of all their rights: They have the right not to live, survive, and die in impoverishment ... The other side of this equation is that *all governments and other powerful actors have obligations with respect to what they do: They must be held accountable for policies and actions that contribute to rights violations* ... Thus, *addressing all rights in terms of their economic, political and social contexts, and holding all actors accountable, constitute critical steps towards challenging the conditions that create and tolerate impoverishment* and repression across the globe.[1006]

1 Sifting the matrix of non-state actors

Throughout the previous chapters of this discourse, the focus has been on the role of states in implementing and securing the protection of economic, social and cultural rights in Africa and, in a comparative way, elsewhere. This should be understandable as all the treaties and legal instruments thus far considered vest the primary responsibility for these rights in states, and it is in this light that scholars interpret the obligations of states.[1007] However, to advance the discourse beyond the purview of states, and to present holistic understanding of the subject in consonance with the objectives of my research, I recognise that there is a correlative need to examine the impact of *non-state actors* and the parameters of their responsibilities for human rights generally and economic, social and cultural rights in particular.[1008]

1006 Russell (n 625 above) 1 3 (my emphasis).

1007 See eg Maastricht Guidelines (n 49 above) para 18; Dankwa *et al* (n 49 above) 720; R Künnemann *et al* (n 111 above) 158 159.

1008 The use of this expression must not confuse the reader. While 'non-state actors' have been employed by various writers to refer to institutions and groups in different contexts, I have employed the phrase as a *convenient* terminology that covers a wide range of private sector entities, including transnational corporations (TNCs), multinational enterprises (MNEs), international financial institutions (IFIs) and trade institutions, local non-governmental organisations (NGOs), international non-governmental organisations (INGOs) and other civil

The essence of my attempt at examining the roles and responsibilities of non-state actors lies in the recognition of the weakened notions of sovereignty and political autonomy in the advent of powerful transnational networks that are increasingly impacting policy making in the areas of governance, development and social welfare, in diverse contexts and to varying degrees.[1009]

Complex and diverse as the nature and structures of non-state actors might be, some scholars have categorised these entities into three groupings, namely, public-interest-oriented non-governmental actors; profit-oriented corporate actors; and public inter-governmental organisations.[1010]

Since the advent of enlarged economic globalisation following the collapse of communism, human rights scholars and activists have increasingly been identifying diverse non-state actors as formidable role players in the implementation of human rights generally.[1011] In the field of economic, social and cultural rights, in particular, advocacy for the protection of these rights has relentlessly pointed in the direction of some identified non-state actors as potential

society groups, inter-governmental development agencies, and similar bodies that have come to represent the pluralism of interests in the interactive fields of human rights, law, politics, public policy, economics and development, particularly as they directly or indirectly impact the implementation of economic, social and cultural rights in Africa. I say 'convenient' because the use of 'non-state' avoids the semantic difficulties that could arise by the use of similar but non-identical expressions such as 'non-governmental' or 'inter-governmental'. In most literature, as would be seen in the course of this chapter, the term 'non-governmental actors' assumes technical reference to NGOs. See eg M Noortmann 'Non-state actors in international law' in B Arts *et al* (eds) *Non-state actors in international relations* (2001) 59 60; JM Russell 'The ambivalence about the globalisation of telecommunications: The story of Amnesty International, Shell Oil Company and Nigeria' (2002) 1 *Journal of Human Rights* 405; C Jochnick 'Confronting the impunity of non-state actors: New fields for the promotion of human rights' (1999) 21 *Human Rights Quarterly* 56 57; R Brett 'Non-governmental actors in the field of human rights' in Hanski *et al* (n 37 above) 399.

1009 See generally C Jonsson 'International organisation and co-operation: An inter-organisational perspective' (1993) 138 *International Social Science Journal* 463 471. See also B Deacon *et al Global social policy: International organisations and the future of welfare* (1997) 60.

1010 B Reinalda *et al* 'Non-state actors in international relations: Do they matter?' in Arts *et al* (n 1008 above) 1 3.

1011 Some of the relevant literature that have explored the impact of non-state actors on human rights generally include R Sullivan *Business and human rights: Dilemmas and solutions* (2003); M Robinson 'Human rights, development and business – An introduction' International Symposium on Human Rights and the Private Sector (27 November 2003) http://www.foundation.novartis.com/german/symposium/speech_mary_robinson.pdf (accessd 12 June 2009). See also Jochnick (n 1008 above) 64-65.

beneficiaries of human rights and yet, along with states, bearers of duties.[1012]

In his Final Report in 1992, Danilo Türk, the UN Special Rapporteur on Economic, Social and Cultural Rights, had painted the picture of the inevitable intercourse between economic, social and cultural rights and the vicissitudes of the free market-induced neo-liberal reforms of the 1980s and 1990s as follows:

> The flurry of many states romantically to embrace the market as the ultimate solution to all of society's ills, and the corresponding rush to denationalise and leave economics, politics and social matters to the whims of the private sector ... inevitably have an impact upon the full realisation of economic, social and cultural rights.[1013]

Goldewijk and Fortman also emphasise the necessity of evolving a 'horizontal functioning' of economic, social and cultural rights by stating that

> [t]he struggle for [economic, social and cultural rights] involves not only states but also international governmental organisations, multinational corporations, non-governmental organisations and international NGOs. These actors also have duties in regard to people's basic entitlements.[1014]

But while discussions about non-state actors' direct or indirect involvement with economic, social and cultural rights tend to emphasise their roles as 'violators', I consider that perception as becoming stereotyped and unhelpful to the evolution of an interactive, interdisciplinary rights-based approach to human development. Economic, social and cultural rights advocacy that is heavily oriented towards 'violator-bashing' without an empirical analysis cannot enhance the validation of economic, social and cultural rights claims in the intervening fields of macro-economics, international trade and finance and public policy. A balanced view of the role of all actors critical to the implementation of economic, social and cultural rights can only crystallise when arguments and perceptions on both sides of ongoing debates are juxtaposed and subjected to objective analysis. As experience tends to show, legalistic rhetoric so far directed at making certain significant non-state global entities amenable to human rights issues have not yielded

1012 See generally Steiner *et al* (n 59 above) 220-221. See also Leckie (n 657 above) 72, drawing a 'list of potential violators' of economic, social and cultural rights categorised into 'five distinct groups', namely (1) the state and public actors; (2) private actors; (3) international financial and other institutions; (4) transnational corporations (TNCs); and (5) the international community.

1013 D Türk 'Realisation of economic, social and cultural rights; final report prepared by Mr D Türk Special Rapporteur' UN Doc E/CN.4/Sub.2/1992/16 (1992) para 98.

1014 Goldewijk *et al* (n 45 above) xii-xiii. See also Jochnick (n 1008 above) 56 57.

results in *tangible* terms.[1015] Moreover, while human rights scholars and advocates readily ascribe bad faith to certain non-state actors, others praise what they regard as positive aspects of those same actors' programmes and policies.[1016]

While it will continue to engage scholars that 'third parties' (that is, natural and artificial persons outside the state *versus* individual equation) may owe obligations under human rights law, my analysis proceeds from the premise that the primary responsibility for providing the legal or other framework for the protection and implementation of economic, social and cultural rights is vested in state entities in the first instance. After all, under international law, only states do negotiate treaties.[1017] Nevertheless, whether as potential violators or as potential protectors, this chapter accentuates the unmistakable influence that existing and emerging human rights standards portend for holding non-state actors accountable under a rights-based development framework in Africa.

To facilitate a coherent presentation of the significance of the activities of non-state actors for the protection and implementation of economic, social and cultural rights and, invariably, their impact on a rights-based approach to human development in Africa, I have classified them according to the diversity and similarity of the interests they represent. In sequence, I discuss international financial and trade institutions, principally consisting of the World Bank and the International Monetary Fund, the World Trade Organisation, intergovernmental development agencies and aid donors, private sector business interests, under which I deal with TNCs and MNEs and other natural and artificial persons in the private sphere and, finally, civil society *vis-à-vis* its role with regard to economic, social and cultural rights implementation in Africa.

The extension of this discourse to the terrain of non-state actors must not in any way becloud my primary focus on the responsibility of states for the protection of economic, social and cultural rights and, indeed, of *all* human rights for that matter. All I attempt to do here is to propose a conceptual framework for understanding and assessing the performance of the economic, social and cultural rights

[1015] M Ssenyonjo 'Accountability of non-state actors in Uganda for war crimes and human rights violations: Between amnesty and the International Criminal Court' (2005) 10 *Journal of Conflict and Security Law* 405.

[1016] See eg IFI Shihata 'The World Bank and human rights: An analysis of the legal issues and the record of achievements' (1988) 17 *Denver Journal of International Law and Policy* 39 48-50. See also SP Leite 'The International Monetary Fund and human rights' http://www.imf.org/external/np/vc/2001/090401.htm (accessed 12 June 2009).

[1017] See Dankwa *et al* (n 49 above) 724; Alston & Quinn (n 836 above) 165; Leckie (n 657 above) 76. See also *Barcelona Traction, Light & Power Co Ltd (Belgium v Spain)* 1970 ICJ 3.

obligations of African states in a holistic manner that would facilitate appropriate strategic outcomes. It must also be borne in mind that, since an exhaustive analysis of the diverse activities of all identifiable non-state actors will not find a proper forum within the scope of this discourse, this chapter basically highlights some of the salient issues that should engage the minds of human rights scholars and activists in fashioning multidimensional responses to the challenges of economic, social and cultural rights in Africa.

2 The basis of the economic, social and cultural rights responsibilities of non-state actors

In chapters II and III, I extensively set out and analysed the frameworks of international, regional and national human rights instruments and mechanisms upon which I construct the approach in this discourse. While I have asserted that the obligations created by that broad array of instruments are primarily the responsibility of states, that assertion does not diminish the extension of those obligations to non-state actors, relying on the language employed in those various instruments.[1018]

Although classical liberal thinking considers that non-state actors are exempted from human rights responsibility,[1019] that thinking is becoming rather obsolete. However, while there now exists a growing consensus among scholars and human rights bodies on the binding nature of human rights obligations generally and economic, social and cultural rights particularly on non-state actors,[1020] the scope and extent of that bindingness is still in question. One formidable impediment to holding many of the most important non-state actors to human rights responsibility is the absence of an explicit human rights mandate or the exclusion of same in their founding instruments.[1021]

1018 See Maastricht Guidelines (n 49 above) paras 18-19, for a consensus of views on the moral and legal basis for the economic, social and cultural rights responsibilities of non-state actors.

1019 See generally ZA Karake-Shalhoub *Organisational downsizing, discrimination, and corporate social responsibility* (1999) 13-52.

1020 See generally Hunt (n 612 above) 196-203, analysing the various theories and approaches on the responsibility of IFIs, TNCs and MNEs for economic, social and cultural rights; ESCR Committee, General Comment No 12 (n 638 above) para 20.

1021 See eg art IV, sec 10, Articles of Agreement of the International Bank for Reconstruction and Development (IBRD) and art V, sec 6 of the International Development Association (IDA), both of which provide that the bodies 'shall not interfere in the political affairs of any member; nor shall they be influenced in their decisions by the political character of the member or members concerned. Only economic considerations shall be relevant to their decisions, and these considerations shall be weighed impartially in order to achieve the purposes stated in this Agreement.'

I contend that notwithstanding arguments to the contrary, by the mere fact of many non-state actors being specialised agencies or affiliated bodies of the UN, such bodies are morally and legally bound to respect the human rights obligations emanating from human rights treaties and other instruments adopted by the UN.[1022] Moreover, apart from the argument based on the connectivity of the IFIs and specialised agencies to the UN, there is another robust conceptual basis for holding these bodies responsible for human rights obligations, namely, general principles of international law.[1023]

Although non-state actors do not come within the purview of customary international law as entities whose consent must be sought in the formation of treaties, there are plausible indications that certain non-state actors (for example, the IMF, World Bank and UN specialised agencies) are nonetheless bound to respect human rights as norms of general international law.[1024] In an opinion given by the International Court of Justice in the interpretation of the agreement of 25 March 1951 between the WHO and Egypt,[1025] the Court had declared that '[i]nternational organisations are subjects of international law and as such, are bound by any obligations incumbent upon them under general rules of international law, under their constructions, or under international agreements to which they are parties'.[1026] By the very nature of the composition, structures and purposes of the IFIs, trade institutions, development and aid agencies that I examine in this chapter, it is logical to argue that they are *persons* in international law, indicating that they acquire rights, privileges and obligations in that regard under the broad spectra of international human rights law.[1027] My contention also finds support

1022 My argument here is not novel. See Vienna Declaration (n 38 above) part II, para 2; ESCR Committee 'International technical assistance measures (art 22 of the Covenant)', General Comment No 2, UN Doc E/C.12/1990/23 (2 February 1990) in *Compilation of general comments* (n 81 above) 11 para 8(d); D Bradlow & CI Grossman 'Limited mandate and intertwined problems: A new challenge for the World Bank and the IMF' (1995) 17 *Human Rights Quarterly* 411 428 442; Skogly (n 90 above) 760. See also M Darrow *Between light and shadow: The World Bank, the International Monetary Fund and international human rights law* (2003) 2 & n 6.

1023 For an extensive argument on this reasoning, see J Humphrey 'The international Bill of Rights and implementation' (1976) 17 *William and Mary Law Review* 259; M Cogen 'Human rights, prohibition of political activities and the lending policies of the World Bank and International Monetary Fund' in SR Chowdhury *et al* (eds) *The right to development in international law* (1988) 379 385-389. See also M Delmas-Marty *Global law: A triple challenge* (1998) 34-36; D Quiroz 'Expanding international law to non-state actors (The corporation)' (2007) 32 *South African Yearbook of International Law* 66.

1024 See ESCR Committee 'Statement on globalisation and economic, social and cultural rights' 18th sess (11 May 1998), para 11. See also Darrow (n 1022 above) 126-132.

1025 *WHO v Egypt* (1980) ICJ Reports 89-90.

1026 As above.

1027 See SI Skogly *The human rights obligations of the World Bank and International Monetary Fund* (2001) 93-109.

in the combined effect of articles 55, 56 and 57 of the UN Charter, the Universal Declaration and the entire corpus of international human rights emanating from them, all of which oblige international organisations, specialised agencies and other influential non-state actors to promote and secure the realisation of the purposes of the UN.[1028] Of particular significance to this discourse are the provisions of ICESCR that pointedly identify certain non-state actors as critical agencies of its implementation.[1029] Article 22 emphatically imports the critical role of

> organs of the United Nations, their subsidiary organs and specialised agencies concerned with furnishing technical assistance [on] any matters ... which may assist ... in deciding ... on the advisability of international measures likely to contribute to the effective progressive implementation of the [ICESCR].[1030]

Extrapolating from the tripartite typology of obligations that I considered in chapter II, the responsibility to *respect* translates into an obligation for non-state actors to avoid carrying out activities or policies that would undermine economic, social and cultural rights and to refrain from encouraging the adoption by governments of policies inimical to economic, social and cultural rights.[1031]

As would be seen in the course of my analyses, this interpretation has been subjected to rigorous contestation on diverse grounds, at various times, and by various persons and entities. While the debate may continue on the status of certain human rights norms in

1028 See generally D Shelton 'Hierarchy of norms and human rights: of trumps and winners' (2002) 65 *Saskatchewan Law Review* 301 306-308. See also A Blackett 'Mapping the equilibrium line: Fundamental principles and rights at work and the interpretive universe of the World Trade Organisation' (2002) 65 *Saskatchewan Law Review* 369 373-375.

1029 See, eg, art 16(2)(b) that mandates the UN Secretary-General to transmit copies of the state reports, or any parts of them, to specialised agencies where such reports fall within the scope of the responsibilities of such agencies; art 17(1) which contemplates 'consultations' between state parties and the appropriate specialised agencies in the implementation of ICESCR; arts 18-21 which create extensive procedural collaboration among states, specialised agencies and ECOSOC in the implementation of ICESCR.

1030 I acknowledge the significant dimension of art 24 of ICESCR which has served as bedrock for the objections of IFIs to economic, social and cultural rights responsibility. See generally 'Economic, social and cultural human rights and the International Monetary Fund, Working Paper submitted by F Gianviti, General Counsel, International Monetary Fund' 7 May 2001, UN Doc E/C.12/2001/WP.5, para 27. While the article indeed seeks to preserve the constitutional mandates of specialised agencies, I contend that by the legal interpretative rule of *expressio unius est exclusio ulterius*, specialised agencies cannot interpret this provision to negate the fundamental objects and purposes of ICESCR. An agreement between a state and an agency of the UN that violates the principles of non-discrimination and equality will, eg, be unsustainable from the perspective of art 53 of the VCLT.

1031 See SI Skogly 'The position of the World Bank and the International Monetary Fund in the human rights field' in Hanski *et al* (n 37 above) 231 243-244; Darrow (n 1022 above) 129-132.

international law or the ascendancy of human rights generally, and economic, social and cultural rights in particular, to the status of obligations *erga omnes* or *jus cogens*,[1032] there have been forceful arguments that a violation of the UN Charter's obligation on its member states to promote higher standards of living and conditions of economic and social progress and development through the activities or policies of IFIs might constitute a violation of *jus cogens*.[1033] Francisco Martin even went further to classify some economic, social and cultural rights ('rights to ... food, shelter and other basic needs') as 'derivative *jus cogens* norms because of their necessity in ensuring the protection of other *jus cogens* norms'.[1034] I find it difficult to align myself with the arguments on the status of all economic, social and cultural rights as being part of *jus cogens* in the hierarchy of international human rights law, having regard to the problematic question of their normative interpretation, the manifest lackadaisical attitude of states toward implementation and even the unresolved dispute on whether economic, social and cultural rights are rights at all. While the economic, social and cultural rights norms of equality and non-discrimination may qualify as peremptory norms, it will be unrealistic to make a blanket assertion for all economic, social and cultural rights.

Be that as it may, against the backdrop of the highlighted theoretical basis for the legal responsibility of non-state actors, I proceed to examine its practical implications for the activities of diverse entities, efforts aimed at addressing human rights problems arising therefrom, problematic issues involved in their accountability and to analyse the linkages of their human rights responsibilities to

1032 Despite her rigorous discourse on 'the primacy of human rights law' in international law, Shelton admits that '[w]hile the supremacy of human rights law is being pressed by human rights bodies, international financial and trade institutions have shown no indication of their willingness to accept the proposed hierarchy, nor have international tribunals shown a willingness to override the customary laws of sovereign and diplomatic immunity in order to give priority to asserted *jus cogens* norms'. See Shelton (n 1028 above) 321. Compare M Koskenniemi 'Hierarchy in international law: A sketch' (1997) 8 *European Journal of International Law* 566 573, limiting his perception about the status of human rights in the hierarchy of international legal norms to 'the right to life'). For a thorough theoretical analysis of the characteristics of peremptory norms as they relate to international human rights law, see L Hannikainen *Peremptory norms (*jus cogens*) in international law: Historical development, criteria, present status* (1998) 315-520. See also Dugard (n 52 above) 40.

1033 See 'The realisation of economic, social and cultural rights: Globalisation and its impact on the full enjoyment of human rights' preliminary report submitted by J Oloka-Onyango and D Udagama, in accordance with Sub-Commission Resolution 1999/8, UN Doc E/CN.4/Sub.2/2000/13 (15 June 2000) para 41. See also Commission on Human Rights 'Effects of structural adjustment policies and foreign debt on the full enjoyment of all human rights, particularly economic, social and cultural rights' Res 2000/82, UN Doc E/CN.4/Res/2000/82 (April 2000), para 6.

1034 FF Martin 'Delineating a hierarchical outline of international law sources and norms' (2002) 65 *Saskatchewan Law Review* 333 348-351.

the focus of this discourse. Since my approach here does not isolate a particular category of non-state actors, it helps an analytic grasp of the issues I address to classify my discussions under distinct headings.

3 International financial and trade institutions

There exists an abundance of well-researched literature on the relevance and impact of the policies and activities of the World Bank, the International Monetary Fund (IMF) and the World Trade Organisation (WTO) on human rights generally.[1035] As far as Africa is concerned, there has also been a considerable level of intellectual activity directed at the same subject.[1036] I do not intend to review such a vast array of works. What is, however, unsettling is that, while virtually every piece of rights-based critique of the activities of these institutions underscores the need for reforms within these institutions under the regime of international human rights law,[1037] the

1035 See eg O Kirshner *The Bretton Woods-GATT system: Retrospect and prospect after fifty years* (1995); C Caufield *Masters of illusion: The World Bank and the poverty of nations* (1996); R Culpeper *et al Global development fifty years after Bretton Woods: Essays in honour of Gerald K Helleiner* (1997); SI Skogly *The human rights obligations of the World Bank and International Monetary Fund* (2001); DD Bradlow *et al Limited mandates and intertwined problems: A new challenge for the World Bank and the IMF* (1995) 17 *Human Rights Quarterly* 411; ER Carrasco 'Critical issues facing the Bretton Woods system: Can the IMF, World Bank and the GATT/WTO promote an enabling environment for social development? (1996) 6 *Transnational Law and Contemporary Problems* i vii-xi; DD Bradlow 'The World Bank, the IMF, and human rights' (1996) 6 *Transnational and Contemporary Problems* 47; M Chossudovsky 'World Trade Organisation (WTO): An illegal organisation that violates the Universal Declaration of Human Rights' http://www.derechos.org/nizkor/doc/ articulos/chossudovskye.html (accessed 12 June 2009); N Gunewardena 'Reinscribing subalternity: International financial institutions, development, and women's marginality' (2003) 7 *UCLA Journal of International and Foreign Affairs* 201; J Morgan-Foster 'The relationship of IMF structural adjustment programmemes to economic, social and cultural rights: The Argentine case revisited' (2003) 24 *Michigan Journal of International Law* 577; JW Head 'The future of law and policy in global financial institutions: The changing role of law in the IMF and the multilateral development banks' (2007) 17 *Kansas Journal of Law and Public Policy* 194; N Wahi 'Human rights accountability of the IMF and the World Bank: A critique of existing mechanisms and articulation of a theory of horizontal accountability' (2006) 12 *University of California Davis Journal of International Law and Policy* 331; PJ Keenan 'Financial globalisation and human rights' (2008) 46 *Columbia Journal of Transnational Law* 509..

1036 As above. See also Skogly (n 90 above) 751-788; M Gravelle *et al* 'Africa and the Uruguay Round' (1996) 6 *Transnational Law and Contemporary Problems* 123.

1037 Some of the ample literature that exists on rights-based criticisms of these institutions and the clamour for institutional reform measures include B Rajagopal 'Crossing the Rubicon: Synthesising the soft international law of the IMF and human rights' (1993) 11 *Boston University International Law Journal* 81; J Williamson 'Reforming the IMF: Different or better?' in RJ Myers (ed) *The political morality of the International Monetary Fund: Ethics and foreign policy* (1987) 1-7; A Caliari *et al* 'Reform proposals for the governance structures of the international financial institutions: A new rules for global governance briefing paper' http://www.new-rules.org/Docs/ifigovernancereform.pdf (accessed 12 June 2009).

theoretical basis for appropriate responses has never been clearly defined nor identified *vis-à-vis* Africa. Again, apart from emphasising the adversities of the domestic policies induced by the conditionalities of these institutions, *how* to integrate human rights (principally economic, social and cultural rights) into the human development challenges engendered thereby remains under-theorised, under-explored and vaguely defined for Africa. This book seeks to fill that *lacuna*.

3.1 Bretton Woods Institutions[1038]

Rather than reviewing the history, organisational structures or other philosophical arguments about the role of IFIs in the north-south conflict over global economic policies, or the desirability of their involvement in Africa's development goals,[1039] my effort in this segment is aimed at evaluating the impact of the policy outlook of these twin institutions on the implementation of economic, social and cultural rights in Africa, weighing their intentions against outcomes and highlighting the critical dimension of their responsibilities.

It is important to note from the onset that both the World Bank and the IMF had at one time or the other, if not repeatedly, offered rhetoric for their commitment to human development and the eradication of poverty – two core issues located in the philosophical realm of economic, social and cultural rights – despite the allegation that they both evade explicit reference to human rights.[1040] While there exists a wide range of other grounds for the scepticism and

1038 Bretton Woods Institutions is the name tag ascribed to the World Bank and its twin institution, the IMF, based on the location of their birthplace, Bretton Woods, New Hampshire, US, in June 1944. For narratives on the history of the Bretton Woods Institutions, see K Knoor 'The Bretton Woods Institutions in transition' (1940) 2 *International Organisation* 35; AF Lowenfeld *International economic law* (2002) 502-506. For the purposes of this discourse, Bretton Woods Institutions and IFIs are used interchangeably and both refer to the IMF and World Bank.

1039 See generally African Forum and Network on Debt and Development (AFRODAD), PRSP Technical Paper 2003 - Africa's experience with the PRSP: Content and process (2003); Deacon (n 1009 above) 67-69. A vast number of civil society groups also exist that are devoted to the scrutiny of the policies and programmemes of these institutions.

1040 In 1998, eg, the World Bank found the important event of the 50th anniversary of the Universal Declaration to declare its recognition of that global instrument and to assert its commitment to the Universal Declaration's goals. See World Bank *Development and human rights: The role of the World Bank* (1998) 2. Earlier in 1993, at the World Conference on Human Rights held in Vienna, Austria, the World Bank had stressed its 'positive' attitude towards 'helping developing countries to make the enjoyment of economic and social human rights a reality'. See World Bank 'The World Bank and the promotion of human rights' UN Doc A/Conf.157/PC/61/Add.19 (1993). Compare G Brodnig 'The World Bank and human rights: Mission impossible?' (2002) 17 *Fletcher Journal of Developmental Studies* 1 3. In its 1994 Annual Report, the Governing Board of the IMF 'reaffirmed its recognition that some policy measures may have important distributional

criticisms that have continued to harass the operations and policies of the IFIs,[1041] it is the failure of those policies to substantially mitigate the economic distress in African states, and the tendency for those policies to aggravate socio-economic adversities and deepen governmental neglect of human rights, especially economic, social and cultural rights, that have been pivotal in the Afro-centric dimension of such criticisms.[1042] It therefore becomes necessary to examine the pertinent dynamics of some of the programmes and policies of IFIs that have exerted and are still exerting a considerable impact on economic, social and cultural rights and human development in Africa.

3.1.1 Structural adjustment programmes

Structural Adjustment Programmes (SAPs)[1043] were introduced by the IFIs as a strategic response to the artificial debt crises that engulfed many states of the developing world in the late 1970s and early 1980s.[1044] Usually formulated as loan conditions by IFIs, SAPs compel

implications, that such distributional effects can undermine public support for the reforms, and that the design of [IMF] supported reform programmemes should valuate and seek to mitigate the short term adverse effects of policy measures on vulnerable groups'. See IMF *Annual report 1994* (1994) 120. See also M Camdessus 'From crisis to a new recovery' IMF, 1999, quoted in JD Taillant 'Human rights and the international financial institutions' paper presented at the conference on Implementing International Sustainable Development Law, Montreal, Canada, 13-15 June 2002 3-5.

1041 See eg S George *et al Faith and credit: The World Bank's secular empire* (1994) 199; Caufield (n 1035 above) 189; D Kapur *et al The World Bank: Its first half century* (1997) 2; Caliari (n 1037 above); Bradlow (n 1035 above) 74-75; EM Denters *Law and policy of IMF conditionality* (1996) 130-131; VA Leary 'Globalisation and human rights' in J Symonides (ed) *Human rights: New dimensions and challenges* (1998) 265 266. For a critique of the IMF-inspired value added tax system in Africa, see R Krever (ed) *VAT in Africa* (2008). For the responses of IFIs to some of these criticisms, see Deacon (n 1009 above) 65; Shihata (n 1016 above) 40-48; JW Head 'For richer or for poorer: Assessing the criticisms directed at the multilateral development banks' (2004) 52 *Kansas Law Review* 241.

1042 See generally Skogly (n 90 above) 755; Head (n 1041above).

1043 The purely economic dimensions of SAPs have been debated over several years. Some of the useful references in that regard include GA Cornia *Adjustment with a human face* (1987) 52; V Corbo *et al* 'Structural adjustment, stabilisation and policy reform: Domestic and international finance' in J Behrman *et al* (eds) *Handbook of development economics* (1995) 2845 2847; DM Schydlowsky *Structural adjustment: Retrospect and prospect* (1995); ER Carrasco 'Income distribution and the Bretton Woods institutions: Promoting an enabling environment for social development' (1996) 6 *Transnational Law and Contemporary Problems* 1 28-33; P Mosley *et al Aid and power: The World Bank and policy lending, analysis and policy proposals* (1991) 65-66.

1044 See R Fletcher 'Adjustment experiences: An overview' in K Haq *et al* (eds) *Adjustment with growth: A search for an equitable solution* (1984) 83-85; Gunewardena (n 1035 above) 213-214.

changes in macroeconomic policies that obligate recipient nations to liberalise their trade and investment policies at home and abroad.[1045]

In his Second Report, the UN Special Rapporteur on Economic, Social and Cultural Rights had drawn a concise linkage between SAPs and economic, social and cultural rights in the following terms:

> Structural adjustment programmes continue to have a significant impact upon the overall realisation of economic, social and cultural rights, both *in terms of the ability of people to exercise these rights, and of the capability of governments to fulfil and implement them.* While significant and positive changes have taken place concerning the design and nature of adjustment, these have yet to result in a marked shift sufficient not only to protect fully the rights of the most vulnerable, but also actually to decrease levels of impoverishment. *Human rights concerns continue to be conspicuously underestimated in the adjustment process.*[1046]

As far as Africa is concerned, his finding could not have been more accurate. The collapse of export products and other harsh economic realities of the 1980s impelled a host of African states to seek refuge under the IFIs for economic development reform strategies.[1047] More than two decades after the introduction of SAPs, the social and economic consequences of the SAPs experiences in Africa and their propensity to weaken government capacity for social services that are keenly linked to economic, social and cultural rights implementation have become pronounced.[1048]

1045 See Gunewardena (n 1035 above); Skogly (n 90 above) 756; CJ Dias 'Influencing the policies of the World Bank and the International Monetary Fund' in Rehof *et al* (n 184 above) 61-62.

1046 Second Report prepared by Mr Danilo Türk, Special Rapporteur (n 863 above) para 185 (my emphasis).

1047 See SJ Burki 'Debt and adjustment: The experience of South Asia and sub-Saharan Africa' in Haq *et al* (n 1044 above) 129-135; Skogly (n 90 above) 751-778; B Ibhawoh 'Structural adjustment, authoritarianism and human rights in Africa' (1999) 19 *Comparative Studies Asia, Africa and Middle East* 158.

1048 See L Tshuma 'The impact of the IMF/World Bank-dictated economic structural adjustment programmemes on human rights: Erosion of empowerment rights' in P Nherere *et al* (eds) *The institutionalisation of human rights in Southern Africa* (1993) 213; A Adepojo *The impact of structural adjustment on the population of Africa: The implications for education, health and employment* (1993); Agbakwa (n 46 above) 196-199. See also B Onimode *The IMF, the World Bank and the African debt* (1987); NJ Udombana 'How should we then live? Globalisation and the New Partnership for Africa's Development' (2002) 20 *Boston University International Law Journal* 293 312-318; J Lobe 'World Bank, IMF held responsible for health crisis in Africa' http://www.twnside.org.sg/title/twe279g.htm (accessed 12 June 2009); Jochnick (n 1008 above); GA Cornia *et al Africa's recovery in the 1990s: From stagnation and adjustment to human development* (1992) 16; M Okumu 'Structural adjustment programmemes: Which way up for Africa?' paper presented at the Heinrich Böll Foundation Gender Forum, Nairobi, Kenya, 26 September 2002 6 (my emphasis); N Osundare 'The critic as scapegoat' 12 *Newswatch* 1 February 1998 38.

While it may be erroneous to point at SAPs as the cause of poverty in Africa, it is undeniable that they have occasioned tremendous negative repercussions on social welfare conditions and indeed the entire spectrum of labour rights across the African continent.[1049] Empirical research shows that, apart from lowered labour standards and social dislocations, state and non-state entities are steadily evolving a culture of impunity in the treatment of people of the working class in Africa.[1050] Women's rights, children's rights, environmental rights and the broad range of economic, social and cultural rights have generally suffered a similar fate.[1051]

Against the backdrop of the *privatisation* of public sector enterprises, a phenomenon that was a key component of SAPs,[1052] the realisation of economic, social and cultural rights, particularly the rights to health, housing and water, have largely been jeopardised since access to basic social services to which they are inherently linked have steadily been curbed.[1053] I contend that, by cutting down on the basic services previously enjoyed by individuals and families either for free or at subsidised rates (for example, education, water, electricity, health, etc) and replacing them with restricted and more expensive services, African governments have continually breached their obligation to respect and to protect the connected economic, social and cultural rights and to refrain from taking retrogressive steps.

Although scholarly views remain divergent regarding the desirability and dynamics of privatisation,[1054] I avoid getting entangled in the protracted debate on whether governments should

1049 See generally D Percival 'The changing face of trade unionism in Africa' (1996) 156 *The Courier ACP-EU* 76-77, reporting the catalogue of state repression of labour rights in the advent of SAPs in Africa. For a relevant bibliography on the impact of SAPs on human and labour rights in Africa, see World View *Labour's role in Africa: Policies, laws and practices* http://worldviews.igc.org/awpguide/labour.html (accessed 12 June 2009).

1050 See Ibhawoh (n 1047 above) 164.

1051 See generally K Frostell *Globalisation and the human rights of women* (2002) 56-59; SI Skogly 'Human rights and economic efficiency: The relationship between social cost of adjustment and human rights protection' in P Baehr *et al* (eds) *Human rights in developing countries: yearbook 1994* (1994) 43 57-63; Udombana (n 1048 above) 293 312-318; S Baden 'The impact of recession and structural adjustment on women in developing countries' ILO Paper (1993); FL Osunsade 'Impacts of adjustment programmemes: Concerns for the human condition' in VP Nanda *et al* (eds) *World debt and the human condition: Structural adjustment and the right to development* (2003) 107.

1052 See JS Guseh 'The public sector, privatisation, and development in sub-Saharan Africa' (1999) 5 *African Studies Quarterly* 1.

1053 See generally S Tsemo 'Privatisation of basic services, democracy and human rights' (2003) 4 *Economics and Social Rights Review* 3.

1054 See generally MO Chibundu 'Law and the political economy of privatisation in sub-Saharan Africa' (1997) 21 *Maryland Journal of International Law and Trade* 1; Tsemo (n 1053 above) 3; R Ram 'Government size and economic growth: A new framework and some evidence from cross-section and time-series data' (1986) 76 *American Economics Review* 191-203.

play larger or minor roles in the process of economic development. Resonating with the Universal Declaration, ICESCR and the African Charter, my approach contemplates that to entrench a 'human' component in any agenda for economic development only requires that, whether large or small, African governments are obliged to create an enabling legislative and institutional environment for the realisation of the goal of authentic development. Economic, social and cultural rights provide a facilitative framework for that process.

It is pertinent to note that in more than half of African states where SAPs have been applied, none had popular participation in the negotiation processes.[1055] This in itself undermines the integrative approach that I canvass in this work. Indeed, in many instances, popular protests against the introduction of SAPs were met with repressive force, resulting in many casualties across Africa.[1056] Even though the IFIs openly stress the value of broad-based consultations between governments and their peoples,[1057] such admonitions usually end up as mere rhetoric as such consultations are never made prerequisites for obtaining or renewing loan facilities.[1058] It would be apt to state that the IFIs have, through their SAPs, given leeway to many African governments to perpetuate malevolent governance patterns without regard to public opinion.[1059] Since the IFIs are not influenced by the legitimacy or reputation of the government negotiating their loans,[1060] it is not difficult to discern how unpopular regimes in Africa could have kept renewing World Bank/IMF loans, thereby perpetuating the steady slide of their respective countries into socio-economic gloom and despair.

3.1.2 The highly indebted poor countries (HIPC) initiative

A pertinent derivative of the SAPs is the HIPC initiative of both the IMF and the World Bank. According to the IMF:

> The HIPC initiative was first launched in 1996 by the IMF and World Bank, with the aim of ensuring that no poor country faces a debt burden it cannot manage. The initiative entails co-ordinated action by the international financial community, including multilateral organisations

1055 See generally Jochnick (n 1008 above) 69-70, observing that, despite the 'broad ramifications for development policies ... [SAPs] are ... exclusively carried out behind closed doors with only the involvement of the finance ministries'.

1056 See generally Ibhawoh (n 1047 above) 160-161; Agbese (n 452 above) 152-154.

1057 See eg World Bank *Development and human rights* (n 1040 above) 11.

1058 See generally U Kirdar 'Impact of IMF conditionality on human conditions' in Haq *et al* (n 1044 above) 229 232.

1059 See generally Ibhawoh (n 1047 above) 161.

1060 As above 160; Agbese (n 452 above) 160 and accompanying n 65.

> and governments, *to reduce to sustainable levels the external debt burdens of the most heavily indebted poor countries.*[1061]

The World Bank equally explained the essence of the HIPC initiative as follows:

> The HIPC framework marks an important change in traditional approaches to debt relief in that it *focuses on debt sustainability*, and on the need for joint action in providing debt relief by all creditors, including, for the first time, multilateral institutions. The initiative reduces the overall amount of debt owed and cuts debt servicing payments within a sustainable development strategy ... As part of an improved economic environment, HIPC debt relief will be used to expand programmes aimed directly at poverty reduction. By helping to sustain better economic policies, it will also increase private investment and generate domestic enterprise.[1062]

As at 31 December 2008, African HIPC countries were 29 out of the entire 33 states listed on the global HIPC initiative table.[1063] While the IFIs claim that the HIPC initiative will reduce the debt of the world's most impoverished countries to 'sustainable' levels, the initiative manifests as a recycled form of the SAPs.[1064]

Moreover, just like the SAPs, the initiative is negotiated exclusively among government technocrats and the 'experts' of the IFIs. Popular participation is largely nil – resulting in an asymmetry of proclaimed intentions and actual outcomes.[1065] Equally critical is the fact that, despite whatever pretensions the IFIs might be making about the situation of Africa's indebtedness under these prescriptive

1061 IMF 'Debt relief under the Heavily Indebted Poor Countries (HIPC) initiative: A factsheet' October 2008 (my emphasis) http://www.imf.org/external/np/exr/facts/hipc.htm (accessed 12 June 2009).

1062 World Bank *Development and human rights* (n 1040 above) 9 (my emphasis).

1063 These states are Benin, Burkina Faso, Burundi, Cameroon, Central African Republic, Chad, Congo, Democratic Republic of the Congo, Côte d'Ivoire, Ethiopia, The Gambia, Ghana, Guinea, Guinea-Bissau, Kenya, Liberia, Madagascar, Malawi, Mali, Mauritania, Mozambique, Niger, Rwanda, São Tomé and Príncipe, Senegal, Sierra Leone, Tanzania, Uganda and Zambia. See 'Heavily indebted poor countries debt initiatives' last updated 12 June 2009 http://www.imf.org/external/np/hipc/index.asp (accessed 22 November 2008).

1064 See UN Commission on Human Rights 'The Highly Indebted Poor Countries (HIPC) initiative: A human rights assessment of the Poverty Reduction Strategy Papers (PRSP)': report submitted by Mr Fantu Cheru, independent expert on the effects of structural adjustment policies and foreign debt on the full enjoyment of all human rights, particularly economic, social and cultural rights, 57th sess, UN Doc E/CN.4/2001/56 (18 January 2001)12 para 27.

1065 n 1064 above, paras 29 & 31, observing that to the knowledge of both the World Bank and the IMF, most 'HIPC countries simply do not have the necessary up-to-date poverty data ... to undertake extensive poverty monitoring and integrate poverty reduction strategies into a macro-economic framework ... [and that even] the construction of a poverty profile is difficult since a recent national household survey is not available in the majority of HIPC countries'.

programmes, empirical evidence abound that the hope of economic recovery for Africa is forlorn.[1066]

It is now beyond polemic that, with the restrictions placed on the budgets of HIPC countries, most African states listed under the initiative are forced to commit more of their scarce resources to the IFIs and other creditors. For instance, impeccable research undeniably projects that 'Senegal, Tanzania and Zambia will emerge from the HIPC debt relief process in the perverse position of paying more on debt servicing ... [and that debt] repayments will continue to absorb a disproportionately large share of government revenue ... to over 40% in Zambia, Cameroon and Malawi'.[1067] According to Oxfam International:

> Debt servicing will continue to absorb a large share of government revenue in most countries, amounting to 40% of total revenue in Zambia; 25-35% of the total in Cameroon, Guinea, Senegal and Malawi; 15-20% in ... Mozambique, Tanzania and Mauritania; 13-14% in Burkina Faso and Mauritania.[1068]

Comparing what these imply for the implementation of economic, social and cultural rights after the HIPC process, the research shows that in 'Zambia, Tanzania, Senegal, Mauritania and Cameroon, debt repayments will exceed the combined health and education budgets after debt relief'.[1069]

It is thus obvious that by setting rigid limits for public sector spending in African participating states, the HIPC initiative indirectly curtails whatever preparedness such states may seek to exert in meeting the basic welfare and social needs of their peoples which are the critical goals of economic, social and cultural rights.[1070]

1066 See generally Africa Action 'Critique of the Heavily Indebted Poor Countries (HIPC) initiative' http://www.africaaction.org/desk/hipc0206.htm (accessed 12 June 2009).

1067 Oxfam Community Aid Abroad 'The link between aid and human rights', submission to the human rights sub-committee of the Joint Standing Committee on Foreign Affairs, Defence and Trade, January 2001 http://www.caa.org.au/campaigns/submissions/aid2001/ (accessed 12 June 2009).

1068 As above.

1069 As above.

1070 See generally A Frankovits 'Economic, social and cultural rights and international financial institutions' http://www.hurights.or.jp/asia-pacific/no_22/03_escr.htm (accessed 12 June 2009); 'Zambian government blames IMF/WB for lack of teachers' *The Post* 2 February 2004, to Africa Files, info@africafiles.org (7 February 2004); A Bathily 'Senegal's structural adjustment programmeme and its economic and social effects: The political economy of regression' in Onimode (n 1048 above) 131.

3.1.3 Poverty reduction strategy papers

In response to the gale of criticisms against the SAPs and HIPC initiative, particularly as regards popular involvement, the IMF and World Bank in 1999 evolved a 'new' agenda for poverty reduction – the Poverty Reduction Strategy Papers (PRSPs).[1071] Since its inception, 29 African states, representing more than 50% of the continent and its islands, have enlisted in the PRSPs programme.[1072]

The World Bank defines a PRSP as a description of

> a country's macro-economic, structural and social policies and programmes to promote growth and reduce poverty, as well as associated external financing needs ... *prepared by governments through a participatory process involving civil society* and development partners, including the World Bank and the International Monetary Fund (IMF).[1073]

In the wisdom of both the IMF and the World Bank, the PRSP mechanism

> is designed to ensure that ... lending will be conditional on national development plans that focus on poverty reduction. It is intended that through a widespread process of national consultation, a country will draw up plans that will prioritise poverty reduction.[1074]

It is significant to note that, despite their frenetic avowal of 'poverty reduction' through the PRSP mechanism, the IFIs have declined to embrace human rights language or mechanisms in interpreting the dynamics of their agenda, and many African participating states have

1071 For a scholarly analysis of the PRSPs process, see Taillant (n 1040 above) 7. See also A Frankovits 'Rules to live by the human rights approach to development' (2002) 17 *Fletcher Journal of Developmental Studies* 1 3.

1072 These states are Benin, Burkina Faso, Burundi, Cameroon, Cape Verde, Central African Republic, Chad, Democratic Republic of the Congo, Côte d'Ivoire, Ethiopia, The Gambia, Ghana, Guinea, Guinea-Bissau, Kenya, Lesotho, Madagascar, Malawi, Mali, Mauritania, Mozambique, Niger, Rwanda, São Tomé and Príncipe, Senegal, Sierra Leone, Tanzania, Uganda and Zambia. See World Bank 'Poverty reduction strategies and PRSPs: Africa – Sub-Saharan' http://poverty.worldbank.org/prsp/index.php?view=reg&id =4 (accessed 12 June 2009). It is interesting to note that except for Burundi, Cape Verde, Central African Republic and Lesotho, all these states are also participating in the HIPC Initiative.

1073 World Bank 'Poverty reduction strategies and PRSPs' http://www.worldbank.org/poverty/strategies/index.htm (accessed 12 June 2009) (my emphasis).

1074 Frankovits (n 1071 above) 2. Broadly defined, a country's PRSP should describe (i) the country's participatory process towards the formulation of the PRSP; (ii) a diagnosis of poverty in the country; (iii) targets, indicators, and monitoring systems for the PRSP; and (iv) the priorities of state actions emanating from the populace. See IMF 'Poverty reduction strategy papers: progress in implementation', report prepared by the staff of the IMF and the World Bank, 7 September 2000 4.

also been encouraged to follow suit.[1075] While the IFIs contend that PRSPs are based on 'a participatory process involving civil society', what African governments present to them are far from being products of popular input.[1076] Rather than reflecting the genuine aspirations of ordinary citizens or their *authentic* representatives, African PRSPs have effectively been the products of finance department officials and other servants of the ruling class.[1077] Indeed, in very many instances, governments only present predetermined data that they know will secure the approval of the IFIs.[1078]

The futility of the PRSP mechanism to address, let alone reduce, the poverty crisis in Africa, has been exposed in a number of writings.[1079] The lack of transparency in the manner of the collaboration between IFIs and African states also remains a particularly huge challenge.[1080] Even though the IFIs readily cite the 'successes' of the PRSP process,[1081] every indication from African participating states shows that the mechanism is sterile and out of tune with local realities and priorities.[1082] While the rhetoric of human rights linkage to the PRSPs' central focus on the 'attainment of basic levels of human dignity' is rife, that linkage has never

1075 See Darrow (n 1022 above) 89 n 142. See generally L Elliot 'Poor nations' rights are wronged' *The Guardian* 3 April 2000 5; 'Zambian Government blames IMF/WB for lack of teachers' (n 1070 above).

1076 See generally DM Dembele 'The myths and dangers of PRSPs' 7 September 2003, http://www.brettonwoodsproject.org/article.shtml?cmd%5B126%5D=x-126-19091 (accessed 12 June 2009); F Cheru (n 1064 above) para 32.

1077 See generally C Thomas 'Poverty reduction, trade, and rights' (2003) 18 *American University International Law Review* 1399; T Thomas Law 'Free trade agreements and the poverty reduction and growth facility: How these institutions target poverty in developing countries' (2006) 12 *Law and Business Review of the Americas* 571..

1078 As above.

1079 See eg AFRODAD (n 1039 above); Dembele (n 1076 above); F Cheru (n 1064 above) paras 23-24; Elliot (n 1075 above).

1080 See generally C Denny 'West's fine words leave debts piled high' *The Guardian* (London) 21 July 2000 quoted in Darrow (n 1022 above) 88 n 133.

1081 See eg IMF/World Bank 'Review of the poverty reduction strategy paper (PRSP) approach: Early experience with interim PRSPs and full PRSPs' 26 March 2002 http://www.imf.org/external/NP/prspgen/review/2002/032602a.pdf (accessed 28 June 2008).

1082 See N Thin *et al* 'Sub-Saharan Africa's poverty reduction strategy papers from social policy and sustainable livelihood perspectives: A report for the Department of International Development' Oxford Policy Management March 2001 11. See also AFRODAD (n 1039 above).

materialised and thus, policy and outcomes have been at variance.[1083] It is difficult to see how states that have had no sustainable culture of democratic debate would open up such crucial issue as external borrowing that implicates the control of national economic power and resources to otherwise 'insignificant' masses.

The IFIs would have done creditably well had they first considered the popularity and legitimacy of a negotiating African government before even considering its proposal for credit facilities. On a continent replete with unpopular regimes, the IFIs will be seen to be operating above board only when they make democratic auditing one of the essential prerequisites for loan and credit assistance to African borrowing states.

3.1.4 Infrastructural 'development' projects

Apart from the lending activities of the IFIs, another very critical area of concern to economic, social and cultural rights is the impact of the IFIs' (essentially the World Bank's) foray into infrastructural development projects.[1084] Even though the World Bank takes pride in its investment 'in people',[1085] there ends whatever bright side exists on the Bank's balance sheet of performance from the perspective of an ordinary African. In pursuit of their 'development' agenda in conjunction with the states of the south, the IFIs' infrastructural project activities have more often than not directly interfered with human rights, particularly economic, social and cultural rights. In many instances, these projects have led to wanton abuse of economic, social and cultural rights, particularly the rights to

1083 See Taillant (n 1040 above). It is interesting to note that in most of the 29 African PRSPs, the words 'vulnerable people', 'disabled persons', 'marginalised groups', 'homeless', 'unemployed', 'people living with HIV/AIDs', 'AIDS-orphans' were never used. See eg Burundi Poverty Reduction Strategy Paper (PRSP), IMF country report 07/46, February 2007 http://imf.org/external/pubs/ft/scr/2007/cr0746.pdf (accessed 12 June 2009); Cape Verde Poverty Reduction Strategy Paper (PRSP), IMF country report 05/135, April 2005, http://imf.org/external/pubs/ft/scr/2005/cr05135.pdf (accessed 22 November 2008); Ghana Poverty Reduction Strategy Paper (PRSP), IMF country report 06/225, June 2006, http://poverty.worldbank.org/files/Cameroon_-_PRSP1.pdf (accessed 22 November 2008).

1084 For a comprehensive view of the World Bank's activities in the 'infrastructure sector' and a long list of references in that regard, see Darrow (n 1022 above) 72-74. Compare Centre for Housing Rights and Evictions (COHRE) 'World Bank funded project linked to atrocities and mass evictions in Guatemala' (2003) 1 *Housing Rights Bulletin* 1.

1085 See n 1040 above, 6 7.

housing, health, food and a clean and safe environment.[1086]

While there is an indication that the World Bank had decreased its lending programmes for major infrastructural projects since the late 1990s,[1087] there is no suggestion that the Bank has chosen to desist from sponsoring or partaking in 'development' projects that portend a serious threat to economic, social and cultural rights. An ongoing reference is the Chad/Cameroon Oil Pipeline Project that the World Bank is fully sponsoring alongside some other powerful non-state actors.[1088] Despite all the scientific, political and cultural concerns being raised by environmental rights activists and other civil society groups that the project would harm the environment, the World Bank has decided to continue with the project.[1089]

1086 See Bradlow (n 1035 above) 59. See generally Jochnick (n 1008 above) 69. The Maroko incident in Nigeria remains an indelible black spot on whatever the true intentions of the World Bank could have been. On 15 July 1990, some 300 000 people were forcibly evicted from their abodes as the entire Maroko area, reputed to be Nigeria's largest slum settlement (and perhaps Africa's largest), was flattened by bulldozers on the orders of an infamous military administration, contrary to court orders, and without any compensation or relocation arrangement for the mass of illegally dispossessed families – a blatant disregard for the right to adequate housing. See ESCR Committee: Concluding Observations – Nigeria (n 131 above) para 42, where the ESCR Committee reprimanded the Nigerian government for 'massive and arbitrary evictions'. A World Bank urban 'development' project had purportedly been earmarked for the area. Up until this day, the project is yet to take off, but the scars of that incident linger. It is also pertinent to remember how, in 1997-1998, under the purported Lagos Drainage and Sanitation Project, the World Bank tenaciously funded and supported the compulsory eviction of individuals and families from 15 slum communities in Ijora, Lagos. Even though civil society resistance ensured the abandonment of that massive violation of the right to housing, two of the communities, (Ijora Oloye and Ijora Badiya) had been levelled under the command of the Lagos State Government of Nigeria.

1087 See Darrow (n 1022 above) 72.

1088 This project has engaged the attention of a number of NGOs. For critiques and analyses of the project, see Africa Energy Intelligence *The Chad/Cameroon Oil Project* http://www.africaintelligence.com/dossiers/energy/dos_aif_energy_tchad_cam.asp (accessed 12 June 2009); Amnesty International *Chad and Cameroon: Oil pipeline threatens local communities and fragile ecosystem*, http://www.amnestyusa.org/justearth/chad-cameroon.html (accessed 22 November 2008); Bank Information Centre 'Chadians call for national day of mourning as pipeline is inaugurated' http://www.bicusa.org/africa/ pppchadcameroon.htm (accessed 22 November 2008).

1089 See 'World Bank sticks by Chad-Cameroon pipeline' 12 September 2002http://www.planetark.com/dailynewsstory.cfm/newsid/17729/story.htm (accessed 22 November 2008). See also JC Owens 'Government failure in sub-Saharan Africa: The international community's options' (2003) 43 *Virginia Journal of International Law* 1003 1042-043.

Even though the World Bank launched an Inspection Panel in 1993 to look into people's grievances in cases involving its sponsored projects,[1090] the inspection process falls gravely short of alleviating the immediate and long-term hardships of those whose rights and livelihood are directly affected.[1091]

What is discernible from all that I have said about IFIs in this segment is that these institutions have fast emerged as atavistic anomalies. At their formation more than five decades ago, world capital markets were skeletal, decentralised and incoherent. Now they are hyperactive, integrated and burgeoning.[1092] Where then lies the legal platform through which these entities may *directly* be subjected to human rights accountability?

This question has engaged many human rights scholars and it has engendered identical responses despite the diverse background experiences of concerned writers and institutions. The recurring decimal in all the theories and proposals put forward so far has been the placement of the human rights responsibilities of IFIs in the *interpretive context* of the various human rights treaties' provisions on 'international assistance and co-operation'.[1093] It is, however, perturbing to observe that, even though such theories resonate with diverse UN, regional and domestic concerns about the impact of IFIs on economic, social and cultural rights, all the many years of such efforts have not moved beyond the precincts of rhetoric. There is a need to address the problem from other perspectives.

While I do commend the efforts of human rights groups and scholars towards establishing a rights-based regime that would secure

1090 See World Bank *The World Bank Inspection Panel*, Resolution 93-10, 22 September 1993 http://www.worldbank.org/inspectionpanel (accessed 12 June 2009). For literature reviewing the World Bank Inspection Panel, see Skogly (n 1031 above) 235-241; Åkermark (n 90 above) 523-526; DL Clark *A citizen's guide to the World Bank inspection panel* (1999). For an uncritical narrative on the World Bank inspection panel, see LB de Chazournes 'Public participation in decision making: The World Bank inspection panel' in EB Weiss *et al* (eds) *The World Bank, international financial institutions, and the development of international law* (1999) 84-94.

1091 See Skogly (n 1031 above) 236-240.

1092 Lowenfeld (n 1038 above) 500-501.

1093 See eg Åkermark (n 90 above) 527; Jochnick (n 1008 above) 71; Skogly (n 1031 above) 245; Skogly (n 90 above) 758-762; Brodnig (n 1040 above) 5; Darrow (n 1022 above) 234-264; Bradlow (n 1035 above) 86-87. See also UN Commission on Human Rights 'Question of the realisation in all countries of the economic, social and cultural rights contained in the Universal Declaration of Human Rights and in the International Covenant on Economic, Social and Cultural Rights, and study of special problems which the developing countries face in their efforts to achieve these human rights: ways and means to carry out a political dialogue between creditor and debtor countries in the United Nations system, based on the principle of shared responsibility', report of the Secretary-General, UN Doc E/CN.4/1996/22 (1996) para 50, attributing the responsibilities of IFIs for human rights to arts 55 and 56 of the UN Charter and 'other international instruments.

binding obligations for IFIs, I am nonetheless of the opinion that it is to states that the human rights movement must look for answers as to why and how IFIs have become so insensate to economic, social and cultural rights and human development goals in Africa. My argument is informed by the reality of African governments' perennial desire to obtain 'quick fixes' for endemic socio-economic crises rather than seeking more credible and transparent structured approaches to sustainable solution.[1094] I contend that the acceptance by African states of the imposition of monotonous economic models by IFIs is a breach of the principles of self-determination and international co-operation enunciated by the International Bill of Rights. After all, the primary violation of those human rights norms in Africa occurs through the *acts or omissions of states*. It is therefore from within domestic and perhaps regional territories that the struggle to break the shackles of IFIs must begin. A rights-based approach to the adversities brought upon ordinary Africans through IFIs' conditionalities must be built on the ramparts of states' human rights responsibilities than on some controversial, if not imaginary, obligations for IFIs. Responsive human rights strategies should be directed at borrowing states and *all* those countries that are members of the IMF, the World Bank, and all state parties to ICESCR and the African Charter, as the case may be, simultaneously. While efforts towards the establishment of an obligatory human rights regime for IFIs should be sustained, the accountability and level of transparency of the borrowing African governments should form the core of immediate concern.

3.2 The World Trade Organisation

The activities of the World Trade Organisation (WTO) *vis-à-vis* the position of developing countries have not escaped the scrutiny of scholars and activists in the field of international trade and development economics and, lately, human rights.[1095] Since the emergence of the WTO in 1994 as successor to the General Agreement

1094 See generally F Cheru (n 1064 above) para 25; Skogly (n 90 above) 756. Compare E Davidson 'IMF and third world governments: A relationship of coercion or collusion?' 7 October 1999 http://www.globalsolidarity.org/articles/imf thirdworldgovhtml (accessed 22 November 2008).

1095 See eg Oloka-Onyango *et al* (n 1033 above) para 13. Some of the literature providing background information on the history, general outlook and policies of the WTO include JH Jackson *The world trading system: Law and policy of international economic relations* (1989); K Adamantopoulos *An anatomy of the World Trade Organisation* (1997); AM Babkina *World Trade Organisation: Issues and bibliography* (2000); P Gallagher *Guide to the WTO and developing countries* (2000); D Palmeter *The WTO as a legal system: Essays on international trade law and policy* (2003); G Orcalli 'A constitutional interpretation of the GATT/WTO' (2003) 14 *Constitutional Political Economy* 141-154. The International NGO Committee on Human Rights in Trade and Investment (INCHRITI) was one of the first networks to advocate for coherence between human rights obligations and trade policies. Its website, http://www.inchriti.org, provides a wealth of useful

on Tariffs and Trade (GATT),[1096] there has been active scholarly engagement in linking the activities and policies of the WTO to human rights concerns.[1097] Although the full import of the WTO regime is yet to be thoroughly explored within the African human rights discourse, some of the salient issues at stake portend direct implications for the rights-based approach conceptualised in my work. With the WTO proclaiming itself as 'the only global international organisation dealing with the rules of trade between nations ... [having at] its heart ... the WTO agreements, negotiated and signed by the bulk of the world's trading nations and ratified in their parliaments',[1098] and with the body controlling 'over 90% of the world's merchandise trade',[1099] consisting of 152 member states (including 41 African states),[1100] the organisation cannot but be an important actor in the protection and implementation of economic, social and cultural rights. In another significant way, the mandate of the WTO to 'co-operate fully, and on an equal footing, with the International Monetary Fund and the World Bank for the furtherance of economic *policymaking*'[1101] makes the body equally critical to any meaningful discourse on economic, social and cultural rights implementation in Africa.[1102]

While there is little debate about the WTO being a subject of international law,[1103] locating the basis of the human rights

references. Others are Global Exchange, http://www.globalexchange.org; Silicon Valley Toxic Coalition, http://www.svtc.org; Funders Network on Trade and Globalisation, http://www.fntg.org/index.php.

1096 See Agreement establishing the World Trade Organisation, opened for signature 15 April 1994 33 ILM 1144 (1994), entered into force 1 January 1995 (WTO Agreements). See Adamantopoulos (n 1095 above) 1-27.

1097 See generally M Mehra 'The intersection of trade and human rights' in D Barnhizer (ed) *Effective strategies for protecting human rights: prevention and intervention, trade and education* (2001) 75 80-81; M Møllmann 'Trade rights conditionalities and human rights' in Barnhizer (above) 113 118-119; Petersmann (n 323 above) 23-34; Chossudovsky (n 1035 above); GM Chunakara *Globalisation and its impact on human rights* (2000); A Brysk *Globalisation and human rights* (2002).

1098 WTO 'What is the WTO?' http://www.wto.org/english/thewto_e/whatis_e/whatis_e.htm (accessed 22 November 2008).

1099 Wilson (n 1095 above) 1. Compare L Sek 'The World Trade Organisation: Background and issues' in Babkina (n 1095 above) 7 8, ascribing '95% of world trade' to the WTO).

1100 As of 23 July 2008, there were 41 African member states in the WTO; seven (Algeria, Cape Verde, Equatorial Guinea, Ethiopia, São Tomé and Principe, Seychelles and Sudan) were observer states and four (Comoros, Eritrea, Liberia and Reunion) were neither involved as members nor as observers. See WTO 'Understanding the WTO: The organisation members and observers, 152 members on 23 July 2008' http://www.wto.org/english/thewto_e/whatis_e/tif_e/org6_e.htm (accessed 7 August 2008).

1101 Adamantopoulos (n 1095 above) 30 (my emphasis).

1102 See ESCR Committee, Statement of the United Nations Committee on Economic, Social and Cultural Rights to the Third Ministerial Conference of the World Trade Organisation (Seattle, 30 November to 3 December 1999) 47th mtg, 21st Sess, UN Doc E/C.12/1999/9 (26 November 1999) para 6 (my emphasis).

1103 See Martin (n 1034 above) 373-374.

responsibilities of the WTO remains problematic. This is because the WTO operates as a fluid system on multiple trade agreements and negotiations whose implications often manifest beyond the borders of the contracting states.[1104] Whereas the notion of state sovereignty is a core pillar of international law, the regime of international trade as portrayed through the WTO persistently seeks to eradicate states' sovereign control on the rules governing the movement of goods and services.[1105] While the constitutive instruments of the WTO as well as its agreements generally ignore human rights rhetoric, there have been remarkable efforts at establishing a theoretical linkage among WTO mandate, human rights, and social responsibility.[1106]

I contend that, whatever the pretensions of this dominant economic body might be towards human rights, since its member states are bound by the UN Charter and the mass of human rights instruments that I have considered in this work, it is unconscionable for the WTO to promote trade agreements that directly or indirectly violate the guarantees in those standards. I am therefore of the view that, while theoretical debates may continue on the responsibility of the WTO for economic, social and cultural rights, a practical analysis of the body's influence on Africa and Africans, particularly in the advent of globalisation, deepens the case for holding the body accountable.[1107]

During the Uruguay Round of Multilateral Trade Negotiations (Uruguay Round) that preceded the transition of GATT to WTO, some scholars had argued that 'Africa will be unable to take advantage of new market access opportunities from the Uruguay Round because of their lack of a manufacturing base'.[1108] That apprehension might have been well placed.

Since the primary aim of the WTO is to liberalise and secure the liberalisation of global trade through the elimination of a broad range of trade tariffs and other barriers, the consequent 'rat race' for competitiveness gives an undue advantage to industrialised

1104 See, eg, WTO trade topics, http://www.wto.org/english/tratop_e/tratop_e.htm (accessed 12 June 2009).

1105 See JT Gathii 'Re-characterising the social in the constitutionalisation of the WTO: A preliminary analysis' (2001) 7 *Widener Law Symposium Journal* 137.

1106 See eg JE Alvarez 'How not to link: Institutional conundrums of an expanded trade regime' (2001) 7 *Widener Law Symposium Journal* 1 14-15; M Cohn 'The World Trade Organisation: Elevating property interests above human rights' (2001) 29 *Georgia Journal of International and Comparative Law* 427 438-440. See also Global Exchange *World Trade Organisation* http://www.globalexchange.org/campaigns/wto/ (accessed 22 November 2008).

1107 For a critical analysis about the impact of trade liberalisation under the WTO regime on vulnerable groups in Africa, see Y Tandon 'The World Trade Organisation and Africa's marginalisation' (1999) 53 *Australian Journal of International Affairs* 83-94; Oloka-Onyango *et al* (n 1033 above) para 27.

1108 Gravelle *et al* (n 1036 above) 124.

nations.[1109] With lowered labour wages, and less scrutiny of goods from the industrialised states, the misery and poverty of Africans is aggravated.[1110] Indeed, despite the rhetoric of freer access to the global market under the WTO regime, African states have had to bear the larger brunt of the terms of the Uruguay Round relating to quota-hopping investment under the Multi-Fibre Agreement, textile imports, and barrier-related terms of trade.[1111]

One of the terms of the Uruguay Round is the reduction in the subsidies on food products in the industrialised states, particularly in Europe.[1112] The consequence of this has been a steady rise in the prices of food items, with significant implications for the implementation of the right to food in Africa. It is also noteworthy that in an updated study on the right to food, the UN Special Rapporteur on the Right to Food had warned about the potential for the intellectual property regime of the WTO to become a tool in the hands of powerful economic entities in controlling economically weak producers of food items and agricultural products, and thus impeding the circulation of food.[1113]

Perhaps the most controversial aspect of the Uruguay Round relates to health care and access to essential medicines – a strong concern for the right to the highest attainable standard of health in struggling states as those in Africa. Under the WTO's Trade-Related Aspects of Intellectual Property Rights (TRIPS) Agreement, its member states are obliged to provide patents 'for any inventions, whether products or processes, in all fields of technology, provided that they are new, involve an inventive step and are capable of industrial application'.[1114] The natural consequence of such a broad restrictive framework has been the increased consolidation of the

1109 See Leary (n 1041 above) 267. See also Hunt (n 612 above) 35.

1110 See generally OXFAM 'Eight broken promises: Why WTO isn't working for the world's poor' OXFAM International Briefing Paper No 9 October 2001 http://www.caa.org.au/ campaigns/trade/wto/index.html (accessed 12 June 2009); 'Africa: WTO at 50, Africa not celebrating' http://www.sunsonline.org/trade/process/followup/1998/05260198.htm (accessed 12 June 2009).

1111 See Gravelle *et al* (n 1036 above) 130-131. See also Esterhuysen (n 715 above) 49 54 57-58.

1112 See Agreement on Agriculture, Annex 1A, WTO Agreement (n 1096 above).

1113 Eide (n 80 above) para 120f.

1114 TRIPS Agreement, art 27(1). For a comprehensive assessment of the WTO's TRIPS Agreement and its multidimensional impacts, see S Walker, International Union of Conservation of Nature and Natural Resources (IUCN) 'The TRIPS Agreement, sustainable development and the public interest' discussion paper, 15-40 (IUCN, Cambridge, UK, IUCN Environmental Policy and Law Paper 41, 2001). Following unceasing criticisms from human rights NGOs and other civil society groups, the WTO recently took an impromptu decision relaxing the rule on TRIPS, which now allows developing countries that have no pharmaceutical manufacturing capacity to import cheap generic drugs. See WTO 'Decision of the WTO General Council of 30 August on the TRIPS Agreement and Public Health' WT/L/150, 1 September 2003 http://www.wto.org/english/tratop_e/trips_e/implem_para6_e.htm (accessed 28 June 2008). It is also pertinent to mention

control of the global market for essential medicines in the hands of pharmaceutical conglomerates that are now at liberty to fix the prices of such medicines (for example HIV/AIDS anti-retrovirals and other anti-protozoals) as they deem fit.[1115] With the costs of the required treatment for HIV patients running at 'hundreds of times average salary levels' in Africa,[1116] the unfortunate plight of the millions of Africa's HIV/AIDS victims is not difficult to conjecture.

Even though there is little or no basis for believing that African states will take any radical step that would constitute sufficient ground for radical review in the WTO system,[1117] activism towards a rights-based socially responsive agenda in the WTO remains nonetheless the viable option.[1118]

4 Development agencies and aid donors

It is safe to posit that an ample legal framework exists in international law for the obligation of states to render assistance to other states in the realisation of human rights generally, and economic, social and

that the worldwide clamour against the huge negative impact of WTO's TRIPS on public health compelled the WTO Ministerial Conference in November 2001 to adopt the Doha Declaration on the TRIPS Agreement and Public Health, which acknowledged the hardships caused by the agreements and the need that they be interpreted in such a manner as would protect public health and promote health for all. See WTO 'Doha Declaration on the TRIPS Agreement and Public Health' WT/MIN(01)/DEC/W/2 (14 November 2001) para 4. See also C Ochoa 'Advancing the language of human rights in a global economic order' (2003) 23 *Boston College Third World Law Journal* 57 94; CM Correa 'Implications of the Doha Declaration on the TRIPS Agreement and public health' Health Economics and Drugs, EDM Series 12, 19-35 (WHO, Geneva, June 2002).

1115 See generally US Food and Drug Administration 'Drugs used to treat complications of HIV/AIDS, http://www.fda.gov/oashi/aids/stat_app.html (accessed 12 June 2009), for the broad spectrum of drugs used in HIV/AIDS complications and their manufacturers. None of these is located in Africa. See also UNDP *Human development report 1999* (1999) 35, indicating that 'the TRIPS agreement ... provides an enabling environment for multinationals, tightening their dominant ownership of technology, impeding and increasing the cost of transfer to developing countries'. see also Walker (n 1114 above) 24-25.

1116 See Walker (n 1114 above) 24.

1117 See generally Lowenfeld (n 1038 above) 106-107.

1118 See generally Petersmann (n 323 above) 35; M Robinson 'Towards development: Human rights and the WTO agenda' Cancun, Mexico, 12 September 2003 http://www.eginitiative.org/documents/wtocancun.html (accessed 12 June 2009); Steiner *et al* (n 59 above) 941-942; 'South Africa says no to WTO' http://www.foodfirst.org/ progs/global/trade/wto2001/southafrica.html (accessed 28 June 2008); Chossudovsky (n 1035 above).

cultural rights in particular.[1119] The UN Charter charges all UN member-states to

> [t]ake joint and separate action in co-operation with the Organization for the achievement of ... (a) higher standards of living, full employment, and conditions of economic and social progress and development; (b) solutions of international economic, social, health and related problems; and international cultural and educational co-operation; and (c) universal respect for, and observance of, human rights and fundamental freedoms for all.[1120]

In its interpretation of the phrase 'to take steps, individually and *through international assistance and co-operation*, especially economic and technical' under article 2(1) of ICESCR, the ESCR Committee had emphasised that

> in accordance with articles 55 and 56 of the Charter of the United Nations, with well-established principles of international law, and with the provisions of the Covenant itself, *international co-operation for development ... for the realisation of economic, social and cultural rights is an obligation of all states.*[1121]

In the post-Cold War era, intergovernmental development agencies and bilateral aid donor states have gained renewed significance since the Vienna Conference in 1993, where the necessity for greater co-operation among states and specialised agencies towards the goal of rights-based development reverberated.[1122] I must remark that at the

1119 See G Alfredsson 'Technical co-operation in the field of economic, social and cultural rights' in Eide *et al* (n 29 above) 473. See also Dankwa *et al* 'Commentary by the Rapporteur on the nature of and scope of state parties' obligations' (1987) 9 *Human Rights Quarterly* 136 140. For a fuller discussion of the legal framework for the recognition of the obligation to co-operate in respect of economic, social and cultural rights within various national and multilateral jurisdictions, see C Jochnick 'The human rights challenge to global poverty' http://www.cesr.org/text%20files/actors.PDF (accessed 12 June 2009).

1120 UN Charter, arts 55 & 56 paraphrased. See also art 22 Universal Declaration, recognising the right of every human being 'to realisation, through national effort and *international co-operation* and in accordance with the organisation and resources of each state, of the economic, social and cultural rights indispensable for his dignity and the free development of his personality'; and art 3(2) UN Declaration on the right to development (n 186 above), providing that '[t]he realisation of the right to development requires full respect for the principles of international law concerning friendly relations and co-operation among states in accordance with the Charter of the United Nations.' See generally M Bedjaoui 'The right to development' in M Bedjaoui (ed) *International law: Achievements and prospects* (1991) 1177.

1121 General Comment No 3 (n 91 above) para 14 (my emphasis).

1122 Vienna Declaration (n 38 above), Preamble para 4, and paras 1, 11 & 72. It will be apt, eg, to recall that in his recommendations following his extensive study of the impact of SAPs on economic, social and cultural rights, Fantu Cheru had unequivocally canvassed the idea that '[t]he World Bank and IMF should not be given the exclusive role as overseers of poverty reduction programmemes in poor countries. Other United Nations agencies, such as UNDP, UNICEF, UNCTAD and ILO should be brought into the process ...' See F Cheru (n 1064 above) para 47(b).

levels of the UN system, various intergovernmental and international institutions, and regional arrangements, efforts based on co-operation and assistance towards development in Third World states have been on the increase. The irony of this trend, however, is the emergence of new problems that often result in ambivalent, counter-productive and negative outcomes, holding enormous implications for economic, social and cultural rights and, invariably, for human development.[1123]

Despite the manifest tendency among African human rights scholars to ignore the impact of development agencies and aid donors on economic, social and cultural rights protection and implementation, there is a need for broadened consciousness in responding to the probable hindrances in the work of these species of powerful actors to the effective implementation of economic, social and cultural rights, not the least in Africa. I attempt to highlight the role of some development agencies in economic, social and cultural rights implementation as well as some of the salient problematic concerns.

4.1 International development agencies and aid donors

Previously, I had mentioned the significance of the work of many specialised agencies of the UN in conceptualising a rights-based approach to development in Africa.[1124] In this regard, the role of the UNDP has been outstanding. Even though the UNDP was not originally committed to human rights,[1125] it has increasingly become a potential role actor in the implementation of human rights generally, and economic, social and cultural rights in particular.[1126] Its direct

[1123] See generally General Comment No 2 (n 641 above) para 7. See also MS Diokno 'Challenges and opportunities: A response' in Human Rights Council of Australia, 'Symposium papers – A human rights approach to development' http://www.hrca.org.au/symposium.htm#The%20Rights%20Framework%20and%20Development%20Assistance (accessed 12 June 2009); CJ Dias 'The rights way to development: Challenges and opportunities' in Symposium papers (n 1123 above).

[1124] See ch II above.

[1125] See generally P Alston 'The rights framework and development assistance' in 'Symposium papers – A human rights approach' (n 1123 above), noting that '[t]he [UNDP] was not prepared to have anything to do with human rights prior to 1990. This is illustrated by the fact that you will almost certainly not find human rights mentioned in any UNDP statement prior to 1990.' See also Gallagher (n 182 above) 156-157, noting that it was not until the 1990s that the UNDP experienced a paradigm shift 'from economic development to *sustainable human development* ... [which] aims at expanding people's choices and improving their quality of life' (emphasis in the original).

[1126] See generally HJ Steiner 'Social rights and economic development: Converging discourses?' (1998) 4 *Buffalo Human Rights Law Review* 25 36-37.

involvement through a wide range of country-based operations is of strategic importance.[1127] The effort of the UNDP, particularly since the inception of its annual Human Development Reports in 1990, is also becoming increasingly significant in the evolution of a rights-based approach to human development. Through its statistical data-based methodologies for measuring the 'essential components of human well-being',[1128] the indices emanating from its annual reports have become veritable information resources for calibrating real-life application of economic, social and cultural rights values across states and regions of the world, including Africa.[1129]

In yet another remarkable way, the UNDP has been actively involved in Africa's struggle to accomplish its Millennium Development Goals.[1130] Regrettably, however, even though the UNDP's commitment to Africa is commendable, its ambivalent attitude towards employing the language of human rights, and particularly economic, social and cultural rights, has not been encouraging.[1131] While the UNDP emphasises the creation of 'an enabling environment in which all human beings lead secure and creative lives' as its 'central purpose',[1132] the body itself acknowledges that there is yet 'a need ... to systematically address and focus the [UNDP's] human rights content and dimensions ... [and to] develop a human rights-based framework in its antipoverty, prosustainable human development work'.[1133]

In any event, despite the general tendency to accuse UN specialised agencies of ambivalence in the pursuit of an inclusive

1127 Ranging from participating in electoral processes to judicial reforms, and to gender empowerment activities, the UNDP has acquired tremendous relevance as a resource base for development-oriented projects at national levels. See generally UNDP 'Linking human rights and development' http://www.undp.org/rbap/rights/enghr.pdf (accessed 22 November 2008), detailing a long list of individual programmemes carried on in diverse countries by UNDP.

1128 UNDP *Human development report 1996* (1996) 54.

1129 There is ample literature where the indices in the UNDP reports have been applied as background information for measuring the level of human growth, human capabilities, and the material well-being of human beings, in different national, regional and global contexts. Such references include AE Yarmin 'Reflections on defining, understanding and measuring poverty in terms of violations of economic and social rights under international law' (1997) 4 *Georgetown Journal on Fighting Poverty* 273; A Sen 'Development thinking at the beginning of the XXIst century' in L Emmerij (ed) *Economic and social development into the XXIst century* (1997) 531 540-542; M Nussbaum 'Capabilities and human rights' (1997) 66 *Fordham Law review* 273.

1130 See UNDP 'Helping the people of sub-Saharan Africa build a better life' http://www.undp.org/rba/ (accessed 12 June 2009). See also UNDP Press Release, 'UNDP bolsters NEPAD with nearly $2 million financial contribution' 13 February 2003 http://www.undp.org/dpa/pressrelease/releases/2003/february/13feb03.html (accessed 12 June 2009).

1131 See generally Steiner (n 1126 above) 38.

1132 UNDP 'Integrating human rights with sustainable human development: A UNDP policy document' January 1998 3.

1133 n 1132 above, 10.

agenda for human rights in their work, there is every indication that most UN specialised agencies are beginning to adopt a rights-based approach to the goals of development.[1134]

However, if human rights scholars consider the ambivalence of UN specialised agencies towards human rights to be problematic, the activities of development assistance and aid donor agencies constitute a more challenging issue in the implementation of economic, social and cultural rights.[1135]

Although a subject of reticent inquiry, a causal link is gradually being drawn by some scholars and activists between development assistance and human rights.[1136] Since African states are arguably the most notorious for donors' development assistance,[1137] the subject becomes one of primary concern in a discourse of this nature.

1134 See generally Gallagher (n 182 above) 165-166. See also I Houghton 'Promoting, respecting and fulfilling human rights: The challenge before intergovernmental agencies' Report of the Workshop on Human Rights and the Intergovernmental Agencies, 24 September 2002, Washington, DC, USA, 8.

1135 Outside the UN system, the critical national and intergovernmental aid donor agencies include the Australian International Development Assistance Bureau (AIDAB), the Canadian International Development Agency (CIDA), the Danish International Development Agency (DANIDA), the Finnish International Development Agency (FINNIDA), the Japan International Co-operation Agency (JICA), the Norwegian Development Agency (NORAD), the Organisation for Economic Co-operation and Development (OECD), the Swedish International Development Agency (SIDA), the United States Agency for International Development (USAID), and such others. For general background reading on international development agencies and the general outlook of their role in the implementation of economic, social and cultural rights, see Rehof *et al* (n 184 above); JCN Paul 'International development agencies, human rights and humane development projects' (1988) 17 *Denver International Law and Policy* 67.

1136 Of particular importance here have been the rigorous efforts by the Human Rights Council of Australia in establishing development aid and donor assistance as critical human rights issues since 1995 when it published a study titled *The rights way to development: A human rights approach to development assistance* (1995). See'Activities of the HRCA: Human rights and development: rights way to development', http://www.hrca.org.au/activities.htm# Development (accessed 12 June 2009).

1137 See generally Esterhuysen (n 715 above) 58-59, analysing the historical attachment of African States to Cold War support-inducing 'development aid', and its tragic decline after the Cold War. See also P Esterhuysen *Africa at a glance* (1997-1998) 54-55, providing a graphic description of the amounts of aid received by African states and noting that, despite a decline in the sums, many 'sub-Saharan countries [still] rely heavily on foreign aid'.

Plausible as the justification for development assistance and donors' aid for developing states might appear,[1138] it masks other perturbing concerns underlying the entire concept. Studies have shown that, while the home governments of many development agencies and donor states proclaim commitment to human rights obligations, they often shirk or repress human rights considerations in aid or development negotiations.[1139] More than that, there is a robust perception that most donor governments 'view development assistance essentially as a vehicle for perpetuating their geopolitical sphere of influence or for maintaining and strengthening their international comparative advantage and international competitive edge in respect of trade and investment'.[1140]

What thus emerges from the foregoing assessment is a bird's eye view of the manifest disconnection between the goal of economic growth and development, which donor countries and agencies often present as motivation for their involvement in developing states, on the one hand, and the consequences of such purported development projects for human rights protection, on the other.[1141] This could not but have been the consequence of a warped approach to development.[1142]

The current beggar-thy-neighbour system of development assistance to African states models a top-down prescriptive approach to development. It does not recognise that genuine development must

1138 In his succinct description of the rationale for development co-operation and aid assistance, FINNIDA chief, Kourula, had stated that '[d]evelopment co-operation activities were born out of the lessons learned from history. The turmoils [*sic*] brought about by the social and economic injustices suffered by the former colonies and the threats posed thereby to world peace led international action to advance the economic and social progress in the world at large. Development co-operation should thus also be seen as a means to minimise the sources of conflict and confrontation and to alleviate the suffering of individuals in cases where aggressive actions have been resorted to. Development co-operation can thus have both a preventive and a curative meaning and effect.' See P Kourula 'Finnida's view on the relationship between development and human rights' in Rehof *et al* (n 184 above) 35 37.

1139 See generally Diokno (n 1123 above). See also Rehof (n 184 above) 8.

1140 Dias (n 1123 above). See also P Baehr 'Dutch human rights policy' in Rehof *et al* (n 184 above) 41. Compare K Arts *Integrating human rights into development co-operation: The case of the Lomé Convention* (2000) 134; Alston (n 1125 above); Paul (n 1135 above) 81; JCN Paul 'Incorporating human rights into mainstream "human" development strategies: Why? And how?' in *Human rights and human development: Report on the Oslo symposium* (n 25 above) Annex 1.

1141 See generally Oxfam Community Aid Abroad (n 1067 above).

1142 See Esterhuysen (n 715 above) 41 45; C Santiso 'Good governance and aid effectiveness: The World Bank and conditionality' (2001) 7 *Georgetown Public Policy Review* 1; VP Nanda 'International processes: The "good governance" concept revisited' (2006) 603 *Annals* 269.

reflect only what its ultimate beneficiaries consider as development.[1143] How can any critical observer of prevalent levels of human misery in Africa justify the construction of a multimillion dollar incinerator as true development in a locality where farmlands will have to be destroyed for the purpose of that construction?[1144] Or what correlation exists between the addition of soon-to-be-abandoned megabuck national stadia and millions of hungry and HIV-ridden Africans?

Furthermore, despite the intractable rhetoric of development by UN specialised agencies (notably the FAO's World Food Programme and the ILO's World Employment Programme) and other development agencies and donor countries since after World War II, a coherent human rights response to rural development has remained elusive, meaning that the rural component of development has suffered total neglect.[1145] This will always remain a critical issue for meaningful development in Africa.

I contend that the guiding principle in assessing the value of development assistance projects should be its overall direct impact on the quality of human life.

4.2 African regional development agencies

Without doubt, the African Development Bank (ADB) is the most visible development agency that has a continent-wide mandate in the African region.[1146] Created in 1964 by the defunct OAU, the ADB has

1143 See JS Wilson 'Why foreign aid fails: Lessons from Indonesia's economic collapse' (2001) 33 *Law and Policy in International Business* 145 169 (my emphasis). See also Kourula (n 1138 above) 35 37. Compare I Axell 'SIDA's view on the relationship between development assistance and human rights' in Rehof *et al* (n 184 above) 31 37, affirming that 'Sweden rejects the thought of using democracy and human rights as some sort of grading instrument for [considering] poor countries' for development assistance eligibility. The US agreed with the government of Zambia to 'forgive' its $500 million debt under the HIPC Initiative provided that Zambia reduces its expenditure on social services and privatise public services. See 'US offers conditional $500m debt write-off' *The Times of Zambia* 17 February 2004.

1144 The case of one of the palaces built by the inglorious Life President of Malawi, Hastings Kamuzu Banda, at the cost of '195 million American dollars ... skimmed from aid money' comes to mind. See S Loosley 'Human rights and aid: An Australian parliamentary perspective' in 'Symposium papers - A human rights approach' (n 1123 above).

1145 For a general theoretical view on the need for development to relate to rural communities in the developing world, see R Plant 'Human rights and rural development: Problems and policy issues' in Rehof *et al* (n 184 above) 97-108.

1146 See D Bradlow 'Should the international financial institutions play a role in the implementation and enforcement of international humanitarian law?' (2002) 50 *Kansas Law Review* 695 702. While there is an East African Development Bank, its operations and mandate are strictly limited to the three sponsoring states of Kenya, Uganda and Tanzania. The Bank was established in 1967, by art 21 of the Treaty for East African Co-operation, adopted 6 June 1967, reprinted in 6 ILM 932.

steadily emerged as the leading African development finance institution to foster economic expansion and social development in Africa.[1147] Curiously, however, the work of the ADB has only attracted the attention of economists and development experts. But like any other development agency, and more so because of its very close affinity to the World Bank,[1148] the ADB deserves scrutiny under human rights spotlight. The Bank's practices and policies are exclusively economic and none of its policy statements or projects has ever been defined in rights-based terms. Indeed, the current ADB's Strategic Plan for 2003-2007 makes no reference to such words as 'human rights', 'vulnerable/marginalised groups', 'rural', 'children' or 'women'. Ostensibly drawn by development economists, the Strategic Plan leaves no one in doubt about the ADB's commitment to a singular goal: market access. In the Bank's own words:

> In order to better achieve ... converging and mutually reinforcing objectives, the Plan embodies the following guiding principles that will govern the Bank's activities over the period 2003-2007 and beyond ... to bring the benefits of globalisation to [regional member countries] in terms of both market access and economic diversification as well as ... medium and long-term debt sustainability.[1149]

It is also somewhat unsettling that the ADB's approach to poverty reduction is patterned so closely after the World Bank and IMF model of borrow-more-to-offset-your-debt:[1150] The adverse consequences will manifest just along familiar experiences. It is equally disquieting that the ADB appears to be quite as distant from African grassroots realities just as the identified IFIs have been, if not more.

For an analysis of the Bank's role within the East African 'development goals', see S Fitzke 'Note: The Treaty for East African Co-operation: Can East Africa successfully revive one of Africa's most infamous economic groupings?' (1999) 8 *Minnesota Journal of Global Trade* 127 135. There is also a fledgling sub-regional bank, the Ecobank Transnational Incorporated, established in 1985 as 'a private sector regional banking institution' by the Economic Community of West African Countries (ECOWAS). See ECOBANK http://www.ecobank.com/English/About_En_fr.htm (accessed 12 June 2009).

1147 For background information on the ADB's history, organisational structures and mandate, see 'The African Development Bank [ADB]' http://www.afdb.org/knowledge/about/ about_adbgroup_ADB.htm (accessed 12 June 2009).

1148 The ADB has collaborated with the World Bank on a series of 'development' programmemes. The ADB even co-hosted the Second Roundtable on Managing for Results at Marrakech, Morocco, in February 2004. The interaction between these two financial bodies remains strong from all indications. See Statement by Omar Kabbaj, President of the African Development Bank Group, at the Opening Session of the Second Roundtable on Managing for Results, 5 February 2004, Marrakech, Morocco 2 4. See also Bradlow (n 1146 above) 703, observing that the ADB is 'engaged in the same four types of activities as the [World] Bank'.

1149 ADB 'ADB strategic plan 2003-2007' in *Brief*, June 2003 15-16 para 3.4.

1150 See generally ADB, Press Release 'International development organisations endorse results plan' 6 February 2004.

As an organisation to which all the state parties to the African Charter are affiliated, the tenor of the African Charter as regards people-centred development should be resonant in its policies and activities.[1151] While the 'development' projects being sponsored and executed by the ADB might be well meant, the Bank will do well when it redefines its focus to directly engage African peoples. For now, the ADB represents a statist approach to development that totally excludes and marginalises ordinary Africans. The ADB should design modalities for ascertaining the relevance and short- and long-term benefits of its financial and development projects to the vast majority of Africans.

While it may sound far-fetched, the ADB should retain the services of in-house human rights experts to give the Bank's development agenda a human face. African human rights scholars and activists will also have to direct their attention to the propensity of the ADB to be a potential actor in enhancing economic, social and cultural rights and a rights-based approach to development in Africa.

Undeniably, I concede that development can be 'a vehicle for ... correcting historically-skewed patterns of distribution of resources, wealth and power'.[1152] But then, in making development serve the ends of social justice, development agencies, aid donors and recipient states alike will have to realise that when they practically inject human rights into development, that merger will result in a self-enhancing whole. Initiatives for development and economic growth will be sustainable and meaningful only when due regard is paid to the basic rights of the human inhabitants of affected the territories – to livelihood, fulfilment and happiness.

Although the much-vaunted justification for development assistance is that it is useful for the promotion of commerce and investment in recipient countries, Africa's experience does not reflect that generalised expectation, and may not radiate such fantasies under current global trading regimes.[1153]

While there may continue to be moral justifications for developed states to render development assistance to developing states, focus

1151 Art 22 of the African Charter guarantees: '(1) All peoples shall have the right to their economic, social and cultural development with due regard to their freedom and identity and in the equal enjoyment of the common heritage of mankind. (2) States shall have the duty, individually or collectively, to ensure the exercise of the right to development.'

1152 Dias (n 1045 above) 53.

1153 See generally K Ewert 'Review: Perpetuating poverty: The World Bank, the IMF and the developing world' http://www.u-turn.net/3-3/poverty.html (accessed 22 November 2008). See also F Foroutan *et al* 'Intra-sub-Saharan African trade: Is it too little?' (1993) 2 *Journal of African Economics* 74-105; Udombana (n 1048 above) 322 340-343.

must not be lost on the non-negotiable necessity for developing states as those in Africa to publicly account for how such assistance aids are disbursed. Development assistance should not become a subsidy for shoddy economic policies in Africa. At the levels of donor agencies, governments and recipient states, a positive human rights ethos must resonate in the contemplation of development assistance projects.

On another plane, an important principle that is yet to be fully integrated into development co-operation programmes with African states is that the *primary responsibility* for development in any country rests with the country itself. While other states and development agencies might possess an ethical responsibility to help struggling African states, aid-recipient states must not become exclusively dependent on such handout arrangements, particularly when conditionalities attached to assistance and aid negatively affect the implementation of economic, social and cultural rights.

5 Economic, social and cultural rights in the private sphere

Apart from the marked progress witnessed in the normative and conceptual development of human rights in the 1990s, that period was also remarkable for the simultaneous extension of the global human rights discourse to the private sphere. Contrary to the conservative perceptions and notions of earlier days that human rights belonged strictly in the realm of public law,[1154] private enterprise and activities are increasingly becoming the subjects of human rights concerns.[1155] In his extensive inquiry into the operation of human rights in the private sphere, Clapham demonstrated that 'it is no longer viable to cling to [that] traditional view that [human rights law] only covers ... violations by states'.[1156] Basing his arguments on dual approaches, Clapham concluded that first, under international law, there is a recognition that individuals or private bodies can commit human rights violations and, second, that practice has shown

1154 See eg L Henkin *The rights of man today* (1979) 2, asserting that human rights are 'rights against society as represented by government and its officials'; J Donnelly *The concept of human rights* (1985) 6, contending that 'human rights are held or at least exercised, primarily in relation to the state'; R Higgins *International law and how we use it* (1996) 39-46, discussing the principle of state responsibility as the guiding rule of human rights protection in the formative stages of international law.

1155 See generally Leckie (n 657 above) 75-76, observing that 'human rights law has irretrievably entered the private domain'.

1156 A Clapham *Human rights in the private sphere* (1993) 93. See also A Clapham *Human rights obligations of non-state actors* (2006).

that distinctions between the private and public sphere would 'leave a *lacuna* in the protection of human rights'.[1157]

I must also point out that the rapid growth in the interference by individuals as well as many other powerful private actors in the human rights sphere has rendered unhelpful any distinction between human rights in the private sphere and human rights in the public domain.[1158]

In this prevailing age of globalisation in which we are witnessing a series of privatisation programmes, free trade regionalism, with tremendous impetus from the volatile growth of TNCs and MNEs, the capacity of states to fully guarantee every aspect of human rights has greatly dwindled, albeit at the behest of states themselves.[1159] In view of the above, I examine the implications of TNCs and MNEs for economic, social and cultural rights and human development in Africa and the efficacy of the concerted efforts aimed at making these colossal economic entities accountable for human rights obligations.

5.1 Transnational corporations and multinational enterprises

If arguments that the increased significance and influence of IFIs, the WTO and other institutions of global governance has either been the product of globalisation or has been aided by the process of globalisation are justifiable,[1160] then it will be appropriate to posit

1157 Clapham (n 1156 above) 93-94. Even though Clapham's analysis relates specifically to the European Convention context, and particularly to civil and political rights, it is nonetheless useful for theoretical purposes of my work. See also JJ Paust 'The other side of right: Private duties under human rights law' (1992) 5 *Harvard Human Rights Journal* 51.

1158 The Commission on Global Governance explained the inexorably blurred and blunted distinction as follows: 'When the United Nations system was created, nation-states, some of them imperial powers, were dominant ... The world economy was not as closely integrated as it is today. The vast array of global firms and corporate alliances that has emerged was just beginning to develop. The huge global capital market, which today dwarfs even the largest national capital markets, was not foreseen. *The enormous growth in people's concern for human rights, equity, democracy, meeting basic material needs, environmental protection, and demilitarisation has today produced a multitude of new actors who can contribute to governance.*' Commission on Global Governance *Our global neighbourhood: The report of the Commission on Global Governance* 3 (1995) (mt emphasis).

1159 See generally Türk (n 1046 above) para 185.

1160 See eg R Honey 'An introduction to the symposium: Interrogating the globalisation project' (2002) 12 *Transnational Law and Contemporary Problems* 1 9; O Aginam 'Global village, divided world: South-north gap and global health challenges at century's dawn' (2000) 7 *Indiana Journal of Global Legal Studies* 603; Oloka-Onyango (n 707 above) 885. See also T Dunne 'Symposium on globalisation at the margins: Perspectives on globalisation from developing states: The spectre of globalisation' (1999) 7 *Indiana Journal of Global Legal Studies* 17 20-22.

that the increasing incursion of TNCs and MNEs[1161] into diverse social, economic and cultural spheres in the twilight of the twentieth century and at the dawn of the twenty-first century continues that trend of economic globalisation. That TNCs and MNEs are the driving force behind the wheels of globalisation in this century can hardly be disputed. But despite the giant strides of 'progress' recorded so far in the fields of commerce, technology and communication through new age globalisation, human rights scholars and even institutions have not failed to identify these entities as potential players in the realisation of human rights generally, and economic, social and cultural rights in particular.[1162] With empirical statistics revealing that some TNCs and MNEs are even more powerful than the governments of most countries in which they operate,[1163] scholars and activists readily infer that these entities have acquired enormous and even 'inordinate influence over local laws and policies [and their] impact on human rights ranges from a direct role in violations, such as abuses of employees or the environment, to indirect support of governments guilty of widespread repression'.[1164] From the perspective of activists in the global south, the crux of the agitation against the rapid growth of TNCs and MNEs is the failure of states to curb the excesses of these bodies and, sometimes, the collusion of other global institutions with TNCs and MNEs in sustaining the

1161 In the assemblage of literature on the influence of TNCs and MNEs on human rights, particularly economic, social and cultural rights and labour issues, the two nomenclatures have been used interchangeably. See generally *Norms on the Responsibilities of Transnational Corporations and Other Business Enterprises with Regard to Human Rights* (*UN Norms*) UN Doc E/CN.4/Sub.2/2003/12/Rev2 (26 August 2003) (UN Norms on the Responsibilities of TNCs and Others); ILO Tripartite Declaration of Principles Concerning Multinational Enterprises and Social Policy, adopted by the Governing Body of the International Labour Office, 204th sess, November 1977 para 6, reprinted in R Blanpain (ed) *Multinational enterprises and the social challenges of the XXIst century* (2000) 305 306; 'The OECD Guidelines for Multinational Enterprises (Annexed To The Declaration of 21st June 1976 by Governments of OECD Member Countries On International Investment and Multinational Enterprises As Amended in 1979, 1984 and 1991)' reprinted in Blanpain (above) 317 318; UNCTAD 'Multinational Corporations (MNCs) in least developed countries (LDCs)' http://www.globalpolicy.org/reform/2002/ modelun.pdf (accessed 12 June 2009).

1162 See eg Trubek (n 76 above) 225; G Roebeling 'Economic globalisation, civil society and rights' in Carbonari (n 40 above) 211; Steiner *et al* (n 59 above) 1349; D Barnhizer 'Trade, environment and human rights: The paradigm case of industrial aquaculture and the exploitation of traditional communities' in Barnhizer (n 1097 above) 137-154; Aginam (n 1160 above) 612-620; Honey (n 1160 above) 5-7; Russell (n 625 above) 2; ILO Tripartite Declaration (n 1161 above) para 1.

1163 See generally S Anderson *et al The top 200: The rise of global corporate power* (1996) 5, observing that among all the 100 largest economies in the world as at 1996, the topmost 51 were TNCs and MNEs; WH Meyer 'Human rights and MNCs: Theory and quantitative analysis' (1996) 18 *Human Rights Quarterly* 368 370; H Schrama en K Vos 'Globalisation, human rights and the government' in W van Genuten *et al* (eds) *Division of roles in the international economic and legal order* (2000) 81 87; Symonides (n 90 above) 151; Leckie (n 657 above) 79.

1164 Jochnick (n 1119 above). See also Oloka-Onyango (n 707 above) 897; UNDP *Human development report 1999* (n 1115 above) 81.

dominance of these entities in the areas of food security, pharmaceutical industry and world markets that have resulted in adverse consequences for ordinary people in the Third World.[1165]

Virtually every civil war and insurgency recorded in Africa since 1990 has had a linkage to the question of *who* controls natural resources.[1166] In almost every such instance, credible pieces of evidence exist to show the involvement of some TNCs and MNEs.[1167] In the Nigerian military years, for example, oil companies were regularly implicated in the armed suppression of protesting local communities.[1168] Even in the current civilian dispensation, such conduct is still rife.[1169]

1165 See UN Commission on Human Rights 'Economic, social and cultural rights, written statement submitted by North South XXI, a non-governmental organisation in special consultative status 22 December 2000', UN Doc E/CN.4/ 2001/NGO/15 (16 January 2001) para 7. See also Symonides (n 90 above) 154; C Whitenton 'Trans-national corporations and the violation of human rights' http:// humanrights.gatech.edu/ TNCHR1.htmlUNCTAD (accessed 12 June 2009).

1166 See generally I Gary Catholic Relief Services *et al Bottom of the barrel*: Africa's *oil boom and the poor* (2003) 24.

1167 See generally C Forcese 'Human rights mean business: Broadening Canadian approach to business and human rights' in Merali & Oosterveld (n 37 above) 71 78 90-91. See also Human Rights Watch 'The International Monetary Fund's staff monitoring programmeme for Angola: The human rights implications' http://www.hrw.org/press/2000/06/ango-0623-back.htm (accessed 12 June 2009); J Lobe 'Global businesses profit from Congo war, groups charge' *Oneworld* US, 28 October 2003http://us.oneworld.net/article/ view/71424 (accessed 12 June 2009); 'Sierra Leone: Another African diamond war' http:// www.markswatson.com/Website/diamondsFrame2Source1.htm (accessed 12 June 2009); V Hawkins 'Stealth conflicts: Africa's World War in the DRC and international consciousness' (2004) *The Journal of Humanitarian Assistance* 5 http://www/ jha.ac/articles/a126.htm (accessed 12 June 2009). It is an open secret that some TNCs and MNEs have been involved in the unseemly activity of sponsoring, or enhancing the capacity of repressive regimes in Africa, in their efforts to protect their economic interests at all cost. See generally A Olukoshi 'Guilty through and through: Shell and the plight of the Ogoni people' (1996) 23 *Review of African Political Economics* 471-472; Okonta *et al* (n 716 above) 79-82.

1168 See generally Human Rights Watch *World report 1997* (1997) 360, observing that the 'Royal Dutch/Shell provided both increased financial investment and a diplomatic public relations shield for the Nigerian government'.

1169 Recently, there was a major oil spillage near Effurum in the Delta State of Nigeria caused by a rupture in Shell Oil Company's pipelines conveying crude oil gas from Forcados to Warri Refinery. In response to the peaceful protest and demand for compensation by the people of Maroko Community, who suffered severe damage to sea resources that constituted their source of livelihood, Shell claimed the entire community land belonged to it and went ahead to mobilise soldiers to forcefully evict the entire community. Over 2 000 families were rendered homeless in that barbarous act, and without remedy to this day. For a brief insight into details of this incident, see Environmental Rights Action 'Shell evicts Maroko residents with soldiers: Renders over 2 000 people homeless' 15 February 2003 http://www.covalence.ch/docs/10514c.htm (accessed 12 June 2009).

However, it is not only in the sphere of conflicts that TNCs and MNEs affect Africa. In the fields of environmental rights, labour rights, housing and health, the immense influence of these entities is felt day by day, and with impunity.[1170] The enormous oil spillages, arbitrary evictions of vast populations from traditional homelands, the destruction of ocean life and farmlands, and other human rights consequences resulting from the heavy oil exploration activities of TNCs, particularly the Shell Petroleum Development Corporation in Nigeria (a division of Shell International, the Anglo-Dutch petrochemical conglomerate), have received such extensive attention that I do not need to revisit them.[1171] What makes the situation grave is that there does not appear to be any coherent rights-based reprieve in sight. Is this merely an untoward expression of pessimism? Not likely. Even though the petition before the African Commission in *Ogoni* expressly cited the Shell Petroleum Development Corporation as a co-violator along with the Nigerian government of the African Charter's provisions,[1172] the African Commission deftly avoided any mention of the company in its decision and recommendations.

Furthermore, in the face of grave economic difficulties compounded by weak legal frameworks for consumer protection, most Africans have had to contend with contaminated or substandard goods flowing from MNEs and TNCs with reckless abandon – endangering human health, safety, and diminishing the capacities of

1170 See generally Udombana (n 1048 above) 318, noting that TNCs and MNEs 'continue to enjoy *de facto* impunity and immunity from their criminal negligence and are able to lower intra- and international standards, due to their financial strengths'.

1171 Virtually all existing literature in the post-Ken Saro Wiwa execution saga of November 1995 on human rights and TNCs would cite the Shell Oil Company. The atrocities are well documented. But for purposes of linkage with background information, the following works are informative: Human Rights Watch 'The price of oil: Corporate responsibility and human rights violations in Nigeria's oil producing communities' (1999); JM Russell 'The ambivalence about the globalisation of telecommunications: The story of Amnesty International, Shell Oil Company and Nigeria' (2002) 1 *Journal of Human Rights* 405-416; A Ganesan 'Human rights, the energy industry and the relationship with home governments' in A Eide *et al Human rights and the oil industry* (2000) 47 54-60; B Wright 'Non-governmental organisations and indifference as a human rights issue: The case of the Nigerian oil embargo' (2002) 1 *Journal of Human Rights* 231. For an image-laundering version of Shell Petroleum Development Company's response to mounting criticisms, see The Shell Petroleum Development Company of Nigeria Ltd *People and the environment annual report 1999* (1999). For other national perspectives on TNCs in the oil industry, see M Kaldor *et al* 'Oil and human rights in Azerbaijan' in A Eide *et al Human rights and the oil industry* (2000) 91-113; P le Billon 'The oil industry and the state of war in Angola' in A Eide *et al Human rights and the oil industry* (2000) 115-138.

1172 The Summary of Facts had stated that 'the military government of Nigeria has been directly involved in oil production through the state oil company, the Nigerian National Petroleum Company (NNPC), the majority shareholder in a consortium with Shell Petroleum Development Corporation (SPDC), and that these operations have caused environmental degradation and health problems resulting from the contamination of the environment among the Ogoni People'. See *Ogoni* (n 143 above) para 1.

local producers.[1173] A related but largely neglected area of impact is the menace of toxic waste dumping.[1174] Despite the commendable efforts of the UN Special Rapporteur on the Adverse Effects of the Illicit Movement and Dumping of Toxic and Dangerous Products and Wastes on economic, social and cultural rights to expose the culpable MNEs and TNCs,[1175] these entities have largely frustrated her attempts at holding them accountable, sometimes, under protection by their home governments or in collusion with some African governments.[1176]

Another recondite aspect is that, despite global efforts aimed at curbing or eradicating child labour, evidence abound on how MNEs have promoted the use of children on cocoa farms, coffee plantations, mining quarries, and other areas of extractive activities

1173 The tragic Pfizer drug test incident in Nigeria of 1996 is illustrative here. At the outbreak of a meningitis epidemic in Kano, Nigeria, Pfizer, one of the largest pharmaceutical companies in the world, sent in a team of doctors to administer its new drug, *Trovan*, containing *cephtiaxone*, on some 200 children. Massive casualties ensued as a result of the medical experiment, and yet the Nigerian government failed to bring Pfizer to account. High-level diplomatic undercurrents aborted the efforts of the relations of the deceased children. See generally *Report of the Secretary-General on the relationship between the enjoyment of human rights, in particular, international labour and trade union rights, and the working methods and activities of transnational corporations* UN Doc E/CN.4/Sub.2/1995/11; UN Commission on Human Rights *Report Submitted by the Special Rapporteur on toxic waste, Mrs Fatma-Zohra Ouhachi-Vesely* UN Doc E/CN.4/2001/55 (19 January 2001), para 48, observing that '[p]oorer, heavily indebted countries are particularly vulnerable to external pressures [from TNCs and MNEs], which can take the forms of promises of easily acquired foreign exchange in hard currency, employment creation, installation of enterprises for waste recycling'. For a discussion on the impact of milk products from such giant MNEs like Nestlé, particularly in the third world, see J Richter *UNICEF holding corporations accountable: Corporate conduct, international codes, and citizen action* (2001) 44-59.

1174 See generally C Hitz *et al* 'Transboundary movement of hazardous wastes: A comparative analysis of policy options to control the international waste trade' (1991) 3 *Environmental Affairs* 29, observing that, whereas the capacity of MNEs and TNCs in the European Union to eliminate wastes is limited to 10 million tones per year, they generate 30 million tones per year - indicating the necessity for them to find hapless alternative dumping sites. Some of the particularly tragic consequences of hazardous wastes dumped in many African countries in the 1980s continue until this day. The 1988 dumping of toxic wastes in Koko, Nigeria by Italian MNEs resulted in the deformities of newborn children for many years after. The dumping contracts in 'at least 15 African countries' are also well documented. See *Report Submitted by the Special Rapporteur on Toxic Waste, Mrs Fatma-Zohra Ouhachi-Vesely* (above) paras 18-19. See also D Olowu 'Environmental governance and the accountability of non-state actors in Africa: A rights-based approach' (2007) 32 *South African Yearbook of International Law* 261 271.

1175 See *Report of the Special Rapporteur on the adverse effects of the illicit dumping of toxic and dangerous products and wastes on the enjoyment of human rights* UN Doc E/CN.4/1999/46, containing her recommendations on effective measures against involved culprits.

1176 See also D Olowu 'The United Nations Special Rapporteur on the adverse effects of the illicit movement and dumping of toxic and dangerous products and wastes on the enjoyment of human rights' (2006) 8 *Environmental Law Review* 199 215.

in Africa that require manual work. This practice continues in defiance of internationally accepted human rights standards.[1177]

5.1.1 *Codification of responsibilities*

Against the background of the indices that assure the continuing role and significance of TNCs and MNEs for economic, social and cultural rights, for labour practices, for environmental protection, and for human development generally, the inescapable consensus among development economists and the human rights community had been the need to prescribe modalities for the legal responsibilities of these entities.[1178]

It is remarkable to note that even long before the post-Cold War processes of globalisation, it had been a concern among writers and various institutions that TNCs and MNEs must be made accountable to social ethics, human rights and the rule of law.[1179] Regrettably, however, apart from few and isolated instances,[1180] how to establish the obligations of TNCs and MNEs to respect human rights, and to bring them to account when they fail to do so, is a subject that has generally not gone beyond the pedestal of rhetoric in many

1177 The phenomenon of child labour in the agro-allied activities of TNCs and MNEs has been considered in some literature. Some of the notable writings on the subject include D Olowu 'Child trafficking, children's rights and the crisis of state interventionism: The West African experience' (2004) *Nottingham Human Rights Law Review* 62 64-65 (Special Issue); A Jacobs 'Child labour' in Blanpain (n 1161 above) 199 204.

1178 See eg UNDP Human development report 1999 (n 1115 above) 100; R Thüsing 'Codes of conduct - A growing concern for enterprises?' in Blanpain (n 1161 above) 95; BR van der Loeff 'The enterprise, man and human rights: In search of rules' in Van Genuten *et al* (n 1163 above) 57 62.

1179 The Brookings Institution in this regard took one of the most outstanding initiatives in 1974 when it 'invited a panel of nine economists, a political scientist, and a legal scholar to examine the question of the social responsibility of business from a variety of viewpoints'. The outcome of that exercise was published as the 'eleventh [book] in the Brookings Series of Studies in the Regulation of Economic Activity'. See K Gordon 'Foreword' in JW McKie (ed) *Social responsibility and the business predicament* (1974) vii-ix.

1180 Some of the most outstanding reference points are the Bhopal (Union Carbide) gas disaster in India, Cape Asbestos compensation cases, and *Doe v UNOCAL*, 110 F Supp 2d 1294 (CD Cal 2000). For a detailed analysis of the *Bhopal* and *Cape Asbestos* cases, see D Bergman 'Corporations and ESC rights' in *Circle of rights* (n 111 above) 486 492 496. For an analysis of more such cases involving TNCs and MNEs, see C Scott 'Multinational enterprises and emergent jurisprudence on violations of economic, social and cultural rights' in Eide *et al* (n 29 above) 563-594.

countries.[1181] The lull in approaches to this problem has been the result of either the enormous influence wielded by these colossal entities,[1182] perceptions about the capacity and capability of governments to monitor compliance,[1183] or the unending cacophony of debates on the philosophical basis for holding TNCs and MNEs accountable at all.[1184]

Whatever reasons economic objectionists to the social responsibility of TNCs and MNEs might have as to why these entities should not be subjected to social control,[1185] the reality of the twenty-first century is that TNCs and MNEs are increasingly responding to the need to adopt ethical rules; and are actually adopting 'codes of conduct'.[1186]

However, the growing phenomenon of 'codes of conduct' must not yet lead to the suggestion that all is well. I should raise a number of observations. Even though over the last decade, TNCs and MNEs have been responding to consumers' and civil society concerns about their social responsibility by adopting 'codes of conduct', the bigger challenge from that experience has been, and will continue to be, how to hold these entities to the standards they have set for themselves. For one, most of the existing codes are mere statements of intent, crafted in nebulous terms and not expressed in any form to ground legal accountability.[1187] In fact, many of them neither refer

1181 See B Hepple 'The importance of law, guidelines and codes of conduct in monitoring corporate behaviour' in Blanpain (n 1161 above) 3; JA Paul *et al* 'Making corporations accountable. A background paper for the United Nations financing for development process' Global Policy Forum, December 2000, http://www.corporate-accountability.org/docs/MakingCorporationsAccountable.htm (accessed 22 November 2008); A Clapham *et al* 'The obligations of states with regard to non-state-actors in the context of the right to health' WHO, Health and Human Rights Working Paper Series 2 5-8; UNCTAD 'Multinational corporations (MNCs) in least developed countries (LDCs)' (n 1161 above); Scott (n 1180 above) 572-594.

1182 See Leckie (n 657 above) 79.

1183 See generally Steiner *et al* (n 59 above) 1349.

1184 See generally G Chandler 'The responsibilities of oil companies' in Eide *et al* (n 1171 above) 6 16; Oloka-Onyango (n 707 above) 898; M Ottaway 'Reluctant missionaries' *Forum Policy* July/Aug 2001 44 54.

1185 See eg LO Kelso *et al The capitalist manifesto* (1958) 211; R Vernon 'Foreign operations' in JW McKie (ed) *Social responsibility and the business predicament* 275 292.

1186 See WJM van Genugten *The status of transnational corporations in international public law in* Eide *et al* (n 1171 above) 71. See also G van Liemt 'Codes of conduct and international subcontracting: A "private" road towards ensuring minimum labour standards in export industries' in Blanpain (n 1161 above) 167 172-173; C Engels 'Codes of conduct: Freedom of association and the right to bargain collectively' in Blanpain (n 1161 above) 207 230. For a theoretical review of codes of conduct and its influence on corporate responsibility under OECD, see OECD *Corporate responsibility: Private initiatives and public goals* (2001).

1187 See M Colucci 'Implementation and monitoring of codes of conduct: How to make codes of conduct effective' in Blanpain (n 1161 above) 277 282.

to the word 'rights' nor define the extent of their corporate responsibility.[1188]

Since it became apparent that these 'voluntary' codes of conducts were largely adopted to smother public criticism, the natural reaction had been a sustained clamour for an international legal regime of corporate responsibility standards.[1189] At the UN level, the outcome of the protracted process of drafting, negotiating and adopting a coherent normative framework was the Norms on the Responsibilities of Transnational Corporations and Other Business Enterprises with Regard to Human Rights (UN Norms), adopted in August 2003. [1190] The Norms are significant in many ways. For the first time, a coherent global framework proclaims that MNEs and TNCs have an obligation to respect national sovereignty and *all* human rights obligations as well as to contribute to their realisation.[1191] The Norms oblige TNCs and MNEs to ensure the protection of the rights to equality and non-discrimination,[1192] the security of persons,[1193] workers' rights to organise and bargain collectively,[1194] consumers[1195] and the environment.[1196] To assert that these Norms are not cosmetic, they

1188 See eg 'The NIKE code of conduct' revised version 1 January 1999' reprinted in Blanpain (n 1161 above) 369-371, making no mention of the right to organise and to bargain collectively; 'Philips general business principles' April 1998, reprinted in Blanpain (n 1161 above) 375-378, providing that 'Philips wishes to be a responsible partner in society acting in integrity towards its shareholders, customers, employees, suppliers, competitors, governments and their agencies and others who can be affected by its activities'. But see 'The Body Shop Trading Charter' reprinted in Blanpain (n 1161 above) 341, referring even to the Universal Declaration in its '*aim* to ensure that human and civil rights ... are respected throughout [its] business activities'. For a critique of Shell's response to human rights demands, see K Tangen *et al* 'Confronting the ghost: Shell's human rights strategy' in Eide *et al* (n 1171 above) 185-198.

1189 See Van Genugten (n 1186 above) 73-78; DP Forsythe 'The political economy of human rights: Transnational corporations' (2001) 14 *Human Rights Working Papers* 1. Some of the efforts towards that end included the OECD guidelines for multinational enterprises (n 1161 above); ILO Tripartite Declaration of principles concerning multinational enterprises and social policy (n 1161 above); 'The realisation of economic, social and cultural rights: The impact of the activities and working methods of transnational corporations on the full enjoyment of all human rights, in particular economic, social and cultural rights and the right to development, bearing in mind existing international guidelines, rules and standards relating to the subject matter Report of the Secretary-General, UN Doc E/CN.4/Sub.2/1996/12 (2 July 1996); letter from K Roth, Executive Director, Human Rights Watch, to His Excellency, Kofi Annan, UN Secretary-General 'Corporations and human rights: Corporate social responsibility' 28 July 2000 http://www.hrw.org/advocacy/ corporations/; 'Acts and conclusions of the seminar on the activities of transnational corporations: The need for a legal framework' 4-5 May 2001, http://www.cetim.ch/activ/engpart1.pdf (accessed 12 June 2009).

1190 *UN Norms* (n 1161 above). See Forsythe (n 1189 above). For a history of the drafting process, see Tsemo (n 1053 above) 7.

1191 *UN Norms* (n 1161 above) paras 10-12.

1192 n 1191 above, para 2.

1193 n 1191 above, para 3.

1194 n 1191 above, 9.

1195 n 1191 above, para 13.

1196 n 1191 above, para 14.

are to be monitored and implemented through UN and 'other international and national mechanisms already in existence or yet to be created'.[1197] Under the Norms, TNCs and MNEs are obliged to 'adopt, disseminate and implement internal rules of operation in compliance with the Norm'[1198] and states are expected to 'establish and reinforce the necessary legal and administrative framework for ensuring ... [compliance by TNCs and MNEs]'.[1199] But then, the Norms open up questions of implementation and compliance. How will an aggrieved individual enforce these Norms? What will be the appropriate forum for enforcing the provisions of the Norms? What, in fact, is the status of the Norms, within both international and domestic legal systems? These are questions that will engage scholars and activists for a long time to come.[1200] But I do not hesitate to argue that while these Norms may not *ipso facto* transmit the same weight as a treaty, they should nonetheless be a strong instrumentality for civil society activism in Africa. In matters before national courts and regional human rights bodies where economic, social and cultural rights are at issue against TNCs and MNEs, for example, litigants and advocates could cite these Norms as persuasive authority or apply them as strategic advocacy tools.[1201]

However, while the human rights community is still grappling with how to interpret these Norms, there should be a drive towards reinforcing the accountability agenda on other fronts. Activism should be directed at demanding that the voluntary codes of conduct of each TNCs and MNEs must be filed along with, or incorporated into, their Articles of Association in every country where they hold a franchise or have an outlet. This would translate those 'statements of intent' into legal instruments. But then, even where TNCs and MNEs are 'willing' to respect national laws, tenuous national legal frameworks of labour rights may not enhance the freedom of workers to associate, organise,

[1197] n 1191 above, para 16.

[1198] n 1191 above, para 15.

[1199] n 1191 above, para 17.

[1200] From the pronouncements of the defunct UN Commission on Human Rights, it is evident that, even though the *Norms* were primarily intended to bind TNCs and MNEs, their *actual* enforcement against these non-state actors is left to the proactive efforts of states. This betrays the incapacity of international law to directly seek the enforcement of the *Norms* against TNCs and MNEs outside the purview of states. See, eg, Commentary on the norms on the responsibilities of transnational corporations and other business enterprises with regard to human rights UN Doc E/CN.4/Sub.2/2003/38/Rev2 (2003) para 17, where the Commission squarely placed the implementation and monitoring of the *Norms* on states.

[1201] See generally T Meron *Human rights and humanitarian norms as customary law* (1989) 89, pointing out how an implicit recognition of international human rights obligations may crystallise through the doctrine of acquiescence. See also D Shelton *Commitment and compliance: The role of non-binding norms in the international legal system* (2000) 448-463, emphasising that even though 'soft law' are generally considered as lacking the force of treaties, they could nonetheless turn out to be efficacious in ensuring compliance.

and bargain collectively. It should be possible for states to enact the Norms into national legal processes and stipulate sanctions.

Global human rights movements should demand that all states adopt *positive* legislative and structural frameworks that will make all the human rights treaties to which they are parties effective. If this demand is vigorously pursued within the territories of all countries – developed, developing, underdeveloped, or least developed – simultaneously, the 'race to the bottom' argument will give way to a positive response to human rights standards by these entities.[1202]

5.2 Sundry actors

Even though there are other categories of actors that may not fit into Grahame Russell's 'powerful actors' concept, there are sufficient indications to compel an enquiry into the role of small-scale entrepreneurs, professionals and even private individuals in the protection and implementation of economic, social and cultural rights.

The ESCR Committee had recognised the potential for the violation of a broad range of economic, social and cultural rights claims by entities in the private sphere when it proclaimed in General Comment No 5 that state parties are obliged to ensure 'that private employers, private suppliers of goods and services, and other non-public entities be subject to both non-discrimination and equality norms'[1203] In the same vein, in his second interim report, the UN Special Rapporteur on Impunity had recognised that '[v]iolations of economic, social and cultural rights can also be perpetrated by private individuals'.[1204] There is no reason to controvert his

1202 A critical dimension to this approach will be for human rights NGOs to investigate, document, analyse, report and publicise their findings on the latent and manifest negative activities of TNCs and MNEs in their respective countries. Through networks across the globe, the message will become clearer that, while globalisation cannot move anti-clockwise, it must be complemented by human rights considerations. See generally Richter (n 1173 above) 87, stating that 'whether or not the human rights approach will help to prevent the harmful market practices of infant food manufacturers depends on ... [whether] transnational corporations can be held accountable'. See also D Shelton Human rights, health and environmental protection: Linkages in law and practice: A background paper for the World Health Organisation WHO Health and Human Rights Working Paper Series 1 2002 6-10.

1203 ICESCR 'The right of persons with disabilities' General Comment No 5, UN Doc E/ C. E/1995/22 (9 December 1994) in *Compilation of general comments* (n 81 above) 25 para 11.

1204 See The realisation of economic, social and cultural rights, second interim report on the question of the impunity of perpetrators of human rights violations, prepared by Mr El Hadji Guissé Special Rapporteur, UN Doc E/CN.4/Sub.2/1996/ 15 (3 July 1996), para 135.

assertion.[1205]

It is gratifying to note that, in the course of advancing the economic, social and cultural rights discourse beyond states, scholars have begun to examine the horizontal applicability of these rights: to corporate and non-corporate entities as well as to natural persons in their individual or professional capacities.[1206] However, in much of Africa, this understanding has not crystallised either in literature or in the work of the human rights movement. The challenge for Africans, from the emerging paradigm, is the need for the internalisation of economic, social and cultural rights at microcosmic social levels. In strengthening the efficacy of economic, social and cultural rights in Africa, therefore, these claims should become central issues in the determination of disputes involving land, inheritance, succession, and other miscellaneous private endeavours that are hitherto not seen as human rights contestations. Legal practitioners, surveyors, architects, engineers, health workers, small-scale business people, farmers, peasants, traditionally marginalised minorities and others should be made to understand the basics of economic, social and cultural rights as tools for social empowerment and human development. When ordinary Africans begin to appreciate economic, social and cultural rights as their personal rights and begin to appropriate these rights in their private social interactions, a deeper and broader orientation towards these rights as legitimate claims would evolve.

[1205] I might add here that art 28 of the African Charter makes it a 'duty' for 'every individual ... to respect and consider his fellow beings without discrimination, and to maintain relations aimed at promoting, safeguarding and reinforcing mutual respect and tolerance'. While this duty may arguably extend to the duty to respect the human rights norms in the Charter, it has not yet been so defined.

[1206] See generally Limburg Principles (n 48 above) para 40, interpreting art 2(2) of ICESCR as demanding 'from state parties that they prohibit private persons and bodies from practising discrimination in any field of public life'; Maastricht Guidelines (n 49 above) para 18, identifying 'individuals' as capable of violating economic, social and cultural rights; Clapham (n 1156 above) 212 218-220, contending that violations of the provisions of the European Convention can be made applicable to cases involving private individuals; Leckie (n 657 above) 76, suggesting that 'employers, corporations, landlords, teachers, doctors and any other citizen capable of violating an individual's rights ... [should be] held accountable'; Liebenberg (n 31 above) 68-69, analysing the 'possibilities for [the] horizontal application' of economic, social and cultural rights under the South African Constitution.

6 Civil society[1207]

In most of the critical literature so far considered in this book, as well as many others related to the sub-themes of this work, a common strategic indicator is discernible: that the praxis for effectual responses to the challenges confronting economic, social and cultural rights implementation, engendered by the acts of states and non-state actors, lies with *the people* themselves – through their organised formations.[1208] This cannot but be an inevitable conclusion because, even with the best intentions of a truly democratic government, a state would still require popular feedback processes to identify appropriate priorities in actualising a rights-led approach to development. But then, the ancient Greek city centre idea of democracy can no longer sustain the immense demands of policy formulation and decision-making processes of the modern age.[1209] Apparently, this is why the notion of the organised civil society, as both a channel of popular responses and as an alternative 'voice' to statist governance, has continued to attract substantial attention in

1207 I recognise that the term 'civil society' has acquired chequered interpretations by various writers. Within different paradigms, it has been used to denote NGOs, community-based organisations (CBOs), peoples' organisations (POs), governmental non-governmental organisations (GONGOs), international non-governmental organisations (INGOs), etc. See generally S Rasheed & E Chole 'Human development: An African perspective' UNDP Occasional Paper 17 (1994), identifying the potential roles of POs, CBOs, NGOs and other people-based organisations in pursuing a coherent human development agenda in Africa. In the context of my analysis, however, the terminology encompasses independent groups of activists, private individuals, scholars, African writers, professional groups, research institutes, media, artisans, religious organisations, local leaders, traditional societies, unaffiliated persons, and networks existing within the African region, or outside Africa but with focus on Africa, without subservience or duty of allegiance to any ruling administration or government in Africa.

1208 See eg Deacon (n 1009 above) 158; Darrow (n 1022 above) 284; D Barnhizer 'Human rights strategies for investigation and 'shaming', resisting globalisation rhetoric, and education' in Barnhizer (n 1097 above) 1 6; Ochoa (n 1114 above) 68-69; K Flinterman 'The trade unions and non-governmental organisations (NGOs): A reaction to Tom Etty's presentation' in Van Genuten *et al* (n 1163 above) 29 31; K Tomaševski 'Measuring compliance with human rights obligations' in Rehof *et al* (n 184 above) 109 115; OC Okafor 'Re-conceiving "third world" legitimate governance struggles in our time: Emergent imperatives for rights activism' (2000) 6 *Buffalo Human Rights Law Review* 1 34; P Takirambude 'Building the record of human rights violations in Africa: The functions of monitoring, investigation and advocacy' in Barnhizer (n 1097 above) 11-19.

1209 See J Boli-Bennett 'Human rights or state expansion? Cross-national definitions of constitutional rights 1870-1970' in VP Nanda *et al* (eds) *Global human rights: Public policies, comparative measures, and NGO strategies* (1981) 173-193; W Safran 'Civil liberties in democracies: Constitutional norms, practices, and problems of comparison' in Nanda *et al* (above) 195-210.

political discourses.[1210] The civil society concept has now grown in relevance and significance in discussions about governance, democracy, the rule of law, social justice, human rights and, of course, human development. Indeed, it has been suggested that civil society is a 'necessity' because 'governments are increasingly [becoming] inadequate expressions of the collective will of the people'.[1211]

I have highlighted the impact of states and state institutions, inter-governmental agencies, powerful international institutions, and otherwise latent sectors of the society with a view to identifying the related implications of their roles in the protection and implementation of economic, social and cultural rights in Africa. It is in the light of the foregoing that it becomes appropriate and compelling to examine the possible role of civil society and its significance for the implementation of economic, social and cultural rights, and a rights-based approach to human development in Africa.[1212]

The role of the organised civil society in the approach being canvassed here cannot be overemphasised. Across the world, both within regional arrangements as well as institutions of global governance, the paradigm is consistently shifting towards an effective partnership between governments and civil society groups to the ends

1210 See generally HJ Steiner *Diverse partners: Non-governmental organisations in the human rights movement* (1991) 51, the 'special situation' of NGOs that make them agents for 'redemocratisation'; K West *Agents of altruism: The expansion of humanitarian NGOs in Rwanda and Afghanistan* (2001) 1-10; L Gordenker *et al* 'Pluralising global governance: Analytical approaches and dimensions' in TG Weiss *et al* (eds) *NGOs, the UN, and global governance* (1996) 17 18-25; FD Gaer 'Reality check: Human rights NGOs confront governments at the UN' in Weiss *et al* (above) 52-66.

1211 SN Hart *et al* 'The role of non-governmental organisations in implementing the Convention on the Rights of the Child' (1996) 6 *Transnational Law and Contemporary Problems* 373 374. See also B Reinalda 'Private in form, public in purpose: NGOs in international relations theory' in Arts *et al* (n 1008 above) 11; A Blaser 'Assessing human rights: The NGO contribution' in Nanda *et al* (n 1209 above) 261 262; B Reinalda *et al* 'Theorising power relations between NGOs, inter-governmental organisations and states' in Arts *et al* (n 1008 above) 145-158. Compare R Fatton Jr 'Civil society revisited: Africa in the new millennium' (1999) 1 *West African Review* 4.

1212 See generally HM Scoble 'Human rights non-governmental organisations in black Africa: Their problems and prospects in the wake of the Banjul Charter' in C Welch Jr *et al Human rights and development in Africa* (1984) 177-203; S Dicklitch *The elusive promise of NGOs in Africa: Lessons from Uganda* (1998); BP Ambrose *Democratisation and the protection of human rights in Africa* (1995) 99-118; Welch Jr (n 131 above); C Welch Jr 'Human rights NGOs and the rule of law in Africa' (2003) 2 *Journal of Human Rights* 315-327.

of creating a conducive atmosphere for good and responsible governance through strong and active civil society participation.[1213]

At the UN level, this trend culminated in the Declaration on the Rights and Responsibility of Individuals, Groups and Organs of Society to Promote and Protect Universally Recognised Human Rights and Fundamental Freedoms (UN Declaration on Human Rights Defenders), after almost 20 years of diplomatic negotiations.[1214] The Declaration not only stresses the crucial role of individuals, groups and associations in the promotion and protection of all human rights and freedoms,[1215] but goes further to define the limitations on the rights proclaimed therein as only those in consonance with international law.[1216] To demonstrate its commitment to the theme of the UN Declaration on Human Rights Defenders, the defunct UN Commission on Human Rights appointed a Special Representative as a thematic mechanism to monitor restrictions placed by states on independent groups and private individuals who are engaged in human rights promotion and protection.[1217]

Within the African regional system, there is no dearth of legal frameworks for civil society partnership in governance and

1213 See M Kaldor 'Civil society and accountability: Occasional paper for human development report 2002' Occasional Paper 2002/6 (UNDP 2002). See also P Sollis 'Partners in development? The state, NGOs, and the UN in Central America' in Weiss et al (n 1210 above) 189-206.

1214 Declaration on the rights and responsibility of individuals, groups and organs of society to promote and protect universally recognised human rights and fundamental freedoms UNGA Res 53, UN GAOR Suppl, 85th mtg, UN Doc A/RES/53/144 (1999). The Declaration is more popularly known as the UN Declaration on Human Rights Defenders. For an appraisal of this instrument (even though written at draft stage), and its significance for human rights advocacy, see A McChesney 'Protecting the rights of all human rights defenders' (1995) 55 *Review of the International Commission of Jurists* 39-57. For a detailed history of civil society involvement in the UN human rights system since 1945 up to the Vienna Declaration in 1993, see W Korey *NGOs and the Universal Declaration of Human Rights: A curious grapevine* (1998) 1-306.

1215 See UN Declaration on Human Rights Defenders (n 1214 above) arts 1, 5, 6, 7, 8, 9, 11, 12 & 13. Art 16 expresses this role more succinctly as follows: 'Individuals, non-governmental organisations and relevant institutions have an important role to play in contributing to making the public more aware of questions relating to all human rights and fundamental freedoms through activities such as education, training and research in these areas.'

1216 n 1214 above, arts 4 & 17.

1217 See generally Commission on Human Rights Resolution 2000/61, UN Commission on Human Rights, 56th sess, 65th mtg at 1-2, UN Doc E/CN.4/RES/2000/1 (2000). Pursuant to this instrument, Ms Hina Jilani from Pakistan was appointed and she assumed office on 18 August 2000.

development.[1218] However, those subsisting instruments and platforms are yet to attain any remarkable level of use or relevance.

A challenge before African human rights groups, scholars and activists must be how to mobilise rhetoric and action in responding to distorted approaches to development. Research should thus be directed at showing the aggravated repercussions of development assistance, multilateral loans and donors' aids, not only from the perspective of African regimes, but also from the dimension of the governments of donor countries. The perpetuation of corruption and poverty should become central issues in the evaluation of aids and loans to African states. Again, both academic literature and activists' efforts should emphasise that IFIs, development agencies, aid donors and recipient states make explicit reference to integrative human rights in their negotiations. The devaluation of human rights through such vague expressions as 'human well-being', 'good governance' and 'human security' should be discarded. What will empower human beings are legal *entitlements* to the basic necessities of life.

Alternative human rights reporting should also begin to highlight how developed states weaken the competitive capacity of African manufacturers, and invariably the potential of ordinary Africans in export trade. This has generally been lacking or negligible in human rights reporting in Africa.

On a continent laden with astounding levels of illiteracy and ignorance, the organised civil society groups and activists will have to shoulder the responsibility of popular awareness, mass mobilisation, grassroots education and participation founded on existing platforms. It has been demonstrated that the success of any endeavour that seeks to address the deprivations and needs of human beings will invariably depend on its level of patronage from and co-operation with the affected people.[1219] This is highly instructive for an African rights-based agenda to human development.

[1218] Apart from the African Charter and the host of other human rights instruments that I have mentioned in ch II, a number of other development-related instruments abound. Others include the Lagos Plan of Action (LPA), 1980; the African Economic Community (AEC) Treaty, 1991; and the New Partnership for Africa's Development (NEPAD), 2001. For an extensive discussion of the objectives outlined in these instruments, see Udombana (n 284 above) 185. See also Olowu (n 619 above) 216 n 150, for the argument that each of these instruments makes room for civil society involvement.

[1219] See eg SR Osmani 'Participatory governance and poverty reduction' in A Grinspun (ed) *Choices for the poor: Lessons from national poverty strategies* (2001) 121 125-137; J May 'Lesotho, Uganda, Zambia and Maldives' in Grinspun (above) 231 241-244; E Ostrom *et al* 'Coping with asymmetries in the commons: Self-governing irrigation systems can work' (1993) 7 *Journal of Economic Perspectives*

7 Concluding remarks

The explorations into the role of non-state actors portray my holistic approach to economic, social and cultural rights protection and implementation. While I do not fail to underscore the central importance of the obligation of states, I have nonetheless demonstrated that a thorough analysis and understanding of the subject must move beyond the narrow confines of state-centricism if viable strategic parameters are to evolve. Even though I attempted in this chapter to establish the unequivocal legal responsibilities of non-state actors for economic, social and cultural rights, I have also highlighted the formidable impediments arising from entities that are not immediately prone to control by ordinary national legal and political processes, and how African civil society might intensify the struggle towards making such entities a little more malleable to economic, social and cultural rights concerns.

Despite seemingly insurmountable challenges, I have identified the platforms of legal and people-oriented responses that would secure the ends of economic, social and cultural rights and rights-based development in Africa. Africa and its bevy of international sympathisers must recognise that only by embedding discussions of human rights in the locally meaningful struggles that daily confront impoverished Africans, and by promoting broader and direct participation, and invariably self-determination, can any African agenda for development acquire success and sustenance.

Beyond its theoretical propositions, my approach, thus far, facilitates both a basis upon which an integrative human rights approach to development in Africa should be grounded, and a modest pedestal for strategies.

93-112. For purposes of mere analogy, see RL Woodson 'The importance of neighbourhood organisations in meeting human needs' in JA Meyer (ed) Meeting human needs: Toward a new public philosophy (1982) 132 133-135, analysing the impact of the 'New Deal' policy in the United States to the Great Depression of the 1930s, particularly its relevance to the affected class of society. See also JC Scott *Seeing like a state: How certain schemes to improve the human condition have failed* (1999).

7

Conclusion

Surely there must be politicians and business people, youth and women activists, trade unionists, religious leaders, artists and professionals from Cape to Cairo, from Madagascar to Cape Verde who are sufficiently enraged by Africa's condition in the world to join the mass crusade for Africa's renewal. It is to these we say, without equivocation, that *to be a true African is to be a rebel in the cause of the African Renaissance*, whose success in the new century and the millennium is one of the greatest challenges of our time.[1220]

1 Final reflections

I have emphatically demonstrated that, against the background of peculiar African circumstances, it is certainly not enough to adopt normative standards and establish institutions to secure the implementation of economic, social and cultural rights. The most fundamental question is and should be whether, ultimately, these rights are realised in practice, that is, whether the standards and institutions help to bring about the urgently desired changes that would enhance human freedom, human rights and human capabilities – all critical components of human development – in Africa.

In clear detail, I have attempted to analyse some of the legalistic impediments to the proper conceptualisation of economic, social and cultural rights obligations with regard to African states and attempted at disproving the critical theoretical legal questions, namely, justiciability and resource constraints. In chapter II, I highlighted the broad assemblage of international and regional human rights frameworks that could promote an integrative rights-based approach to human development in Africa, indicating the legal and political considerations that should guide the performance of economic, social and cultural rights obligations.

[1220] Address of President Thabo Mbeki of South Africa, 12 August 1998, quoted in G le Pere *et al* 'Making foreign policy in South Africa' in P Nel *et al Power, wealth, and the global order* (1999) 205 (my emphasis).

In chapter III, I examined diverse domestic normative and institutional frameworks that could enhance economic, social and cultural rights in Africa, pointing out that, contrary to the prevalent notion of weak standards, the challenge is more about adequate utilisation of existing legal mechanisms and structures to address development priorities in Africa.

Against the backdrop of an incoherent interpretative approach to economic, social and cultural rights in Africa, chapter IV extensively considered how diverse juridical organs within the UN, various regional human rights arrangements and national bodies across the world, have adopted a holistic approach to the interpretation of all human rights, strengthening their interrelated values, and reinforcing my contention that economic, social and cultural rights are *legal* entitlements with a definable scope and content.

Recognising the prevalent positivist approaches to the implementation of human rights generally, chapter V critically examined scholarly and juridical efforts aimed at defining the standards of measuring the performance of economic, social and cultural rights obligations at the UN level. I have highlighted why current approaches are problematic for Africa within the peculiar context of the African Charter. The chapter strongly canvassed an integrative approach to the measurement of economic, social and cultural rights implementation in Africa, emphasising a *remedial* understanding that would ensure the *actual* realisation of the promises of economic, social and cultural rights. The 'trilogical' approach proposed in the chapter (that is, performance evaluation from legal and policy perspectives; basic needs; and administrative justice) responds to the age-long debate on resource constraints by accentuating practical legal considerations that should guide the assessment of African states' performance, indicating a plausible basis for balancing the demands of human rights law and policy on governments. Moving away from conventional *ex post facto* legal approaches to human rights violations, chapter V introduced the dynamic of preventive implementation for economic, social and cultural rights.

Beyond the bureaucratic complexities and institutional inertia at the level of states, chapter VI identified a broad range of non-state actors whose mandates and activities directly and indirectly portend strong implications for the implementation of economic, social and cultural rights in Africa. Highlighting the formal and informal legal responsibilities of this diversity of non-state actors for economic, social and cultural rights and, invariably, in the evolutionary process of rights-based development in Africa, the chapter makes a case for increased rights-based scrutiny of the activities of *all* actors.

In all, I emphasise that the array of international, regional and domestic human rights instruments considered in this discourse unequivocally create legal economic, social and cultural rights obligations for African states that cannot, in law and in fact, be evaded by arguments based on normative imprecision or resource limitations. However, confronting the human development crisis in Africa remains a formidable challenge indeed, for all Africans as well as for all humanity in this age. My approach to this challenge proceeds on the understanding that the promotion of a rights-based approach to human development in Africa is not to be interpreted merely as a legal question, but also as a moral obligation for all humanity. How then do we tackle the broad gamut of issues highlighted in this work?

I have canvassed a holistic human rights framework that will promote investment in the *people* of Africa in respect of their health, nutrition, shelter, education, and overall well-being. I conceive of an agenda that will strengthen the capacity, responsibility, sensitivity, and the willingness of African governments to pursue the welfare aspirations of their peoples. My approach contemplates an era of increased civil society input in the governance process towards ensuring public accountability that would in turn encourage and foster the political and socio-economic environment required for human growth within broader schemes of national development.

I contended that if governments in Africa would *respect*, *protect* and *fulfil* all those rights that will enhance the value and dignity of every African, it will have to be the result of concerted activism. Towards that end, my discussion has attempted to establish a causal relationship between development dynamics and a human rights ethos, and has identified such linkage as a basis for synergy between development economists and human rights advocates.

In similar tenor, this discourse accentuated the notion that the emergence and sustainability of a rights-based approach to human development in Africa will be contingent on the interplay of several key factors, namely, a proactive approach to the interpretation of human rights generally and economic, social and cultural rights in particular; a free flow of information and accelerated popular participation in decision-making processes; transparent policies genuinely aimed at promoting equity, public accountability, tolerance, the rule of law and human dignity; and a redirected effort towards strengthening social capital by encouraging creativity and collaboration among diverse civil society groups. These are all components of the governance paradigm that will usher in the new type of modernism essential for human development as I envisage for Africa.

I have attempted to demonstrate that efforts aimed at improving the lot of Africans should be taken beyond the lofty heights of legalism to the social and moral planes. Beyond being a matter confined to macro-economics and political propositions, my approach ardently contends that the development theme in Africa is a pursuit that must be nurtured in the minds of the people. This mind-set certainly requires a syndication of multidimensional, multi-disciplinary, ideology-neutral strategies, chief among which is the *strengthening of institutional capacity* at diverse levels.

2 Looking towards the future

2.1 Governance in Africa

I have cited much of the considerable amounts of literature depicting the trends that produced the parlous human development scenario in Africa in this work. It has been proven, quite repeatedly, that the bane of governance in much of post-colonial Africa is that holders of public offices operate the machinery of state in such a way that gives little or no consideration to the welfare of the people. This has also been cited as the primary reason for a great deal of the socio-economic crises and political instability.[1221]

There has even been a contention that, immediately after the attainment of independence by many African states in the 1960s, with the preconceived notion that there can be no genuine political independence without economic empowerment, African leaders and nationalists rapidly embarked on initiatives aimed at establishing a firm control over their national economies as well as over foreign capital activities.[1222] These moves were vigorously pursued with the maximum state capacities wielded by African political leaders in their respective domains. The resultant effect was the breeding of neocolonialism as exemplified in the personalisation of governance ('patrimonialism'); heightened intolerance for opposition; culture of patronage; skewed economic policies leading to the collapse of thitherto-vibrant economies; increased dependence on foreign aid

[1221] See eg JH Frimpong-Ansah *The vampire state in Africa: The political economy of decline in Ghana* (1991) 75-85; IE Orji 'Issues on ethnicity and governance in Nigeria: A universal human rights perspective' (2001) 25 *Fordham International Law Journal* 431 450-454; Owens (n 1089 above) 1014; PC Aka 'Africa in the new world order: The trouble with the notion of African marginalisation' (2001) 9 *Tulane Journal of International and Comparative Law* 187 190-196; Gutto (n 197 above) 56-70. This is an antithesis to 'the full-belly thesis' propounded by Howard. See Howard (n 294 above) and accompanying text.

[1222] SS Kozitsky 'Foreign private capital in Africa: Modification of methods' in EA Tarabrin (ed) *Neocolonialism and Africa in the 1970s* (1978) 149-150.

and various degrees of social tensions and conflicts that threatened the very existence of the nascent democracies in Africa.[1223]

The noticeable trend since the end of the Cold War shows a steady attempt to move towards democratisation in many nations of Africa.[1224] However, this euphoria of democratisation has yet to produce positive indices of well-being and happiness for the vast majority of Africans. On a continent where democratisation is more fixated on personalised coalitions of power brokers than on performance, and where political leadership is often recognised as an ascendancy to wealth and power,[1225] the challenge today is to redefine African democratic processes ranging from electoral structures to party systems. This raises a challenge for legislative reforms, particularly in states where legal frameworks are weak.

Besides the lamentations on scarcity and non-availability of funds for those essential social services — water, healthcare, education, housing, social security — that underscore economic, social and cultural rights, African governments should begin to understand that human development is as much about the mobilisation of resources, but much more, about the judicious appropriation of available resources. I have argued that African states have generally failed, neglected or refused to respond appropriately to human development needs because they lack the political will to give concrete expression to policies that would create conducive atmosphere for the common good.

Although there have been neo-liberal arguments canvassing 'destatisation' (weakening of state control of the apparatuses of governance) as an antidote to socio-economic malformations in

[1223] See generally DL Gordon 'African Politics' in AL Gordon & DL Gordon (eds) *Understanding contemporary Africa* (2001) 72, analysing the chain of transfer of power at independence, to the centralisation of power.

[1224] Between 1990 and the end of 2001, elected regimes have emerged in the following African countries which were before 1990 under one-party, apartheid or military regimes: Benin, Ethiopia, Ghana, Kenya, Malawi, Mozambique, Namibia, Nigeria, South Africa and Zambia, to mention a few. For a detailed discussion of multi-party democratisation in Africa in the 1990s, see L Rakner & L Svasand 'Multiparty elections in Africa's new democracies' Report 7 (2002). See also M Cowen & L Laakso *Multi-party elections in Africa* (2002).

[1225] See Wunsch *et al* (n 563 above) 4-5. See also DN Wai 'Human rights in sub-Saharan Africa' in A Pollis *et al Human rights: Cultural and ideological perspectives* (1979) 115, describing how ethnic pluralism and patronage has led to personalisation of state power, and making it a difficult task for state institutions to check their own excesses; JCN Paul 'Participatory approaches to human rights in sub-Saharan Africa' in AA An-Na'im *et al* (eds) *Human rights in Africa: Cross-cultural perspectives* (1990) 213 257, pointing out how historical constitutional structures have become tools for entrenched manipulation of state control and resources, and a weapon for the exclusion of criticism; Gutto (n 197 above) 55-72, analysing how 'domestic authoritarian state machinery', 'economic straightjackets' and '*de facto* impunity policies' have combined to impact any meaningful democratisation in negative ways in Africa.

Africa,[1226] I contend that rolling back state capacity is not the answer. Rather, it is the operation of the machinery of governance that must be overhauled by every legitimate means.

My central concern here is the placement of *all* human rights squarely on the African development agenda in a way that guarantees that all Africans acquire the opportunity to attain their maximum potentials. While I recognise that the typical African government will not accede to peaceable change, African civil society must evolve and pursue the modalities that would galvanise this rights-based approach to development. It is my submission that the much-vaunted 'democratic' gains may not for long endure if the living conditions of human beings in Africa continue to slip into further decadence.

2.1.1 African regional arrangements

Earlier in this work, I highlighted a wide range of initiatives that were adopted to guide the development agenda in Africa. Since the early years of the defunct OAU, there has been an emphasis on the pursuit of development for Africa.[1227] However, despite various brilliant African regional initiatives and international collaborative efforts that proclaim and emphasise clear commitments to democracy, popular participation, good governance, accountable leadership and human development, these efforts have often been unproductive due to lack of political will.[1228]

While there have recently been renewed efforts at advancing good governance, human rights and development through increased regional integration as evident in the AU and the New Partnership for Africa's Development (NEPAD) agenda, concerns still persist about the genuine intentions of African governments and leaders to turn these goals into reality for their peoples.[1229]

1226 See AB Zack-Williams 'No democracy, no development: Reflections on democracy and development in Africa' (2001) 28 *Review of African Political Economics* 213.

1227 Indeed, there has been an indication that the themes of good governance and development within the African regional arrangement preceded the global discussion in many respects. K Wohlmuth 'Good governance and economic development: New foundations for growth in Africa' *Institute for World Economics and International Management* (1998) 18.

1228 See S Rasheed & E Chole 'Human development: An African perspective' Occasional Paper 17 (UNDP 1994) 3. See also Oloka-Onyango (n 31 above) 42-44.

1229 See Udombana (n 284 above) 202-206. For a discussion of the overlapping normative structures of both NEPAD and the AU that could hamper the effectiveness of the African development agenda, see E Baimu 'Human rights mechanisms and structures under NEPAD and the African Union: Emerging trends towards proliferation and duplication' Occasional Paper 15 1-15 (Centre for Human Rights, Pretoria, August 2002).

Rather than churning out more rhetoric, the platforms already designed for action should be made to produce results, and to work with tangible dividends at the levels of the people. Visionary faith must be accompanied by positive works, otherwise it is dead faith.[1230]

In another vein, the African regional system should de-emphasise its exclusively state-centred approach to governance and development initiatives. It is plausible to posit that regional development efforts will gain more recognition and legitimacy when they are people-owned and people-controlled, invariably increasing their chances of success and productivity.[1231]

African regional development programmes should also incorporate a human rights focus into all such initiatives. If African governments are to abide by the enunciated principles and legal obligations to which they have formally committed themselves, they should recognise credible platforms for accountability. The rights-based approach avails such.

Further, beyond the projectionism of Africa's woes solely on IFIs and other multilateral agencies, African institutions and leaderships should squarely place on the regional development agenda not only the attainment of (nominal) democracy but, more essentially, of social justice and economic democracy.

While the sometimes ambivalent involvement of foreign powers in African development is acknowledged and well documented,[1232] the words of George W Shepherd Jr are more apposite in describing what an objective African reaction to the prevailing situation should be: 'The oppressor has not always been the foreigner, and today the most tyrannical systems of human rights violations are often the regimes of the new states themselves.'[1233] The moral is, concerning development, Africa can no longer afford to play the ostrich or to resort to buck-passing in its present circumstances. Its leaders and peoples must conscientiously brace up to the challenges thereby presented, in result-oriented fashion.

Linked to the foregoing is the clearly identifiable potential of the African regional human rights system to advance the rights-based

1230 This is an allusion to the epistelian expression 'faith by itself, if it does not have works, is dead' in *James* 2:17 (New King James).

1231 See generally Scott (n 1219 above) 85-180, contending strongly that human development initiatives have failed in many parts of the world because the design and implementation failed to consider local peculiarities.

1232 See PJ Schraeder 'African international relations' in Gordon & Gordon (n 1223 above) 143-187.

1233 GW Shepherd Jr 'The power system and basic human rights: From tribute to self-reliance' in GW Shepherd Jr & VP Nanda (eds) *Human rights and third world development* (1985) 13.

approach to development through greater commitment to economic, social and cultural rights. Notwithstanding the wide range of criticisms about the inherent structural deficiencies and weaknesses of the African regional human rights system, my argument remains that, since the same structures were relatively functional in assessing civil and political rights violations by repressive and dictatorial regimes across Africa in the 1990s, the same structures should be galvanised towards the positive evolution of an enhanced economic, social and cultural rights culture in Africa. I contend that a viable basis exists for the optimal utilisation of the complaints procedure provided in the African Charter based on the radical consequence of its overthrow of a stereotyped human rights trichotomy.

Of course, the complaint procedures afforded by the African Charter are essentially dependent on its activation by civil society groups. If communications are not brought before the African Commission in respect of economic, social and cultural rights violations, a body of jurisprudence that will enhance the value of these rights across the continent cannot develop, and the mechanisms will only remain window dressings of sorts. The only *caveat* in this trajectory, however, is the necessity of adopting an approach that would eliminate the possibility of subjecting the African corpus of economic, social and cultural rights to the conceptual and methodological limitations of the UN or other comparative regional systems.

Beyond strengthening activism at the level of civil society, the African regional system should begin to critically address ways of enhancing the status of economic, social and cultural rights on the continent. An urgent need specifically arises for the African Commission and the emerging African Court to critically appraise and properly conceptualise the standards of state obligations in respect of the economic, social and cultural rights in the African Charter to accord with the Charter's unique philosophy and outlook.

In reinforcing these efforts, the AU should identify and provide adequate resources that would strengthen the capacities of both the African Commission and the African Court to promote, protect and secure the implementation of economic, social and cultural rights. Of significance here is the need for a renewed commitment to the implementation of the virtually abandoned Mauritius Plan of Action[1234] which contemplated both vertical co-operation between the African regional human rights bodies and NGOs, on the one hand,

[1234] The Mauritius Plan of Action 1996-2001, adopted by the African Commission, 20th ordinary session 21-31 October 1996, Grand Baie, Mauritius, reprinted in (1996-1997) 6 *Review of the African Commission on Human and Peoples' Rights* 215 224.

and horizontal collaboration among African human rights NGOs, on the other.[1235]

Similarly, in accordance with the vision for a greater understanding of economic, social and cultural rights as expressed in the Mauritius Plan of Action,[1236] a special rapporteur should be appointed on the monitoring and implementation of economic, social and cultural rights in African states. This is a step long overdue and it behoves African human rights NGOs to heighten demand in this regard.

2.1.2 African national juridical bodies

The inestimable value of the judicial process to economic, social and cultural rights activism at the domestic level cannot be overemphasised when one realises that the public nature of judicial review provides a veritable platform for agitation and campaigns against anti-people policies, particularly where such mechanism is independent and efficient. At one of the most remarkable workshops convened at the twilight of the last millennium aimed at identifying ways of strengthening economic, social and cultural rights, the participating NGOs, jurists, scholars, development experts and other activists had recognised that 'one obvious way ... to pursue ESC rights claims ... is with the courts'.[1237]

I contend that, in the face of chronic and widespread poverty, massive human suffering and deprivation in Africa, occasioned in most part by the policies and actions of states or state-sponsored or state-supported actors, judicial and quasi-judicial institutions in Africa can no longer afford to ignore the necessity for a critical human rights engagement and, invariably, the development of a coherent approach to economic, social and cultural rights adjudication. After all, the same judicial pedestal that has customarily existed for redressing administrative wrongs and civil suits would in most cases suffice for the examination of economic, social and cultural rights claims and actions related thereto. As Budlender argues:

> Justiciability ... is under the control of the courts. Our law is replete with instances, particularly in the law of delict (tort) and administrative law, where the question which the courts have to determine is whether the defendant or respondent acted 'reasonably'. Where a court has to decide this, it can and should develop the nature and extent of the duty on state officials with due regard to the requirements of the

1235 n 1234 above, paras 60-63.
1236 n 1234 above, para 18.
1237 'Developing a common framework for the promotion of economic, social and cultural rights' Workshop I, summary report 21 (Centre for Economic, Social and Cultural Rights, New York 1995).

> Constitution, and in particular the obligation of the state to 'protect' the rights of people affected by state action or inaction.[1238]

I have shown that in most African states that entrench economic, social and cultural rights as directly enforceable entitlements in their constitutions, the general picture portrays underdeveloped jurisprudence and, in some cases, a cloud of uncertainty. In many African constitutions, the Directive Principles do not confer legal rights and are thus neither enforceable in courts of law, nor may any question of inconsistency of a law with such provisions be raised in courts. Nevertheless, it behoves African judiciaries to engage in a proactive interpretation of fundamental human rights and freedoms in such manner as to harmonise them with the Directive Principles. A harmonious interpretation will not only mean that the state would certainly implement the Directive Principles, but will also entail that the state should do so in such a way that its laws and policies do not take away or abridge the very essence of governance, namely, the happiness of its people. Harmonious interpretation is particularly necessary in many African states because the operation of Directive Principles is subject to enforceability limitations.

Since most legal systems in Africa permit the courts to consider international law principles in the interpretation of constitutional provisions, great potentials lie in the use of international and regional juridical influences in domestic adjudication. In this regard, the African Charter stands out as a significant instrument of economic, social and cultural rights litigation in African states, particularly in states where these rights are non-justiciable or where jurisprudence is not well developed. Even where domestic legal constraints would ordinarily dissuade a court from examining issues of policy, African judges should be willing to seek solace in the direct and indirect application of relevant international legal principles and instruments on human rights where such matters involve the very survival and livelihood of human beings.[1239]

2.1.3 The international community

With the spate of socio-economic misfortunes, governance crises, the HIV/AIDS menace and development mirages that have remained in the repository of Africa against the tide of New Age progress, Africa is indeed one continent that desperately demands global attention. The consequences of the current African socio-economic quagmire cannot

[1238] G Budlender 'Justiciability of the right to housing - The South African experience' in S Leckie (ed) *National perspectives on housing rights* (2003) 207 211.

[1239] See generally NR Jones 'The role of judges in advancing the protection of human rights in domestic courts' in *Developing human rights jurisprudence Vol IV* (n 620 above) 184 185.

be abandoned to Africa to bear alone. One of the formidable pillars for a rights-based approach to human development canvassed in this book is the formation of a collaborative agenda within the international community. More significant in this regard are the concerted efforts of multilateral and bilateral development agencies. But then, there remains the need for a reappraisal of the efforts of these key institutions in the context of this discourse.

Certainly, the prevalent notion of development within the international system views the material contributions of developed states to the alleviation of the plight of people in Third World states as the most viable approach to assisting such people.[1240] With the posture of the UN Charter's mandate, the ICESCR obligations, TICAD II strategy, and many other multilateral frameworks that premise this 'development responsibility' of developed states on 'assistance', usually in the form of aid, it is predictable that the paradigm of hand-outs to African states from Western nations will continue to be the norm. It is, however, regrettable that most aid donors are traditionally not interested in the asymmetry of what recipient states in Africa propose to do with such aids and what they actually do with them.[1241]

The international community needs to realise that when aid is given to unscrupulous and insensate African governments, they indirectly perpetuate the vicious cycle of repression, corruption and profligacy in such instances. The challenge for multilateral and bilateral aid donors and development agencies is to urgently develop coherent and responsive codes of conduct that would govern the administration of foreign aid.

Since the language of the UN Charter and ICESCR connote the intention of delivering the benefits of international assistance and co-operation to human beings, I recommend that, in the face of rampant graft and waste in Africa, aid donors and development agencies should co-opt tested independent joint administrators for development aids and projects rather than leaving African governments as absolute determinants of aid funds. While the fine details of this suggestion may be subject to further discussion and elaboration, it suffices to emphasise that whatever modalities emerge must stress the central role of genuine participation by *every* segment of society in an African state. This is not a tall order at all. Development assistance and aid projects should make human beings central objects and subjects of development as envisaged by the UN Charter, ICESCR and the African Charter. To that end, development

1240 See generally The Congress of the United States, Congressional Budget Office, 'The role of foreign aid in development' May 1997 7 11-12.
1241 Owens (n 1089 above) 1044-1045.

should be people-driven, people-controlled, and people-oriented through genuine, transparent 'bottom-up' participation.[1242] African states' role should be limited to merely facilitating the normative and institutional framework towards that end.

The international community will be *assisting* the cause of genuine development when it begins to approach the subject of development aid and assistance projects on the platform of human rights: to secure free and popular participation, to check governmental abuse of aid, and to pursue credible development programmes that accord with the most pressing needs of affective communities in Africa.

In considering the unwillingness of most African states to fulfil their economic, social and cultural rights obligations, donor agencies should begin to place more emphasis on the level of performance of fund-seeking states in complying with their reporting and other implementation obligations under the applicable human rights instruments.

Related to this is the role of the IFIs. While these bodies have, at various times, emphasised the improvement in social services as a core element of their poverty reduction efforts in Africa, progress is slow and retarded because their approach does not reflect the totality of the social problems within varying African contexts. For instance, most of the World Bank/IMF initiatives heavily rely on the 'intellectual resources' and 'analytical work' entirely produced by academics.[1243] This in itself is problematic. As the World Bank itself confesses, '[p]art of the problem is that the information [they produce] is typically fragmented or hard to access, and sometimes dated, but the broader problem relates to issues of funding and incentives to get the work done'.[1244] While the IFIs' approach lately seeks to make giant strides in creating opportunities for socially relevant initiatives in collaboration with few NGOs in different African countries, these activities are often limited to the input of rather

[1242] See generally *Human rights and human development: Report on the Oslo symposium* (n 25 above) Annex 1, detailing what scholars consider as the summary of 'the content of international law on development', namely, that: 'development must be people-centred'; 'must be participatory'; 'must protect and promote all ... human rights'; 'must work to eliminate all forms of discrimination against women, and cultural, ethnic or other groups'; 'must be concerned with the protection and rehabilitation of environments and it must be environmentally sustainable'; 'must respect and protect cultures and cultural diversity'; 'must promote democratic governance'; and 'must promote rule of law designed to secure the above principles'.

[1243] See Tan *et al* (n 33 above) 16.

[1244] As above.

obscure NGOs or groups surreptitiously thriving on governmental patronage or located in the urban centres of Africa.[1245]

It is no surprise, therefore, that following a critical examination of the development-related activities of IFIs *vis-à-vis* the current trends in the economic reforms introduced at the insistence of IFIs, there has been a suggestion that such activities have actually engendered a steady shifting from a liberal pluralist model of society to one of deepened social division and exclusion in Africa.[1246]

IFIs, aid donors and development agencies dealing with Africa should therefore evolve credible mechanisms that will ensure that the *people* are allowed to speak up for themselves, to organise themselves, and to make an impact on policy making and, thus, make their choices a real-life experience. Not only will this 'bottom-up' strategy strengthen goal achievement and relevance, but it will provide appropriate platforms for verifying assumptions, projections and outcomes.

2.1.4 African civil society

Since I have demonstrably and persistently argued that economic, social and cultural rights are core platforms for the attainment of human development in Africa, African civil society groups need to reappraise their responses in that regard. I have shown that strategies for promoting e in Africa may include, but are certainly not limited to, the legal, monitoring and violations approach used for civil and political rights. The different strategies to which I allude include engaging the people in participation, exploring broader proportions of civil and political rights by moving beyond narrow juridical focus, incorporating more sectors of the civil society, developing creative lawyering skills, using a blend of juridical or other methods, and investing in rational, multi-disciplinary research.

[1245] As above. This is with reference to the World Bank conducting its co-operative efforts with civil society groups in the form of 'collaboration between governments and NGOs, including the *involvement of NGOs in specific activities under subcontracting arrangements* ... by sharing technical resources (such as the PRSP Sourcebook, which is now widely *available via the internet*' (mt emphasis). In view of the pallid state of infrastructures in Africa, the remoteness of these sorts of therapies in meeting the gross socio-economic ailments in grassroots Africa can be conjectured.

[1246] B Campbell 'Governance, institutional reform and the state: International financial institutions and political transition in Africa' (2001) 28 *Review of African Political Economy* 155.

Integrative human rights approach

As already noted, while in other regions of the world there has been an increasing trend towards establishing a nexus between human rights and human development, and invariably, a growing articulation of the interdependence and indivisibility of all human rights, the same does not hold true for Africa. The bifurcated debate about resources and justiciability has largely been responsible for the notion that economic development must precede human rights protection in Africa.[1247] It is difficult to subscribe to that perception.

The traditional focus of human rights groups in Africa has largely been confined to those that directly relate to democracy and the democratic process; notably, elections, trials, press freedom and other elements of civil and political rights. That culture is understandable in view of the long history of repression and monolithic governance in much of Africa. However, after putting elected regimes in office, what next?

While there has been a commendable trend towards the actualisation of economic, social and cultural rights through litigation processes serving as channels of community mobilisation in some African countries, the strategy is still far-fetched as civil society groups in many African states are still labouring under the yoke of the traditional conceptualisation of economic, social and cultural rights as being mere ideals not subject to immediate realisation. Now is the time when civil society groups in Africa must begin to articulate, as a central theme, the indivisibility of all human rights within their respective domestic legal systems as well as the regional human rights system.

The quest for relevance beyond the electoral process is becoming particularly problematic for the popular human rights movement in many African countries. There should have been no dilemma for civil society if all the broad dynamics of governance had been dialectically incorporated into the wider context of democratic struggles.[1248]

Moreover, a stronger platform for governmental accountability and people-oriented governance can be established in Africa through the integrative human rights approach. Although considered a relegated subject in the African human rights discourse, economic, social and cultural rights embody the essential elements required for

[1247] See generally Howard (n 294 above) 469.

[1248] See generally Gutto (n 197 above) 120-138, analysing the conservatism of the African human rights movement and how it has aided a weak culture of popular democracy and highlighting the 'separatist' approach that stunts the growth of developmental rights.

human life, dignity and freedom. This bundle of rights establishes and assures a platform for social justice and the well-being of all. Beyond the phobia of the fiscal implications of economic, social and cultural rights, South African courts have consistently interpreted the scope and content of positive economic, social and cultural rights provisions, and yet the state has not collapsed. I believe that an integrative approach to human rights portends the advantage of keeping civil society movements relevant and vital to overall development in Africa.

I have pointed out the increasing recognition among governments, the UN system, regional arrangements, civil society groups and even international development institutions, of the critical importance of the integrative human rights approach to development. Beyond this, there have been plausible pointers to the capability of that approach to serve as a tool of governmental reform.[1249] This should be of significant insight for the civil society in Africa.

It is the responsibility of scholars and activists on African issues to begin to delve into various aspects of the integrative human rights approach. It should become a pedestal for social and economic democratisation in African states.

While I am not making a case for African human rights scholars and activists to abandon their traditional focus on civil and political rights, I am simply attempting here to sensitise them to the challenge of exploring the means of translating economic, social and cultural rights into tools for the advancement of popular struggles against poverty, inequality and misery in Africa.

Budgetary processes and popular participation[1250]

Given the strong case that has traditionally been made against economic, social and cultural rights on the ground of their fiscal connotations, the implementation of these rights necessarily demands closer budgetary monitoring. The approach I conceptualise here considers the accountability of state institutions and those who operate them as pivotal machinery in matching state resources against the delivery of human needs. As many African states continue

1249 See E Owens *The future of freedom in the developing world* (1987) 33-39.

1250 For background reflections on the strategic intercourse between economic, social and cultural rights and budgetary work, see J Shultz 'Promises to keep: Using public budgets as a tool to advance economic, social and cultural rights' January 2002 9-21 (FUNDAR-Center for Analysis and Research, Mexico City, Mexico). For links to civil society groups that are active in budgetary policy transparency as a means of stronger human rights protection around the world, see 'The international budget process' http://www.internationalbudget.org/index.htm (accessed 12 June 2009).

to wallow under the weight of foreign debt, it cannot be more pertinent that the people who bear the brunt must have a say in the destiny of their states. This is what makes it crucial to evaluate the level of popular participation in the budgetary processes in African states.[1251] Although most African states have statutory regulations for national fiscal arrangements, the legislative capacity for thorough scrutiny is usually weak and haphazard as most parliamentarians lack the technical skills for the volumes of numerical details presented to them.[1252] In an extensive survey of some African democracies, over the space of the last five years, a general pattern emerged: the absence of civil society involvement in budgetary work.[1253]

The connectivity between human rights, development and fiscal budgets in Africa cannot be overemphasised. While I acknowledge that not all 'positive' aspects of economic, social and cultural rights obligations can be *fully* achieved overnight, every government in Africa should be pressured into fulfilling those human rights obligations as would enhance living conditions, to the limits of their *maximum* resource capacity.

The challenge of civil society in Africa is to become deeply involved in the budgetary processes in every country, building the framework of their involvement on the available platforms. Civil society groups will achieve an impact by compiling empirical data with which to confront the governments of respective African states.[1254]

Public pressure as well as litigation and other legitimate non-litigation methods should also complement this effort. Study has shown the successful influences of analytical budgetary work,

[1251] See generally A Fölscher 'Transparency and participation in the budgetary process' in A Fölscher (ed) *Budget transparency and participation, five African case studies* (2002) 29-35.

[1252] n 1251 above, 6 20-24.

[1253] n 1251 above, 46-47, showing that apart from South Africa, civil society involvement in budgetary work has been curtailed by a combination of factors. The comprehensive study covered Ghana, Kenya, Nigeria, Zambia and South Africa, which are all 'new' democracies.

[1254] Civil society groups in some countries prepare and publicise their own alternative or parallel budgets. See generally McChesney (n 47 above) 66-67; N Hijab 'Human rights and human development: Learning from those who act' UNDP, Background Paper 2000 http://hdr.undp.org/docs/publications/background_papers/Hijab 2000.html (accessed 12 June 2009); 'Expectations from the medium term budget policy statement 2008/2009'http://www.sacc-ct.org.za/pbstatement.html (accessed 22 November 2008); 'Peoples Budget Coalition Expectations statement for the 2008-2009 Budget' http://www.sangoco.org.za/site/index2.php?option=com_content&do_pdf=1&id=347 (accessed 12 June 2009); K Creamer 'The impact of South Africa's evolving jurisprudence on children's socio-economic rights on budget analysis' (Cape Town, Institute for Democracy in South Africa, 2002) 1-70.

lobbying and judicial recourse in some countries where civil society groups have chosen to act.[1255]

The stupendous level of official corruption in Africa is a matter relatively well researched and publicised.[1256] Taming the menace of corruption and graft in African states has received some level of official response at both national and regional levels. Many African states have put in place anti-corruption mechanisms aimed at apprehending and punishing corrupt public officials and their accomplices.[1257]

While not undermining the capacity of these broad mechanisms to serve as viable platforms of action, it remains very important that the people themselves combat governmental corruption through concerted efforts. Budgetary participation by civil society will go a long way in advancing the anti-corruption crusade in Africa. The underlying reality that should echo across the continent is that no meaningful human development will take place in Africa without subjecting governmental spending to public scrutiny.

The other aspect of my concern is the almost total neglect of traditional civil society structures in development discourse in Africa. It will be absurd, if not foolhardy, for any so-called expert to believe that only the wisdom of 'learned' elite and technocrats would achieve success for human rights and development in Africa.[1258] Traditional civil society structures should be engaged and equipped in strengthening the rights-based approach. They have the advantage of working through familiar processes to produce broader results.

[1255] See generally Fölscher (n 1251 above) 46-47, showing 'study results' of 'civil society participation' in the budgetary processes of Ghana, Kenya, Nigeria, South Africa and Zambia over a certain period. See also Shultz (n 1250 above) 38-41.

[1256] See eg ABM Marong 'Legal effects of the principles to combat corruption in Africa' (2002) 30 *Denver Journal of International Law and Policy* 99 99-129; KR Hope Sr *et al Corruption and development in Africa: Lessons from country case studies* (2000); D Gordon 'African politics' in A Goedon *et al* (eds) *Understanding contemporary Africa* (2001) 80-82; T Martin 'Corruption and improper payments: Global trends and applicable laws' (1998) 36 *Alberta Law Review* 416; Oloka-Onyango (n 31 above) 3-4; Agbakwa (n 46 above) 189.

[1257] See Marong (n 1256 above) 118-121. It is worthy to note that there is now an AU Convention on Preventing and Combating Corruption, adopted by African Heads of State and Government. See African Union Convention on Preventing and Combating Corruption, AU Doc Min/Draft/AU/Conv/Comb/Corruption (II) Rev 5 (2002) adopted by the AU Assembly, 2nd ordinary session, 11 July 2003, Maputo, Mozambique, not yet in force. For a scholarly analysis of the promise of this treaty, see Olaniyan (n 1129 above) 217-234.

[1258] As an illustration, at the Call to Solidarity with Africa Conference held at the University of Notre Dame, Notre Dame, Indiana, USA, 21-24 September 2003, I had posed this question to the eminent scholars and discussants at one of the sessions on NEPAD: What direct participatory role is NEPAD envisaging for Africans at the grassroots? The response had been one of palpable consternation. The discourse on Africa's development was obviously never meant to involve the unscripted and non-urban!

Scholarly human rights and human development research should therefore work in tandem with the traditional structures of the African civil society. Rather than feeding abstract data reports and recommendations into development policies, efforts must begin to incorporate the input of the unlearned, unskilled populace at the grassroots level. It is illogical to concentrate on a stereotype of formalised monitoring and documentation that excludes the wisdom of the ultimate beneficiaries.

Furthermore, in recognition of the scarcity of funds for civil society activities in Africa, civil society groups should develop collaborative networks. This will go a long way in empowering them for their human development tasks.

Monitoring, research and documentation

Many attempts made by foreign governments, the international community and development agencies alike towards enhancing human development in Africa are predicated on information founded upon formal indices, data and statistics. The fall-out has been an unmistakable disconnection between recommendations and results.[1259]

It is now discernible *why* and *how* many proposed solutions to Africa's myriad problems have often failed the test of implementation and relevance: There is a gulf in the line of communication between experts, policy makers and development agencies on the one hand, and the people at the grassroots level who should be the first in line of policy formulation, on the other.[1260] This still takes place in Africa, despite the robust and persuasive scholarly appreciation of the notion that the success of any endeavour that seeks to address the deprivations and needs of human beings will invariably depend on its level of patronage from and co-operation with the affected people.[1261]

Without doubt, for a rights-based approach to development to be meaningful in Africa, it must be research-driven. However, research in this context can only produce effective results when it focuses on thorough socio-cultural and economic investigations that can provide

1259 See generally K King'ei 'Language in development research in 21st century Africa' http://web.Africa.ufl.edu/asq/v3/v3i3a3.htm (accessed 12 June 2009), contending that most projects carried out at the grassroots are abstractions to those people who should benefit from them.

1260 See n 1219 above and accompanying text.

1261 For purposes of mere analogy, see RL Woodson 'The importance of neighbourhood organisations in meeting human needs' in JA Meyer (ed) *Meeting human needs: Towards a new public philosophy* (1982) 132 133-135. See also Scott (n 1219 above).

vital data, inclusive of grassroots realities. This sort of research approach is necessary to arrive at sound, well-informed, credible policies that will serve as a launching pad for good governance and development.

Multidimensional cutting-edge advocacy

African civil society groups must play a more dynamic role in increasing the effectiveness of the state-reporting procedures through the preparation of alternative or shadow reports at both international and regional levels, particularly in relation to economic, social and cultural rights. In doing so, I recommend that they should begin to produce *issue-specific* reports or modified versions of the format used by states so that there is a correlation with states' reports on a right-by-right presentation, and also to ensure that specialists in diverse fields make technical input to such formats. Related to this is the need for these groups to formulate fundamental questions that would help treaty-monitoring bodies to ascertain the veracity of governments' claims during intergovernmental human rights reviews. Although states are usually required to include copies of their relevant legislation in the reports, where they fail to do so, African civil society groups should furnish such legislation. To add effect, African civil society groups should transmit their 'shadow' reports well in advance to the appropriate bodies, and attend sessions of the monitoring bodies to brief and lobby the members. Attendance of international human rights assessment fora ensures that these groups will have an opportunity to update information and internationalise their concerns.

In the same vein, the inertia of African human rights groups in utilising the complaints mechanism afforded by the African Charter as a pedestal for economic, social and cultural rights activism must be brought to an end. They should begin to critically analyse the potential of litigating cases involving economic, social and cultural rights claims more than ever. This is the only effective way of developing and charting new jurisprudential horizons for the African regional human rights system.

At the domestic level, civil society groups should make co-ordinated efforts to raise awareness of economic, social and cultural rights among the various sectors of the populace. Given the uneven polarities in urban-rural structures and the depth of illiteracy in much of Africa, the need arises to evolve strategies that would take into account local situations, frustrations and priorities. To this end, effective media strategies should be developed to meet the needs of awareness and mobilisation at the grassroots level.[1262] The electronic and print media should be adapted to local languages and local values for maximum effect. Human rights education should target, in particular, the peasantry and pastorals to which the majority of Africans belong; people in urban areas, especially those working in industrial or informal trade sectors, law enforcement agencies and civil servants, and all groups and personalities instrumental in disseminating information, including the media, school teachers, religious and traditional leaders, and other prominent grassroots figures. In the clamour for the integration of human rights education into school curricula from primary to tertiary institutions, human rights groups should be involved in designing appropriate curricula aimed at cognitive and experiential understanding of the subject.

Where there are constitutional guarantees for economic, social and cultural rights, it may become easier to seek their remedial implementation. Similarly, when legislative reforms are carried out to reflect international normative values, states attain a higher threshold for protecting these rights. Civil society groups across Africa should therefore take up the gauntlet in agitating for new rights-based development-oriented treaties, urging the ratification and implementation of existing ones, and maximising major political transition and constitutional review processes to ensure the incorporation of economic, social and cultural rights norms into municipal laws.

Against the background of negative judicial attitudes and a lack of knowledge in relation to economic, social and cultural rights development in many African states, there is the necessity for a radical approach to the use of judicial methods in the enforcement of these rights. Civil society groups at the domestic levels should develop innovative lawyering skills and strategies to change judicial attitudes about the issues of *locus standi* and non-justiciability of economic, social and cultural rights. The frontiers of developing an expansive interpretation of civil and political rights should be explored in promoting and protecting economic, social and cultural rights. This is particularly instructive in states where these rights are couched as directive principles or where there has been no demonstration of the political will to actualise them as *legal* entitlements.

Likewise, human rights groups should begin to activate the national institutional mechanisms for the protection of economic,

[1262] For a robust analysis of the necessity for grassroots education in evolving 'social and economic transformation', see S Koenig 'Human rights education for social transformation: Innovative grassroots programmemes on economic, social and cultural rights' in Barnhizer (n 1097 above) 163 175.

social and cultural rights. The near-total exclusion of economic, social and cultural rights issues before most human rights commissions in Africa does not portend a good omen for a rights-based human development agenda in Africa.

I must also mention that the trajectory of supranational work among African human rights groups and activists is yet to be fully articulated, explored and utilised. African human rights NGOs should learn that none of them can successfully execute a rights-based agenda for human development single-handedly, just as no civil society group can monopolise the costs, expertise, information, data, mobilisation strategies and other resources. The importance of networking as a viable strategy for overcoming the perennial inadequacy of resources can therefore not be overstated.

In the face of the gaping lack of co-ordination and collaboration among local African human rights groups – a phenomenon that breeds unnecessary replication of efforts and costs, break-neck competition, personality cults, unhealthy rivalries over scarce resources, vitriolic mudslinging over limited opportunities, and the desire for dominance – the synergy of efforts and platforms becomes imperative. What is needed are strategic thoughts on what fitting roles international, regional, sub-regional and national groups can best play, in which contexts, and what types of strategic alliances would function finest – without perpetuating any culture of hierarchy, subservience or dominance.[1263] This process calls for cutting-edge initiatives on the part of African activists and researchers.

Far from being an *ex cathedra* pronouncement on all the dynamics that would inform the emergence of a concrete rights-based approach to human development in Africa, it is my expectation that this scholarly exertion will become a vehicle for the evolution of further multidimensional approaches to the diverse legal and policy concerns that I have raised.

[1263] See generally J Gathii *et al* 'Reflections on United States-based human rights NGOs' work on Africa' (1996) 9 *Harvard Human Rights Journal* 285 295. See also Welch Jr (131 above) 75.

BIBLIOGRAPHY

Adjami, ME 'African courts, international law, and comparative case law: Chimera or emerging human rights jurisprudence?' (2002) 24 *Michigan Journal of International Law* 103

Agbakwa, SC 'Reclaiming humanity: Economic, social and cultural rights as the cornerstone of African human rights' (2002) 5 *Yale Human Rights and Development Law Journal* 177

Åkermark, SS 'International development finance institutions: The World Bank and the International Monetary Fund' in Eide A *et al* (eds) (2001) *Economic, social and cultural rights: a textbook* The Hague: Kluwer Academic Publishers

Alston, P 'Peoples' rights: Their rise and fall' in Alston P (ed) (2001) *Peoples' rights* Oxford: Oxford University Press

Alston, P, Steiner, HJ & Goodman, R *International human rights in context: law, politics and morals* (2007) Oxford: Oxford University Press

Alston, P 'Reconceiving the UN human rights regime: Challenges confronting the new UN Human Rights Council' (2006) 7(1) *Melbourne Journal of International Law* 155

Amnesty International Press Release 'World social and economic fora: All human rights for all, everyone's responsibility' AI INDEX: ACT 79/002/2003 (23 January 2003)

Amnesty International and the Law Society, *The United Nations Thematic Mechanisms - Update 2000: An Overview of their Work and Mandates* (AI Index: IOR 40/20/00, London, 2000)

Andhyarujina, TR 'The evolution of due process of law by the Supreme Court' in Kirpal BN *et al* (eds) (2000) *Supreme but not infallible: Essays in honour of the Supreme Court of India* New Delhi: Oxford University Press

An-Na'im, AA (2003) *Human rights under African constitutions: Realising the promise for ourselves* Philadelphia, PA: University of Pennsylvania Press

Arambulo, K (1999) *Strengthening the supervision of the International Covenant on Economic, Social and Cultural Rights: Theoretical and procedural aspects* Groningen: Intersentia

Austin, G (1999) *The Indian Constitution: Cornerstone of a nation* Bombay: Oxford University Press

Baah, RA (2000) *Human rights in Africa: The conflict of implementation* Lanham, MD: University Press of America

Bachman, S (2007) *Civil responsibility for gross human rights violations: The need for a global instrument* Pretoria: Pretoria University Law Press

Bahdi, R 'Globalisation of judgment: transjudicialism and the five faces of international law in domestic courts' (2002) 34 *George Washington International Law Review* 555

Baqwa, SAM 'The role of the Public Prosecutor *vis-à-vis* other institutions that redress grievances in South Africa' (1999) *3 International Ombudsman Year Book* 129

Barnhizer, D (2001) *Effective strategies for protecting human rights: Economic sanctions, use of national courts and international fora and coercive power* Ashgate: Dartmouth Publishing

Barnhizer, D (2001) *Effective strategies for protecting human rights: prevention and intervention, trade and education* Ashgate: Dartmouth Publishing

Bendor, AL 'On Aristotelian equality, the fundamental right to equality, and governmental discretion' (2003) 8 *Review of Constitutional Studies* 1

Bilchitz, D 'Placing basic needs at the centre of socio-economic rights jurisprudence' (2003) 4(1) *Economics and Social Rights Review* 3

Blackett, A 'Mapping the equilibrium line: Fundamental principles and rights at work and the interpretive universe of the World Trade Organisation' (2002) 65(4) *Saskatchewan Law Review* 369

Blanpain, R (2000) *Multinational enterprises and the social challenges of the XXIst century* The Hague: Kluwer Law International

Bollyky, T 'R If C > P + B: A paradigm for judicial remedies of socio-economic rights violations' (2002) 18(2) *South African Journal on Human Rights* 161

Bradlow, DD 'Should the international financial institutions play a role in the implementation and enforcement of international humanitarian law?' (2002) 50 *Kansas Law Review* 695

Brand, D & Heyns, C (2005) *Socio-economic rights in South Africa* Pretoria: Pretoria University Law Press

Brodnig, G 'The World Bank and human rights: Mission impossible?' (2002) 17 *Fletcher Journal of Developmental Studies* 1

Brysk, A (2002) *Globalisation and human rights* Berkeley CA: University of California Press

Carceles, G *et al* 'Can sub-Saharan Africa reach the international targets for human development?' *African Region Human Development Working Paper Series*, Washington, DC: World Bank (2001)

Chandler, G 'The responsibilities of oil companies' in A Eide *et al* (eds) (2000) *Human rights and the oil industry* 6 Oslo: Institute for Human Rights

Chapman, A 'A "violations approach" for monitoring the International Covenant on Economic, Social and Cultural Rights' (1996) 18(1) *Human Rights Quarterly* 23

Chapman, A *et al* (2002) *Core obligations: building a framework for economic, social and cultural rights* New York, NY: Intersentia

Chunakara, GM (2000) *Globalisation and its impact on human rights* Bangalore: Institute of Human Rights

Clapham, A (2006) *Human rights obligations of non-state actors* Oxford: Oxford University Press

Clapham, A *et al* 'The obligations of states with regard to non-state-actors in the context of the right to health' *WHO, Health and Human Rights Working Paper Series* No 3 Geneva: WHO (2004)

Cohn, M 'The World Trade Organisation: Elevating property interests above human rights' (2001) 29 *Georgia Journal of International and Comparative Law* 427

Colucci, M 'Implementation and monitoring of codes of conduct: How to make codes of conduct effective' in Blanpain R (2000) *Multinational enterprises and the social challenges of the XXIst century* 277 The Hague: Kluwer Law International

Coomans, F 'Economic, social and cultural rights' *SIM Special* No 16 Utrecht: Netherlands Institute for Human Rights (1998)

Corder, H (ed) (2007) *Comparing administrative justice across the Commonwealth* Kenwyn: Juta & Co

Corder, H 'Administrative justice: A cornerstone of South Africa's democracy' (1998) 14(1) *South African Journal on Human Rights* 38

Correa, CM *Implications of the Doha Declaration on the TRIPS Agreement and public health, health economics and drugs, EDM Series* No 12 Geneva: WHO (June 2002)

Council of Europe (2003) *European Social Charter: Collected texts* Strasbourg: Council of Europe

Craven, M 'The protection of economic, social and cultural rights under the Inter-American system of human rights' in Harris D et al (eds) (1998) The inter-American system of human rights 289 Oxford: Clarendon Press

Currie, I & de Waal, J (2005) *The Bill of Rights handbook* Cape Town: Juta & Co

Darrow, M (2003) *Between light and shadow: The World Bank, the International Monetary Fund and international human rights law* Portland, OR: Hart Publishing

Desai, AH *et al* 'Public interest litigation: Potentials and problems' in Kirpal BN *et al* (eds) (2000) *Supreme but not infallible: Essays in honour of the Supreme Court of India* 159 New Delhi: Oxford University Press

De Schutter, O 'The protection of social rights by the European Court of Human Rights' in Van der Auweraert P (2002) *Social, economic and cultural rights: An appraisal of current European and international developments* 207 Antwerp: Maklu

De Vos, P 'Transformative justice: social and economic rights in the South African Constitution' in Van der Auweraert P *et al* (2002) *Social, economic and cultural rights: An appraisal of current European and international developments* Antwerp: Maklu

Djajic, S 'Victims and promise of remedies: International law fairytale gone bad' (2008) 9 *San Diego International Law Journal* 329

Easterlin, RA 'The globalisation of human development' (2000) 570 *Annals* 35

Economic Commission for Africa (ECA) & Africa Action (2000) *International policies and African realities* Addis Ababa: ECA

Eide, A 'Making human rights universal: Achievements and prospects' in Stokke H *et al* (eds) (2001) *Human rights in development yearbook, the millennium edition* 23 Oslo: Nordic Human Rights Publications

Eide, A *et al* (2001) *Economic, social and cultural rights: A textbook* Dordrecht: Martinus Nijhoff Publishers

En Kees, V & Henk, S 'Globalisation, human rights and the government' in Van Genuten, W (2000) *Division of roles in the international economic and legal order* 81 Nijmegen: Wolf Legal Publishers

Eno, RW 'The jurisdiction of the African Court on Human and Peoples' Rights' (2002) 2(2) *African Human Rights Law Journal* 223

Evans, M & Murray, R (2002) *The African Charter on Human and Peoples' Rights: The system in practice 1986-2000* Cambridge, MA: Cambridge University Press

Farris, K 'Human rights and US military interventions' in Wagner T *et al* (eds) (2001) *Fifty years after the declaration: The United Nations' record on human rights* 145 Lanham, MD: University Press of America

Fölscher, A (2002) *Budget transparency and participation, five African case studies* Cape Town: Institute for Democracy in South Africa

Gallagher, P (2000) *Guide to the WTO and developing countries* Boston, MA: Kluwer Law International

Ganesan, A 'Human rights, the energy industry and the relationship with home governments' in Eide A *et al* (eds) (2000) *Human rights and the oil industry* 47 Oslo: Institute for Human Rights

Gary, I Catholic Relief Services *et al* (2003) *Bottom of the barrel: Africa's oil boom and the poor* Baltimore, MD: Catholic Relief Services

Gathii, JT 'Re-characterising the social in the constitutionalisation of the WTO: A preliminary analysis' (2001) 7 *Widener Law Symposium Journal* 137

Gideon, J 'Economic and social rights: Exploring gender differences in a Central American context' in Molyneux M *et al* (eds) (2002) *Gender justice, development and rights* 173 London: Oxford University Press

Gifford, A 'The evolution of social contract' (2002) 13(4) *Constitutional Political Economy* 361

Goldewijk, BK & De Gaay, FB (1999) *Where needs meet rights: Economic, social and cultural rights in a new perspective* Geneva: World Council of Churches Publications

Goldewijk, BK *et al* (2002) *Dignity and human rights: The implementation of economic, social and cultural rights* Antwerp: Intersentia

Gordon, AA (2001) *Understanding contemporary Africa* Boulder, CO: Lynne Rienner Publishers

Gordon, S (1999) *Controlling the state: Constitutionalism from ancient Athens to today* Cambridge, MA: Harvard University Press

Grinspun, A (2001) *Choice for the poor: Lessons from national poverty strategies* New York, NY: UNDP

Grote, R 'The scope of judicial review of administrative action and the changing rule of law: Some comparative reflections' (2004) 19 *SA Public Law* 513

Gunewardena, N 'Reinscribing subalternity: International financial institutions, development, and women's marginality' (2003) 7 *UCLA Journal of International and Foreign Affairs* 201

Gutto, SBO 'Current concepts, core principles, dimensions, processes and institutions of democracy and the inter-relationship between democracy and modern human rights' UN Seminar on the Interdependence Between Democracy and Human Rights, Geneva, 25-26 November 2002

Hardin, R (2003) *Liberalism, constitutionalism and democracy* New York, NY: Oxford University Press

Harrington, J 'Special Rapporteurs of the African Commission on Human and Peoples' Rights' (2001) 1(2) *African Human Rights Law Journal* 247

Harris, D *et al* (2001) *The European Social Charter* Ardsley, NY: Transnational Publishers

Hausermann, J 'A human rights approach to human development' (1998) *Human rights and human development report on the Oslo Symposium* New York, NY: UNDP

Hoexter, C (2007) *Administrative law in South Africa* Cape Town: Juta & Co

Hoexter, C 'Judicial policy revisited: Transformative adjudication in administrative law' (2008) 24 *South African Journal on Human Rights* 281

Holmes, S & Sunstein, CR (1999) *The cost of rights: Why liberty depends on taxes* New York, NY: W W Norton and Company

Hope Sr, Kempe R *et al* (2000) *Corruption and development in Africa: Lessons from country case studies* New York, NY St Martin's Press

Hossain, K *et al* (2000) *Human rights commissions and ombudsman offices: National experiences throughout the world* Dordrecht: Kluwer Law International

Hunt, P (2002) *Reclaiming social rights: International and comparative perspectives* Aldershot: Dartmouth Publishing

IMF 'Poverty reduction strategy papers: Progress in implementation, report prepared by the staffs of the IMF and the World Bank' Washington, DC: IMF (7 September 2000)

International Human Rights Internship Programme (IHRIP) (2000) *Circle of rights economic, social and cultural rights activism: A training resource* Washington, DC: IHRIP

Jaswal, PS 'Public accountability for violation of human rights and judicial activism in India: Some observations' (2002) 3 SCC (Journal) 6

Jochnick, C 'Confronting the impunity of non-state actors: New fields for the promotion of human rights' (1999) 21(1) *Human Rights Quarterly* 56

Jones, P 'Human rights, group rights, and peoples' rights' (1999) 21(1) *Human Rights Quarterly* 80

Joseph, R (1999) *State, conflict and democratisation in Africa* Boulder, CO: Lynne Rienner Publishers

Joshi, PL 'Judicial activism – A critique' (2001) 4(1) *Journal of the Institute of Human Rights* 52

Kaldor, M *Civil society and accountability: Occasional paper for human development report 2002*, Occasional Paper 2002/6 New York, NY: UNDP (2002)

Kennedy, D 'Boundaries in the field of human rights: The international human rights movement: Part of the problem?' (2002) 15 *Harvard Human Rights Journal* 99

Kis, J (2003) *Constitutional democracy* Budapest: Central European University Press

Knop, K 'Here and there: International law in domestic courts' (2000) 32 *International Law and Policy* 501

Koch, IE 'Good governance and implementation of economic, social and cultural rights' in Hans-Otto S *et al* (eds) (2002) *Human rights and good governance* 73 The Hague: Martinus Nijhoff Publishers

Koch, IE 'Social rights as components in the civil right to personal liberty: Another step forward in the integrated human rights approach' (2002) 20(1) *Netherlands Quarterly of Human Rights* 29, 35

Kolodziej, EA (2003) *A force profonde: The power, politics, and promise of human rights* Philadelphia, PA: University of Pennsylvania Press

Krever, R (ed) (2008) *VAT in Africa* Pretoria: Pretoria University Law Press

Lalwani, DP 'Public interest litigation - Offshoot of judicial activism' (2001) 4(1) *Journal of the Institute of Human Rights* 86

Leckie, S 'Another step towards indivisibility: Identifying the key features of violations of economic, social and cultural rights' (1998) 20(1) *Human Rights Quarterly* 81

Leckie, S 'The Committee on Economic, Social and Cultural Rights: Catalyst for change in a system needing reform' in Alston, P *et al* (eds) (2000) *The future of UN human rights monitoring* Cambridge, MA: Cambridge University Press

Leckie, S 'Violations of economic, social and cultural rights' in Van Boven, T *et al* (eds) *The Maastricht guidelines on violations of economic, social and cultural rights* (1998) *SIM Special* No 20 Utrecht: Netherlands Institute for Human Rights

Leckie, S (2003) *National perspectives on housing rights* The Hague: Martinus Nijhoff Publishers

Lenaerts, K *et al* 'Social rights in the case law of the European Court of Justice: The impact of the Charter of Fundamental Rights of the European Union on standing case law' in Van der Auweraert P *et al* (eds) (2002) *Social, economic and cultural rights: An appraisal of current European and international developments* 159 Antwerp: Maklu

Liebenberg, S 'Human development and human rights: South African country study' UNDP, Human Development Report 2000 Background Paper New York, NY: UNDP (2000)

Liebenberg S 'The value of human dignity in interpreting socio-economic rights' 2005 (1) *South African Journal on Human Rights* 173

Liebenberg, S 'Needs, rights and transformation: Adjudicating social rights in South Africa' (2006) 17(1) *Stellenbosch Law Review* 5

Liebenberg, S 'The protection of economic and social rights' in Eide, A *et al* (eds) (2001) *Domestic legal systems, in economic, social and cultural rights: A textbook* The Hague: Martinus Nijhoff Publishers

Liebenberg, S 'The right to social assistance: The implications of Grootboom for policy reform in South Africa' (2001) 17(2) *South African Journal on Human Rights* 232

Loucaides, LG (2007) *The European Convention on Human Rights: Collected essays* The Hague: Martinus Nijhoff Publishers

Manohar, SV 'The Indian judiciary and human rights' in Iyer, V (2000) *Democracy, human rights and the rule of Law* New Delhi: Butterworths

Mapulanga-Hulston, JK 'Examining the justiciability of economic, social and cultural rights' (2002) 6(4) *International Journal of Human Rights* 29

Mbazira, C 'Appropriate, just and equitable relief in socio-economic rights litigation: The tension between corrective and distributive forms of justice' (2008) *South African Law Journal* 71

McBride, J 'The violation of economic, social and cultural rights as torture or cruel, inhuman or degrading treatment' in Van Bueren, G (ed) (1998) *Childhood abused* Aldershot: Ashgate Publishing Company

McCracken, R *et al Standing and fundamental rights: A South Asian perspective* (2002) 7(3) *Judicial Review* 172

Merali, I & Oosterveld, V (2001) *Giving meaning to economic, social and cultural rights* Philadelphia, PA: University of Pennsylvania Press

Mugwanya, GW (2003) *Human rights in Africa: Enhancing human rights through the African regional human rights system* Ardsley, NY: Transnational Publishers

Muralidhar, S 'Justiciability - The Indian experience' in (2000) *Circle of rights* 435 (IHRIP) Washington, DC: IHRIP

Murray, R (2004) *Human rights in Africa: From the OAU to the African Union* Cambridge: Cambridge University Press

Ndulo, M 'The democratisation process and structural adjustment in Africa' (2003) 10(1) *Indian Journal of Global Legal Studies* 315

Newman, DG 'Institutional monitoring of social and economic rights: A South African case study and a new research agenda' (2003) 19(2) *South African Journal on Human Rights* 189

Nmehielle, VOO (2001) *The African human rights system: Its laws, practice, and institutions* The Hague: Martinus Nijhoff Publishers

Ochoa, C 'Advancing the language of human rights in a global economic order' (2003) 23 *Boston College Third World Law Journal* 57

Odinkalu, CA 'Analysis of paralysis or paralysis by analysis? Implementing economic, social and cultural rights under the African Charter on Human and Peoples' Rights' (2001) 23(2) *Human Rights Quarterly*

Okafor, OC 'Re-conceiving 'Third World' legitimate governance struggles in our time: Emergent imperatives for rights activism' (2000) 6 *Buffalo Human Rights Law Review* 1

Oloka-Onyango, J (2001) *Constitutionalism in Africa: Creating opportunities, facing challenges* Kampala: Fountain Publishers

Oloka-Onyango, J 'Reinforcing marginalised rights in an age of globalisation: international mechanisms, non-state actors, and the struggle for peoples' rights in Africa' (2003) 18 *American University International Law Review* 851

Oloka-Onyango, J (2007) *The problematique of economic, social and cultural right in globalized Uganda: A conceptual review* Kampala: University of Makerere

Olowu, D 'Child trafficking, children's rights and the crisis of state interventionism: The West African experience' (2004) *Nottingham Human Rights Law Review* 62

Olowu, D 'Conceptualising a rights-based approach to poverty alleviation in Africa: The platform of social security' (2003) 43(1) *Indian Journal of International Law* 67

Olowu, D 'Human development challenges in Africa: A rights-based approach' (2004) 5 *San Diego International Law Journal* 179

Olowu, D 'Human rights and the avoidance of domestic implementation: The phenomenon of non-justiciable constitutional guarantees' (2006) 69 *Saskatchewan Law Review* 39

Olowu, D 'Privatisation and water governance in Africa: Implications of a rights-based approach' (2008) 4 *TD: Journal for Transdisciplinary Research* 59

Olowu, D 'Protecting children's rights in Africa: A critique of the African Charter on the Rights and Welfare of the Child' (2002) 10(2) *International Journal of Children's Rights* 127

Olowu, D 'Regional integration, development and the African Union agenda: Challenges, gaps and opportunities' (2003) 13 *Iowa Journal of Transnational and Comparative Problems* 211

Olowu, D 'The effect of human rights treaties in domestic courts: the Nigerian Supreme Court decision in *Sani Abacha v Gani Fawehinmi* revisited' (2002) 3 *Nigerian Supreme Court Monthly* 172

Olowu, D 'Emerging jurisprudence on economic, social and cultural rights in Africa: A critique of the decision in *SERAC and Another v Nigeria*' (2004) 2 *Turf Law Review* 29

Orcalli, G 'A constitutional interpretation of the GATT/WTO' (2003) 14(2) *Constitutional Political Economy* 141

Osmani, SR 'Participatory governance and poverty reduction' in Grinpun, A (2001) *Choices for the poor: Lessons from national poverty strategies* 121 New York, NY: UNDP

Osunsade, FL 'Impacts of adjustment programmes: Concerns for the human condition' in Nanda VP *et al* (eds) (2003) *World debt and the human condition: Structural adjustment and the right to development* 107 Westport, CT: Greenwood Press

Ouguergouz, F (2003) *The African Charter on Human and Peoples' Rights: A comprehensive agenda for human rights and sustainable democracy in Africa* The Hague: Martinus Nijhoff

Owens, JC 'Government failure in sub-Saharan Africa: The international community's options' (2003) 43 *Virginia Journal of International Law* 1003

Palmeter, DN (2003) *The WTO as a legal system: Essays on international trade law and policy* London: Cameron May

Pasqualucci, JM 'The right to a dignified life (*vida digna*): The integration of economic and social rights with civil and political rights in the Inter-American human rights system' (2008) 31 *Hastings International and Comparative Law Review* 1

Porter, B 'Judging poverty: Using international human rights law to refine the scope of charter rights' (2000) 15 *Journal of Law and Social Policy* 117

Quashigah, K 'The African Charter on Human and People's Rights: Towards a more effective reporting mechanism' (2002) 2(2) *African Human Rights Law Journal* 261

Raes, K 'The philosophical basis of social, economic and cultural rights' in Van der Auweraert P *et al* (2002) *Social, economic and cultural rights: An appraisal of current European and international developments* 43 Antwerp: Maklu

Reif, LC 'Building democratic institutions: The role of national human rights institutions in good governance and human rights protection' (2000) 13 *Harvard Human Rights Journal* 1

Reinalda, B *et al* 'Non-state actors in international law: do they matter?' in Arts, B *et al* (eds) (2001) *Non -state actors in international relations* 1 Burlington, VT: Ashgate

Richter, J (2001) *Holding corporations accountable: Corporate conduct, international codes, and citizen action* London: Zed Books

Roach, K & Budlender, G 'Mandatory relief and supervisory jurisdiction: When is it appropriate, just and equitable?' (2005) 122 *SA Law Journal* 325

Robinson, M 'Making human rights matter: Eleanor Roosevelt's time has come' (2003) 16 *Harvard Human Rights Journal* 4

Rosas, A *et al* 'Implementation mechanisms and remedies' in Eide A *et al* (eds) (2001) *Economic, social and cultural rights: A textbook* 425 Dordrecht: Martinus Nijhoff Publishers

Rossi, J 'Strategies for enforcing ESC rights through domestic legal systems' in (2000) *Circle of rights* 418 (IHRIP) Washington, DC: IHRIP

Russell, JM 'The ambivalence about the globalisation of telecommunications: The story of Amnesty International, Shell Oil Company and Nigeria' (2002) 1(3) *Journal of Human Rights* 405

Samuel, L (2002) *Fundamental social rights: Case law of the European Social Charter* Strasbourg: Council of Europe

Sarelin, AL 'human rights-based approaches to development co-operation, HIV/AIDS, and food security' (2007) 29 *Human Rights Quarterly* 460

Sarkin, J 'The role of national human rights institutions in post-apartheid South Africa' in Sarkin J *et al* (eds) (2001) *Human rights, the citizen and the state: South African and Irish approaches* 13 Dublin: Round Hall Sweet & Maxwell

Scheinin, M 'Economic and social rights as legal rights' in Eide *et al* (eds) (2001) *Economic, social and cultural rights: A textbook* The Hague: Kluwer Academic Publishers

Scheinin, M (2001) *The welfare state and constitutionalism in the Nordic countries* Copenhagen: Nordic Council of Ministers

Scheinin, M 'The proposed Optional Protocol to the Covenant on Economic, Social and Cultural Rrights: A blueprint for UN human rights treaty body reform - without amending the existing treaties' (2006) 6(1) Human Rights Law Review 131

Scott, C 'Multinational enterprises and emergent jurisprudence on violations of economic, social and cultural rights' in Eide A *et al* (eds) (2001) *Economic, Social and cultural rights: a textbook* 563 The Hague: Kluwer Academic Publishers

Scott, C 'Reaching beyond (without abandoning) the category of economic, social and cultural rights' (1999) 21(3) *Human Rights Quarterly* 633

Scott, C *et al* 'Adjudicating constitutional priorities in a transnational context: A comment on Soobramoney's legacy and Grootboom's promise' (2000) 16(2) *South African Journal on Human Rights* 206

Scott, JC (1999) *Seeing like a state: How certain schemes to improve the human condition have failed* New Haven, CT: Yale University Press

Seleoane, M (2001) *Socio-economic rights in the South African Constitution: Theory and practice* Pretoria: Human Sciences Research Council

Sen, AK (1999) *Development as freedom* Oxford: Oxford University Press

Sepulveda, M (2003) *The nature of the obligations under the International Covenant on Economic, Social and Cultural Rights* Antwerp: Intersentia

Shelton, D (2000) *Commitment and compliance: The role of non-binding norms in the international legal system* New York, NY: Oxford University Press

Shelton, D 'Decision regarding Communication 155/96 *SERAC v Nigeria Case No ACHPR/COMM/A044/1*' (2002) 96 *American Journal of International Law* 937

Shelton, D 'Hierarchy of norms and human rights: Of trumps and winners' (2002) 65(4) *Saskatchewan Law Review* 301

Shelton, D 'Human rights, health and environmental protection: Linkages in law and practice: A background paper for the World Health Organisation' World Health Organization (WHO), *Health and Human Rights Working Paper Series* No 1 Geneva: WHO (2002)

Shelton, D (2001) *Remedies in international human rights law* New York, NY: Oxford University Press

Skogly, SI (2001) *The human rights obligations of the World Bank and International Monetary Fund* London: Cavendish Publishing

Sloth-Nielsen, J (2008) *Children's rights in Africa: A legal perspective* Aldershot: Ashgate Publishing

Squires, J, Langford, M & Thiele, B (2005) *The road to a remedy: Current issues in the litigation of economic, social and cultural rights* Sydney: Australian Human Rights Centre

Steiner, HJ, Alston, P & Goodman, R (2007) *International human rights in context: Law, politics, morals* New York, NY: Oxford University Press

Sullivan, R (2003) *Business and human rights: Dilemmas and solutions* Sheffield, UK: Greenleaf Publishing

Symonides, J 'Globalisation and human rights' (2000) 4 *Mediterranean Journal of Human Rights* 145

Symonides, J (2000) *Human rights: concepts and standards* Burlington: Ashgate Publishing Company

Thiele, B 'Litigating against forced evictions under the American Convention on Human Rights' (2003) 21(3) *Netherlands Quarterly of Human Rights* 463

Thin, N *et al* (2001) *Sub-Saharan Africa's poverty reduction strategy papers from social policy and sustainable livelihood perspectives: A report for the Department of International Development* Oxford: Oxford Policy Management

Thomas, R (2000) *Legitimate expectations and proportionality in administrative* law Oxford: Hart Publishing

Tooze, J 'Aligning states' economic policies with human rights obligations: The ESCR Committee's quest for consistency' (2002) 2(2) *Nottingham Human Rights Law Review* 229

Toth, MA 'The right to dignity at work: Reflections on article 26 of the Revised European Social Charter' (2008) 29 *Comparative Labour Law and Policy Journal* 275

UNDP *Human development report 2007-2008: Fighting climate change: Human solidarity in a divided world* New York, NY: Oxford University Press

United Nations 'Commentary on the norms on the responsibilities of transnational corporations and other business enterprises with regard to human rights' UN Doc E/CN4/Sub2/2003/38/Rev2 (2003)

Vadodaria, RR 'Constitutional crises and judicial activism' (2001) 4(1) *Journal of the Institute for Human Rights* 46

Vandenhole, W 'Completing the UN complaint mechanisms for human rights violations step by step: towards a complaints procedure complementing the International Covenant on Economic, Social and Cultural Rights' (2003) 21(3) *Netherlands Quarterly of Human Rights* 423

Viljoen, F (2007) *International human rights law in Africa* Oxford: Oxford University Press

Wahi, N 'Human rights accountability of the IMF and the World Bank: A critique of existing mechanisms and articulation of a theory of horizontal accountability' (2006) 12 *University of California Davis Journal of International Law and Policy* 331

Welch, Jr CE 'Human rights NGOs and the rule of law in Africa' (2003) 2(3) *Journal of Human Rights* 315

Woodiwiss, A (2003) *Making human rights work globally* London: Glasshouse Press

Woolman, S & Bishop, M (2008) *Constitutional conversations* Pretoria: Pretoria University Law Press

Wright, B 'Non-governmental organisations and indifference as a human rights issue: The case of the Nigerian oil embargo' (2002) 1(2) *Journal of Human Rights* 231

Yeshanew, S 'Combining the "minimum core" and "reasonableness" models of reviewing socio-economic rights' (2008) 9(3) *ESR Review* 8

Young, KG 'The minimum core of economic and social rights: A concept in search of content' (2008) 33 *Yale Journal of International Law* 113

Permissions

All chapters in this book were first published in AIRBAHDA, by Pretoria University Law Press (PULP) by Dejo Olowu; hereby published with permission under the Creative Commons Attribution License or equivalent. Every chapter published in this book has been scrutinized by our experts. Their significance has been extensively debated. The topics covered herein carry significant information for a comprehensive understanding. They may even be implemented as practical applications or may be referred to as a beginning point for further studies.

We would like to thank the editorial team for lending their expertise to make the book truly unique. They have played a crucial role in the development of this book. Without their invaluable contributions this book wouldn't have been possible. They have made vital efforts to compile up to date information on the varied aspects of this subject to make this book a valuable addition to the collection of many professionals and students.

This book was conceptualized with the vision of imparting up-to-date and integrated information in this field. To ensure the same, a matchless editorial board was set up. Every individual on the board went through rigorous rounds of assessment to prove their worth. After which they invested a large part of their time researching and compiling the most relevant data for our readers.

The editorial board has been involved in producing this book since its inception. They have spent rigorous hours researching and exploring the diverse topics which have resulted in the successful publishing of this book. They have passed on their knowledge of decades through this book. To expedite this challenging task, the publisher supported the team at every step. A small team of assistant editors was also appointed to further simplify the editing procedure and attain best results for the readers.

Apart from the editorial board, the designing team has also invested a significant amount of their time in understanding the subject and creating the most relevant covers. They scrutinized every image to scout for the most suitable representation of the subject and create an appropriate cover for the book.

The publishing team has been an ardent support to the editorial, designing and production team. Their endless efforts to recruit the best for this project, has resulted in the accomplishment of this book. They are a veteran in the field of academics and their pool of knowledge is as vast as their experience in printing. Their expertise and guidance has proved useful at every step. Their uncompromising quality standards have made this book an exceptional effort. Their encouragement from time to time has been an inspiration for everyone.

The publisher and the editorial board hope that this book will prove to be a valuable piece of knowledge for students, practitioners and scholars across the globe.

Index